Translating the Social World for Law

OXFORD STUDIES IN LANGUAGE AND LAW

Oxford Studies in Language and Law includes scholarly analyses and descriptions of language evidence in civil and criminal law cases as well as language issues arising in the area of statutes, statutory interpretation, courtroom discourse, jury instructions, and historical changes in legal language.

Series Editor:
Roger W. Shuy, *Georgetown University*

Editorial Board:
Janet Ainsworth, *Seattle University School of Law*
Janet Cotterill, *Cardiff University, UK*
Christopher Heffer, *Cardiff University, UK*
Robert Leonard, *Hofstra University*
Anne Lise Kjær, *University of Copenhagen*
Gregory Matoesian, *University of Illinois at Chicago*
Elizabeth Mertz, *University of Wisconsin Law School and American Bar Foundation*
Lawrence Solan, *Brooklyn Law School*

Translating the Social World for Law

LINGUISTIC TOOLS FOR A NEW LEGAL REALISM

Edited by Elizabeth Mertz, William K. Ford, and Gregory Matoesian

OXFORD
UNIVERSITY PRESS

Published in the United States of America by Oxford University Press
198 Madison Avenue, New York, NY 10016, United States of America.

© Oxford University Press 2016

First issued as an Oxford University Press paperback, 2020

Library of Congress Cataloging-in-Publication Data
Names: Mertz, Elizabeth, editor. | Ford, William K. (Law teacher) editor. |
Matoesian, Gregory M., editor.
Title: Translating the social world for law : linguistic tools for a new legal realism /
Edited by Elizabeth Mertz, William K. Ford, and Gregory Matoesian.
Description: New York : Oxford University Press, 2016. |
Series: Oxford studies in language and law |
Includes bibliographical references and index.
Identifiers: LCCN 2015049060 | ISBN 9780199990559 (hardcover : alk. paper) |
ISBN 9780199990566 (ebook (updf)) | ISBN 9780190619794 (ebook (epub)) |
ISBN 9780190267407 (online content) | ISBN 9780197537367 (paperback : alk. paper)
Subjects: LCSH: Law—Translating. | Law—Language. | Semantics (Law) |
Sociological jurisprudence.
Classification: LCC K213 .T7363 2016 | DDC 340/.14—dc23
LC record available at http://lccn.loc.gov/2015049060

To Michael Silverstein,

whose brilliant insights revolutionized the study of language and discourse. His enthusiasm for this project is testament to his incredibly generous collegial spirit, which has extended to so many of us, across disciplines, languages, institutions, and walks of life. At a law-and-society conference in Chicago, years ago, Michael characterized the law as "practicing linguistics without a license." Our efforts in this book and the group meetings that formed its foundation took inspiration from his insistent encouragement that we demonstrate how practicing linguistics, even without a license, can better translate the social world for law.

CONTENTS

CONTRIBUTORS

Peter Brooks is Sterling Professor Emeritus of Comparative Literature at Yale University and Andrew W. Mellon Foundation Scholar in the University Center for Human Values and the Department of Comparative Literature at Princeton University.

Robert P. Burns is the William W. Gurley Memorial Professor of Law at Northwestern University School of Law.

William K. Ford is Associate Professor at the UIC John Marshall Law School in Chicago, IL.

Susan Gal is Mae & Sidney G. Metzl Distinguished Service Professor of Anthropology, of Linguistics, and of Social Sciences in the Department of Anthropology at the University of Chicago.

M. Catherine Gruber earned a Ph.D. in Linguistics from the University of Chicago.

Gregory Matoesian is Professor in the Department of Criminology, Law, and Justice at the University of Illinois at Chicago.

Elizabeth Mertz is John and Rylla Bosshard Professor of Law at the University of Wisconsin and Senior Research Faculty at the American Bar Foundation.

Christopher Roy is Assistant Professor of Instruction in Anthropology at Temple University.

Michael Silverstein is Charles F. Grey Distinguished Service Professor of Anthropology, of Linguistics, and of Psychology and in the Committee on Interdisciplinary Studies in the Humanities at the University of Chicago.

Winnifred F. Sullivan is Professor and Chair in the Department of Religious Studies and Affiliate Professor of Law at Maurer School of Law at Indiana University, Bloomington.

Translating the Social World for Law

1

Introduction

TRANSLATING LAW AND SOCIAL SCIENCE

William K. Ford and Elizabeth Mertz

1.1 The New Legal Realist Translation Project

This volume emerges from interdisciplinary discussions held over a number of years by a working group focused on the issue of how to translate between law and other disciplines.[1] Participants included scholars from the fields of anthropology, religious studies, philosophy, linguistics, and law—with occasional visitors also from other fields such as psychology. The group locates itself within a current movement calling for a "New Legal Realism (NLR)" designed to encourage better communication between law and the social sciences. Most of the authors in this volume were part of the group and engaged actively in ongoing efforts to talk productively about law across disciplinary boundaries. One of the group's goals was to develop forms of interdisciplinary conversation that would allow us all to achieve more sophisticated and effective understandings of social science in legal settings—and vice versa. From different disciplinary perspectives, we are all concerned with the close examination of language.

As we grappled with communicating across a wide variety of disciplinary approaches, conceptual frames, and ways of talking, we found the metaphor of "translation" to be useful.[2] When we think about the task of interdisciplinary communication as a form of translation, we call attention to the fact that participants are actually operating with very different linguistic habits and analytic starting points. The fact that they seem to be speaking the same vernacular language (English, in our case) only creates more difficulties: when two people are using the "same" word to mean quite different ideas, it may be very challenging just to figure out that they are attaching quite different meanings to this word (if they sort this out at all!). But beyond the simpler level of individual words, there are whole sets of assumptions about why and how we communicate—assumptions that differ among different disciplines. When these wider background norms are ignored, interdisciplinary discussions can founder or even backfire (with participants from each discipline simply concluding that the other disciplinary approaches are essentially worthless or wrong). What a waste of energy and of potential for new insights—especially with all the interest and resources currently being poured into interdisciplinary conferences and work!

This volume is dedicated to exploring—as well as illustrating!—the challenges involved in the process of interdisciplinary translation across legal and social science perspectives. The field of language-and-law has by now produced much insightful research at the intersections of legal and linguistic analysis—research of obvious importance that offers many insights for improving the quality of justice "on the ground," although that knowledge has been slow to penetrate the worlds of legal scholarship and practice (see, e.g., Ainsworth 1993; Eades 2008; Matoesian 2001; Richland 2008; Shuy 2005; Solan and Tiersma 2005—and the list could go on for pages!).[3] And indeed, researchers have noted the failure of law to make use of much relevant social science—and have examined why this might be the case. Along with institutional and political considerations, scholars have pointed to intertwined differences in purpose, epistemology, and discursive conventions between social science and law as key sources of difficulty.[4] At a moment when much renewed attention is being paid within the legal academy to the desirability of incorporating social science work, we used our group's experience in interdisciplinary communication to build on existing insights and develop new ones about the role of language—at many levels—in the recurrent difficulties faced by interdisciplinary legal scholarship.

1.2 Law and Social Science: The Challenges of Interdisciplinary Translation

Incorporating the insights of social science into the heart of legal analysis has seemed to be almost impossible, despite numerous efforts over many years and generations.[5] Perhaps understandably, much legal scholarship focuses on—but also remains constrained to—legal doctrine and procedure, which could arguably be thought of as a core communicative framework—a kind of "grammar" of the law—through which legal ideas are conveyed and negotiated (Mertz 2007a). And yet, attempting to grasp how law works on the ground through doctrinal analysis alone has many of the same shortcomings as attempts to map how we speak by studying only grammatical structures in the abstract. In both cases, we miss key parts of the actual practices on the ground, the embedding of law or language in complex social and cultural settings, as well as the adjustments that abstract "rules" must go through as they are put to use. For many years now, business schools have hired social scientists who can help nascent business professionals understand the institutional and broader social settings within which businesses operate. The core languages of finance and economics remain central, but at least some of these professionals and the schools that train them have recognized that they have much to gain by casting a broader net in drawing on (and creating) social science research pertinent to their specialty.

US legal scholars have been attempting to draw on social science at least since the time of the Legal Realist school during the opening decades of the twentieth century, but have not to date achieved the kind of successful integration found in some other professional fields. This effort has been renewed at the turn of the new millennium, under a number of labels such as "Empirical Legal Studies" and "New Legal Realism" (see Suchman and Mertz 2010). Many scholars working within the new legal empiricist vein have proceeded without much serious or sustained attention to the process of translating between social science and law, assuming that as long as the appropriate social science method is performed correctly, all will be well. However empirical findings on legal problems are not so transparently adaptable to the very normative field of law, which also has an expertise and language of its own that must be considered (see Constable 2014). And the social sciences generally deploy their methods in interaction with underpinning theories, which provide important contexts within which to recognize the limits of what social science methodologies can accomplish. Thus it can be very bad practice to apply social science methods to legal problems with no consideration of the theoretical contexts that give those methods meaning.

New Legal Realism takes the process of interdisciplinary translation to be nontransparent and often deeply problematic (see Erlanger et al. 2005; Macaulay 2005; Mertz 2008). This volume delves into questions surrounding that translation process from the perspective of socially and institutionally grounded analyses of language. Following in the tradition of fields like sociolinguistics and linguistic anthropology, the studies in this volume move beyond analysis of linguistic structure in the abstract to examine how the social and cultural contexts of professional and disciplinary languages affect mutual comprehension. Our primary emphasis is on legal language, asking what might make this particular domain resistant to the insights of social science—and conversely, what social scientists might need to consider when attempting to translate their approaches for legal audiences. Though the authors in this volume come from different disciplinary backgrounds, we converge in the priority we place on close attention to details of legal language. At times, we can lump the "other" (i.e., non-legal) disciplines that we represent together, in that all of them have perspectives in common that differ from typical legal approaches. At other times, we have to pay attention to the specific contours of various social sciences. For example, the first two chapters in the book, and the accompanying commentary, use fairly technical analyses of discourse to point out aspects of a distinctively legal approach to language and culture. The distinctively legal approach uncovered by these analyses stands in contrast to—and fails to take account of—everyday understandings of how people "do things with words," whereas socially grounded linguistic analyses do a better job at capturing and translating those everyday understandings, in the process pointing out systematic failures on the part of the legal system (Table 1.1).

TABLE 1.1

Volume chapters and volume themes

Chapter	Metacommunicative Norms (Linguistic Ideologies)	Language Details and Contexts	Worldviews (Epistemologies)	Interdisciplinary Translation Itself
Ch2. Gruber	-LEGAL: we can read transparently from language form to speakers' intentions; we can examine individual utterances out of context; **just "trust your gut"** -SOC.SCI.: ask what each party thinks the norms of speaking are (and look for mismatches); pay attention to the full linguistic context, not just individual utterances; **don't just "trust your gut"** -LAY: speakers in court can rely on the full context of utterances for apologies, as in **everyday speech**	-in everyday speech, a linguistic feature (*ellipsis*) permits speakers to rely on full contexts of speech to fill in apparent gaps in individual utterances (this is true in the United States but also elsewhere) -erasure of meaning can occur when ellipsis is misread (as happens in court) -overly cursory use of "I'm sorry for . . ." can indicate disrespect; this creates double-binds for defendants	-LEGAL: **"demeanor evidence" provides superior knowledge about truth and character**; no need to track cultural differences that might lead judges and laypeople from different backgrounds to assess demeanor differently -SOC.SCI.: differences in social background affect how we understand emotion & rationality; these differences can create ambiguity, which permits typecasting. . . . **"demeanor" in/of itself is not a reliable source of knowledge**	-unexamined underlying assumptions can make interdisciplinary translation almost impossible -better translations can be achieved by realizing that there are many unconscious assumptions, with accompanying worldviews, and that they matter -those worldviews can become visible through analysis of linguistic details, contexts, & ideologies

Ch3. Matoesian	-LEGAL: assumes that descriptions of behaviors and language transparently reveal the intentions of victims and defendant; assumes that structure of **language in court is neutral &** reveals truth -SOC.SCI.: problematizes **hidden metalinguistic assumptions in court** about women, men, and how they negotiate sexual access; also raises questions about how in-court norms create "inconsistencies" that may not be inconsistent when viewed from multiple vantages	-micro-level linguistic features link individual instances (*tokens*) and categories defined by precedent (*types*), but the link relies on shared underlying ideologies about gendered behavior -the same is true of the contributions of gesture, body position, and other aspects of *multimodal discourse* used by the prosecutor	-LEGAL: no need to overtly question underlying assumptions about how behavior and speech indicate types of people (e.g., virtuous women, rapists); **OK to rely w/o reflection on micro-level, tacit linguistic indicators** which then play important roles in creating legal knowledge and precedent SOC.SCI.: tacit micro-level signals can invoke **knowledge that feels natural and "true" but is actually quite socially structured** and sometimes skewed	-social science and linguistic analysis can help unpack how social prejudices are tacitly played out in apparently "neutral" legal settings -but it's unclear, given (1) their very different epistemological frames, and (2) the micro-linguistic level at which truth is negotiated in the courtroom, whether this social science knowledge can be "translated" for use by judges and attorneys

Ch4. Comment Silverstein

Even when legal professionals are generally aware of the fact that norms from outside the courtroom *leak* into trials, they cannot fully control how sociocultural influences affect legal decisions. The *poetics* (rhymes and rhythms) of speech are just one of many micro-levels at which such influences work. Along with other such minute levels of language, they affect how past events are interpreted within the current courtroom discourse—and whether those events are deemed relevant under frames provided by legal precedent. Given that sociocultural influences from outside of the courtroom are not neutral—but are affected by class, race, gender, and other aspects of context—the unexamined leakage of those influences into legal proceedings is problematic. Social science analysis that reveals this leakage is not easily translated into the less subtle and more action-oriented discourse of law, let alone into "how to fix it" advice of the kind the legal system (for some understandable reasons) prefers.

(continued)

TABLE 1.1
Continued

Chapter	Metacommunicative Norms	Lang. Details/Contexts	Worldviews	Interdisc. Translation
Ch5. Ford	-LEGAL: (in committee hearings) reliable information can come from "reading people" (experts) rather than reading research reports—**give deference to demeanor; it's okay to rely on global assertions** of expertise and summaries rather than undertaking much questioning or examination of details; no need to translate the semiotic context (i.e., the gaming medium itself) -SOC.SCI.: reliable information is only available from **reading the actual research and grasping empirical details and/or from experts with research credentials;** it's important to pay attention to contexts and specific definitions of terms	-even in committee hearings, complex explanations of social science is typically limited to MINUTES; committees ask for CONCLUSIONS rather than explanations -variations in the meaning of "violence" across different settings (research, games, crimes) not questioned in hearings -hearings face a problem of balancing "information overload" w/ need for some detail -subtle imbalances in the hearings' linguistic structures can mean less rigorous examination of the relevant science	-LEGAL: **stated authority of the expert suffices to support research conclusions** described; conclusory language is well-received and failure to discuss the studies' limitations is OK -SOC.SCI.: expertise is in part exhibited by the expert's ability to give details re/ methods, acknowledge limitations on conclusions, and explain how concepts like "violence" are operationalized in context of research; **detailed understanding is essential to expertise**	-legislators accept "expert" translators of relevant research who are not social scientists and who are overt advocates for particular positions—contrary to norms in social science -legal interpretive norms do not favor careful translation of social science, even in legislative committee hearings; courts may sometimes do a better job because the adversarial process promotes presentation of opposing views -to achieve better use of social science, law needs to shift language/translation norms and practices
Ch6. Sullivan	-LEGAL: deference to modernist principles and to experts on Christian theology (espousing **clear dividing line between science and religion**)—but not to social scientists studying religion -SOC.SCI.: science studies researchers and social scientists studying religion have **more contextually sensitive norms** for defining and analyzing religion and science; they problematize simplistic modernist divisions	-struggle between different positions on religion and science evident in the details of school board resolutions, legislation, expert commentary, pronouncements of national scientific organization, court opinions, newspaper stories, and historical discussions -key words such as "faith" used without examination of contexts	-LEGAL: **rely on experts for bright-line definitions** separating science and religion, preference for experts who are not studying science or religion from social scientific vantage -SOC.SCI.: **definitions of religion and law are based in history and social context.** This does not mean that we can't distinguish them, but it does make distinctions less simplistic (and more socially grounded)	-courts' current approach to translation obscures the unavoidably normative or political character of the decision being made -appeal to the social sciences studying religion and science would provide law with a more nuanced way of handling struggles between science and religion (though the resulting complications would pose challenges for law)

Chapter	Metacommunicative Norms	Lang. Details/Contexts	Worldviews	Interdisc. Translation
Ch7. Burns	****THERE ARE MULTIPLE IDEOLOGIES AT WORK IN DIFFERENT ARENAS OF LAW AND OF SOCIAL SCIENCE -LEGAL:** ****THE "RECEIVED VIEW" OF THE TRIAL:** the "semantic content" of rules can be applied in a deductive fashion to determine outcomes in particular cases; **demeanor evidence/oaths/ cross-exam re/relevant perceptual knowledge** are best way to find truth; classic liberal values; if overt normative content is ruled out, then no need to worry about objectivity; "opinion testimony" is okay if from experts (e.g., scientists); it's appropriate for judges to be gatekeepers for scientific evidence … **FITS WITH POSITIVIST SOC.SCI.** ****FULLER (REALIST) VIEW OF THE TRIAL:** truth can be discerned through **highly contextual common-sense moral judgment, mediated by legal language,** and based on practical choice of narratives as played out in practices of courtroom …**FITS WITH INTERPRETIVE SOC.SCI. and with LEGAL REALISM**	-the actual SEMIOTIC STRUCTURE OF THE US COURTROOM (as opposed to the ideological "received view" of how trials supposedly work) CREATES A UNIQUE SITUATION within which particular facts and incommensurable norms can be synthesized in an effort to achieve justice -legal-linguistic structures of the trial require jurors & judges to combine common-sense and contextual assessment WITH linguistic distancing/scrutiny and attention to abstractions of several kinds -the trial is "a set of linguistic practices that make a normative judgment with practical import possible"	-LEGAL: law must **normatively assess** "the human action that lies at the center of the trial"—this is quite different from the social science goal of predicting/reconstructing perceivable events; law "enacts the close relationship between description and evaluation" -SOC.SCI.: good social science appropriately deployed can provide legal proceedings with **social or historical context, correctives to "common sense"**—different kinds of empirical social science make different kinds of contributions: this includes descriptive, interpretive, and positivist approaches	-despite the disparities among the goals & epistemologies of various legal and social scientific approaches, "the language regions which may characterize a human act—of morality, of law, of causal social science, of interpretive social science—are [NOT] absolutely self-contained and [DO NOT] universally resist translation" -whether translation across different disciplines will be "mutually enlightening" depends on context -one cannot achieve "full translation" within or outside of the languages of description, explanation, or evaluation (see Wittgenstein on language games) -soc.sci. may be most useful where it fails positivist tests; where it informs but does not leave the jury "helpless"
Ch8. Comment Gal	The dominant language ideology in a particular institutional context is crucial to how successful a translation between different disciplines will be. Euro-American language ideology privileges *denotation*, artificially separating "facts" of world and words from values. This doesn't fit well with how language actually works, including in trials. When understood through the prism of a particular language ideology (or metacommunicative assumption), not all ways of translating are alike. E.g., they can create authority by modeling. Or subsume practices and texts of one disciplinary language under another by framing them as mere examples of categories (or types) defined by the dominant language (translation-as-voicing): science v. religion v. law. In doing this, it forms part of ongoing competitive contests over where and how those boundaries should be drawn—contests in which social movements also often play a role.			

(continued)

TABLE 1.1
Continued

CHAPTER	Metacommunicative Norms	Lang. Details/Contexts	Worldviews	Interdisc. Translations
Ch9. Mertz	-LEGAL: The point of interdisciplinary exchange is to **extract tools that can be used** to answer questions about the meaning in legal texts with more certainty; however, any interdisciplinary tools must be employed in ways that are congruent with law's broader normative/ pragmatic contexts and practices -SOC.SCI.: the most important goal of interdisciplinary exchange is **an improved understanding of how legal language works**; how that understanding plays out in the world in particular legal cases is secondary	Overt attention to the contextual and metalinguistic demands of interdisciplinary translation cannot always solve the problems caused by the deeply embedded details of different disciplines' linguistic practices Even in small groups, aspects of "performance" invite miscommunication (e.g., demand that disciplines speak in a single voice)	-LEGAL: the value of knowledge is in its utility for solving problems as framed by law; knowledge is most useful when it is detachable, easily summarized, and adapted to the assumptions embedded in law (rather than challenging them) -SOC.SCI.: there are different worldviews, even within a single discipline. It can be difficult—or even self-defeating—to attempt to elide those differences.	When points of fundamental conflict between disciplines' metacommunicative norms and goals go unrecognized, the translation process is hindered A likely question in interdisciplinary exchanges is the degree to which the expertise of one discipline can be "exported" by people who have not been trained in the subject (this is an issue of power as well as epistemology and specialized knowledge)
Ch10. Brooks	Reflecting on years of teaching law-and-literature in three different law school settings, Brooks describes law as "almost Teflon-coated, resistant to deep engagements with other perspectives." This is disturbing given Brooks' observation that this Teflon-coated approach fails to hold legal interpretation to any reliably "realist ethical standards." He asks why law should be taught in a university setting at all, and challenges the idea that teaching the practice of law must be at odds with teaching law as an intellectual and ethical discipline. From this perspective, the position of law training within universities affords law a continuing opportunity to learn from and incorporate the wisdom of other disciplines. Whether it can do that, given its resistance to deep translations, is an open question. Brooks is more hopeful about the opportunities for broader intellectual horizons in the teaching of undergraduates interested in law.			

2.1 Volume Themes

Several overarching themes emerged from our interdisciplinary discussions of the process of legal and other translations, and they can be traced as threads running through the chapters in this volume. First, we pay attention to the *background assumptions* that guide communication in different settings and disciplines: What is the point or goal of any particular communication? How is the process of such communication conceptualized? For example, is it thought of as a battle in which one side must prevail over the other? Is it a search for more accurate mutual understandings, in which multiple and carefully hedged punchlines are the norm? Or are some of the people in the conversation waiting for a couple of sentences that tell them what to do next? The possibilities are endless—and important. Just to give one instance, a speaker can utter the very same words (for example, "Get out of here!") but get very different reactions depending on whether the person being addressed views the exchange as a verbal battle or a friendly conversation. (Hence the importance of metalinguistic corrections such as "I'm just kidding" to ongoing successful communication of shared understandings.) Following the pathbreaking work of Michael Silverstein (1979) in this area, anthropologists refer to these kinds of background assumptions guiding communicative exchanges as *linguistic ideologies*—and one important subset of linguistic ideologies are metacommunicative norms giving us guidelines for the "proper" use of language in professional settings.[6]

Second, the chapters in this book pay close attention to the *details of language and context* in situations where people are trying to translate for legal audiences. Are there particular features of language that seem more important in certain legal settings? Are there ways of using language that cause problems for those who seek to translate in and out of the language of law? In examining language carefully, we pay close attention to settings and contexts: it matters who the people are, where they are, why they are trying to communicate, and what their expectations are. In this sense, we encourage more contextually sensitive guidelines to help improve the translation of social science in legal settings. There may be times and places in which some forms of social science simply are not applicable to legal problems; there may be situations in which it is better not to venture into the translation process at all. At other times, the social sciences may be able to provide valuable guidance to lawyers, judges, and lawmakers—but only if their limitations as well as their utility are fully understood. The authors in this volume demonstrate that we can indeed achieve such an understanding if we develop a sophisticated sense of the cultures and social structures embedded in (and conveyed through) the languages used during interdisciplinary exchanges—*the underlying or implicit worldviews*, the unspoken assumptions, the deeply felt attitudes, the core missions at stake for different participants.

Our approach to interdisciplinary translation is part of a wider conversation that includes fields like translation studies and science studies in addition to the more expected social science disciplines. Although he would not advocate use of the word "translation" for attempts to communicate across disciplinary "languages," translation scholar David Bellos (2011) shares many of the ideas of contributors to this volume. For example, he stresses the importance of language details and contexts: "Two of the key determinants of how an utterance conveys meaning . . . are these: the situation in which it is uttered (the time, the place, and knowledge of the [pertinent conventional] practices. . .); and the identities of the participants, together with the relationship between them" (Bellos 2011, 74). Rather than focusing on abstract definitions ("what is translation?"), or prescriptive advice ("how to do a good translation"), he prefers to explore "what seems to me to be the real issue—understanding what translation *does*" (2011, 4)—that is, translation "in action," and in social contexts. Finally, Bellos reminds us that any stretch of language can have multiple valid translations, depending on the purpose of the translation: "By choosing which dimensions to connect in a relationship of likeness and the extent to which likeness is made visible, a translation hierarchizes the interlocking, overlaying features of the original" (2011, 321). In this volume, Susan Gal makes a very similar point when she suggests that we center attention on "In what way is *this* a translation of *that?*" This requires us to consider the linguistic ideology, or meta-level ideas about language, that are at work in any particular translation occasion.

The authors of the chapters in this volume, in paying attention to metacommunicative norms, communicative contexts, and underlying worldviews, teach us about the process of interdisciplinary translation between legal knowledge and the forms of social knowledge offered by the social sciences. They acknowledge and point to connections with prior work on these issues, setting their own contributions in context. Many of the insights presented are confirmed in other research as well—but sadly, that research has not to date received the recognition it should have within policy and legal domains. Throughout the volume, we contrast the promise of sensitive interdisciplinary translation with problems caused by translation misfires in legal studies. And finally, we ask if a New Legal Realism could draw on this more context-sensitive approach to language to create a stronger, more reciprocal dialogue among professionals from different disciplines—in service of a fuller, more robust conception of law's complex linguistic, social, and normative character as it actually functions in the "real world."

2.2 Volume Structure and Arguments

When we examine the interdisciplinary translation process in detail, we can begin to outline contrasting sets of practices surrounding the use of language and the construction of knowledge in law and in many of the social sciences.

We can also identify what aspects of the social world—and of law—are missed or captured by one or the other set of practices. Although legal professionals and social scientists often proceed as if they can simply pick out facts from each other's fields, without thinking much about the complex worlds they are translating, there are in fact many layers involved. We see those different layers in the organization of this volume, which moves from the level of individuals' speech in courtrooms to wider attempts to translate whole disciplines or fields of thought.

2.2.1 *[PART ONE]* ANALYZING LEGAL TRANSLATIONS ON THE GROUND

We begin very close to the ground, with linguistic analyses of transcripts of actual court proceedings. In these transcripts, we hear individual speakers attempting to convey stories through the language of law. The authors of our first two chapters analyze these transcripts using forms of at-times technical linguistic analysis. They pay attention not only to particular aspects of language, but also to the impact of legal contexts and customs—as well as to wider social and cultural norms and ways of speaking. This rich understanding of language in context yields detailed accounts of how legal translations work and fail to work.

Creating our own experiment in interdisciplinary translation for this volume, we provide "translations" of these two more technical chapters and the commentary that follows, with highlighted "translation" blocks at the start of each section within each chapter. As is the case with many edited volumes, we are also providing summaries of the chapters in this Introduction. We supply glosses for many technical terms in footnotes. In addition, in the volume's Introduction and Conclusion, we explicitly examine how differences in professional languages might make it difficult to translate between law and social sciences like linguistics—and at the end of the Introduction we include a chart that maps how each chapter in the volume fits with the overarching themes of the volume. Thus we pay conscious attention to the task facing our own readers as we invite them to participate actively in interdisciplinary communication. We hope that these combined features will help to bridge disciplinary gaps in language and understanding—or at the very least, to call attention to the existence of those gaps and the challenges they pose.

The first chapter in this section focuses on laypeople who have been given a chance to speak directly to judges. M. Catherine Gruber's chapter takes us into courtrooms where defendants who have previously been convicted of crimes seek to mitigate their sentences through formal apologies to the court. She deals with translation issues at two levels: issues arising from a disjunction between legal and sociolinguistic perspectives (with sociolinguistics paying more attention to communicative contexts); and also issues arising from a disjuncture between lay and legal understandings—a difference revealed by sociolinguistics' more contextual approach. When we examine the fuller context of communication, we can see that laypeople are unlikely to understand the background assumptions and conventions that render one form of apology more legally powerful than another. And at the same time, judges sometimes *erase* parts of what defendants have conveyed, generating ambiguity where none seems to have been intended. In the space created by this ambiguity, judges feel freer to look beyond the language of the in-court apology to other criteria—among which is the degree to which a defendant fits judges' stereotype of a "career criminal." Thus the linguistic performance of an apology in court, when it fails to conform to particular tacit criteria, can actually invite judges to consider aspects of "character" that go far beyond the mere spoken language in court. Gruber uses the tools of sociolinguistics and linguistic anthropology to give us a precise understanding of where and how the problem emerges. Through her analysis, we come to see that one important part of success in translation is a common linguistic repertoire. Courts that do not examine this feature of translation are inviting poor communication. As we see in this chapter, it is a linguistic feature that is visible in one kind of social science analysis but invisible to standard legal approaches. Gruber's analysis raises the question of whether (and then, how) the insights derived from sociolinguistics could be translated to help achieve better communication in legal arenas. Based on her findings, it seems unlikely that judges could be persuaded to stop trusting their "gut" instincts in interpreting defendants' utterances in court (and indeed, legal doctrine encourages them to do just that). Thus Gruber is pessimistic about the possibility of adequately translating this kind of social science knowledge for law. She settles for a more modest outcome, suggesting that perhaps the sociolinguistic findings might help defendants' attorneys advise their clients as to whether they should directly address the court during sentencing hearings.

In the next chapter, Gregory Matoesian dissects a preliminary hearing at a rape trial to analyze how a prosecutor translates real-world events (*tokens*) so that they fit within legal categories dictated by precedent (*types*). The prosecutor in this case is trying to demonstrate to a judge that the behaviors and language of the defendant on multiple occasions fit within the pattern of behavior of a serial rapist—defined, as it turns out, not only legally but also—in very tacit ways—culturally. The prosecutor attempting to perform the translation has obviously been trained in the language of law. Thus, in contrast with Gruber's example, certain shared ground rules and background assumptions about the linguistic exchange between judge and prosecutor can be taken for granted. Unlike a lay defendant, the lawyer here fully understands the ground rules of the linguistic game in court. And yet, the strictures imposed on this prosecutor's choice of language—strictures that emanate from sexist social norms, refracted through legal language and rules—ultimately make it impossible to achieve an effective discussion of rape from the victim's point of view. As in Gruber's example, the courtroom struggle over translation operates at an unrecognized level, and again the stated goals of law are undermined by the misfire. In both cases, social science offers clues to creating better communication in courts—but somehow the available social science knowledge is not itself being translated or heard by legal professionals. The gap between the legal linguistic ideologies implemented in court and the linguistic ideologies of defendants in sentencing hearings or rape victims in a preliminary hearing can be large, leading to seemingly inevitable misfires (both in terms of communication and of justice, in this setting). Thus far, Matoesian is focusing not on translation between disciplines, but on the everyday assumptions do and don't translate within legal institutional settings. Matoesian concludes by moving to the level of translation between disciplines, asking whether his own analysis might be able to aid legal professionals in bridging the large gap he has identified. Perhaps even more than Gruber, Matoesian reaches pessimistic conclusions about the degree to which courts and the legal profession generally will be able to make use of social science knowledge detailing how metacommunicative norms, details of language in context, and underlying worldviews interact to create miscarriages of justice.

This section of the book closes with a Commentary by Michael Silverstein, which further explicates the reasons why some *leakage* of everyday prejudices into courtroom and other legal proceedings is inevitable. His commentary is primarily about a core battle over the translations that occur through the languages of law. On the one hand, the linguistic ideologies that dominate in legal proceedings give a great deal of credence to the power of legal procedures (which are also of course linguistic procedures) to "purify" courtroom proceedings of external prejudices. In this sense, as Silverstein notes, legal procedures are rituals. However, the culture and values of court personnel— because they are also human and members of their own subcultures—sneak in nonetheless. The invisible biases based in gender, class, and other aspects of social background invade and permeate the smallest crevices of language, at levels so subtle and constant that it seems unlikely that juries—or even highly trained judges—will be able to monitor them. Unfortunately, then, linguistic ideologies that place faith in legal rituals often serve to heighten the invisibility of this leakage, while it gives false reassurance to participants. Silverstein's commentary thus echoes Matoesian's pessimism—and Gruber's largely pessimistic views—about the ability of legal language to fight leakage from the prejudices of the world outside of legal proceedings.

It is when we reach this last point that we can indirectly glean yet another lesson about translation from Silverstein's commentary—this time, not about the translation of everyday attitudes through the imperfect sieve of supposedly neutral legal procedures. Silverstein's commentary also demonstrates how in both of the first chapters, social science is able to capture the way this leakage is happening—in details of the poetic structuring of language, in micro-linguistic connections between past and present, and in the constant shape that underlying linguistic ideologies gives to the evolving legal interpretation of evidence. As we saw in Gruber's chapter, the kinds of advice that can actually translate in legal settings tend to be quite crude by comparison with the fine-grained level of analysis needed to uncover implicit biases in the courtroom. Thus we can reasonably conclude that it might be quite difficult to convince legal personnel of the lessons to be had from these social science studies. Is this a positive or negative phenomenon? In a sense, the leakage of everyday values into courtroom proceedings could be thought of as an acceptable aspect of any system of justice rooted in a particular place and time. But on the other hand, these studies clearly show that such leakage can undermine the very goals of the system of justice, and disproportionately injure those who are not part of more privileged or powerful groups. Should or can we use social science in service of a remedy? Or is this likely to just perpetuate the myth that it is possible to cleanse courtroom language of social prejudices? We turn next to some explicit examples of the legal translation of social science, to shed more light on these translation dilemmas.

2.2.2 *[PART TWO]* SYSTEM-LEVEL CHALLENGES: WHEN COURTS AND LEGISLATURES TRANSLATE SOCIAL SCIENCE AND NATURAL SCIENCE

The next three chapters analyze what happens when legal language overtly confronts and attempts to translate the languages of the social and natural sciences. On the one hand, the chapters identify some marked shortcomings in these legal translation efforts. At the same time, the authors begin to suggest how these shortcomings might be addressed—in part through judicious use of social science in legal settings. We move from a more direct and concrete case study—in William Ford's examination of how legislatures (as compared with courts) handle social science in video game violence cases—to more general levels of analysis, in the next two chapters, of what happens when professional discourses meet. The chapter by Winnifred Fallers Sullivan examines the nexus of science and religion in court, while Robert Burns's chapter analyzes the structure of trials. This set of chapters is relatively optimistic about the possibility of overcoming the translation difficulties that were outlined in the first section of the book. All three authors are law professors, and combine this expertise with backgrounds in political science, religious studies, and philosophy. In her Commentary on these three chapters, linguistic anthropologist Susan Gal demonstrates the importance of paying attention to linguistic ideology, to the particular forms that interdisciplinary translation takes, and to the social contexts within which these translations take place. Here we see law policing the boundary that it helps to create among disciplines, as multiple disciplinary languages and practices interact with the particular social and political contexts of their times.

In the opening chapter of this section, political scientist and law professor William Ford provides an in-depth examination of how legislatures have handled social science evidence regarding the effects of violent video games on the game players—in the end also comparing legislatures to courts in this regard. Note that, in keeping with our ongoing experiment with different disciplinary genres and styles in this volume, this chapter differs from the others in its format: it conforms to the longer and more encyclopedic style of law review articles (although there is much more inclusion of social science perspectives, and translation of legal concepts, than would usually be found in such articles). In previous work, Ford (2013) had already analyzed how courts dealt with scientific and social scientific information, demonstrating that both trial and appeals courts commonly made faulty assumptions about how empirical research works.[7] He found that judges' comments revealed a failure to understand scientific meta-analyses combining results from numerous studies; that the judges over-idealized the probative value of having "one good study"; that they lit on particular statistical tests (e.g., multiple regressions) as a kind of gold standard, without considering the different research settings in which that might not be true; and so on. Ford's chapter in this volume picks up where his previous one left off, providing an in-depth picture of how legislatures have fared in comparison with courts when translating the social science pertaining to the relationship between children's violence and violent video games. Ford provides a thoughtful discussion of what we should aim for in working between law and social science:

> A "good" translation is not necessarily comprehensive, one that might turn policymakers into experts, but one that is sufficient to support sensible decisions about public policy. Any more than this would probably be a poor use of limited legislative and judicial resources and would further contribute to the "information overload" of decision makers. (Ford, this volume/1st pg)

In the present chapter, he finds that legislatures facing the same issue (video game violence) have often done an even less satisfactory job than courts of attempting to grasp social science; as he comments, one could achieve a better analysis of the pertinent literature in one meeting of a graduate-level seminar than occurred in the best of the state legislative hearings. This conclusion runs against some accepted wisdom within the field of law, where, as Ford explains, the legislative hearing is often thought to provide superior insights on these sorts of issues. Ford's detailed study gives us an unparalleled opportunity to track in detail the difficulties facing translations between law and social science, "on the ground." As compared with the micro-level of language analysis typical of the linguists in this book, Ford gives us a "mid-range" account, with enough detail that we can see where "misfires" occurred but also stepping back to let us see the translation process in multiple sites. This permits him to trace the similarities beneath apparent differences.

Winnifred Fallers Sullivan, lawyer and religious studies scholar, continues the discussion with a critical examination of how law has dealt with conflicts over the teaching of science and religion in US public schools. She contrasts three worldviews: those of institutionalized science, religion, and law in the United States. A brief historical account tracks earlier views under which many theologians viewed science and religion as compatible, before a time when these fields became framed as more in conflict and competition with each other—within both public and legal discourses. In the United States, the legal system has translated these two fields using a language of strict separation, distinguishing sharply between secular, empirically tested propositions in science and ethical, faith-based propositions in religion. Sullivan notes that although the US legal system has developed its own "separate spheres" theory regarding science and religion, this view contrasts with that of "many religious people," who "do not practice a religion that is either entirely about the meaning of morality, or that is entirely non-empirical"—and she adds that newer perspectives from science studies teach that "science cannot be defined simply by the scientific method." (In other words, science is also performed by human beings situated within cultural contexts that leak into their practices—which is not to say that the methods used by scientists are not also capable of performing as expected in many instances.) If the line between science and religion is not as sociologically and philosophically "objective" or clear as US law has made it seem, how then to deal with the nevertheless persistent problem of how to cope with the legally required separation between the two? In conclusion, Sullivan suggests that the sociological study of religion can help in presenting a more nuanced view of the problem than is currently promoted by legal experts. The choice of how such nuance might be translated in science classrooms, however, she sees as an issue of politics. Her study suggests that law cannot remain neutral in its translation role where religion and science are concerned—and that there are subtleties that are currently lost in legal translation. Here again, we see the importance of attention to the acts of translation into and out of law—and to the complex cultural, structural, and metalinguistic contexts that shape it.

Combining the perspectives of practicing lawyer and philosopher, Robert Burns's chapter examines the diverse language practices that characterize law and social science. He stresses the important point that there are multiple possible views of law, as well as multiple institutionalized social science approaches. Thus it can be useful to examine what happens when different forms of legal and social science knowledge meet in translation. And like Sullivan, Burns critiques a sharp opposition between disciplines—as, for example, between law and social science. His chapter then contrasts the "received" or dominant ideology within law regarding trials with a more complete and realistic view of what happens in actual trials. The received view is evident in formal rules as well as in the way some legal philosophers and judges describe the system—as if real trials could be adequately described by the rules and by formalist descriptions of how the system is supposed to run (i.e., the "grammar" of legal procedure and doctrine, as characterized above). In terms of how courts deal with social science, in keeping with Ford's conclusions, Burns acknowledges that in reality courts have "adhered to their own relatively unexamined traditions" in dealing with expert testimony from the social sciences, often "relying on their own rules of thumb." Standard approaches to understanding the trial share many assumptions with positivist social science, which may lead to a sense that they fit very comfortably together. But Burns casts doubt on whether this is the optimal or even a good use of the information available from the full range of social sciences. Pushed by more positivist and standard approaches, he argues, courts and juries often attempt to perform "complete" translations that may paradoxically bleed social science of its best potential contributions to legal decisions. The hidden language ideology that favors mythical "complete translations" ironically undercuts the very process it purports to promote: the use of social science to inform but not disable the democratic process produced through the tensions structured into the trial.

In her commentary on this section, Susan Gal uses the research of these scholars (and others in this volume) as a springboard for an important rethinking of interdisciplinary translation. Like David Bellos, she asks us to think about translation not as a uniformly straightforward process, but as a form of interpretation that has to vary depending on context and purpose:

> Judgments of similarity and difference are centrally at issue.... any two texts (or objects, practices) have innumerable qualities and properties, many of which can be picked out as similar in some way. Thus, similarity and difference are always judgments relative to those who judge and to their roles, situations, and projects.... We have to ask: In what way is *this* a translation of *that*? What frames of understanding—what priorities, situations, metadiscourses, ideologies, presumptions—enable us to [see two objects/words/ideas as similar or different]? (Gal this volume, pp. 216–17)

This kind of variation—which ought to be quite familiar to any legal audience—does not mean that *any*thing can pass as an adequate translation. Indeed, when we start to focus on the forms that variation takes, we find a whole field of systematic inquiry opening up. Drawing on linguistic anthropological approaches, Gal raises three key issues to consider in such a field of inquiry. First, a theme familiar throughout this volume, namely, what ideas and ideologies about language itself are at work in situations of interdisciplinary translation? Second, as we focus in on different kinds of semiotic approaches to translation, we can begin to distinguish distinct ways that language works to create what Gal calls "equivalence-in-difference." For example, one can use analogies between the practices or texts of different disciplines' languages in order to create authority for one approach by modeling it on another (and here Gal adopts the more technical Silversteinian language to specify this form of translation as *transduction*). One fascinating example Gal gives us is the early transduction of legal evidentiary practices (the use of multiple witnesses and original/primary evidence) into natural science, where scientists drew on the law of evidence to delineate adequate standards for empirical proof in science. And, Gal points out, ironically looping back around, US courts are sometimes now turning to scientific evidentiary models to solidify conceptions of factuality and proof. In contrast with this transduction approach to interdisciplinary borrowing, one could alternatively insist that the overarching categories defining a particular translation come from one disciplinary language, subsuming materials drawn from the other discipline as mere examples that fit within the frame decreed by the more dominant discipline (Gal's *translation-as-voicing*). Finally, the third key issue raised by Gal is the way that legal (and other) contestation over boundaries among disciplines is bound up in social movements, practices, knowledge forms, and identities that create a kind of *looping effect* (or what others might call *recursivity*; see Mertz 2016 for a discussion of the concept of recursivity in NLR scholarship).[8]

If the first section of the volume underscores the difficulties involved in translating social science for law on the ground, the second suggests ways that research on the institutional systems and norms surrounding this translation process can open doors to new possibilities for improved understanding. But a first step toward this would be to actually take the barriers to communication seriously. This issue is explored further in Part Three.

2.2.3 *[PART THREE]* TOWARD IMPROVED TRANSLATIONS: RECOGNIZING THE BARRIERS

One thread that runs throughout the volume is the idea that it is only through a realistic recognition of the barriers to interdisciplinary translation that law can make the best use of social science. Adequate recognition of where and how these barriers block communication will require sustained attention and cooperation among professionals trained in the relevant disciplinary languages (or discourses). The final section of the volume presents two quite different approaches to assessing those barriers and how they might be overcome.

In the first chapter, Elizabeth Mertz analyzes the results of a methodological experiment, in which the interdisciplinary group at the core of this volume worked together, over several meetings in 2009, to read and interpret a transcript of a previous conversation between linguists and lawyers, from a conference held in 1995. That earlier conference represented a concerted and conscious attempt to find common ground between scholars in trained in linguistics and others trained in law (traditions which, despite many differences, share an exacting micro-level attention to the details of language). The fact that the scholars involved in the 1995 conference had published a transcript of their interactions provided a wonderful opportunity for our working group to assess a deliberate attempt to translate between legal and linguistic scholarship. In her chapter, Mertz analyzes the 1995 transcript, using the general perspective developed by the working group whose work is presented in this volume (along with perspectives from her own home discipline of linguistic anthropology). At a number of points in her chapter, Mertz draws on the explicit discussions that this working group held in 2009 when it used the earlier 1995 transcript as its central topic for conversation. (Cross-checking and sharing linguistic observations in working groups as part of transcript analysis is a methodological approach that has been part of law-and-language scholarship from its inception, as Mertz explains.) The core role of linguistic ideologies in interdisciplinary translation becomes evident in Mertz's chapter, as she traces moments of productive exchange but also misfires even within a highly trained and very perceptive group of scholars.

The second chapter in this section is actually itself an edited transcript from an interview with law-and-literature scholar Peter Brooks, as he reflects on "law's resistance to translation." Characterizing legal rhetoric as at times "Teflon-coated," Brooks expresses concern that in law schools' insistence on forms of doctrine and legal practice as central, they miss the importance of their role as homes for law as an intellectual discipline. Law as an intellectual discipline can insist that legal professionals continue to consider what is excluded by standard legal approaches; the legal academy can play a role in reminding lawyers to keep questioning and raising doubts about too-easily-accepted legal certainties. In conclusion, Brooks holds out hope for continued fruitful interdisciplinary conversation for law with other disciplines, despite the admittedly serious barriers that he identifies.

3.1 Themes and Conclusions

In sum, the chapters in this volume make a strong case for the non-transparency of interdisciplinary translation, while advocating for its importance. When we move between the languages of law and the languages of the social sciences, we cannot assume that communication will be simple or straightforward. Just as we would if going to another country where a distinct language is spoken, we need to think first about the customs and assumptions that characterize the new context in which we are speaking—and we need to take seriously the linguistic differences that can separate us from our new interlocutors. Lawyers and legal scholars use a very distinctive, normatively charged set of linguistic practices. These language practices have underlying goals and ethics that diverge sharply from those underlying most (if not all) of the social sciences. Some (not all) trained in law adhere to metalinguistic norms shaped by their profession's role as a source of advocacy, while many (not all) social scientists adhere to metalinguistic norms in which a more cooperative and pensive back-and-forth is valued. From one side, the pugilistic style can seem the opposite of intellectual discussion. From another side, the nuanced and seemingly meandering discussion, which is deliberately open-ended, can seem aimless. Here we consider just a few of the overarching guidelines for interdisciplinary communication that have emerged from the volume authors' careful analyses of legal and social science discourses.

3.2 Meta-Level Communicative Norms

Our first conclusion is that we need to pay better attention to the meta-level norms that guide language in different disciplinary settings. For example, there are questions on which social science arguably cannot offer what law needs, because the reasons and purposes behind communication are just so different. Gruber, Matoesian, Silverstein, and Sullivan all offer examples of these strong divergences, although they might disagree as to whether this should lead to pessimism as to how far social science can go in correcting the problems they identify in the legal translation process. On the other hand, there are issues about which social science can offer good guidance, but where discussion has been curtailed because of inadequate consideration of the meta-norms guiding legal translation, and of the limiting effects of the surrounding institutional settings (see, e.g., Ford, Sullivan, Burns, Gal, Mertz, Brooks).[9] In these situations, it is possible that better analysis could lead to more effective use of social science in law. A first step toward achieving better communication is to at least acknowledge and carefully delineate the different goals and theoretical frames involved.

3.3 Language Details and Contexts

These chapters are replete with discussions of how differences among disciplinary languages can be discerned only through attention to tiny linguistic details and to how those details take on specific meaning within particular contexts. Studying the structured links between disciplinary languages and practices, on the one hand, and institutional and larger social contexts, on the other hand, will be crucial in furthering higher-quality translations of social science—and of the social world—for law. It's admittedly a pain in the neck, but there is just no way around it. Ignoring the need for this kind of systematic attention simply leads to mistaken and misleading invocations of social science—or, perhaps more accurately, it robs interdisciplinary encounters of their potential power to enlighten, and in this particular case, to contribute to more just uses of law.

3.4 Underlying Disciplinary Worldviews (or Epistemologies)

As we deepen our understanding of interdisciplinary translation, we will have to find ways to specify the divergent kinds of demands for certainty found in different disciplines. What seems like waffling to one audience might seem like a required precision as to the bounds of certainty for another. Similarly, the contributors to this volume help us understand the quite different construction of "facts" or pieces of knowledge that form the basis of understandings in various disciplines. This group, having developed practices for attending to their disciplinary differences, was able to find constructive ways of translating across those differences to develop the coordinated conversation evidenced in their contributions here. But watching scholars who hold very different ideas converse with no recognition of the difference is a bit like watching two people banging their heads against a glass wall from different sides, each convinced that the other is the one with the problem. Finally, a crucial point for misunderstanding is the different kind of relationship that disciplines forge between facts and organizing theoretical frames. Plucking findings or methods out of the theoretical contexts that gave them empirical meaning sounds obviously self-defeating, and yet is all too common of a practice. Outlining all of these kinds of epistemological differences with analytic care is an indispensable step toward accurate interdisciplinary translation.

3.5 The Process of Interdisciplinary Translation Itself

Finally, we conclude with the deceptively simple observation that it is important to be thinking consciously about the process of translation itself when working between law and social science. Even within social science fields devoted to the issue of language, scholars often assume that they can converse with scholars from other fields without considering all angles required for a conscious effort at interdisciplinary translation: for example, without first asking what the goals of communication in a particular encounter are, what background assumptions about word meaning and language are operative, and so on. Most would agree that we have to frame what we say differently when addressing different audiences,[10] yet we have a long way to go in thinking rigorously about how to communicate with the quite different audiences that exist for legal and social scientific knowledge. What are the barriers to translation? When should we even try; are there points at which translation is impossible? When is effective translation useful, or even essential? The contributors to this volume have given us some exciting insights into these issues.

Even within this volume, based on work generated by years of discussions by the participants, we can see discipline-based differences that peek through despite the regimentation imposed by conforming to our stated volume guidelines. Indeed, we deliberately permitted some distinctive features to remain. The chapter by Ford crosses disciplines and genres in its lengthy dissection of the legal landscape surrounding the in-depth analysis he performs. Aspects of this format are much more typical of law review articles than of social science ones: it relies on massive numbers of footnotes (consistent with the deference in legal writing generally to authoritative texts, with frequent and precise citations required), and it sets out a problem with full context given for the argument that it makes. As one of us has noted before, law review editors are law students, and they work long hours to trace and check the original sources for each citation (Mertz 2007b, 496–497). It would not be possible for them to verify that what the original sources say is true: this would fall far beyond their expertise. By contrast, when social scientists submit their articles to peer review, the scholars refereeing their work are supposed to be conversant with the relevant research in the field. No number of citations in a long list will suffice to support a proposition if the work in the source material has been discredited. (On the other hand, it is expected that social scientists will police their own footnotes and be sure that the page numbers and publication information are correct.) It's important to note, however, that Ford's chapter departs from the typical law review article in that his research began with a question that was empirically investigated, only coming to a conclusion after the investigation is satisfactorily concluded. (In that sense, it could be viewed as a hybrid effort.) The typical law review article, perhaps predictably, often identifies a problem and then makes an extended argument for the author's preferred solution. This more argumentative and normative format again fits well with legal approaches.

By contrast, the body of social science articles is typically less polemical, focused more on describing the empirical method and research results, and on analyzing what was revealed by the study. It would be considered a strength to note the limitations of the method, and to indicate what still needs to be discovered—whereas putting too many caveats in a law review article might undermine the entire project. In general, as in the peer review process, the format of social science articles presumes a great deal of shared disciplinary knowledge, which allows research questions and results to be presented more succinctly. And of course, the details of formatting for social science articles will vary across disciplines, and even subdisciplines. As noted, even within the narrow compass of this volume, we've tried to give our own audience at least an initial sense of how different approaches (disciplines, genres) can affect the form, kind, and requirements of knowledge they yield.

From our "translation blocks" to inclusion of different genres and added exegetical apparatus such as footnotes (and the attached chart summarizing the volume), we've attempted to demonstrate the kinds of issues that arise in moving among disciplines—even as we've also discussed and exemplified them within the content of the chapters. There is a very strong consensus in the empirical research on law's contact with other disciplines: translation is needed, and many improvements could be achieved within law through judicious application of social science knowledge. The question that remains is whether those carrying on this interdisciplinary conversation will find the willingness and the skill to create more meaningful translations.

Acknowledgements

We thank our colleagues in the Chicago NLR Translation Group for years of rich conversation and insight, and we are particularly grateful to Michael Silverstein and Greg Matoesian for taking time to read and respond to this chapter with very helpful comments.

Notes

1. These discussions were held over a period of four years. There were differences within the group over a number of issues. For example, each disciplinary tradition had its own specialized vocabulary for some of the central issues we were discussing. What we are calling disciplinary "languages" here would generally be referred to as *registers* within fields such as sociolinguistics and linguistic anthropology. We use the less technical vernacular wording here not only as part of our own effort to communicate across disciplinary divisions, but also to highlight a central theme of the volume: that an assumption of easy translation or communication across disciplines is itself a form of linguistic ideology (i.e., meta-level, culturally informed ideas about how language works)—and one that can actively hinder understanding. If we think of the differences in forms of disciplines' communication as differences in "languages" that need "translation," we may take more seriously the divisions that lead to failures in interdisciplinary understandings. Throughout this introduction, any mention of "the working group" refers to the NLR Translation Working Group that met in Chicago during a period from 2005 to 2009 (see Mertz, this volume, for a more in-depth description).

2. Michael Silverstein (2003) has suggested alternatives such as *transduction* and *transformation* that might also have provided terminology for parts of the interdisciplinary communicative process involved here (cf. Gal, this volume). Ultimately, and perhaps ironically, we concluded that use of this more technical vocabulary might make our own "translation" here less accessible to audiences outside of linguistic anthropology.

3. This literature is too voluminous for us to do justice to it here—which only goes to make our point more palpable: there is a great deal of interdisciplinary research that could in theory be used to make law more fair and accessible to all. There are certainly some wonderful examples of productive forensic work—in naming just a few of many, one could mention Diana Eades' work with the government of Australia on Aboriginal English (http://www.une.edu.au/staff-profiles/bcss/deades), or Peter Tiersma's work on jury instructions in California (2001). Roger Shuy's notable series of books based on his own forensic work (see, e.g., Shuy 1993, 2005, 2013) provides many examples of linguists' utility in trials (for example, his analyses of an indirect speech act and the discourse context of topic recycling in the DeLorean case, along with many other insightful applications of linguistic insights in the context of criminal trials where so much is at stake).

We view our volume as another contribution in a continuing stream of research that pushes at the difficult linguistic boundary between law and social science.

4. While many of us were trained in linguistics and linguistic anthropology, this volume does not claim those fields as the only key to understanding the interdisciplinary difficulties on which we focus. Instead, we draw on those fields for some useful tools, as part

of a larger conversation among multiple disciplines. And although much of this commentary focuses on law's failure to pick up on clearly relevant knowledge from social science scholarship on language, law, and their intersection—we readily acknowledge that social scientists have sometimes missed aspects of legal scholarship that is arguably relevant to their work. There is, however, a power difference; when law as a discipline fails to make use of knowledge that could enlighten lawmakers, judges, lawyers, and juries, miscarriages of justice can result. Perhaps also because of this power difference, with law as the dominant discourse, those conversant with law tend to be less careful or even interested in borrowing from other fields. By contrast, it is more frequently the case that social scientists studying legal issues take great care to learn as much as they can about the legal field. Nonetheless, as is noted elsewhere in this chapter, social scientists too often assume that the different (more normatively laden) mission of law and legal scholarship is transparent to interdisciplinary translation—whereas in fact legal epistemologies and languages have deep and important roots within the exigencies of their field. This, too, must be taken into account for good interdisciplinary translations to occur—as we can see in many examples throughout this volume.

5. Of course, the history of attempts to apply social science in law has many interesting ups-and-downs. Some of the attempts thought to have been most successful—as with the famous "Brandeis brief," or *Brown v. Board of Education*—later received fairly convincing critiques in terms of the quality of the social science itself or how it was reframed in addressing legal questions (see Mertz 2008 for further discussion of this conundrum). While some legal scholars claim that "we're all realists now"—implying that the major insights of realism are now commonplace truisms, it's clear that law practice, law teaching, and legal scholarship all lack any systematic approach to incorporating social science in sophisticated ways. Indeed, in the wake of famed cases that require judges to act as gatekeepers for admission of social science evidence, more than one judge has commented explicitly (and ruefully) in their opinions on their lack of appropriate expertise for this assigned task (Yovel and Mertz 2004; Mertz 2008). But as we suggest in this volume, the judges themselves can hardly be held to account for this unfortunate deficiency when the part of the discipline with the most time and resources for working this puzzle out (the academy) has yet to really tackle the meta-level question of how best to bring these discourses together, with only a very few exceptions. (And then it goes without saying that in the absence of a systematic scholarly tradition, law professors have a long way to go in incorporating social science usefully and appropriately into the training of nascent lawyers during law school.)

6. Linguistic ideologies underlie *metapragmatic* language—that is, language that reflexively comments on its own contextually dependent function and/or meaning (Lucy 1993; Mertz 1993; Schieffelin, Woolard, and Kroskrity 1998; Silverstein 1976, 1993). Implicit metapragmatic structuring occurs at many levels, from "micro-levels" at which small shifts in intonation patterns (even when using otherwise identical phraseology) can create or break down understood social distance, to "macro-levels" at which broad shared ideas about identity and language use help listeners to understand what someone is conveying when they shift the kind of language they are using (whether, say, from Swahili to English, or from a local Southern US dialect to the kind of speech style typical of NPR radio announcers). Included within this broader category are norms governing "proper speech"—for example, a shared understanding that yelling and swearing are not appropriate at a professional conference, or the varying degrees of harsh criticism tolerated as "civil" in different professional settings.

7. This observation bridges legal issues that point in quite different political directions, as can be seen through a comparison of the common ground that Ford's critique shares with critiques of Justice Rehnquist's approach to death penalty studies (Baldus, Woodworth, and Pulaski 1990; Mertz 2008). As lawyers and judges frequently assume a world in which arguments vary depending on the result one wants to reach, it might be reassuring to note that social scientists view conservative and liberal judges as equally prone to making serious errors in assessing social science evidence. As Ford notes, "Lawyers are not quick to highlight or even acknowledge the limitations in their arguments. . . . This may explain why the court[s] . . . treated standard scholarly statements about the limitations of their work as something closer to admissions of failure" (2013, 329). Anthropologist James Clifford (1988) gives a telling example of this in demonstrating how a federal court failed to grasp the strength of subtle anthropological testimony on behalf of the Mashpee.

8. Michael Silverstein (pers. comm.) suggests that an apt term here might be emergent "in the sense of performatively entailed," following Ian Hacking's conception of looping concepts in the social sciences.

9. The list of authors following each of these points does not exhaust the way their chapters could be invoked—as some of the more pessimistic chapters nonetheless indicate possible channels for better interdisciplinary translations, while some of the more optimistic chapters nonetheless acknowledge the difficult chasms that would need to be bridged for such translations to succeed.

10. As noted, linguists and many literary scholars would talk about this issue of addressing different audiences in terms of the contextually specific deployment of particular "registers."

References

Ainsworth, Janet. 1993. "In a Different Register: The Pragmatics of Powerlessness in Police Interrogation." *Yale Law Journal* 103: 259–322.

Baldus, David, George Woodworth, and Charles Pulaski. 1990. *Equal Justice and the Death Penalty: A Legal and Empirical Analysis*. Boston: Northeastern University Press.

Bellos, David. 2011. *Is That a Fish in Your Ear?* New York: Faber and Faber, Inc.

Clifford, James. 1988. *The Predicament of Culture: Twentieth-Century Ethnography, Literature, and Art*. Cambridge, MA: Harvard University Press.

Constable, Marianne. 2014. *Our Word Is Our Bond: How Legal Speech Acts*. Stanford: Stanford University Press.

Eades, Diana. 2008. *Courtroom Talk and Neocolonial Control*. Berlin: Mouton de Gruyter.

Erlanger, Howard, Bryant Garth, Jane Larson, Elizabeth Mertz, Victoria Nourse, and David Wilkins. 2005. "Is It Time for a New Legal Realism?" *Wisconsin Law Review* 2005(2): 335–363.

Ford, William. 2013. "The Law and Science of Video Game Violence: What Was Lost in Translation?" *Cardozo Arts & Entertainment Law Journal* 31: 297–356.

Lucy, John. 1993. "Reflexive Language and the Human Disciplines." In *Reflexive Language: Reported Speech and Metapragmatics*, edited John Lucy, 9–32. Cambridge: Cambridge University Press.

Macaulay, Stewart. 2005. "The New versus the Old Realism: 'Things Ain't What They Used to Be.'" *Wisconsin Law Review* 2005(2): 365–403.

Matoesian, Gregory M. 2001. *Law and the Language of Identity: Discourse in the William Kennedy Smith Rape Trial*. Oxford: Oxford University Press.

Mertz, Elizabeth. 1993. "Learning What to Ask: Metapragmatic Factors and Methodological Reification." In *Reflexive Language: Reported Speech and Metapragmatics*, edited by John Lucy, 159–174. Cambridge: Cambridge University Press.

Mertz, Elizabeth. 2007a. *The Language of Law Schools: Learning to "Think Like a Lawyer."* Oxford: Oxford University Press.

Mertz, Elizabeth. 2007b. "Inside the Law School Classroom: Toward a New Legal Realist Pedagogy." *Vanderbilt Law Review* 60: 483–513.

Mertz, Elizabeth. 2008. "Introduction: Toward a Systematic Translation of Law and Social Science." In *The Use of Social Science in Legal Decisions*, edited by Elizabeth Mertz, xiii–xxx. Aldershot: Ashgate.

Mertz, Elizabeth. 2016. "Introduction: New Legal Realism: Law and Social Science in the New Millenium." In *The New Legal Realism: Translating Law-and-Society for Today's Legal Practice*, edited by Stewart Macaulay, Elizabeth Mertz, and Thomas W. Mitchell. Cambridge: Cambridge University Press.

Richland, Justin. 2008. *Arguing with Tradition: The Language of Law in a Hopi Tribal Court*. Chicago: University of Chicago Press.

Scheiffelin, Bambi, Kathryn Woolard, and Paul Kroskrity, eds. 1998. *Language Ideologies: Practice and Theory.* Oxford: Oxford University Press.

Shuy, Roger. 1993. *Language Crimes: The Use and Abuse of Language Evidence in the Courtroom.* Malden, MA: Wiley Blackwell.

Shuy, Roger. 2005. *Creating Language Crimes: How Law Enforcement Uses (and Misuses) Language.* Oxford: Oxford University Press.

Shuy, Roger. 2013. *The Language of Bribery Cases.* Oxford: Oxford University Press.

Silverstein, Michael. 1976. "Shifters, Linguistic Categories, and Cultural Description." In *Meaning in Anthropology*, edited by Keith H. Basso and Henry A. Selby, 11–55. Albuquerque: University of New Mexico Press.

Silverstein, Michael. 1979. "Language Structure and Linguistic Ideology." In *The Elements: A Parasession on Linguistic Units and Levels*, edited by Paul R. Clyne, William F. Hanks, and Carol L. Hofbauer, 194–247. Chicago: Chicago Linguistic Society.

Silverstein, Michael. 1993. "Metapragmatic Discourse and Metapragmatic Function." In *Reflexive Language: Reported Speech and Metapragmatics*, edited by John Lucy, 33–58. Cambridge: Cambridge University Press.

Silverstein, Michael. 2003. "Translation, Transduction, Transformation: Skating Glossando on Thin Semiotic Ice." In *Translating Cultures: Perspectives on Translation and Anthropology*, edited Paula G. Rubel and Abraham Rosman, 75–105. Oxford: Berg.

Solan, Lawrence, and Peter Tiersma. 2005. *Speaking of Crime: The Language of Criminal Justice*. Chicago: University of Chicago Press.

Suchman, Mark, and Elizabeth Mertz. 2010. "Toward a New Legal Empiricism: Empirical Legal Studies and New Legal Realism." *Annual Review of Law & Social Science* 6: 555–579.

Tiersma, Peter. 2001. "The Rocky Road to Legal Reform: Improving the Language of Jury Instructions. *Brooklyn Law Review* 66: 1081–1119.

Yovel, Jonathan, and Elizabeth Mertz. 2004. "Courtroom Narrative." In *Routledge Encyclopedia of Narrative Theory*, edited by D. Herman, M. Jahn, and M. Ryan, Routledge.

PART ONE

Analyzing Legal Translations on the Ground

2

Translating Defendants' Apologies during Allocution at Sentencing
M. Catherine Gruber

2A

Gruber "In Translation"
Frances Tung

2.1 Introduction

2A.1 In this paper, Gruber uses sociolinguistic analysis to explore communication problems that arise in courtroom exchanges between defendants and judges. Specifically, she examines the different possible meanings of apologies made to the court by convicted defendants during their sentencing hearings. Detailed study of these interactions shows that when judges omit consideration of surrounding linguistic contexts, they can misunderstand the meaning of defendants' *I'm sorry* statements. The application of a sociolinguistic perspective requires that attention be paid to those surrounding contexts, whereas the judges' legal approach does not. It is very common for speakers to rely on surrounding utterances when conveying meaning in any particular sentence. Gruber demonstrates that background assumptions embedded in legal frameworks can lead judges to focus on single sentences in defendants' apologies, failing to examine fuller linguistic contexts. In the process, apologies viewed as unambiguous by defendants may be interpreted as ambiguous by judges. Gruber's research indicates that once a particular apology is misunderstood as ambiguous, then it is more likely to be interpreted as reflecting self-interest (as opposed to remorse) if it is uttered by a defendant who more closely fits the stereotype of a "career criminal." Gruber then explores how to translate the difference in perspective between legal and sociolinguistic approaches.

This paper deals with the different ways in which people fill in the gaps and interpret an interlocutor's utterance.[1] That there are gaps in naturally occurring speech is uncontested: we rely on context (which includes the background information known or believed to be known by our interlocutor(s)) to supply a vast range of information ranging from the relevant time period indexed by our use of a present or past tense form, the identities of persons referenced by means of pronouns, and absent or deleted objects, such as what is communicated by "I will, too" when it follows a fellow diner's order of: "I'll have the special." The focus of this paper is one interesting case, supplemented with an analysis of other cases, in which a sentencing judge identified two different meanings of a defendant's brief apology—a bare *I'm sorry* which lacks a complement (e.g., a *for*-clause, such as "I'm sorry for making you wait"). In this case, during her closing remarks, the judge noted that a defendant's bare *I'm sorry* could mean that the defendant was sorry for his/her actions or it could mean that the defendant was sorry to have gotten caught. These two translations carry conflicting implications regarding the stance that the defendant is understood to have adopted. In the context of a sentencing hearing this is critically important because the stance or attitude which the defendant is viewed as having toward his/her crime could impact the judge's decision regarding the sentence that should be applied.

From the perspective of sociolinguistics, in the context of allocution at sentencing—the point at which defendants are invited to address the court—a defendant's bare *I'm sorry* looks considerably different. While the sentencing judge focused on the potential meanings of a single utterance with no reference to the turn of talk as a whole, sociolinguists insist that utterances be assessed in the light of their surrounding context. So, for example, although it is true that nearly 20% of the defendants in the data set used for this study produced bare *I'm sorry* statements, a look at the allocutions as a whole reveals that whenever defendants produced *I'm sorry* statements with reduced argument structure, elsewhere in the allocution they made some kind of reference to their offense. Generally speaking, when an argument of a verb (in this case, an oblique argument, or complement) appears in one sentence, its absence in a parallel structure elsewhere in the same turn of talk (and typically subsequent turns as well) is understood as a deletion in the surface structure; with regard to meaning, however, it is still understood as "there." Thus, in the example presented above, "have the special" is deleted in the surface structure of the fellow diner's order of "I will, too." When a sentencing judge focuses on a single utterance, the elements that fill out the meaning of surface deletions in that utterance can be easily obscured.

Following Irvine and Gal (2000), this appears to be a case of erasure, which they define as "the process in which ideology, in simplifying the sociolinguistic field, renders some persons or activities (or sociolinguistic phenomena) invisible" (2000, 38). In this case, defendants' references to their crimes are erased, thereby making the judge's claim of ambiguity of meaning possible. This paper proposes, following Gruber (2008, 2014), that the context of sentencing hearings functions to impute intentions to defendants, who are often viewed as apologizing out of self-interest with regard to the impending sentence rather than out of remorse. It appears that the more defendants match the image of "career criminal," the more this calculus seems to apply. Merely observing that defendants' references to their crimes are erased, however, misses much of the interesting complexity of the genre of allocutory apologies at sentencing because the references that defendants do make to their crimes are usually quite vague, often consisting of semantically bleached referring constructions such as "what I did" or "my actions." Thus, to take one example in which a defendant produced a bare *I'm sorry*, earlier in her allocution she referred to the offense, saying: *I know and I admit, uh, what I did was wrong and I'm sincerely sorry for it.* While these nonspecific references may appear from a judge's perspective to reflect either a lack of awareness or a denial of responsibility, a close look at the context of sentencing hearings and commonly used rules of information structure help to explain the predominance of these forms.

When it comes to sharing these findings and translating between the field of sociolinguistics and the courtroom, a number of issues surrounding the interpretation of affect (or emotion) arise. These issues are rooted in the many and diverse ideologies surrounding emotion, which often conflict in fundamental ways. Thus, following Labov and Fanshel (1977), although individuals are often viewed as undisputed experts on the topic of their own feelings (1977, 34), Goffman (1986) observes that an individual's thoughts and feelings make their appearance through both intended and unintended expressions (1986, 216). This feature of emotions positions both speaker and addressee in privileged positions when it comes to the assessment of someone's emotional state. Case law has long supported judges' individual assessments of defendants' demeanor at sentencing and considered that assessment as a legitimate factor in sentencing. This paper explores some of the issues surrounding the translation of the insights of sociolinguistics when these insights conflict with ideologies of role identity and performance of emotion.

2.2 Allocution at Sentencing

2A.2 Defendants at sentencing are given an opportunity to address the court (an act known as an *allocution*), and many defendants use this opportunity to make an apology. Although this option can provide benefits for defendants, it can also open the door to negative perceptions—as, for example, if the allocution does not convey a sufficient sense of remorse or responsibility. Because these apologetic allocutions occur just before sentencing, defendants also often start out having to combat a perception that their apologies are self-interested, just by virtue of the contextual (or metapragmatic) framing involved. For this project, Gruber collected

52 apologetic allocutions from a set of three judges. Within her data set, the phrase *I'm sorry* without any additional elaboration (or *complements*) is not an uncommon format. Because *I'm sorry* can precede two very different complements—one in which the speaker takes responsibility for the misdeed (e.g., *I'm sorry for what I've done*) and one in which the speaker expresses sympathy for something he/she did not cause (e.g., *I'm sorry you feel that way*) a bare *I'm sorry* produced by a defendant at sentencing can be viewed by a judge as an attempt to mask a lack of responsibility for the crime.

The practice of giving defendants the opportunity to address the court at sentencing is known as the right of allocution. Allocution is viewed as being primarily a benefit for the defendant because it provides an opportunity to make a statement in his/her own behalf and to present any information in mitigation of punishment. Allocution also comes with risks, however. As noted by O'Hear (1997) and Natapoff (2005), one of the main risks for defendants—especially those who have pleaded guilty (and this is the vast majority[2])—is that the defendant might speak in such a way as to suggest that she/he had not fully accepted responsibility for the crime.

At federal sentencing hearings, judges generally impose sentences based on the Federal Sentencing Guidelines. Defendants get assigned a particular range of months of incarceration based on the intersection of their total offense level and their criminal history category. The Federal Sentencing Guidelines used to leave judges little discretion. Apart from the lowest sentences, the maximum of a sentencing range does not exceed the minimum by more than 25%. In most cases, it is this 25% of the lower end of the range over which the judge exercises discretion, and upon which a defendant's allocution could have an effect. In January 2005, in the case of *United States v. Booker*, the Supreme Court held that the Federal Sentencing Guidelines were no longer mandatory; as a result, a judge now has greater freedom to impose a sentence that is below the guidelines when she feels such a sentence is warranted.[3] The Sourcebook of Federal Sentencing Statistics reveals, however, that the Guidelines appear to be used in much the same way that they were before *Booker*.[4]

If defendants choose to address the court, they often use their allocution to make some sort of apology to the judge, their families, the victim(s), and/or the government. Allocution provides a non-prototypical context for the production of an apology for a number of reasons (here I mention just a few): in the context of a sentencing hearing, defendants are offering an apology many months after the offense to someone who was not directly harmed by their actions. Further, given that the purpose of the sentencing hearing is to impose a sentence of imprisonment, it will be presumed that defendants seek to minimize their sentences. As a result, when defendants make apologetic allocutions—as most of those who make an allocution do—the metapragmatic[5] framing supplied by the context of the courtroom already functions so as to weight what defendants say in the direction of self-interest. Speech act theorists such as Austin (1962) and Searle (1975) have observed that successful apologies depend upon the perception that speakers are sincere. Because sincerity conflicts with self-interest, the apologies produced at sentencing can be understood as handicapped to a significant degree. Lastly, we know from the work of Coulmas (1981) and others that apologies typically occur in a three-part sequence: the misdeed, the apology, and some kind of response by the addressee. In the context of the sentencing hearing, judges usually do not respond to the content of defendants' allocutions. This lack of interaction makes a defendant's allocution monologic in many respects, in contrast with more typical apologies, which are usually part of a dialogue.

Between November 2004 and March 2006, Gruber collected 52 apologetic allocutions in the courtrooms of three different US District Court judges to whom she refers as Judge X, Judge Y, and Judge Z.[6] She collected 17 allocutions in Judge X's courtroom, 17 allocutions in Judge Y's courtroom, and 18 allocutions in Judge Z's courtroom. Gruber attended and took notes on each of the sentencing hearings and afterwards used recordings of the hearings to make her own transcripts for analysis. The defendants consisted of 41 men and 11 women. In terms of race (using the category names employed by the district courts), 26 (or 50%) of the defendants were Caucasian; 16 (31%) were African-American; eight were Native American; one was Hispanic; and one was Asian. The convictions that led to the sentencing hearings that Gruber observed were obtained by guilty pleas for 48 of the defendants and by trials for four of the defendants. The three most common categories of crimes for which they were being sentenced related to drugs, firearms, or fraud/embezzlement. The allocutions ranged between 4 seconds and 186 seconds; the average allocution lasted for about 30 seconds. To protect defendants' identities, allocutions are generally referred to by the letter X, Y, or Z, depending on the judge that presided, plus a number.

In one of the cases that was observed, the defendant, who had pleaded guilty to selling drugs, had submitted a letter in advance of the hearing which Gruber was permitted to see. As part of the two-page letter which he submitted to Judge X, the defendant, a 30-year-old Native American man, wrote:

> ... I would like for this letter to be my voice and let all the people I hurt with my actions to know that I am truly sorry for what I have done. I would like my experience here [in jail] to teach others, which is why I am sending a copy of the letter to the [name of local newspaper], the local newspaper of my native people. .. I hope that by relaying this information to them, that the people of the [name of reservation] Reservation will think twice before using or selling drugs. (X20)

During the sentencing hearing Judge X offered the defendant (referred to here as Mr. T) the opportunity to address the court and the following exchange ensued:

> JUDGE X: Mr. T, is there anything you'd like to say in your own behalf before I sentence you?
> MR. T: Uh, you did, did you receive the letter that I wrote .. to you?
> JUDGE X: I think so; are you talking about the letter that was sent on, um
> MR. T: The same.
> JUDGE X: November .. we received it on November 22.
> MR. T: Yeah, that'd be the one. And that's what I would like to say to the court. That's everything that I would like to say to the court.[7]

Thus, although Mr. T spoke during his sentencing hearing, he did not make a statement in his own behalf. At the beginning of her closing remarks Judge X said:

> ~Mr. T, it is, as ~Mr. Jones [the defense attorney] pointed out often the case that people come into the court and say "Ah, now I'm really sorry" and it's often hard to distinguish between "I'm really sorry I ever did this and I understand the harm it caused" and the "I'm really sorry I did this and got caught—and have to come to court and take the consequences of my actions." I hope that your remorse is the former kind, that you understand just how much harm you have caused the reservation, the people on the reservation. (X20)[8]

For the record (and contrary to Judge X's claim—and defense attorney Jones's, for that matter), Mr. T did not produce a bare *I'm sorry* in either the letter he submitted to Judge X before the sentencing hearing or during his allocution. Judge X, who located the letter during the sentencing hearing (as evidenced by her reference to receiving it on November 22) but did not spend time rereading it, appears to have reduced the meaningful elements of Mr. T's letter to a bare *I'm sorry*. An examination of the data set of 52 apologetic allocutions reveals that a bare *I'm sorry* from defendants was not uncommon: 10 defendants produced 12 tokens in which *I'm sorry* lacked a complement of any kind (Table 2.1). (A token is defined as an utterance consisting of an optional subject, a verb (or verbs if they are conjoined), and its complement(s), which is usually demarcated by pauses.) The tokens of *I'm sorry* which lack a complement are presented below, following an explanation of the transcription symbols used (Table 2.2).

1. No matter how many times I can say it, .. I'm sorry. (X13: 4)
2. From the bottom of my heart, .. I'm sorry. That would be it. [end of allocution] (Y1: 3–4)
3. And (1.0) I just wanna say that .. I'm sorry, (Y2: 8)
   (H) And I'm sorry, (Y2: 12)

4. (TSK) (1.2) Um, I'd just like to say I'm sorry, (Y8: 1)
5. I'm so sorry. [end of allocution] (Y18: 8)
6. and say that I'm sorry, (Z5: 7)
7. but I am sorry, and [end of allocution] (Z6: 10)
8. but (1.0) I'm sorry. [end of allocution] (Z16: 32)
9. I'm sorry.>> [end of allocution] (Z20: 8)
10. ((turns to family)) (1.0)
    I'm sorry. (Z21: 5)
    (SNIFF) and I'm sorry.>> [end of allocution] (Z21: 8)

TABLE 2.1
Defendant demographics for the defendants whose speech is represented in this paper

Defendant	Gender	Age	Race	Education Level	Main Charge
X12	F	41	Caucasian	Some college	Theft of mail by employee
X13	M	47	Native American	GED	Selling controlled substance
X16	M	26	African-American	11th grade	Selling controlled substance
Y1	M	28	Caucasian	11th grade	Selling controlled substance
Y2	F	25	Native American	10th grade	Selling controlled substance
Y8	F	31	Caucasian	11th grade	Bank robbery
Y18	F	40	Caucasian	2 yrs college	Frauds & swindles
Z2	M	37	Caucasian	Some college	Submitting false financial statement
Z5	M	27	African-American	GED	Selling narcotics
Z6	M	48	Caucasian	High school	Explosives used in destruction of personal property; unlawful possession of firearm
Z16	M	56	African-American	Unknown	Conspiracy to commit election fraud
Z20	F	30	African-American	1 yr college	Conspiracy to distribute controlled substance
Z21	F	29	African-American	1 yr college	Conspiracy to distribute controlled substance

TABLE 2.2
Meaning of transcription symbols (largely following Du Bois 2006)

Transcription Symbol	Meaning
#	Unintelligible; one per syllable
#word	transcribed word is uncertain
(1.2)	intra-sentence pause duration in seconds and tenths of seconds
..	intra-sentence pause lasting less than 1 second
(H)	audible inhalation
(Hx)	audible exhalation
<	beginning of wavery/unsteady voice
>	end of wavery/unsteady voice
<<	beginning of crying-while-talking
>>	end of crying-while-talking
word	boldface indicates emphasis via loudness or contrastive pitch

In the data set as a whole, 29 defendants produced 43 tokens which contained a form of the phrase *I'm sorry*. No other construction was used by more defendants. Approximately one fourth of these 43 tokens lacked a complement: thus, as noted above, 10 of the 29 defendants produced 12 tokens of a variant of *I'm sorry* that had no complement.

2.3 Interpreting a Bare *I'm Sorry*

2A.3 In the case example above, the judge remarked that the phrase *I'm sorry* could be interpreted in two ways: as an expression of remorse for committing the offense (which is viewed as more valued because it indicates the individual's potential to be rehabilitated) or as a feeling of sorrow about the consequences of getting caught. Given the pattern of references evident in defendants' allocutions, a judge would have to interpret the bare phrase *I'm sorry* in isolation from the rest of the allocution in order to understand that phrase as only indicating sorrow about the consequences of getting caught. From a sociolinguistic perspective, the meaning of this phrase can only be understood when considering the whole allocution. Gruber provides examples of the way contextual information illuminates the meaning of each allocution. When the context is included, the meaning of the apology is better understood: defendants actually are often referring to their offenses in seemingly "bare" apologies, using conventions that pervade everyday speech. However, the apparent ambiguity of bare apologies gave judges increased freedom to "erase" defendants' other parts of their allocutions, increasing the likelihood that individuals who fit the profile of a "career criminal" would be viewed as apologizing more out of self-interest than remorse.

In her closing remarks Judge X identifies two different meanings that she understands as consistent with a bare *I'm sorry*: the defendant is sorry for the offense, or the defendant is sorry to have gotten caught. (Notice that it can't be both: according to this schema, defendants can't be sorry for their actions *and* be sorry about the consequences that they face.) Judge X makes it clear that the first meaning—the "I'm sorry I ever did this and I understand the harm it caused" meaning—is of course what the court wants to hear. Natapoff (2005) explains that the reason that remorse in defendants is valued is because it is viewed as an index of rehabilitative potential. She writes:

> Acceptance of responsibility and rehabilitation are intertwined, central goals of the criminal justice process. A defendant's acceptance of responsibility or remorse for his crime is usually seen as a necessary precursor to rehabilitation because it reflects an internalization of the wrongfulness of his actions. According to the Supreme Court, "[a]cceptance of responsibility ... demonstrates that an offender 'is ready and willing to admit his crime and to enter the correctional system in a frame of mind that affords hope for success in rehabilitation over a shorter period of time than might otherwise be necessary.'" (2005, 1494–1495)[9]

Judge X's comments point to the problem that the deletion of arguments supposedly presents for sentencing judges: if a defendant produces a bare *I'm sorry*, there is presumably no way for a judge to differentiate between two very different complements that work equally well grammatically, but carry conflicting implications for the stance that the defendant is understood as inhabiting. From this perspective, a bare *I'm sorry* can be viewed as a strategic move by defendants who are leaving out the part of the predicate that would reveal them to be self-focused and more interested in the impending sentence than in expressing remorse for their offenses.

A defendant's bare *I'm sorry* in the context of allocution at sentencing looks quite different from the perspective of the discipline of sociolinguistics. While Judge X focused on the potential meanings of a single utterance with no reference to the turn of talk as a whole, sociolinguists insist that utterances be assessed in the light of their surrounding contexts. So, for example, although it is true that 10 of the 52 defendants produced bare *I'm sorry* statements, a look at the allocutions as a whole reveals that when defendants produced *I'm sorry* statements with reduced argument structure, elsewhere in the allocution they made some kind of reference to their offense. Below Gruber has reproduced the list of bare *I'm sorry* utterances and added the lines containing defendants' references to their offenses as well as some additional contextual material necessary for understanding these references:

1.	X13:	4	No matter how many times I can say it, .. I'm sorry.
		5	It's not gonna change anything.
		6	(COUGH) .. Uh, I wanna apologize .. to everyone that hurt .. and .. people
		7	that .. I've hurt.
		8	Um, .. I want the court to realize that .. um I did .. some things that .. I'm
		9	not proud of.
2.	Y1:	1	(1.5) (COUGH) <I'm sorry that> .. I have any part in the situation,
		2	and I regret it to the fullest extent.
		3	From the bottom of my heart, .. I'm sorry.
		4	That would be it. [end of allocution]
3.	Y2:	2	I know and I admit .. uh what I did was wrong (1.0)
		3	and I'm <sincerely sorry for it.> (1.8)
		4	I just (2.2) # the crime that I am being charged for is <not my character at all.>

5   It's just a matter of me (1.4) hookin up with the wrong guy at the *wrong* time (2.0)

6   and I didn't—I wa-I wasn't even with him very long,

7   I didn't know .. his criminal background.

8   And (1.0) I just wanna say that .. I'm sorry,

13   (H) And I'm sorry,

14   and I know what I did was wrong.>> (7.3) (SOB) [end of allocution]

4.   Y8:   1   (TSK) (1.2) Um, I'd just like to say I'm sorry,

2   that I didn't mean <to (1.2) scare the ladies> or put them in .. any danger.

5.   Y18: 4   I would just like to say I am very sorry .. for what I have done.

5   And I am willing—I am (1.1) ready to pay restitution.

6   It'll take a significant amount of time, but .. we can pay it .. back.

7   I am very sorry for all the lives I have touched .. in a negative way.

8   I'm so sorry. [end of allocution]

6.   Z5:   6   Your Honor, I would like to .. apologize and say that I'm sorry,

7   Uh, .. sometimes .. it's hard to do right, #know #what #I'm #sayin, (2.2)

8   I just wanna .. let you know # I regret ## what I did (1.1)

9   and (1.7) that (1.1) I let myself down as well as my family.

18   I just wanna say, you know, uh, .. I just made the wrong choice ..

19   – again, you know, (2.0)

20   I sincerely want you to know ## .. that I-I would give anything to correct it,

21   but, .. you know, I know every action carries a reaction.

7.   Z6:   2   I'd like to apologize for what I've done ..

3   and take responsibility, ..

4   apologize to you and my family and ..

5   anybody that I might have involved in this.

6   And I just—(1.3) I just can't believe that I, .. you know, (1.1) I never had

7   any idea that it would ever come to something like this.

		8	#Just .. I really didn't .. think things out, .. you know, like I should.

8   #Just .. I really didn't .. think things out, .. you know, like I should.

9   I just took things too lightly, I guess, I don't know, (1.1)

10   but I am sorry, and [end of allocution]

8.   Z16:   15   People have to be**lieve** that there's some way out, that some way .. they can

16   improve upon their lot.

17   That something could happen .. positive for **them**.

18   And much of that .. has been taken away from ~City A.

19   Perhaps by people like myself .. who've made some stupid mistakes, made error.

20   Uh, .. and I am repentant for those things (1.2) uh, that I have done (1.0)

21   incorrectly? (1.0)

22   Uh, I apologize to **each** and **every** resident of the city of ~City A .. first and

23   foremost, for bein a part of this. (1.1)

29   Uh, (1.0) and uh, (1.5) I've been uh,—it's been .. one year, 17 days .. uh, today

30   (1.0) uh, (1.0) and I am repentant.

31   I am repentant **every** um .. day of that one year and 17 days.

34   but (1.0) I'm sorry. [end of allocution]

9.   Z20:   4   ((wipes eye)) (SOB) (H) (11.7) <<I'm sorry for what I did (Hx).

5   It was wrong and I knew that. (SNIFF)

6   I'm sorry for puttin you through all this stress, Mama. (SOB)

7   I'm not gonna do it again.

8   I'm sorry.>> [end of allocution]

10.   Z21:   1   (SNIFF) (SOB) ## (6.1) (SNIFF) <<I just wanna say that I apologize to

2   the USA for my #waywardness, (1.0)

3   and I would like to apologize to my family and friends, (SNIFF)

4   ~Judge Z; There, there, why don't you turn around and apologize to them ..

5   ((defendant turns to family)) (1.0) I'm sorry.

8   (SNIFF) and I'm sorry.>> [end of allocution]

A close look at these more complete transcripts reveals that in every case in which defendants produced an *I'm sorry* lacking in complements, elsewhere in their allocutions they made some kind of reference to their offense.[10] In most of these cases, the reference to the offense precedes the bare *I'm sorry*, as can be seen in examples numbered 2, 3, 5, 7, 8, 9, and 10. Interestingly, in six of these seven allocutions (numbers 2, 5, 7, 8, 9, and 10), the defendants' bare *I'm sorry* constitutes the last content line of their allocutions, suggesting a formulaic "closing" quality of this construction. More importantly, however, is the fact that in each of these seven allocutions, before the defendant produces a bare *I'm sorry*, he/she produces either an *I'm sorry* construction which contains a complement referring to the offense (examples 2, 3, 5, and 9) or uses a construction with a meaning similar to *I'm sorry* (such as a variant of *I apologize*) that contains a reference to the offense (examples 7, 8, and 10). Thus, in example 2, the defendant says *<I'm sorry that> .. I have any part in the situation* in line 1 and then in line 3 he produces a bare *I'm sorry* construction: *From the bottom of my heart, .. I'm sorry*. In examples 7, 8, and 10, the defendant's bare *I'm sorry* is preceded by a construction similar to *I'm sorry* which makes reference to the offense. Thus, in example 7, the defendant begins his allocution by saying, *I'd like to apologize for what I've done* and he ends his allocution by saying, *but I am sorry, and*; similarly, in example 10, the defendant begins her allocution by saying, *<<I just wanna say that I apologize to the USA for my #waywardness* and she ends her allocution with, *and I'm sorry*. The similarity or even overlap of these constructions is quite striking. Generally speaking, when an argument of a construction appears in one sentence, its absence in a parallel structure elsewhere in the same turn of talk is understood as a deletion in surface structure; it is still present in the "deep structure" of the utterance, however. As a result, with regard to meaning, it is still understood as "there." From a linguistic perspective, then, these bare *I'm sorry* constructions have complements that are understood from the context.

In three of the allocutions (numbers 1, 4, and 6), the reference to the offense follows the defendant's bare *I'm sorry*.[11] In these cases, the defendants make reference to their offenses within the next two lines. Thus, in example 1, the defendant's *I'm sorry* lacks a complement in line 4: *No matter how many times I can say it, .. I'm sorry* but in lines 6–7 he produces a similar *apologize* construction with reference to his offense: *I wanna apologize .. to everyone that hurt .. and .. people that .. I've hurt*. Due to the close proximity of the reference to the offense to the bare *I'm sorry* constructions in these three examples (and, of course, the absence of language that undermines a remorseful stance), the reference to the offense can be understood as applying to the bare *I'm sorry* constructions. From the perspective of sociolinguistics, then, and in contrast to

Judge X's assertion, these bare *I'm sorry* constructions are not consistent with a meaning of "I'm sorry I got caught."

Following Irvine and Gal (2000), this problem in translation is an example of erasure, which they define as "the process in which ideology, in simplifying the sociolinguistic field, renders some persons or activities (or sociolinguistic phenomena) invisible" (2000, 38). In this case, following Gruber (2008), the ideology at work here centers on the premise that the context of sentencing hearings functions to impute intentions to defendants, who are often viewed as apologizing out of self-interest with regard to the impending sentence rather than out of remorse. In my data, I found that the more a defendant's profile aligned with that of a "career criminal," the more skeptical judges were that the apology expressed true remorse. From this perspective, the lack of an argument in an *I'm sorry* construction is viewed as a defensive strategy of defendants who want to mask their real interest in the impending sentence by using a grammatical construction that is consistent with a remorseful stance. For this process to work, judges need to "erase" the references that defendants make to their offenses in apologetic-type utterances.

2.4 Defendants' References to Their Offenses

2A.4 Although defendants refer to their offenses in their allocutions, most are considered vague (85% in Gruber's sample) in that they do not provide specifics of the offenses committed. Gruber provides examples of the ways in which defendants refer to their offenses in the data set. Vague references to the offense can be understood in very different ways. On the one hand, the use of vague references could be viewed as a defensive and advantageous strategy for the defendant who wishes to avoid explicitly apologizing for the crime committed. On the other hand, from a sociolinguistic perspective, vague apologies can be seen to function differently. In everyday speech, there is a limit to the severity of an injury for which one apologizes: a mere *I'm sorry* might not seem to suffice for injuries or crimes that are to be taken very seriously. And it is usually the case that the specifics of the crimes have already been mentioned. The use of vague constructions prevents defendants from seeming flippant, and also from engaging in a kind of repetition or redundancy that would often be avoided in normal conversation. Although references to the offense in these allocutions may be vague, defendants do commonly provide a negative value judgment of the crime, which can be viewed as the "new information" in their utterances.

While it is true that defendants do refer to their offenses during their allocutions, it is striking that these references are generally quite vague. In most cases, defendants' allocutions give no indication of the specific crimes for which they are being sentenced. Typically, defendants' references to their offenses are accomplished by means of semantically bleached constructions—that is, constructions that rely on low-content verbs such as "do," "make," and "happen." Of the 102 tokens in which defendants referred to the crime in some way, the majority were semantically bleached: 85 tokens or 83% contained no identifying information regarding the crime for which the defendant was being sentenced. The other 17% offered varying degrees of identifying information about the crime in question—about half of them delimited the scope of possibilities or identified the basic type of crime involved; the other half was more explicit. The semantically bleached constructions took a variety of forms. The most frequently used construction was employed by 19 of the 52 defendants (37%). It consisted of a form of "what I DO,"[12] with the present perfect ("what I have done") being the most frequently used form.

11. I know and I admit .. uh what **I** did was wrong (Y2: 4)

12. I would just like to say I am very sorry .. for what I have done. (Y18: 4)

13. I just wanna .. let you know # I regret ## what I did (Z5: 8)

14. I'd like to apologize for what I've done .. and take responsibility, (Z6: 2–3)

15. Uh, .. and I am repentant for those things (1.2) uh, that I have done (1.0) incorrectly? (Z16: 20–21)

16. <<I'm sorry for what I did (Z20: 4)

Apart from example 12, these defendants did not refer to their offenses in more specific ways elsewhere in their allocutions.[13]

In addition to DO-constructions, constructions involving semantically bleached MAKE were also popular choices. Thirteen defendants (25%) produced semantically bleached utterances using MAKE. In all of these examples, MAKE co-occurs with a limited set of nouns: either "mistakes," "decisions," or "choices," and often with modification that communicates a critical stance, e.g., "poor," "wrong," "bad," "stupid." Below Gruber presents several examples of MAKE-constructions.

17. Well, I know I made a mistake (X12: 1)

18. I—(1.2) you know, I know I did this to myself, I made mistakes (X16: 5–6)

19. I just wanna say, you know, uh, .. I just made the wrong choice—again, you know (Z5: 18–19)

20. And much of that .. has been taken away from ~City A. Perhaps by people like myself .. who've made some stupid mistakes, made error. (Z16: 18–19)

These defendants did not refer to their offenses in more specific ways elsewhere in their allocutions.

The remaining semantically bleached references to defendants' crimes used other nonspecific noun phrases and verb phrases. Four examples are presented below:

21. (COUGH) <I'm sorry that> .. I have any part in the situation (Y1: 1)

22. I just—(2.2) # the crime that I am being charged for is <not my character at all.> (Y2: 4)

23. I just .. would like to say that uh .. I realize what hap-occurred was wrong (Z2: 2)

24. (SNIFF) <<I just wanna say that I apologize to the USA for my #waywardness (Z21: 1–2)

These defendants did not make more specific reference to their offenses elsewhere in their allocutions.

Defendants' general practice of making indeterminate references to their criminal activities can be understood in different ways. From one perspective, because allocution is a largely monologic speech event as opposed to a dialogic one, the use of semantically bleached referring expressions could be understood as a defensive strategy. Consider an utterance such as the one in example 23, above: *I just .. would like to say that uh .. I realize what hap-occurred was wrong* (Z2: 2). In this case Mr. ZB was being sentenced for misrepresenting his financial situation on bank records and claiming that he was bonded for more money than he actually was. As was noted earlier, there was no prior (or subsequent) identification of exactly what Mr. ZB meant by *what hap-occurred*. Because allocution is largely a monologic speech event, it was highly unlikely that Judge Z would ask the defendant to clarify what he meant. (And he didn't.) As a result of these factors, Judge Z would have had to play an active role in selecting which of the possible relevant events Mr. ZB was referring to. If the judge co-constructs what defendants are sorry for, however, defendants can't be accused of "getting it wrong." (As Natapoff (2005) has observed, defendants who "get it wrong" during allocution risk receiving sentences above the minimum for which they are eligible.) From this perspective, the use of broad referring constructions during allocution could constitute one way in which defendants use the structural feature of monologicality to their advantage. In cases in which defendants have contested the government's depiction of the offense, referring to the offense by means of vague constructions during allocution at sentencing allows them to avoid explicitly offering an apology for behavior which they had earlier denied.

Understanding defendants' vague references to their offenses as a defensive strategy forefronts and reifies the adversarial aspects of the legal system, but other interpretations are also possible, such as those grounded in a sociolinguistic approach to language use. From this perspective, we can ask what a more crime-specific allocution might look like. Example 23: *I just .. would like to say that uh .. I realize what hap-occurred was wrong* might become "I just .. would like to say that uh .. I realize that misrepresenting my financial situation was wrong." As another example (number 17), *Well, I know I made a mistake* (X12: 1) might become "It was a mistake to take that check" or "I made a mistake by taking that check." And (number 7) *I'd like to apologize for what I've done* (Z6: 2) might become "I'd like to apologize for blowing up Mr. Smith's mailbox." These variants sound distinctly odd—and they suggest that the use of semantically bleached constructions might function very differently from the point of view of the defendant.

First of all, some types of actions (criminal and non-criminal) lend themselves to representation more easily than others: "robbing a bank," for example, contrasts with "misrepresenting one's financial situation on bank documents." A related factor is whether the offense in question has a clear victim (such as a robbery) compared to those that do not (for example, possession of a firearm). From this perspective, it should be easier to offer a specific apology for a robbery than for illegally possessing a firearm. Another factor also at play here is a conflict in terms of semantic load: studies on apologies such as those by Trosborg (1987) and Schlenker and Darby (1981) have noted that there appears to be a limit in terms of the degree of severity of offense that can occur in an *I'm sorry* frame. In other words, if a very severe injury has occurred, use of the *I'm sorry* frame can seem to trivialize that injury. The same principle could apply to other kinds of apologetic-type utterances. In the context of allocution, where an apology of some kind seems to be expected, one way in which defendants could meet the conflicting constraints on producing an apology but not exceed the propositional content limit for a formulaic expression of an apology is to produce an *I'm sorry* or *I apologize* utterance with a semantically bleached reference to the offense.

There is another reason defendants might not make specific references to their offenses. In his discussion of the "one new idea" constraint, Chafe (1994) refers to the role that low-content verbs play in framing new information, noting that these verbs are more usually employed to reference already-introduced information rather than to introduce new information. Applying these insights to defendant allocutions, we see that the semantically bleached MAKE and DO constructions (as well as the other examples) fit into the class of low-content verbs. When we consider the context and the way in which sentencing hearings function as institutional responses to defendants' crimes, we can understand the crimes themselves as being "activated" in this context independent of whether they have been explicitly articulated during the sentencing hearing itself. Further, all of the defendants have participated in preceding case-related events—either a plea hearing for 48 defendants, or a trial for four defendants—which, in most cases, occurred in the same courtroom and before the judge who now presides over the sentencing hearing. From this perspective, the choice of a low-content construction to refer to the crime makes sense because it is not "new" information.

If the reference to the crime is accessible or old information, then the new idea of the apologetic utterance can be found in the evaluation or the commentary that defendants make with regard to the offense. All of the examples presented above convey some type of critical stance toward the offense. Defendants do this in different ways: some use lexical items that convey criticism semantically such as by means of words and phrases like "mistake(s)," "bad decisions," and "what I did was wrong." Others offer an implicitly critical response to their actions through the use of conventional apologies. Still other defendants combine these strategies. In fact, it is through this critical evaluation of their actions that defendants accomplish what Goffman says people do when they apologize: "an individual splits himself into two parts, the part that is guilty of an offense and the part that dissociates itself from the delict and affirms a belief in the offended rule" (1971, 113). By criticizing their actions, defendants position themselves as different from the person who committed the crime and, as a result, able to rejoin the community by virtue of knowing the rules of proper behavior.

2.5 Ideologies Surrounding Emotion

2A.5 The communication of emotion plays a central role in successful apologies, so the ways in which individuals understand and interpret emotion need to be considered in this analysis. Emotion can be juxtaposed with "rational thought" but also with estrangement/isolation; these two contexts generate quite different attitudes toward emotionality. Similarly, emotion can be viewed as an internal event; in this case, the individual feeling the emotion is considered to be the expert. By contrast, emotions can also be understood as evident externally in ways that individuals who feel those emotions don't have conscious access to. In parallel fashion, emotions can be tracked in two different ways: through the language used to express internal feelings (i.e., verbally, such as *I'm sorry* statements) and through external indications visible to others (i.e., nonverbal cues such as facial expressions, tone, rate of speech, demeanor). Nonverbal cues of emotion may be interpreted in different ways depending on the context, but observers may think of these cues as more reliable, despite the fact that their interpretations are far from certain. In Gruber's study, judges' individual impressions of defendants' nonverbal cues sometimes took precedence over what defendants actually said during allocution. Interestingly, case law permits this, because it mirrors the linguistic ideology that privileges nonverbal cues over overtly spoken words.

When it comes to translating insights from sociolinguistics to the courtroom, a number of issues surrounding the interpretation of affect arise. These issues are rooted in the many and diverse ideologies surrounding emotion, which often conflict in fundamental ways. To briefly sketch a complex landscape, emotion appears to play opposite roles in two dualities currently operative in Western society. On one hand, emotion and "rational thought" have traditionally been opposed to each other. As a result of the way rational thought (or better, the belief in rational thought) has been privileged in Western societies, emotion has tended to be viewed negatively (Lutz 1988; Oatley 1992). The other dualism in which emotion takes part is that between emotion and estrangement/isolation. In this opposition, emotion is perceived more positively than estrangement. Lutz points to the Romantic tradition as reflecting this weighting:

> In the Romantic tradition, the natural (including emotion) is depicted as synonymous with the uncorrupted, the pure, the honest, the original. Nature and emotion are seen as fountains of high truths, while culture, conscious thought, and disengagement are all viewed as disgust, artifice, or vise [sic] . . . (Lutz 1988, 68)

Both of these oppositions involving emotion play a role in the various and complex ways emotion is communicated and understood.

Further, within psychology, emotion has been understood from different perspectives over time. On the one hand, following William James, emotion has been viewed as an entirely interior phenomenon, but one which is given privileged status because it is perceived as being connected with Nature and therefore seen as uncorrupted and a source of truth. On the other hand, more recently, emotions have been understood as fundamentally social because they are linked to specific contexts, and they are seen as providing access to an individual's evaluations of events in relation to his/her goals and beliefs (Oatley 1992).

One of the results of emotions having been viewed as primarily internal human events is that speakers have consistently been treated as authorities when the subject is their own emotions. As Labov and Fanshel (1977) point out, this has important ramifications for conversations of all kinds:

> In ordinary conversation, we are always subject to being contradicted on matters of fact, and we may expect contradiction most often if we speak about areas where the other person is known to be expert and we are not. But a speaker can be confident that there are many areas where he himself

is the undisputed expert. These are his personal and private emotions, experience, and all of the events that make up his biography. If he chooses to speak of his innermost feelings, his fatigue, his anger or guilt, the other party is not as free to contradict him as if he had spoken of the temperature or predicted an economic recession. (1977, 34)

Oatley problematizes this issue of authority in regards to emotion with his observation that "... we have private, conscious experience of our emotions that is not available to anyone else. On the other hand, experience of our own emotional expressions is visible to others but not fully available to us" (1992, 9). These emotional expressions are communicated by means of paralinguistic channels (which include facial expressions, tone of voice, and body language).

Thus, when we talk about emotions in speech, we are talking about at least two different kinds of affect. One type of affect is conventionally implicated by means of role inhabitance and the projection of various states onto grammatical roles (referred to as affect$_1$ here)[14]—the language in which people talk about their feelings. This type of affect is perceived as being consciously employed by the speaker to achieve her communicative goals. Speakers are generally held accountable for what they communicate through this medium. As mentioned above, the bar of truth is set relatively low in Western society for claims of having certain feelings or emotions, given that individuals are generally granted authority in this realm considered inaccessible to others. The many *I'm sorry* statements discussed above are examples of this kind of affect. The other type of affect refers to the panoply of emotional expressions that is visible to addressees, but is perceived as being not fully available to the speaker (referred to as affect$_2$ here). These are the moment-to-moment interactional indexes of affect that are projected largely via paralinguistic channels of communication. As Emerson points out, the messages communicated via affect$_1$ and affect$_2$ must be consistent:

> In general, mere verbal expressions of remorse and contrition do not adequately communicate the commitment to the role of wrongdoer expected by court officials. A totally consistent performance is required, and this demands that the repentant delinquent convey a properly deferential and remorseful attitude by his demeanor. (1969, 192)

Besnier identifies some additional attributes of affect$_2$: he claims that many affective signs are "bewildering[ly] multifunctional" and that this feature can be accounted for due to the semiotic nature of indexical vehicles, which are fundamentally dependent on the context in which they are embedded (1990, 429). As a result of this crucial dependence on context, an affective sign may index several affective experiences ambiguously. This feature would appear to be responsible for the very different readings of a speaker's affect that different addressees can make on the basis of the same input.

Speakers and addressees alike understand that emotion conveyed in communication can have very different "sources" and these different sources (rhetorical device [affect$_1$] vs. "true self" [affect$_2$]) affect the reliability which addressees accord their respective messages. As many studies have shown, messages conveyed via paralinguistic channels (i.e., affect$_2$: rate of speech, prosody, volume, the perception of hesitation, gestures of all kinds) tend to be perceived as much more reliable (Besnier 1990, 430). This is consistent with the Romantic tradition which privileges the "natural" (and emotional) over the "non-natural" mentioned above. Thus, while culture and conscious thought have enjoyed an about-face in the way they are perceived in modern society since the period of Romanticism, momentary interactional indexes of emotion seem to have maintained their upper hand in the realm of reliability of message communicated.

This brief sketch of some of the conflicting ideologies surrounding emotion helps to explain how a judge might feel certain that her reading of a defendant's demeanor is the correct one—even when that reading conflicts with the words that the defendant speaks during allocution at sentencing. The judge would be privileging information conveyed via paralinguistic channels (affect$_2$) over that conveyed via propositional content (affect$_1$), which is entirely consistent with US cultural ideologies concerning emotion. Not surprisingly, it is also consistent with case law, which has supported judges' individual assessments of defendants' demeanor at sentencing and considered that assessment a legitimate factor in sentencing. Thus, in the landmark case of *Green v. U.S.* (1961), which had the effect of making it mandatory for federal judges to offer defendants the opportunity to make an allocution at sentencing, the court writes: "[t]he most persuasive counsel may not be able to speak for a defendant as the defendant might, with halting eloquence, speak for himself" (304). The only person who determines what constitutes "halting eloquence" in the context of a sentencing hearing is the individual sentencing judge. Similarly, in the case of *U.S. v. Clemmons*, a case decided in 1995 by the US Court of Appeals for the Seventh Circuit, Judge Skinner balanced the risks associated with making an allocution with the latitude that judges have in imposing sentences and concluded that the court could consider any information, including the attitude and demeanor of the defendant during allocution. A similar finding was made in *U.S. v. Li* (Second Circuit) in 1997.

2.6 Conclusion

2A.6 In conclusion, this paper examined the ways in which apologetic allocutions are understood and the impact that they can have on sentencing. Through a sociolinguistic analysis, Gruber showed that even in "bare apologies," defendants are actually constructing their allocutions in ways that refer to their offenses, albeit through surface "deletions" that refer to other parts of the utterances, and/or in vague ways. These approaches make sense when understood in the context of common rules of everyday speech. However, when this happens, judges may "erase" previously explicit references to offenses; they may also privilege their own interpretations of defendants' nonverbal emotional cues. All of this can render the phrase *I'm sorry* ambiguous, which in the context of sentencing hearings can feed a somewhat dubious presumption that defendants are apologizing out of self-interest. Given this analysis, which she views as reflecting more broadly shared perspectives in society, Gruber is not optimistic about translating the wider findings of sociolinguistics (urging judges and others not to just trust their gut reactions) in legal settings. She does, however, offer the more easily absorbed, narrow suggestion that allocutions have the most potential benefit for first-time offenders who have committed less serious crimes. For other defendants, allocutions are likely to either convey no benefits or possibly a negative effect.

This paper has focused on two different translations of meaning that a sentencing judge provided for a defendant's bare *I'm sorry* during allocution at sentencing. The two different meanings identified by the judge have distinctly different implications for the stance that the defendant is understood as having adopted: "I'm really sorry I ever did this and I understand the harm it caused" is consistent with a remorseful stance—which presumably correlates with less likelihood of recidivism, while "I'm really sorry I did this and got caught" is consistent with defiance of the law—and possibly a greater likelihood of recidivism. Obviously, these different stances have quite different implications with regard to the type of sentence that is viewed as appropriate.

Applying the analytical techniques of sociolinguistics and examining allocutions as whole as opposed to focusing on individual utterances revealed that defendants do in fact refer to their offenses in their allocutions—many by means of other *I'm sorry* or *I apologize* constructions with complements that make reference to the offense. Following Irvine and Gal (2000), it was proposed that Judge X's claim that a bare *I'm sorry* construction is ambiguous required the judge to "erase" the defendant's reference(s) to his offense elsewhere in the allocution. As noted above, erasure is the process in which ideology renders some persons or activities (or sociolinguistic phenomena) invisible (Irvine and Gal 2000, 38). In this case, the ideology at work isolates defendants' utterances, robbing them of context and then reinterpreting them as indices of defendants' insincerity. This reading of allocutions gains even more force when the utterances are understood in the different context provided by defendants' criminal histories.

While defendants do consistently make reference to their offenses during allocution, these references tend to be quite vague. Depending on the perspective one adopts, these broad references can be understood in very different ways. The use of semantically bleached referring constructions such as "what I did" and "my actions" could reflect a compromise between the expectation of an apology and an offense that exceeds the typical severity limit for an *I'm sorry* frame. From a defendant's perspective, the deletion of arguments in apology constructions could also reflect the deletion of information that is assumed to be accessible or already activated in this context; in these utterances, it appears that the focus (for defendants) is on the critical stance that they take toward their actions. From the perspective of the sentencing judge, however, an apologetic stance by a defendant could very well be expected. Judge X's comments suggest that she, for example, would like to hear a defendant recount the specifics of the offense and demonstrate an awareness of how the offense affected others. As a result, the use of semantically bleached referring expressions and the deletion of arguments could be viewed by judges as part of an (insincere) defensive strategy. Such a strategy could have the unintended consequence of indexing defendants as unwilling or unable to talk about their crimes in specific kinds of ways.

In order to understand the force behind the powerful process of erasure, some of the ideologies surrounding the performance of emotion were explored. By showing how multifunctional paralinguistic signs such as facial expressions, tone of voice, and demeanor (affect$_2$) can trump affective messages that are viewed as being more under the control of the speaker (affect$_1$), the chapter fleshed out the way in which erasure might be working in the context of a sentencing hearing. Judges are able to "erase" defendants' explicit references to their offenses in order to render ambiguous an *I'm sorry* utterance lacking in complements because the paralinguistic affective signs that constitute a person's demeanor are particularly susceptible to multiple and diverse interpretations. In this case, lexical referents (overt references to the particularities of the crime) that in other contexts would be understood to be present—even if they aren't explicitly mentioned—are erased, thereby making a defendant's affective performance consistent with an ideology that privileges the view that defendants are apologizing out of self-interest rather than out of sincere remorse. The forces at work behind the phenomenon of erasure during allocution at sentencing are also at work in other legal contexts, which makes the prospect of translating the findings of this chapter for a broader audience quite daunting. It is not an easy sell to convince people that they should not rely on their "gut" (i.e., ideologically based) readings of the demeanor of others.

Given these conflicting forces at work, it may be more possible to translate the findings of sociolinguistics as shorter, more action-oriented advice about the specific context of sentencing hearings: how should defense attorneys advise their clients with regard to allocution? Although more data and further research are necessary, as noted above, Gruber (2008) suggests that allocution holds the greatest potential benefit for defendants who most diverge from a "typical" criminal profile—first-time offenders who have committed relatively less serious crimes and who have the support of family and friends. In these cases, the judge is probably already positively disposed toward the defendant and the allocution can act to support the judge's decision to impose a sentence at or below the low end of the guidelines. (But note, however, that the potential for a misstep during allocution—and hence a longer sentence—still exists for these defendants.) For defendants who do not meet these criteria, even the "best" allocution is unlikely to sway a judge's assessment of the defendant's character. Once a defendant's previous offenses exceed a certain threshold, allocution does not offer much potential for affecting a sentence in a positive way, but it does offer opportunities for affecting it negatively. This is not to say that allocution has no value for these defendants—or any defendant— for that matter. Natapoff (2005), for example, argues that defendants who decline the opportunity to speak at sentencing (and hence remain silent throughout the legal process) "are less likely to understand their own cases, engage the dictates of the law intellectually, accept the legitimacy of the outcomes, feel remorse, or change as a result of the experience" (2005, 1451). Different attorneys will weigh the risks and benefits for their clients differently in this matter.

Notes

1. Some of these ideas were presented on January 4, 2007 at the annual meeting of the Linguistic Society of America in Anaheim, CA. The audience in attendance provided helpful comments and suggestions, as did the Translation Working Group at the American Bar Foundation when I presented part of this material on July 3, 2007. Other ideas appear in my 2014 book, *"I'm Sorry for What I've Done": The Language of Courtroom Apologies*. I am grateful to Beth Mertz for orchestrating this project and to Beth and Bill Ford for helpful suggestions for this version.

2. According to government statistics, from 10/1/04—9/30/05 (a large portion of the period of this study), 96% of all convictions of federal defendants resulted from guilty pleas (see http://www.uscourts.gov/judbus2005/appendices/d7.pdf). The rate has remained at 96% since then.

3. Before *Booker*, a judge could depart from the Guidelines only when the court found that there was "an aggravating or mitigating circumstance of a kind, or to a degree, not adequately taken into consideration by the Sentencing Commission in promulgating the Guidelines." 21A *American Jurisprudence 2d*, §840.

4. Before *Booker* was decided, the Sourcebook reports that the percentage of federal sentences that fell within the applicable guideline range was about 70%. After *Booker*, during fiscal years 2006–2008, that rate fell to about 60%. The rate of above-guideline sentences stayed near 1.5% while the rate of below-guideline sentences was responsible for the 10% change. The 2010 Sourcebook reports that in fiscal year 2010, 55% of all federal sentences fell within the Guidelines.

5. The term *metapragmatic* refers to the way contextual features of an instance of language are working at a "meta-level" to comment on and change the meaning of the surface-level speech. So, for example, in these courtrooms, the surface level of the spoken language should convey the message that a defendant is "sorry." However, aspects of the context provide another level that in effect comments on the apparent surface-level meaning. At the broadest level here, the context of the upcoming sentence becomes quite important in

framing the meaning of the spoken words *I'm sorry*. These contextual or metapragmatic cues can operate at multiple levels, from more macro-levels created by overall social hierarchies implicated in race, gender, and class—all the way to very micro-levels. For example, if a defendant had a calm and unexpressive facial expression while uttering an apology, this in itself might also contribute contextually to how the words will be interpreted (in effect saying to some observers: "The words I'm saying are not deeply felt."). Note that the almost automatic imputation of meaning based on meta-level contextual cuing can be hard to dispute but can also be quite mistaken (as, for example, with someone who is generally impassive in demeanor, or who dislikes putting on a dramatic tone in such settings because it feels fake or manipulative).

6. I am very grateful for a dissertation improvement grant from the National Science Foundation's Law and Social Science Program which covered the costs of travel and the purchase of official transcripts. I am also grateful to the University of Chicago's Language Laboratories and Archives for the use of recording equipment.

7. Because the defendant did not make an allocution during his sentencing hearing, this case was not included in the data set of 52 apologetic allocutions.

8. Mr. T had a total offense level of 23 (26 for the base offense less 3 points for acceptance of responsibility) and a criminal history category of III, so the guideline sentence for which he was eligible was 57–71 months. Because the quantity of marijuana involved in the offense was not agreed upon, Judge X explained that the sentencing guidelines could not be applied in this case. The sentence she imposed upon Mr. T was 57 months of confinement plus 3 years of supervised release.

9. See Proeve, Smith, and Niblo (1999) and Bagaric and Amarasekara (2001), however, for an argument that there is no evidence of an association between remorse and reduced recidivism.

10. There is clearly much more going on in these allocutions than I discuss here. See, for example, Gruber (2008), which proposes that the discursive context of allocution in conjunction with defendants' positional role identity functions to limit both the effectiveness with which defendants can speak on their own behalf and the kinds of things that they can say, and Gruber (2009), which explores intersections between the socio-interactional functions of formulaic and non-formulaic language and the stigmatized institutional role identity of criminal defendant.

11. The allocution excerpt in example 3 contains two tokens of bare *I'm sorry* so it falls into both categories: it has a reference to the offense that precedes the bare *I'm sorry* as well as a reference to the offense that follows it. This allocation was categorized according to the pattern that appears first—a reference to the offense that precedes the bare *I'm sorry*.

12. When a verb is written with capital letters, it should be understood as a stand-in for all of the various tenses/forms that the verb can appear in.

13. The defendant in example 12 did not identify the specific type of fraud to which she pleaded guilty, but by referring to her plan to pay restitution, she indicated the monetary nature of her offense: *And I am willing—I am (1.1) ready to pay restitution. It'll take a significant amount of time, but .. we **can** pay it .. back.*

14. This subscripting convention is adapted from the anthropological linguistic convention introduced by Silverstein (1979) in discussing a parallel distinction between two types of pragmatic function.

References

Austin, J. L. 1962. *How to Do Things with Words*. Cambridge, MA: Harvard University Press.

Bagaric, Mirko, and Kumar Amarasekara. 2001. "Feeling Sorry?—Tell Someone Who Cares: The Irrelevance of Remorse in Sentencing." *The Howard Journal* 40(4): 364–376.

Besnier, Niko. 1990. "Language and Affect." *Annual Review of Anthropology* 19: 419–51.

Chafe, Wallace. 1994. *Discourse, Consciousness, and Time: The Flow and Displacement of Conscious Experience in Speaking and Writing*. Chicago: University of Chicago Press.

Coulmas, Florian. 1981. "Poison to Your Soul. Thanks and Apologies Contrastively Viewed." In *Conversational Routine*, edited by Florian Coulmas, 69–92. The Hague: Mouton.

Du Bois, John W. 2006. *Representing Discourse*. Available at: http://www.linguistics.ucsb.edu/projects/transcription/representing. Accessed August 13, 2011.

Emerson, Robert. 1969. *Judging Delinquents*. New York: Aldine.

Goffman, Erving. 1971. *Relations in Public: Microstudies of the Public Order*. New York: Basic Books, Inc.

Goffman, Erving. 1986 [1974]. *Frame Analysis*. Boston: Northeastern Press.

Gruber, M. Catherine. 2008. "Contextual Constraints on Defendants' Apologies at Sentencing." *Studies in Law, Politics, and Society* 45: 47–74.

Gruber, M. Catherine. 2009. "Accepting Responsibility at Defendants' Sentencing Hearings: No Formulas for Success." In *Formulaic Language, Volume 2, Acquisition, Loss, Psychological Reality, and Functional Explanations*, edited by Roberta Corrigan, Edith A. Moravcsik, Hamid Ouali, and Kathleen M. Wheatley, 545–566. Amsterdam/Philadelphia: John Benjamins Publishing Company.

Gruber, M. Catherine. 2014. *"I'm Sorry for What I've Done": The Language of Courtroom Apologies*. New York: Oxford University Press.

Irvine, Judith T., and Susan Gal. 2000. "Language Ideology and Linguistic Differentiation." In *Regimes of Language: Ideologies, Polities, and Identities*, edited by Paul V. Kroskrity, 35–83. Santa Fe: School of American Research Press.

Labov, William, and David Fanshel. 1977. *Therapeutic Discourse*. New York: Academic Press.

Lutz, Catherine A. 1988. *Unnatural Emotions*. Chicago: University of Chicago Press.

Natapoff, Alexandra. 2005. "Speechless: The Silencing of Criminal Defendants." *New York University Law Review* 80: 1449–1504.

Oatley, Keith. 1992. *Best Laid Schemes: The Psychology of Emotions*. Paris: Cambridge University Press.

O'Hear, Michael. 1997. "Remorse, Cooperation, and 'Acceptance of Responsibility': The Structure, Implementation, and Reform of Section 3E1.1 of the Federal Sentencing Guidelines." *Northwestern University Law Review* 91: 1507–1573.

Proeve, Michael J., David I. Smith, and Diane Mead Niblo. 1999. "Mitigation without Definition: Remorse in the Criminal Justice System." *The Australian and New Zealand Journal of Criminology* 32(1): 16–26.

Schlenker, Barry, and Bruce Darby. 1981. "The Use of Apologies in Social Predicaments." *Social Psychological Quarterly* 44(3): 271–278.

Searle, John R. 1975. "A Taxonomy of Illocutionary Acts." In *Minnesota Studies in the Philosophy of Science, Vol. VII, Language, Mind and Knowledge*, edited by K. Gunderson, 344–369. Minneapolis: University of Minnesota Press.

Silverstein, Michael. 1979. "Language Structure and Linguistic Ideology." In *The Elements: A Parasession on Linguistic Units and Levels*, edited by Paul R. Clyne, William F. Hanks, and Carol L. Hofbauer, 193–247. Chicago: Chicago Linguistic Society.

Trosborg, Anna. 1987. "Apology Strategies in Natives/Non-natives." *Journal of Pragmatics* 11: 147–167.

Cases Cited

Green v. United States, 365 US 301 (1961).

United States v. Booker, 543 US 220 (2005).

United States v. Clemmons, 48 F.3d 1020 (7th Cir. 1995).

United States v. Li, 115 F.3d 125 (2d Cir. 1997).

3

Translating Token Instances of "This" into Type Patterns of "That"

THE DISCURSIVE AND MULTIMODAL TRANSLATION OF EVIDENCE INTO PRECEDENT

Gregory Matoesian

3A

Matoesian "In Translation"—From Instances of "This" to Patterns of "That": Translating Evidence into Legal Precedent

Christopher Roy and Elizabeth Mertz

3.1 Introduction

3A.1 Common-law legal systems rely on the notion of precedent, understood by linguistic anthropologists to result from processes in which spoken or written "texts" are detached from their original settings (*decontextualized*) and then redeployed in a new sociolinguistic context (*recontextualized*). Matoesian illustrates this insight, and its analytic utility, by examining how the "Williams Rule" (allowing juries to hear testimony about defendants' prior conduct) was invoked in William Kennedy Smith's 1991 rape trial. This was no simple matter, as the prosecuting attorney (PA) had to establish that allowing testimony about Smith's prior conduct in this case would establish a pattern of criminal behavior, and thus be permissible under the Williams Rule. The prior conduct could then be considered by the jury as part of the evidentiary record of the trial; otherwise it would have to be excluded. This chapter presents a micro-level analysis of the words and nonverbal communication used by the prosecution to establish particular instances of behavior as fitting within categories established by legal precedent. In the process of doing this, the prosecution forges links between the texts of past cases and the account that is emerging during the trial, demonstrating the complex way precedent influences courtroom battles. This is also a process of translation in which particular activities are transformed into instances [tokens] of legal categories [types]—as for example, when a particular physical action is categorized as an "assault." Noting that the translation of a token into a type necessarily entails the transformation of existing relationships and identities through legal discourse, Matoesian identifies distinct parts of that linguistic process, which involves (1) decontexualization, (2) reconfiguration of indexicality (or contextual aspects of language), and (3) a recontextualization in which particular behaviors are reinterpreted as instances of a pattern as defined by precedent.

When making a decision, courts in the United States and other common-law countries draw upon precedent—upon previously established rules and principles that deal with similar issues, facts, and cases. In technical legal terms, a precedent is a "narrow holding in a prior case that controls the disposition of the case before the court."[1] Indeed, scholars consider precedent as the hallmark of common-law reasoning, a system of formal rationality that allows legal actors to calculate, predict, and plan a subsequent case based on analogized continuity with historically authorized rules and principles (Weber 1978). But, even in a system of formal rationality, such continuity only emerges dynamically and interactively in the concrete details of situated legal practice: a creative process of extracting text from some historical setting and naturalizing and authorizing it as the same in the here-and-now speech event. In the process, precedential text both shapes and is shaped by the indexical particulars[2] and interactional contingencies of the current case under consideration (Mertz 2007, 46). As Mertz (2007, 46; see also White 1990, 254) observes: "The invocation of precedent involves an inevitable transformation at some level."

In this chapter, I examine how a PA invokes precedent in a rape trial: more specifically, how she decontextualizes and recontextualizes evidence from three other rape victims to prove that the defendant possesses a *modus operandi* or pattern of criminal behavior. Under the "Williams Rule" (*Williams v. Florida* 1959) prior conduct of a criminal defendant can be introduced as evidence if it shows a pattern of criminality (or *modus operandi*) rather than mere propensity to engage in such behavior. If the PA succeeds in establishing such a pattern and the precedential link—the putative stability across multiple laminations of context—then the testimony of the three other victims would be introduced in the current case. This would have the effect of moving from the evidence of a single witness (in the he-said-she-said style typical of acquaintance or date rape trials) to evidence from four witnesses against the defendant, a favorable advantage for the prosecution even before the trial begins.

In analytic terms, I address the following issue: how does an instance (or *token*) of "this" evidence from all four victims translate into a *type*-level pattern of "that" behavior on the part of the defendant?[3] As Michael Silverstein (2003) notes, translation always involves cultural and discursive transformation of social relationships and identities; it is never a simple matter of matching propositional content or denotational text from one language to the next. This chapter analyzes precedential translation as a microdiscursive form of identity transformation in which evidence is placed under auspices of a rule, thus forging a connection with prior texts and legal principles. I demonstrate how the PA brings *multimodal resources*—the integration of verbal and visual conduct—to bear on the constitution of legal evidence, identity, and sociocultural relationships in an intertextual drive to shape a coherent, precedential narrative against the defendant. I show how the PA (1) selectively extracts prior segments of talk, (2) reconfigures indexical facts from historical speech events, and (3) recontextualizes these in the current speech event to mobilize an authoritative account of defendant behavior fitting under auspices of the rule—to invoke precedent as a meaning-making strategy.

3.2 Intertextuality and Multimodality as Legal Language

3A.2 Matoesian begins this section by explaining the importance of relationships between texts (*intertextuality*) to law. In a closely related sense, *intratexual* continuities may also emerge within a segment or between segments of a single text. Examples include not only making connections to prior texts designated as legal precedents, but also the use of prior utterances within a trial to cast doubts on newer utterances. In the courtroom, forging continuity and discontinuity between texts is a matter of creative strategizing and contestation. Matoesian uses an example from his prior work to illustrate how this kind of intertexuality can alter a speaker's relationship to her own speech (or *footing*). This can occur in courtroom dialogue when an attorney creates a discontinuity between different statements by a witness, making them appear to be in conflict. Even within one speaker's narrative, attention to intertextuality draws our attention to crucial linguistic complexities, particularly language's indexical functions, which convey contextual meaning beyond the more obvious "dictionary" (or referential) meanings of words and sentences. (For example, we can say a phrase like "No way" with different intonations and convey quite different things despite the apparent equivalence of surface meanings.) Matoesian's analysis includes a consideration of the role of both verbal and nonverbal communication (*multimodal resources*), as employed by the PA in her quest to establish a pattern of previous criminal behavior, per the *Williams* test.

Words and speech from historical settings constitute the evidential infrastructure of the adversarial system. Thus written documents, verbal statements, and electronic recordings from prior depositions, affidavits, interviews, and testimony form the evidential basis of legal order. Linguists refer to this felt continuity between historical text and its recontextualization in a current text as *intertextuality* (that is, how structural features of a text come to resemble prior or historical discourse). In a closely related sense, *intratextual* continuities may also emerge within a segment of text and between segments in a single text along with multiplex inter(intra)textual hybrids.[4] Prototypic forms of intertextuality would include direct and indirect quotes; repetition; formulaic words as in greeting, closing, or oath-taking sequences; forms of address (like *Your Honor* or *Ladies and Gentlemen of the Jury*); and stylistic manipulations of represented speech, to mention but a few. In each case, the current use of language relies on and connects with some prior text for its full meaning (in the case of repetition, for example, the connection made might be within the same sentence).

Such continuities are always designed and negotiated with an eye toward the strategic interactional tasks at hand; that is to say, legal participants not only build textual linkages but contest and transform them as well, creating discontinuities and continuities across speech events as they frame, position, and evaluate their own speech and the speech of others to foster a particular impression on the jury. In this sense, extracting and recontextualizing elements of talk as either the same or different affects how forms of participation, real and/or imaginary, are projected in the interactive constitution of evidence and in the organization of dialogue. In his seminal work on participation, Goffman (1981) demonstrated how traditional conceptions of speaker and hearer were too simple to account for the complexity of talk. With his concept of footing, he permitted analysts to make distinctions within the constellation of discursive roles and figures in concrete instances of talk. Thus, using concepts such as animator, author, and principal, he was able to specify how speakers position themselves and others relative to one another and to their utterances, embedding multiple laminations of participation even within a single utterance.[5]

To illustrate, I have elsewhere shown how a witness may attempt to establish an intertextual continuity with her prior trial testimony to reframe a striking inconsistency and rehabilitate her credibility (stating that "I would like to complete my testimony from yesterday") (Matoesian 2008, 201). On the other hand, in this particular instance, the cross-examining attorney recalibrates that prior testimony as an intertextual discontinuity to further impeach and discredit her (stating "You mean you want to answer a question that I had asked you yesterday after thinking about it overnight?"). In so doing, he conveys the inference that her current testimony involves "coaching" with her attorney (Matoesian 2008). In this case, the attorney projects a form of participation involving not just himself questioning the witness on the stand (in the current speech event) but an imaginary organization of participation including the witness animating (or merely mouthing) the words from her coaching during the prior evening. Her coach thus appears to be both *author* and *principal* (or authority) behind the witness's words, so that her testimony becomes marked as evidentially "contaminated," representing an inferior source of sociolinguistic authority and authenticity in the legal order. This example focused on an exchange between two people, but even in the narrative of a single speaker, as we will see, intertextual discourse reveals a thoroughly interactive and *metapragmatic* dialogue of participation—beyond its mere referential function—that evaluates the source of evidence, indexes epistemic stance, and contextualizes legal identity.[6]

Drawing on a quite different analytic dimension, I also investigate how the PA's narrative creatively deploys multimodal semiotic resources in contextually situated ways to authorize social relationships and position evidence so that it fits within precedential rules. That is to say, I illustrate the dynamic and creative emergence of precedent not only through mobilization of language but through the integration of verbal and visual conduct: the multimodal resources that speakers bring to bear on the constitution of institutional authority. While studies of language-and-law or forensic linguistics have developed at a brisk and productive pace since the groundbreaking works of William O'Barr (1981) and Atkinson and Drew (1979), they have neglected how language and embodied conduct work together as co-expressive semiotic partners—as multimodal resources—in the dynamic performance of legal meaning (see Matoesian 2010). Along with verbal and written modes, language in court includes gesture, gaze, and material artifacts in the production of legal identity, identity not as a static or passive individual attribute but as a dynamic interactional achievement. In this process, people come to occupy new, legally circumscribed identities as victim or false accuser, perpetrator or exonerated defendant. Focusing on speech alone neglects the role of multimodal activities in the precedential narrative—how language and embodied conduct mutually contextualize one another—and leaves researchers with an incomplete understanding of legal conduct.

3.3 Background to the Case and Data

3A.3 The transcripts analyzed here come from the trial of William Kennedy Smith, who stood accused of raping a woman named Patricia Bowman, after he met her at a bar and she gave him a ride home. During preliminary motions, the prosecution sought to include evidence from three other women who claimed that Smith had previously sexually assaulted them. This analysis uses segments from the trial transcript to examine how the PA decontextualizes and recontextualizes details from the testimony of these three women, connects them with evidence from Bowman, and then attempts to show how all four display the kind of pattern that would allow evidence from the other three women to be included in the trial at hand. With Segment 1, Matoesian examines how the PA's rhetoric structurally mirrors a dimension of timing in Smith's alleged behavior (in technical terms, this creates an *iconic* or mirroring connection between the PA's language and the temporal opposition that characterizes bio-polar behavior). Segment 2 is used to illustrate how the PA portrays Smith as a sexual predator through the use of contextual (or indexical) features of language, developing the idea that a particular style of speech used by Smith to "entice" victims into his "territory" reveals him to be a predator. Matoesian's analysis of Segment 3 centers on PA's use of multimodal communication (through both verbal and visual channels) to convey how the defendant fosters trust in victims in a characteristic linguistic style, thus adding more evidence of the sexual predator pattern required by the Williams Rule. Across all of these segments (and the segment of the PA's closing remarks then analyzed at the end of the chapter), the PA uses a pattern of *type-token reflexivity* in which she moves rhythmically back-and-forth to connect particular instances with type-level categories (which are then linked to more instances), returning repeatedly so that each segment frames the next. At a metalinguistic level (more specifically, a *metapragmatic* level, where language signals about its own contextual meaning), this both enacts and encourages the listener to perceive—through the form as well as the content of the language—a pattern as required by *Williams*. This kind of metalinguistic signaling "naturalizes" the message that the PA attempts to convey, making it seem more taken-for-granted by virtue of its fit with very subtle aspects of the rhetoric.

On Easter weekend in March 1991, William Kennedy Smith met Patricia Bowman at the trendy Au Bar nightclub in West Palm Beach, Florida. After the bar closed, Bowman gave Smith a ride home to the Kennedy home, where she claimed that he raped her at roughly 4 a.m. on the lawn of the estate. During preliminary motions in early December, 1991, the prosecution announced that three other women—Lisa, Lynn, and Michele—had come forward to claim that Smith had sexually assaulted them in the past. As we've seen, under the Williams Rule (*Williams v. State of Florida* 1959), relevant evidence is admissible if it shows that the defendant displays a pattern of criminal behavior, not just a propensity to engage in such conduct (or bad moral character). If the prosecution could make a case for admitting the testimony of the three other women, this could be damaging to the defendant because it would show that he possessed a unique signature or clear pattern for committing sexual assault. In other words, the prosecution may prove the victim's state of mind pertaining to consent or lack of consent by the states of mind of the three other women and whether they had consented to sex with Smith on prior occasions. But to do so, the prosecution must extract (that is, decontextualize and recontextualize) the relevant particulars of evidence from each woman's testimony, link these with evidence from the current victim, and then show how all four cases fall under auspices of the rule. How does the PA assemble a coherent narrative of sameness that displays a pattern of criminality? How does she translate or transform the indexical particulars of each woman's discourse to establish a unique signature to the offense?

In what follows, I examine several extracts of the prosecution's precedential narrative that flow in a linear ordering of segments. While it would be important, of course, to analyze all segments of her argument as well as the defense attorney's response, such an undertaking would require book-length treatment, if not more.[7] With this space limitation in mind, Segment 1 focuses on the contrastive rhetoric in the PA's narrative and how this powerfully conveys an *iconic* (or mirroring) form of temporal opposition in the defendant's "bipolar" personality: a "one moment he was x, then next minute he was y" format. In Segment 2, I analyze how the PA rhetorically activates a sexual predator identity in which the defendant "entices" or lures victims into his "territory," an identity constructed through a rapist speech register or style.[8] Segment 3 focuses on the multimodal integration of verbal and visual conduct as the PA argues that the defendant fosters trust in the victims before the attacks, consolidating the sexual predator pattern. In the final section of the chapter, I consider how power and "culture in action" (Ehrlich 2010, 279) figure prominently in the production of gender and sexual identity during the PA's summary of the *modus operandi* she needed to establish, an issue "lost in translation." More specifically, I demonstrate how she positions herself into double-bind configurations indexed by stance adverbs, in a counter-hegemonic bid to denaturalize and pathologize patriarchal structures of sexual rationality. While the grammatical-lexical and text-metrical encoding of *stance* (the speaker's attitude or degree of commitment toward a proposition) has preoccupied linguistic analysis, I demonstrate how stance also embodies and reproduces sociocultural context.

Most importantly, talk within and across the ensuing segments is not autonomous but synchronizes with the others in a rhythmically integrated form of type-token reflexivity. Each segment begins with a metapragmatic utterance type that categorizes (or classifies) the defendant and victim's words, which, in turn, contextualizes a reflexive interpretive frame for connecting each subsequent token with the type within a segment (Silverstein 2005). Each completed type-token segment then contextualizes the discursive frame for the ensuing type-token segment across the series, which, in turn, reflexively recalibrates the prior type-token segment as continuous with the ongoing litany (and so on recursively), as an instance in a progressively interwoven horizontal-vertical (*syntagmatic-paradigmatic*) linguistic pattern. Together, each vertical and horizontal increment in the inter(intra)textual pattern bears an iconic correspondence to the defendant's escalating pattern of sexually violent behavior. As these patterns collide and fuse, they synchronize a subtle yet iconic naturalization between social structure—patterns of interaction across space and time—and discursive patterning. In other words, the linguistic pattern makes the social patterning seem more natural through very subtle signaling devices.

A final note before proceeding. My objective is not to assess the correctness or incorrectness of the legal judgment allowing or disallowing the testimony of the three other women. That is, I do not analyze the outcome of the precedential argument in a prescriptive sense—what the judge should have done—and the various pro and con claims. Instead, I address the linguistic, ideological, and multimodal resources that the PA brings to bear on the legal translation of evidence as an instance of following a rule. I illuminate how this process integrates crisscrossing, polyrhythmic currents of intertexual relations in the naturalization of precedential reality (see Table 3A.1).

TABLE 3A.1

Overview of Matoesian's key points "translated" for readers

	Types	Tokens	Token Frames
Segment 1	*Defendant's behavior abnormal, sexual predator TYPE: changes in time from gentle to violent *PA uses same type-frame for each example or token	*Intratextual pattern for each of four women: (1) name of woman, (2) quotes from woman's testimony showing temporal before/after shift in defendant's behavior in each case (including quoted material from what defendant said to victim)	*Opening frame is a TYPE level characterization of "all four of these girls" and emphasis on how they stre:::sed the same temporal description (creates intertextual continuity)
Segment 2	*Defendant's speech is of sexual predator TYPE: enticing or luring victims *PA uses two different framing types	*Intratextual pattern for each of four women reports what defendant said to each to lure them "into his territory" *Intra- and intertextual patterning links the tokens *within* each segment (vertically) and then *between* segments (horizontally) as examples of same overall type (sexual predator behaviors/speech)	*Opening frame is TYPE level characterization of type of speech used by defendant to all women: [he] *enti::ced* the victims into his territory with false pretenses *Closing or post-token frame continues this type-level theme with slightly varied structure: *Every single one of these people he got to his house by false pretenses*
Segment 3	*Defendant fosters false trust of TYPE sexual predators develop in victims *PA uses multimodal signals to solidify frame	*Begins each token with the woman's name, followed by reasons for trust, linked explicitly by phrase *no reason not to trust him* *Multimodal signals embody victims' innocent trust, placed in opposition to putative attitude toward stranger, demonstrated through "objective" evidence on easel	*Opening frame sets up TYPE of sexual predator behavior that preys on victim trust to connect token examples of trust-based, relational connections (*cousin of her boyfriend, fellow medical student* (not *stranger on the street*), fellow student who acted like a *big brother*, mother consulting defendant *as a physician*)

3.4 Segment 1: Discursive Organization of Temporal Contrast

3A.4 In his analysis of Segment 1, Matoesian notes how the PA uses many micro-linguistic devices to create a similarity among the reported experiences of four different women with the defendant. She does this through parallel descriptions at the surface level (denotatively or semantically) but also through the structure of her language. For example, she creates an iconic or mirroring connection among the women's reported experiences by stressing and lengthening her own words to echo the emphasis (on the startlingly quick change in Smith's personality) that she attributes to the four women. After this opening frame, the PA goes on to create narrative similarity among the accounts of the four women, structuring each description of Smith's explosive change in character as a token of a general type of behavior. Matoesian summarizes: each instance, or token, not only represents the type being constructed by the PA, but intertextually elaborates the overall argument, not only through the testimony being reviewed, but iconically as well, as the pattern of behavior identified by the PA is reflected in the structure of the discourse. Each token reinforces the type, and this in turn constructs the interpretive frame of each successive segment. The language structure echoes and describes a dramatic shift from gentlemanly, trustworthy behavior to violent, coercive sexual assault, setting up a repeated temporal contrast that in turn signals a type of behavioral pattern.

TABLE 3.2

Transcription conventions

Transcription Symbol	Meaning
:::	indicates sound prolongation
(1.9)	numbers in parentheses mark duration of silence in tenths of seconds
(.)	indicates a very short untimed pause
- hyphen	refers to a cut-off
[]	marks simultaneous speech and/or simultaneous speech and bodily conduct; alignment of above/below brackets indicates bodily actions and gestures occurring simultaneously with the speech
> <	encloses speech produced at a faster delivery
=	refers to an immediately latched utterance
(())	indicates bodily conduct or some other relevant aspect of context
Word	*italics* indicates emphatic stress
Word	**boldface** refers to increased loudness

The PA's argument for introducing the testimony of the three other women begins with a type classification, summarizing prior deposition questioning, of the defendant's change in behavior (see Table 3.2).

Segment 1: Williams Rule Evidence 1, PA (00:21–01:24)

001   A::ll four of these girls *stre:::ssed* (.) the change in personality.

002   (0.6)

003   Lisa (.) "he was charming. I danced with him. I felt completely

004   comfortable with him (.) Once at his parent's home (.) one moment-

005   moment he was standing in front of me talking with me, saying goodnight

006	to me (.) and the next minute he would- (.) had tackled me onto the bed."
007	Apologized. Seemed OK. *Re*peated the act.
008	(1.0)
009	Lynn (.) "he seemed quiet, attractive, a well dressed, very
010	gentlemanly young man (.) Later I saw a ***complete*** change in character (.)
011	We were on the back side of the couch. At that point without any
012	warning (.) he grabbed my- (.) grabbed me by the wrist (.) ***threw*** me over
013	the couch" (.) Composed afterwards (.) unlocked the door n'let her out.
014	(0.8)
015	Michele (.) "He said '*NO::* (.) you can stay upstairs' (.) I just thought he was
016	goin to be a gentleman and let me sleep in his bed (.) Once upstairs he was
017	***such*** a ***ferocious*** (1.0) almost ***animal like*** look to him." Composed the next
018	day, very indifferent toward her.
019	(1.0)
020	Patricia (.) "talked and danced with him. Very interesting to talk to, very
021	nice (.) had a nice demeanor." The defendant went skinny dip-ping, invited her in.
022	She declined, he grabbed her ankle, tackled her onto the lawn (.)
023	Described him as *ferocious* composed afterwards (.) very indifferent.

In line 1, the PA mobilizes the quantifier (*all four of*) + specific determiner (*these*) + collective noun (*girls*) type-level classification to show how each victim **stre:::sed** the defendant's change in behavior. Here she moves beyond a focus on individual instances to unify the arguably different occasions and people as part of a single type. Notice how she delivers the main verb with marked stress and vowel lengthening to emphasize the proposition and, in so doing, instructs listeners that each woman did not merely notice or mention the behavioral change but accentuated it to create a distinct intertextual continuity. Still more specifically, we see in vivid detail how the PA authorizes an interpretive template for the ensuing tokens not only through denotational text but also in the iconic correspondence between the proposition and noticeably marked stress in the reporting verb. She offers a poignant demonstration of intertexuality in motion as she *enacts* the represented word in the current narrative, a symbolic interaction in which what was said becomes what we are doing or what Silverstein (1998, 266) calls a "mapping of denotational text to interacting text."

After a short pause in line 2, the PA unpacks the type classification with an incremental and progressive listing of tokens from each victim (also drawn from prior deposition interviews taken some months previously), a repetitive litany occurring as a temporal contrast. The litany begins in lines 3–7 with a proper name, a short pause, and then a quote drawn from Lisa's speech: an intratextual pattern repeated for each subsequent victim statement. Put another way, the PA omits the reporting verb and instead deploys the simple first name and short pause to contextualize the direct report. Notice how the quote consists of a parallel structure that assembles a contrast between the defendant's initial mild demeanor and subsequent rough assault. More explicitly, the quote lists the defendant's positive attributes along with Lisa's actions and feelings: *he was charming. I danced with him. I felt completely comfortable with him.* Just as important, her sense of certainty about those attributes—indexed through the degree adverb (*completely*)—contextualizes and intensifies the contrast via the temporal locator noun phrases or NPs (*one moment* and *the next minute*). In this iconic correspondence between linguistic form and behavioral pattern, the PA instructs listeners that such dramatic mood swings constitute an abnormality—a unique criminal signature—in the defendant's personality, perhaps a bipolar disorder or split personality indexed by the poetic (or intratextual, rhythmic) construction. To complete Lisa's testimony, the PA moves out of the direct quote and produces two additional behavioral anomalies in elliptical format, a format repeated in each ensuing victim account: first he *apologized* for his behavior and second, after the apology, *repeated the act.* Although the defendant apologized for his untoward behavior, he repeated it nevertheless, displaying total disregard for his victim(s) and a complete lack of self-control—another increment to the emerging *modus operandi.*

In the next token of the unfolding litany, after a one-second pause, the PA moves from Lisa to Lynn, once again, repeating the *turn-shape format* (proper name+ micro pause+ direct quote). She then repeats and recalibrates the epistemic verb from line 7 (*seemed*) followed by a poetic listing of positive attributes through the predicative adjectives—including the degree adverb on the last adverbial—that intensifies the forthcoming contrast: (*he seemed quiet, attractive, a well dressed, very gentlemanly young man*). However, while Lisa's contrast above consists of juxtaposing the temporal locator NPs, Lynn's statement involves something different. After the temporal adverb, the PA uses the evidential verb *saw* (in line 9) to generate an appearance/ uncertainty versus reality/certainty contrast (*Later I saw a complete change in character*), grammatically marked through the temporal deictic (*later*), variation in perception verbs (*seems, saw*) and, most important, absolute quantifier (*complete*). On the one hand, the epistemic stance verb (*seems*) marks the degree of certainty in the proposition: Lynn's inference about the defendant's character based on appearance. The evidential verb (*saw*), on the other, marks the source of information: her sensory evidence about those attributes that becomes the reality. As the oppositional structure develops, we see that what Lynn initially presumed turned out to be inaccurate and later "corrected" via sensory experience. After elaborating the details of the attack, the PA withdraws from the direct quote format to produce, once again, two post-attack descriptions that delete the subject and *be*-verb in an elliptical construction (*Composed afterwards (.) unlocked the door n'let her out*).[9]

In line 15, the PA turns from Lynn to Michele with the same repetitive representation. However, rather than use a direct quote referring to the victim's initial impressions, she introduces a direct quote from the defendant ('*NO::* (.) *you can stay upstairs*') embedded in Michele's direct quote from the historical deposition. Here we see multiple laminations of participation, multiple forms of embedded social organization, across an intertextual medley of speech events, each designed for strategic interactional effect; the defendant's talk in the rape event is embedded in Michele's deposition testimony which is, in turn, embedded within the PA's current precedential argument. Increased loudness, vowel lengthening, and stress in the defendant's *NO::* indexes a conversation with Michele in the rape incident where the defendant appears emotionally concerned about her leaving his apartment (as we will see in Segment 2, he does so because she is in an intoxicated state and he invites her to stay in his bedroom as a matter of "safety").

As it turns out, however, affective marking in rejecting her reported request (to leave) reveals something other than the defendant's altruistic motives. While multifunctional *just* (*I just thought he was going to be a gentleman*) may operate as a modal discourse particle, locative or temporal construction (among other functions), it possesses, in this context, an intensifying function designed to "tone up" an argumentative strategy (Aijmer 2002, 158–173). The epistemic mental verb *thought* prefaced by the *just*-adverb contextualizes and intensifies the impending opposition, repeating the discursive patterning from both Lisa and Lynn. And that contrast escalates full force in marked degree modification (*such*) of the stressed extreme adjectives (*ferocious* and *animal like*) to evoke an image of the defendant as a dangerous, violent predator—not only to characterize him as a psychopath with uncontrollable sexual impulses, but also to pathologize the unfolding pattern (*Once upstairs he was **such** a ferocious (1.0) almost **animal** like look to him*). As in the prior two statements, the post-rape depiction of the defendant departs from the direct quote with clause-final *ellipsis* (or omission of part of the quote), though this time repeating the degree modifier (*very indifferent*)—just as we would expect an *animal* to display no emotion after an attack.

In line 20, the PA describes the defendant with the same contrastive rhetoric, starting with sentence initial first name, micro-pause, and extracts of Patricia's prior police statement. Those extracts consist of, first, ellipted direct quotes with repetition of the degree adverbs and modifiers of the defendant's attributes (*very interesting, very nice*) and, second, movement of the second adjective to modify the clause-final noun (*nice demeanor*) for a third repetitive structure. Following this, the PA moves from the direct quote into a description of the sexual assault by repeating the stressed evaluative lexical item (***ferocious***) from Michele's statement followed by the ellipted post-rape recitation (*composed afterward/indifferent*).

To sum up the points made thus far: The type utterance frames an intertextual continuity for the ensuing token, which, in turn, foregrounds the next token as another instance of "that" type as they mutually elaborate one another and the framing type in a recursively interwoven intratextual structure. Inter(intra) textual continuity in linguistic form and content naturalizes an iconic continuity of sexual violence and, as this microcosmic gestalt unfolds, type-token calibrations and recalibrations yield a recursive ensemble of inter(intra)textual coherence to "pathologize" the defendant's behavior, building up a polyrhythmic temporal pattern of charm, violence, and indifference to bestow a unique criminal signature to his actions. As we are beginning to see, inter(intra)textual repetition not only or even primarily functions as a referential link with the past—building up a coherent pattern—but provides a dynamic sense of persuasive involvement and evaluation in current text as well. As we will next discover, type-token repetition within Segment 1 furnishes the reflexive frame for interpreting Segment 2 (and so on recursively and reflexively) in the progressively linked linear pattern.

3.5 Segment 2: Enticing the Victims into His Territory

3A.5 In Segment 2, Matoesian isolates another example of the type-token-type construction (one in the ongoing series of such constructions he analyzes in this chapter). Whereas in the previous segment, the PA used an identical frame for each token example, here she uses two different frames, but in each case she employs verbs of speaking to report the defendant's speech either directly or indirectly. Those token instances of individual speech events are linked, in the larger frame of this segment, with an overall type of speech (enticement) in order to build a picture of the defendant as the type of person (predator) who would use that speech style (or register). Matoesian points out how the intratextual structure within each segment (which he calls "vertical") builds upon the prior segment (in what he calls a "horizontal" connection across different segments of text). This creates an ongoing reflexivity within the textual language, with successive features building upon (and pointing back to) features from prior segments—a process that permits the PA to make connections among the individual token-to-type pairings so that they all seem to naturally fit into an overarching pattern of sexually predatory behavior/speech.

In Segment 2, the PA presents another type classification—this time characterizing the defendant as a sexual predator not by virtue of his reported behavioral pattern, but in terms of a pattern in his speech. Instead of simply re-presenting the victim's statements, she translates the defendant's verbal action using direct and indirect quote formats: what he told each victim to lure them into his territory for the attacks. As in Segment 1 above, she deploys heavily marked stress, increased volume, and vowel lengthening in the main verb (*enti:::ced*) and then proceeds to list what he told each victim in chronological order.

Segment 2: Williams Rule Evidence 2, PA (01:47–02:26)

001   The **defendant** *enti:::ced* the victims into his territory with false
002   pretenses judge.
003   (0.9)
004   He offered Lisa a place to stay? in- in the guest room of his family's
005   home (.) after the people she was supposed to stay with had left.
006   (1.1)
007   He told *Lynn* there was a party at his house (.) when in reality there
008   was no party (.) But he invited her there.
009   (0.7)
010   Michele (.) he told her (0.5) "I'll give ya a place to stay
011   for the night" ya'know "You're too drunk to go home."
012   (1.3)
013   And with *Patricia* (.) he told her he needed a ride home (.) and once
014   there he invited her in to see the Kennedy estate and then to walk
015   onto the beach.
016   (0.6)
017   *Every single* one of these people he *got* to his house by false
018   pretenses.

While the PA uses one type frame in Segment 1, she employs two framing types for Segment 2, enclosing the tokens with variant repetition of the initial type to mark beginning and closing of the segment (lines 1 and 17–18) (*enticed ... by false pretenses; got to his house by false pretenses*). That is, she bounds the tokens by type-framing clauses in an inter(intra)textual repetitive structure that foregrounds the defendant's planning for the attacks, so that each example within the frame is set up as a token of the larger type (predator's speech). Moreover, type-to-token translation functions not only through repetition of the type-frame enclosure but through repetition of the reporting verb (*told*) in triplet. Much like the extreme adjectives from Segment 1 (*ferocious* and *animal-like*), the marked verb *enticed* and locative phrase *into his territory* suggest that the defendant "lured" the victims to his "lair" for the attacks, as a predator would, recalibrating and repeating the intertextual imagery from Segment 1 but adding the theme of intentional and premeditated false statements. In a very transparent sense, such specialized lexical items percolate through her narrative to build a type-level conception that there is a sexual predator speech style or register which can be traced through many different instances of the defendant's speech.

We can make several observations about the intertextual litany. First, type-token reflexivity produces a cumulative effect, building up the predator identity and criminal pattern vertically (or intratextually) within each segment through stressed verbs, linear ordering of each victim, pausing, quotes, and reported speech. Second, each type-token segment reflexively generates a horizontal cumulative effect as it frames the next segment, recalibrates and stabilizes our interpretation of the prior one, and builds up the pattern intertexually across segments. Such patterning organizes reflexive continuities between the segments, a prior segment shaping the next as next shapes the prior as both shape one another through repetition and variation of linguistic features. And last, in this dense constellation of sense-making resources, inter(intra)textual continuities—in both form and content—combine with type-token reflexivity to synchronize the developing criminal pattern.[10]

3.6 Segment 3: Fostering Trust in Multimodal Detail

3A.6 Segment 3 permits Matoesian to widen his analysis to include signaling that goes beyond just the words spoken, instead examining many facets of the communication (i.e., *multimodal* communication). This can include everything from gesture and gaze to body position and the speaker's connection with objects in the room. As the PA develops a type-level account of how the defendant fostered trust in the women he allegedly then raped, she uses gesture and gaze to emphasize her overarching framing of individual instances as examples. In particular, she uses multimodal communication to partially enact and give physical embodiment to the victims' choices to trust or not trust, attempting to signal that they would reject overtures from mere strangers. By contrast, they chose to trust the defendant because he gave them *no reason not to trust them*. The PA also uses an easel with textual evidence to distance herself from the facts she is asserting, physically indicating the evidence as objectively out there rather than as subjectively part of her own opinion. All of this implicitly addresses cultural norms surrounding acquaintance as opposed to stranger rape. If Segment 2 showed how the PA enticed victims into his territory through language, Segment 3 builds on that to show in multimodal detail how the defendant took advantage of the reasons the women had to trust him. The PA mobilizes many modalities to link the different reasons each woman had for trust as tokens of the general type: reasons upon which a crafty sexual predator could capitalize in enticing his victims—also reasons setting up a situation that would make sexual advances improper. The multimodal type-token linkages here play upon and reinforce prior linkages to build the developing image the PA crafts of the defendant as a sexual predator.

To entice the victims into his territory the defendant must first gain their trust, and in this segment I illuminate how multimodality, identity, and participation figure in the PA's logic as it makes connections with legal precedent.

Segment 3: Williams Rule Evidence 3, PA (02:27–03:08)

001   The defendant fostered trust in his victims.
        [((gazes at board)) [((closed hand point at the board))
002   (.)
003   Lisa trusted him- (.) he was a cousin of her boyfriend (.)
        [((gaze to judge)) [((gaze to board))
004   No reason not to trust him
        [((gaze at judge))
005   (1.25)
006   Lynn (.) he was a fellow medical student (.)
                        [(((left arm bent at elbow/waist level.
                        extended outward.
        open palm facing judge/fingers spread.))
007   No reason not to trust him=
        [(((fully extends arm))][(((moves to point at blackboard
        with closed palm facing downward + gaze at judge))
008   =as compared to some stranger on the street=
                    [(((left arm thrust backward in a waving "flip"))
009   =that would come up and ask you out
        [(((hands return to home position in front of body))
010   (0.8)
011   Michelle (.) she attended Georgetown with him (.) He was
        acting
012   like a bi- big brother (.) No reason not to *trust* him
                        [(((gaze to judge))
013   (0.6)
014   Patricia (.5) she discussed the medical condition of
        her child
015   that's one of the first things that she discussed with
        Mr. Smith (.)
016   that she had a child and that the child had a problem at

017   birth (.) and that the child was very ill (.) She completely trusted
         him
018   as a physician and as a person (.) There was no reason not to.
         [(gaze to judge))

As noted earlier, multimodal discourse refers to the integration of bodily conduct—gesture, gaze, and postural orientation—and speech in the coordination of coherent courses of improvised action. Gesture or speech-synchronized gesticulations consist of idiosyncratic or *ad hoc* hand movements that occur generally, though not invariably, with speech. Their meaning co-occurs only in concert with their speech counterparts, in contrast to quotable gestures or emblems (like the "OK" sign or sign languages of the deaf, etc.) that rely on form-meaning conventions and convey meaning independently (McNeill 1992, 2005). But although co-occurring with speech, co-speech gestures do not merely replicate the spoken word. More accurately, they add a visual dimension of meaning to their lexical counterparts; they complement or clarify the message, perform distinct speech acts, foreground information, coordinate the rhythm of speech, and intensify commitment to the proposition, among other functions (Kendon 2004). Along with gesture, gaze and postural orientation often accompany speech to contextualize additional aspects of meaning in interaction, such as creating a focus of joint attention and generating emergent forms of participation in the unfolding dialogue (Goodwin 1981). As integrated discursive resources, bodily conduct and speech represent different yet complementary modes of semiotic expression that yield a more vivid performance of meaning in discourse (Kendon 2004; McNeill 2005). In the courtroom, attorneys may employ bodily conduct to insert their own voice and evaluation into the evidence and thus circumvent legal constraints on their speech.

With these points in mind, note how the PA (in Segment 3) stands to the right of, and parallel with, an artist's "easel" that consists of a large sketchpad with an inscription of each victim's first name, while simultaneously facing the judge with arms held down and hands folded in front of her body—what is often referred to as "home" or base position (Sacks and Schegloff 1972). To gaze at the easel, she must torque her upper body and tilt her head upward to the left. In line 1, her type utterance (*The defendant fostered trust in his victims*), telling us what overarching type of behavior each subsequent example fits into, coincides with gaze and closed hand point at the easel in perfect alignment with production of the verb.[11] After a short pause, she begins the token listing with Lisa (line 3)—but rather than mention how the defendant fostered trust, the PA produces an explanation based on a triangulation of kinship reference (*he was a cousin of her boyfriend*) followed by utterance-initial ellipsis (ellipting *there*-existential and *be*-verb—in other words, leaving out *there was*) and post-token frame (the negative adverb + infinitive clause *No reason not to trust him*)—directing gaze shift from easel toward judge at the infinitive. This post-token frame (based on the "no reason" theme) represents a final expansion and a variation on the single type-frame we witnessed in Segment 1, and the type boundary-repetition we saw in Segment 2. At a finer level of granularity, a series of unmarked lateral head nods accompanies gaze toward the judge to reinforce and stabilize the co-equivalence relation between type ("fostering trust") and post-token frames ("no reason not to"), on the one hand, and corresponding tokens on the other.

As the incantation unfolds, the PA includes Lynn and the defendant (line 6) as co-incumbents in the student identity (*fellow medical student*) followed by repetition and expansion of the post-token type with the comparative (*as compared to some stranger on the street*) and relative clause (*that would come up and ask you out*). By virtue of their shared student status, the victim inherits legitimate grounds for the trusting the defendant, as if mere student identity naturally "extends" their relationship to a higher level of trust.

Similarly, if we consider lines 6–10 in more detail, notice that speech-gesture synchronization expresses not only an affective layering of emphasis but a laminated form of participation unavailable from just the spoken word, demonstrating how forms of bodily conduct integrate with speech to produce an additional dimension of meaning in courtroom interaction. At the modifier *fellow* (Figure 3.1) the PA produces a pleading, open-palm gesture (arm down with wrist bent, parallel to her waist and directed to the judge) and then extends her left arm (with palm still open and fingers spread vertically at waist level and still directed toward the judge) on *medical student* (Figure 3.2), suspending the gesture for a moment in a post-stroke hold, as if extending the initial pleading gesture to invite or implore the judge to agree with her position (see Figures 3.1 and 3.2).[12] Much more speculatively but not so remotely, arm extension may constitute a metaphoric gesture of how co-identity would extend or expand into a trusting relationship (as it simultaneously synchronizes with phrase expansion).

As her arm gesture decays, the PA, first, shifts the open palm into a closed and downward palm point toward the easel, extending her arm in its direction on the post-token frame *no reason not to trust him* (see Figure 3.3 below), and, second, shifts gaze from the judge to the material artifact. On the phrase (*to some stranger*) she redeploys the pointing gesture to execute a backward hand toss (a "brush-off" gesture that takes the outstretched arm pointing toward the easel, bends it at the elbow, and then flings it past the head with the palm facing upward and fingers spread), and in the process projects—better yet *enacts*—an imaginary participation structure to demonstrate in vivid detail how Lynn would have summarily brushed off such an advance or "come-on" by a stranger on the street (see Figure 3.4 below). In an intricate display of multimodal

FIGURE 3.1 **Gesture with *fellow*.**

FIGURE 3.2 **Gesture with *medical student*.**

FIGURE 3.3 **Gesture with *no reason not to trust him.***

dexterity, the PA expands the *trust* proposition with the comparative plus relative (*as compared to some stranger out on the street that would come up and ask
you out*) as she simultaneously expands the brush-off gesture in perfect synchronization with utterance-final clause, integrating verbal and visual expansion by putting participation and epistemic stance *in motion* in the very details
of their multimodal realization. In a strikingly nimble gestural movement, she
adds an intricate lamination of participation and embodied stance that would
be unavailable from the spoken word to show not just "what" Lynn would have
done with the imaginary stranger but *performs* how she would do it in the here
and now, performing epistemic and affective stance in the deictic immediacy of
multimodal action. In more symbolic terms, the brush-off gesture appears as
a metaphor representing how Lynn would have brushed off such an advance
for casual sex (before the PA's hands return to "home" position in front of her).

But the PA's verbal representation and gestural reenactment of Lynn involve
much more than the integration of language and gesture, for any discussion of
embodied activity would be incomplete without understanding the role of material artifacts and how they penetrate the stream of visual and verbal conduct—
what Heath and Hindmarsh (2002, 117) refer to as the "local ecology of material
artifacts." As they mention, while material artifacts appear to possess a physical
facticity based on mere presence in context, they function, much more dynamically, as discursive resources only at specific moments within unfolding courses
of action. While researchers often consider material artifacts as stable and passive features of context that encapsulate action, this ignores their active role in

FIGURE 3.4 **Gesture with *compared to some stranger.***

the multimodal network: how participants utilize them as dynamic resources to enliven distinct interactional tasks. In this sense, the easel functions as a disembodied semiotic resource that directs gaze to it, creating a joint focus of attention that channels evidential orientation. Just as important, when the PA gazes at the easel she executes another crucial form of interactional work. She projects and naturalizes a "passive" animator footing toward the evidence, that she is merely animating Lynn's figure in the narrative (Lynn's brush-off reaction to the stranger), rather than inserting her own voice—her own position and evaluation as author and/or principal—in the imaginary multimodal dialogue, circumventing legal constraints on attorney speech in the process. Thus the artifact's meaning comes into play as the PA animates its relevance and punctuates its significance through verbal and visual resources, gearing distinct spheres of institutional relevance into discursive prominence, setting into motion the circulation of discourse across time, space, and speech events. In this instance, easel, talk, and bodily conduct mutually elaborate one another in the embodied materialization of meaning to *perform* behavior that fits within governing precedent.

More theoretically, the PA extracts, lists, and positions relations in the ongoing dialogue not just through language but in the contextually situated and multimodally emergent construction of precedential evidence, creating a joint interplay of polyrhythmic voices and intertextual continuity. More symbolically, she orchestrates what we might think of as an improvisational, melodic, and staccato "gestural phrase" (see Kendon 2004)—a four-part multimodal excursion that flows in tight, crisp phrases—in which the criminal pattern percolates through variant forms of inter(intra)textual repetition. More practically, but no less interestingly, the intertextual link to the victim's statement superimposes an allusive participation structure that instructs the judge on the role of trust in understanding acquaintance or date rape (in stark contrast to stranger rape) and how that figures prominently in the application of precedent—the precedent applicable in this case.[13]

Turning to Michelle and Patricia, notice the same identity translation regarding the "foster trust" frame. After the pause in line 10, the PA repeats the co-student identity structure (*she attended Georgetown with him*), adds kinship analogy (*He was acting like a big brother*), and ends with the ellipted *reason*-clause and gaze redirection toward the judge.

The PA employs a more complex construction in discussing Patricia. First, she brings up the medical problems associated with her premature child, packaged in a parallel repetition of *that*-complements (*that she had a child, that the child had a problem at birth, and that the child was very ill*): a mother worried about a sick child. While the PA initially refers to the defendant with formal address (*Mr. Smith*) in line 15, she switches reference first to occupational identity (*physician*) and second to the prepositional complement *person,* inserting occupational identity and person reference prior to the post-token type as an "internal" expansion. The victim trusted neither Mr. *Smith* nor even, for the most part, the defendant *as a person* but trusted him, most critically, as a physician, someone who helps patients. Second, the PA foregrounds maternal identity with the degree adverb (*completely trusted him*), parallel repetition of the adverbials (*as a physician, as a person*), and flip-flop repetition of the *reason*-clause from clause-initial to clause-final ellipsis (*There was no reason not to*), ellipting the infinitive. In so doing she constructs a participation structure that portrays a mother consulting her sick child's physician, and this makes the defendant's behavior even more deplorable, more despicable: that he is violating doctor-patient trust and exploiting a distraught mother for criminal purposes. And last, this displays how person reference functions to construct legal identity and to craft persuasive work in contextualizing precedent—more specifically, how maternal identity translates in the process of fostering trust through doctor-patient identities and multimodal performance.

3.7 Finale: Lost in Translation

3A.7 Here Matoesian uses a segment from the PA's closing comments at the hearing to launch an analysis of the larger barriers to success in persuading the judge that the defendant's prior behavior fit with a sexual predator pattern, despite the complex use of type-token framing traced throughout the chapter. Because of the dominance of unarticulated male cultural norms, the PA has to persuade the judge that there were absolutely no sexual innuendos exchanged in the defendant's encounters with the four women involved (despite the fact that such innuendos need not, from a woman's point of view, amount to any kind of consent to sex). And given a norm more common among men that any flirting might well indicate consent, the adversarial structure of the hearing then added to the challenge; that structure permitted any indications of imputed sexual interest to be introduced as being inconsistent (or discontinuous) with the PA's overall account of serial rapes—without ever addressing the underlying presumed norms. Indeed, even the facts of the encounter, with the women accompanying the defendant to his home, could be read (according to one tacit logic) as contradicting the asserted lack of sexual interest. Thus the extreme assertion of absolutely no sexual innuendo, while in one way necessitated by patriarchal logic, is also not credible under that same logic—leading to a double-bind that was invisible within the adversarial hearing format. Beneath the overt structure of the discourse, there were tacit underlying linguistic ideologies at work—first in the way legal adversarial hearings allow for the formulation of "inconsistencies," which then in turn allowed unexamined linguistic ideologies about gendered speech and behavior to be interpolated without examination. The extreme denial of any sexual innuendo, along with the need to pathologize seemingly "normal" male sexual desires and overtures, creates an ongoing mismatch under which many of the PA's subtle linguistic moves are open to instant reinterpretation or "recalibration" that undermines her overall account. Much, then, is lost in the courtroom translation of the women's experiences of sexual violence.

We have seen how intertextual circuits repeat form, content, and imagery and how that process is stabilized, calibrated, and recalibrated in type-token reflexivities not only across historical texts but within and across current text segments. In the process, the PA produces an iconic correspondence between discursive patterning on the one hand and legal identity under auspices of the Williams Rule on the other. Still, the translation is ever problematic as she must maneuver an ambivalent gauntlet of norm and counter-norm and steer an interpretive route through this discursive maze. Consider her concluding comments:

Segment 4: Williams Rule Evidence 4, PA Finish

001   Judge there was absolutely no sexual innuendos exchanged

002   between any of these victims and the defendant at any ti::me.

003   And I submit to the court that this is the defendant's pla:::n

004   to meet unescorted young women at some kind of social
        gathering,

005   to lure them to his house under false pretenses and once there

006   to make a violent, swift, sudden attack with absolutely no sexual

007   innuendo beforehand

In this concluding meta-intertextual frame, the PA once again delivers a multilayered poetic structure consisting of parallel repetition of the *to*-infinitives (*to meet, to lure, to make*), including alliteration in the first and last lines (*meet, make*), repetition of the *any*-modifiers (*any of these victims/at any time*), and a parallel listing of the modifiers in line 6, with alliteration in the final adjectives (*swift, sudden*), to summarize and foreground the predator image. Just as impressively, she repeats the intratextual imagery from the main verbs in Segments 1 and 2 but this time in the stressed ***pla:::n*** in line 3, producing an iconic alignment in vowel lengthening in the NP on the one hand and a lengthy amount of planning for the violent attacks on the other.

But the most interesting repetition lies with the epistemic stance adverb in lines 1 and 6–7 (*absolutely*) and what the PA indexes about her utterance—perhaps even what she indexes about her entire precedential narrative—with this grammatical choice. As mentioned previously, stance refers to positioning of speaker's utterance and to the degree of certainty regarding the proposition: how speaker grounds the authority of knowledge. I argue here that it also encodes broader forms of sociocultural context and dominational configurations. And it is this latter dimension that will occupy our final analytic concerns for understanding legal identity and the performance of precedent, for while the PA's interlaced lyricism and lush impressionism are doubtless sophisticated, several socially structured issues are "lost in translation."

First, while the jury in the adversary system understands that parties will only select evidence that best supports their case, they also expect attorneys to present a persuasive argument of facts brought before them. In Goffmanian terms, attorneys must manage the impressions of the judge or jury by projecting an appearance of objective neutrality rather than presenting an argument that appears too *explicitly* biased. Komter (2000, 420) captures this ambivalence as follows: "The task of both prosecution and defense is to present the jury with the more convincing story. The problem is that too conspicuous orientation to 'winning the case' might undermine the persuasiveness of their story. Thus establishment of the facts is managed by implicit persuasion and persuasion is disguised as 'establishing the facts.'" In other words, if persuasion appears too persuasive—too oriented to winning at the expense of truth—it undermines the facticity of the legal narrative and "spoils" the impression management performance; the PA has to find the seam between coherence and fracture to cultivate the threshold of objective neutrality for the jury.

Second, superimposed on this aspect of the adversary system lies a system of power, of domination, infused with the adversary system in such a way to conceal itself. I have referred to this system of domination elsewhere as the patriarchal logic of sexual rationality (Matoesian 2001). The patriarchal logic of sexual rationality constitutes a linguistic ideology—an interpretive template—for assessing the victim's and offender's actions during the rape event, a representational logic of power based on male standards of sexual preference contingently enacted in the courtroom to accomplish distinct interactional tasks.[14] Most important, patriarchal logic conceals itself within the adversary system—as it simultaneously misrepresents itself—*as the adversary system*. Any form of "sexual innuendo" or "interest" or innocent flirtation (and so on) is interpreted, according to male logic, as granting sexual access and is *misrepresented* and *concealed* as an inconsistency—as a *logical incongruity* among aspects of evidence—when claimed otherwise.[15]

Third, given the dominational logic of this system, the PA must stabilize translations among type and tokens (and between these types and precedent) within and across each segment of her narrative to avoid intertextual "ruptures" or "fractures" that would expose even minute forms of sexual "innuendo." Her narrative must bleach the account of any hint of sexual interest between the victims and defendant—any conspicuous orientation to or relevance of sexual identity. The women must appear as completely devoid of sexual interest or identity. More sharply put, the PA must bleach out all sexual references, pathologize male heterosexual desires, and sanitize sexual content from each woman's narrative. Any exposed sexual residue (of even the most innocent form of flirtation) will be governed by calibrations and recalibrations emanating from patriarchal logic and *colonized* as a legal inconsistency.

And, in each segment, we can see this process at work in dynamic detail. The PA attempts to give date or acquaintance rape the characteristics and moral status of stranger rape and blur the artificial distinction between the two, as the lexical items *ferocious* and *animal-like* suggest. Through her invocation of the type-level rapist register or speech style, the PA recalibrates characteristics of stranger rape, superimposes these on the date rape scenario, and thereby displaces normative male sexual preferences as to how flirtatious cues should be interpreted. More pointedly, her translation must pathologize not only the defendant's actions but also his male-hegemonic form of sexual desire. The problem is this: her counter-hegemonic tactics (attempting to undercut a more male view of consent) still yield intertextual ruptures that reinforce and naturalize hegemonic sexual rationality.[16] That the victims, in Segment 1, were in the bedroom or near the bed or sitting on the couch could lead to some degree of sexual interpretation, though not necessarily sexual consent. Of course, an intoxicated woman sleeping in a young man's bed could lead to more direct sexual interpretations, and that he was *indifferent* afterwards could lead to the motivational issue of fabricating the charges. Her claim of *no sexual innuendo* is inconsistent according to the ideological order of male standards of sexual access, under which information such as the fact that the women went with the defendant into more intimate settings would be interpreted as the giving of consent.

When the PA switches reference from the victim to defendant in Segments 2 and 3 more problematic representations arise with the "enticed into his territory" and "fostered trust" frames. Given that it would be inappropriate for a man engaged in a "normal encounter" to expose sexual interests blatantly (or at least be inadvisable), then he would have to be more or less indirect and "entice" a woman with an offer of a drink or cup of coffee or an invitation to walk on the beach (and so on) as an avenue for obtaining sexual access later. Notice in particular how the PA uses the verb "entice" instead of the more generic "seduce." Even so, according to the *OED*[17] the verb "entice" carries connotations of "allure" or "seduce" and "to attract physically" (not to mention the connotation of "tempt" and the connotation of "getting someone to do something that is morally questionable").

The "fostering trust" frame, for example, could represent a "pick-up line" that men use (as a ruse) to attract women, once again with an eye to sexual conquest. Moreover, since *foster* is an active verb one would expect a degree of defendant agency; yet the sole impetus behind the frame is identity co-membership with the victims: a passive relational attribute. Indeed, PA must "stretch" considerably to stabilize asexual translations when "normal" male heterosexual behavior often involves using a "line" (or *foster trust*) to "pick up" a woman at a bar or elsewhere (*entice*), get them over to his place (or *territory*) and try to have sex with them (see Matoesian 2001).

Fourth and with the above points in mind, why would the PA deploy such extreme or absolute representations, permitting no gradations on the ordered scale, leaving all other degrees ripe for the DA to exploit? Why not simply state that the women were interested in the defendant for any number of reasons but not sexual interest? Why not admit that there was, perhaps, some sexual innuendo but nothing in the way of sexual consent? The patriarchal logic of sexual rationality erases the female perspective in the gendered order, displaces it with male standards of sexual access, and governs any type of interest as sexual interest, the way men are interested in women (see Ehrlich 2001; Matoesian 2001). In this ideological process, the woman is interested in the man the same way that he is interested in her: sexually. The patriarchal logic of sexual rationality is not just a system of logic but logic of power that shapes discourse as discourse shapes it, even as it submerses itself under auspices of the adversary system. In the legal-linguistic ideology of inconsistency, no moderate position is possible; the PA must commit to the most extreme end of the ideological spectrum, leaving her mired in the sexual abyss she so studiously sought to avoid, leaving her with no interpretive latitude. This is how the stance adverb *absolutely* encodes quite more than a grammatical or text-metrical or interactive way to signal the degree of commitment to or level of certainty about the proposition. In this context *absolutely* incorporates broader forms of sociocultural domination, indexes the patriarchal logic of sexual rationality, and drives the ambivalence in the PA's discursive representation.

Last, this ambivalence imperils the PA's extreme representations and precedent-framed narrative, leaving her in a dominational double-bind and dangerously exposed to the defense attorney's more "modest," objective, and thus "neutral" counterclaims, with all remaining gradational points to exploit.[18] That is to say, if we consider this as an ordered scale, the defense attorney can exploit everything after the extreme representation (absolutely no sexual innuendo) and thus maneuver in much wider field of opportunity. The PA's melodic attempts to bleach sexualized identity, pathologize the defendant's actions via type-token reflexivity, and mobilize stance/degree adverbs demonstrate how the patriarchal logic of sexual rationality is normatively oriented to and relevant to discursive practice even in absence; that is, it is not just absent but, to adapt a line from Sacks (1992), noticeably and powerfully absent. Indeed, we can see how type-token reflexivity functions to not only create a predator identity but, just as importantly, bleach sexualized identity from representation organized around precedent—a representation that turns out to be problematic because type-token relations will recalibrate, under auspices of patriarchal logic, as type-token mismatches. Indeed, the PA not only attempts to pathologize the defendant but to denaturalize normative male sexual preferences—a system of domination—in the translation process.

She loses either way, an issue lost in translation, and that's why the judge denied the motion to introduce the testimony of the three other women. On the one hand, her claim of *absolutely no* sexual innuendo is incredible; on the other hand, if she admits innocent flirting or some sexual innuendo, the patriarchal logic of sexual rationality recalibrates such action as sexual interest and thus sexual access—yet hidden under the auspices of the linguistic ideology of inconsistency. These reciprocally infused ambivalent systems—the adversary system and the patriarchal logic of sexual rationality—pressure the PA into extreme translations of the events using characterizations like *absolutely*, making her precedential narrative appear too persuasive, too conspicuously oriented to winning the case. In the process, it shapes and co-opts resistance and re-channels it into male-hegemonic forms, concealed as legal inconsistency. Because of the dynamic interpenetration of social structure and linguistic structure, there is no way to translate precedential narrative by taking a more moderate stance. Despite the intricate and artful type-token coordination, articulated at times in dense multimodal form, the PA could not overcome the intertwined sociocultural and linguistic barriers to translation encountered in this courtroom.

Notes

1. Matthew Lippman, personal communication. See also *Black's Law Dictionary* 1991: 814.

2. *Indexical* refers to the way parts of language signal meaning through pointing to aspects of their contexts. Words like *this* and *that*, for example, rely heavily on the contexts in which they occur for their actual meanings. Those kinds of words are known as *deictics*. Nonverbal signals can also function as deictics—perhaps the quintessential example being a finger pointing at an object that the speaker wishes to talk about. Note that this chapter generally uses the term *multimodal* signaling to discuss nonverbal communication, which includes gestures, gaze, bodily position, and the like. The kinds of cues commonly talked about by linguists as *paralinguistic signals* (intonation, stress, etc.) are analyzed as part of verbal communication. The word *semiotics*, which refers to the study of *signs*, is also used

to indicate the wider study of all kinds of signaling that form a part of communication—whether linguistic or not.

3. The distinction between token and type can be traced to the idea of "category" and "instances" subsumed under its auspices (see Silverstein 2005, 9). Thus we can distinguish between the word *door* in the abstract (the *type* level) and an utterance of the word *door* in a particular instance (a *token* of the more abstract word *door*).

4. For simplicity's sake, I am using the term *intertextuality* to refer to what is more accurately called *interdiscursivity* or the continuity across different genres or speech events and the use of one genre in another (Matoesian 2001, 2008).

5. The *animator* physically produces the words; the *author* composes the words; and the *principal* authorizes those roles as the responsible party (Goffman 1981). The concept of *lamination* allows us to track how negotiating roles and meanings while talking is frequently a complex, multilayered process. The concept of participation structure indicates the social organization of discursive roles.

6. Participation refers to the projection of discursive roles performed in speech; epistemic stance captures the speaker's degree of commitment to his or her words; and referential function applies to the role language plays in denoting some state of affairs in some universe (see Silverstein 1979).

7. For instance, one of the segments deals with what Susan Ehrlich (2001) has analyzed in illuminating detail in her work on rape trials: cultural mythologies relating to the "utmost resistance standard."

8. When sociolinguists talk about speech style or register, they are referring to types of speech that are peculiar to a given social situation.

9. On a theoretical note, while the linguistic debate rages on about the difference between epistemic stance (one's degree of certainty about the proposition) and evidentiality (the source of information)—and if they bear any conceptual relationship to one another, we can see in the above example how the contrastive structure functions to combine both evidentiality and epistemic stance as a strategic persuasive device. Perhaps a more interesting way to proceed would be to consider how social actors use these concepts to accomplish distinct interaction work.

10. This is done through perfectly balanced syntagmatic and paradigmatic structure—i.e. = sameness and difference. Notice too how defendant agency and victim passivity are marked in the grammatical structure of each of the above statements (see Ehrlich 2001 for an overview of how this operates in a similar manner).

11. This shows how the gesture stroke (McNeill 1992) or meaning conveying phrase of the gesture aligns with its lexical counterpart so that both arrive simultaneously at the main moment of meaning making.

12. According to McNeill (2005), the post-stroke hold suspends or "freezes" the stroke for emphasis.

13. Note too, in this regard, how PA shifts gaze from the easel back to the judge on "compared to some stranger . . ."

14. The term *linguistic ideologies* (Silverstein 1979) refers to folks rationalizations of language and how these may interact with social context and power.

15. As I have demonstrated previously (Matoesian 2001), while inconsistency in the rape trial cross-examination of the victim is taken as a natural juxtaposition of contradictory facts, I argue that, in reality, it is also a legal linguistic ideology that conceals a massive

system of power and domination. This should not be taken to mean, in some absolute or generic sense, that inconsistency always interacts with power. This is only a possible reading of inconsistency in this data, in the interactional contingencies of this context and at this specific moment.

16. Susan Ehrlich (2003) describes this issue from another direction. She notes accurately that non-stranger rape lacks a "well-developed sense making framework" and how victims of this type of sexual assault (and judges or attorneys) frequently describe their experience in terms of "'normal' heterosexual sex" rather than violent assault. Here we can see a similar strategy to articulate a coherent narrative, an attempt to translate date or acquaintance rape into the stranger rape speech register, but with the same unfortunate consequences for the prosecution and victims.

17. *Oxford English Dictionary.* Online at http://www.oed.com/view/Entry/62887?redire ctedFrom=entice#eid. Accessed February 15, 2016.

18. Although more modest on the face of it, the defense argument tacitly bears the dominational imprint of patriarchal logic, only recalibrated as the facts.

References

Aijmer, Karin. 2002. *English Discourse Particles.* Amsterdam: John Benjamins.
Atkinson, J. Maxwell, and Paul Drew. 1979. *Order in Court.* New York: MacMillian.
Black's Law Dictionary. 1991. St. Paul, MN: West.
Ehrlich, Susan. 2001. *Representing Rape.* New York: Routledge.
Ehrlich, Susan. 2003. "Normative Discourses and Representations of Coerced Sex." In *The Language of Sexual Crime*, edited by Janet Cotterill, 126–128. New York: Palgrave.
Ehrlich, Susan. 2010. "Rape Victims: The Discourse of Rape Trials." In *Routledge Handbook of Forensic Linguistics*, edited by Malcolm Coulthard and Alison Johnson, 265–280. New York: Routledge.
Goffman, Erving. 1981. *Forms of Talk.* Philadelphia: University of Pennsylvania Press.
Goodwin, Charles. 1981. *Conversational Organization.* New York: Academic Press. Cambridge University Press.
Heath, Christian, and Jon Hindmarsh. 2002. "Analyzing Interaction." In *Qualitative Research in Action*, edited by Tim May, 99–121. London: Sage.
Kendon, Adam. 2004. *Gesture.* New York: Cambridge University Press.
Komter, Martha. 2000. "The Power of Legal Language: The Significance of Small Activities for Large Problems." *Semiotica* 131 (3/4): 415–428.
Matoesian, Gregory. 2001. *Law and the Language of Identity.* Oxford: Oxford University Press.
Matoesian, Gregory. 2008. "You Might Win the Battle but Lose the War: Multimodal, Interactive, and Extralinguistic Aspects of Witness Resistance." *Journal of English Linguistics* 36 (3): 195–219.
Matoesian, Gregory. 2010. "Multimodal Aspects of Victim Narration in Direct Examination." In *Routledge Handbook of Forensic Linguistics*, edited by Malcolm Coulthard and Alison Johnson, 541–557. New York: Routledge.
McNeill, David. 1992. *Hand and Mind.* Chicago: University of Chicago Press.
McNeill, David. 2005. *Gesture and Thought.* Chicago: University of Chicago Press.
Mertz, Elizabeth. 2007. *The Language of Law School.* New York: Oxford University Press.

O'Barr, William. 1981. *Linguistic Evidence.* New York: Academic Press.

Sacks, Harvey. 1992. *Lectures in Conversation. Volumes 1 & 2.* Oxford: Blackwell.

Sacks, Harvey, and Emanuel Schegloff. 2002. "Home Position." *Gesture* 2: 133–146.

Silverstein, Michael. 1979. "Language Structure and Linguistic Ideology." In *The Elements: A Parasession on Linguistic Units and Levels*, edited by Paul R. Clyne, William F. Hanks, and Carol L. Hofbauer, 193–247. Chicago: Chicago Linguistic Society.

Silverstein, Michael. 1998. "The Improvisational Performance of Culture in Realtime Discursive Practice." In *Creativity in Performance*, edited by Robert Keith Sawyer, 266–312. London: Ablex.

Silverstein, Michael. 2003. "Translation, Transduction, Transformation." In *Translating Cultures*, edited by Paula G. Rubel and Abraham Rosman, 5–108. Oxford: Berg.

Silverstein, Michael. 2005. "Axes of Evals: Token versus Type Interdiscursivity." *Journal of Linguistic Anthropology* 15(1): 6–22.

Weber, Max. 1978. "The Formal Qualities of Modern Law." In *Economy and Society*, Vol. 2, edited by Guenther Roth and Claus Wittich, 880–900. Berkeley: University of California Press.

White, James. 1990. *Justice as Translation.* Chicago: University of Chicago Press.

Cases

Williams v. Florida, 110 So. 2d 654 (Fla. 1959).

4

Part One Commentary
PERFORMATIVE RISKS IN RISKING PERFORMANCE
Michael Silverstein

4A.

Silverstein "In Translation"
Elizabeth Mertz

4.1 Introduction

4A.1 When speaking in court, both the lay defendant apologizing to the
court (in Gruber's chapter) and the prosecutor in a rape case (in Matoesian's
chapter) wind up caught in linguistic dilemmas that defy the capacity of law to
separate legal communication from the wider social world around it. Courtroom
language is constrained by procedures that attempt to bound off trials as
distinct and special linguistically—and yet everyday communicative (*semiotic*)
norms continue to leak in—as happens within all such ritual performances.
Of course, legal professionals know about this *leakage*, and take advantage of
it—as when they play to the jury. But even so, certain aspects of the dominant
culture's views (whether of sexuality, sincerity, or how language itself operates)
can be impossible to escape. This creates a serious problem for justice that is
supposed to be even-handed across social divisions (i.e., race, class, gender).
Surrounding, within, and beneath the overt language of the courtroom are what
Silverstein calls *sociocultural affordances*—that is, the hidden limits of possible
interpretations of what is overtly said in court, limits based on tacit sociocultural
norms and understandings. Added to this is the fact that when speakers in
court use *performative* language (language that does something in-and-by the
uttering of it), there are often very serious consequences. (For example, if
I apologize to a passerby on the street, and my apology fails because we don't
share similar background sociocultural norms, the result is different than if a
criminal defendant's attempted apology fails due to a similar divergence of shared
norms.) Silverstein's commentary proceeds in three parts: (1) an analysis of how
details of patterned language structure (*poetics*) contribute to this dilemma; (2) a
discussion of the crucial role played by the relationship (created in the language

of the courtroom) between past and present actions and actors; and (3) a
demonstration of how the sociocultural world around the courtroom enters into
courtroom language despite, or sometimes because of, trial procedures.

Whether performed by a legal professional such as a prosecuting attorney (as
in Matoesian's material) or by a hapless and scared layperson about to receive
a federal judge's sentence for a crime (as in Gruber's), segments in the procedurally framed events called trials, like all ritual moments, borrow their very
material—communicative signs and their consequentiality—from everyday
life while transforming it in the process of transposition. And, no matter how
much we can recognize the massive bounding-off work that is designed to guar-
antee to the ritual of trial, as to any such ritual, performative autonomy and
hence authority to determine and to ordain, the actors inhabiting ritual roles
are dogged by those everyday facts-of-semiotic-life, cultural commonplaces
that inevitably turn out to play a major if perhaps unrecognized role in determining the course of "justice." To be sure, legal professionals have long since
strategically used such "leakage" to their client's advantage, across the boundary of, say, the everyday sociocultural realities of jurors' value systems and their
charge of attentive focus in their roles at trial, which might reinforce a certain
cynicism about case law's proceduralism. But here, in both Matoesian's and
Gruber's reports, we find examples of semiotic "leakage" simply impossible
to counter yet, as they argue, decisive for understanding the actual course of
things in trial procedures such as those they analyze—in a sense, the clouding
of the chaliceful of clear justice with everyday impurities.

To the anthropological eye, the material in Matoesian's and in Gruber's
papers reveals at once the rich discursive poetics[1] common to courtroom
interaction, discursive poetics central to its "ritual" character as interlocutors
move through procedural segments fixed by the orderliness of a decision tree.
Matoesian's chapter concerns itself with a pre-trial motion, the attempt by a
prosecuting attorney in a rape trial to secure permission to introduce deposed
evidence of defendant's prior—and arguably recurrently patterned—behavior
as a sexual predator. Gruber's chapter concerns itself with a trial segment
immediately preceding the meting out of a sentence, the first-person courtroom
allocution of a defendant now determined to be guilty of a federal crime, for
which he or she frequently feels compelled to issue a kind of apology.

Both of these chapters focus on what we might term the *performative*
(doing in-and-by saying) characteristics of the courtroom roles that play out in
verbal interactions of trials, giving us a careful empirical record of what is said
and, in-and-by the saying, what—if successful—will have been done or effectu-
ated.[2] As well, Matoesian and Gruber emphasize the respective multiple sociocultural affordances framing what is said-and-done, affordances that license a
courtroom move's possible efficaciousness and also that allow us to understand

its risk of failure. What both studies reveal is that, no matter how scripted the proceduralism of adversarial legal institutions, the actual cause-and-effect risks of doing-by-saying in the courtroom are the same as those we are elsewhere subject to, even as the outcomes loom more starkly and consequentially for the participants. In each author's careful analysis of particular micro-segments of trials certain perduring frameworks of American bourgeois cultural values about everything from sexuality to sincerity to language itself are brought to bear in motivating and explaining the said and the unsaid, the effective and the ineffective in what transpires in court under their analytic gaze.

Let me organize my elaboration of these points in order. First, I wish to address the poetic texture of what is revealed in the transcript material, its organizational characteristics as ventures into rhetorically effective ritual discourse directed by speakers to certain interested ends and, for Gruber's convicted defendants no less than for Matoesian's polished prosecuting attorney, ultimately falling somewhat short of the mark. Next, I want to discuss what we might term the denotational "aboutness" of trials as they become yet one more event of—to be sure, highly circumscribed—representation of past events in the present circumstance, with which the current ritual event is in an interdiscursive relationship involving at least some of the very same individuals who are characters in the represented states-of-affairs. How this relationship shapes the material we see here (and all other trial material) is central to both of these chapters. Third, I wish to elaborate on the permeability of trial ritual procedure revealed in these authors' analyses of what goes right and what wrong in the instances they treat, seeing the "culture" in the courtroom as much as the culture of the courtroom, in other words.

4.2 Macro- and Micro-"Poetics" in the Context of Trial

4A.2 The very brief snippets of language analyzed by Gruber and Matoesian are embedded within the larger macro-structures of the trials, which designate how and when each party is supposed to talk, listen, or perform some other *interaction role* in the ongoing legal drama. As Silverstein points out, even the names for actors in this drama (*judge, defendant, prosecutor*, etc.) are in one sense metalinguistic terms, in that they indicate the linguistic roles each person is to play in court. (Indeed, they are *metapragmatic* terms in that they are instances of language referring to and designating its own social-contextual structure.) The speakers analyzed by Matoesian and Gruber inhabit those interaction roles, in the process linking their micro-level utterances to the macro-level of the legal-linguistic trial structure that shapes not only their roles but also how evidence can be presented and assimilated (and much more). Silverstein notes that the everyday *poetics* (rhythms and rhymes) of criminal defendants' apologies to the court often do not work well with the legal system's expectations, set in place at the macro-structural level—and so Gruber's defendants risk significant misfires when apologizing to the court. By contrast, Matoesian's prosecutor is well-versed in legally structured discourse, and employs elegantly constructed micro-linguistic parallel poetic structures to perform the very equivalence she is also attempting to establish descriptively among the experiences that four different women had with the alleged rapist. Silverstein tracks the way the prosecutor enacts what she is describing, as she tightly combines contextual structuring (at the *pragmatic* or *indexical* level) with the content of what she is saying (*denotational* or *semantic* content). Even in the trained voice of the prosecutor, however, this often-powerful mirroring of language content in language structure (an *iconic* relationship), winds up falling short for reasons discussed later in the chapter.

Notwithstanding the short duration of the moments examined—Gruber's 52 defendants' allocutions range from 4 seconds to just over 3 minutes, averaging 30 seconds; each of Matoesian's three substantive excerpts from the prosecutor's preliminary motion took about a minute—each event is embedded within a dense macro-structure of trial procedure organized into interactional roles with rights to speak and responsibilities to watch and listen and weigh that take differential salience as a case serially moves through its phases. The very names for the statuses of people in respect of a case— judge; plaintiff; complainant; defendant; prosecuting attorney; defense attorney; etc.—are *metapragmatic* terms, terms that describe the relational role incumbencies and their rights and responsibilities relative to the various interactional phases of the history unfolding around the case and how it got to trial.

As Gruber notes, once "guilty" by virtue of trial or plea, during the sentencing phase of a proceeding a criminal defendant in federal court has the right to speak, presumably in his or her own behalf, prior to the presiding judge's issuance of a sentence. Here is a performance slot, as it were, in a determinate position in the whole; it is more or less the one time other than the utterance of the plea itself when the individual him- or herself— as opposed to his or her attorney, acting on the client's behalf—is written into the script of role incumbencies as authorized speaker, given the floor or licensed a turn-at-talk. But what, Gruber asks, is the nature of that turn-at-talk? Whether after a whole evidentiary trial or no, whether by jury trial or bench, the now—as agreed upon by all parties—"guilty" individual is about to learn what punishment is to be exacted by the state by the authorized delegate of state authority who speaks in this respect *ex cathedra*. Is the guilty party now speaking to the state? To the person of the presiding judge? To his or her familiars "back home," as it were? To no one in particular in a kind of staged soliloquy of remorse, regret, or revisionist autobiography? And of what is the now-guilty party speaking?

Such matters are of central interest precisely because, as Gruber points out, the illocutionary act of *apology*, performable in-and-by the utterance of a specific verbal formula, seems to figure centrally both in what now-guilty defendants offer in the instance and what the legal professionals seem to counsel and to expect from the guilty. A canonical formula would be something like

"I apologize to you for [. . .]," where one can fill in a descriptor of the delict of commission or omission for which one is now taking responsibility and offering a repair of social relations. In the instance, Gruber finds that defendants use the alternative formula with the predicate *be- sorry*, one that at least denotationally focuses on the speaker's current state of mind, as in *I am sorry that [. . .]*, or *I am sorry for [. . .]*, where a full—and fulsome—role performance requires filling in with a clause or participial complement specifying the speaker's offense as describable. Note that apology is, in the normal everyday world, understood to be an act requiring, as J. L. Austin would have it, *uptake*; the party to whom the apology is directed needs to acknowledge it and, in the quickest resolving instance, accept it by uttering a formula, for example, "Oh, all right. [But don't do it again or [. . .]!" before social relations can be restored to *status quo ante*. This is hardly what is going on in courtroom procedure.

So regardless of the fact that the formula for apology is both sought after and duly delivered in the segment allocated to defendant *allocution* (or formal apology), the poetics of sentencing is such that the defendant is hardly apologizing; he or she is performing an act of supplication before a powerful entity who determines one's fate in-and-by the following illocutionary act, *sentencing*. The defendant is thus a specimen of humanity being examined by the powerful entity, the judge, who is in no ritual sense an interlocutor to whom an apology is being directed, as in the everyday one-two structure of *{apology; [non]acceptance}* (though several allocutions include actual apologies to family, to victims, etc., along with other material). What the guilty defendant has to offer in the plea, the supplication for leniency, is only evidence of some saving human virtue despite (or because of) having—as admitted or having been "proved" at trial—committed acts the state deems criminal.

So what are the outward indexical signs of inner residual virtue at this point that might figure in mitigating the state's—the judge's, that is—meting out of punishment? Can the guilty party create the image of someone basically good though temporarily having gone astray, with the capacity to be redeemed through incarceration? It is interesting that in Gruber's transcribed material such indexical demonstration before the court as a supplicant takes the canonical form of descriptors of inner states, among the several examples one of the vernacular formulas for performing an actual apology, *I'm sorry*, that frequently constitutes the culminative and final moment of the allocutionary turn at talk, summing up the whole.

But, to be sure, these are laypersons' vernacular supplicating performances of redeemability, sometimes rambling and requiring their own poetic parsing to see where the indexicals are germane to the task at hand. As Gruber points out, we must look to such discourse structures to understand what the guilty individuals are communicating about themselves, rather than to fixed, formal performative formulas in which the legal register abounds and to which, we might surmise, legal personnel are attuned. And indeed, if we study the transcripts we see how richly and how repetitively, in their own sometimes unartful and not quite syntactically well-formed phraseology, the guilty aver and index inner states bespeaking a reformed—or at least reformable—intentionality, cognizant of and affected by their culpability. The speakers are all very eloquent in using the poetics of repetition and variation of discourse partials, even if they may be deficient in syntax and connectedness of legal expository prose.

By contrast, Matoesian's prosecuting attorney at the preliminary evidentiary hearing of the William Kennedy Smith trial is superbly able in the poetics of trial discourse. In the instance, Matoesian draws a parallel with the abductive mode of reasoning in common-law–based jurisprudence, whereby a collection of specific cases become tokens or instances of a general principle or type criterion—a "covering law!"—that legal reasoning in a sense extracts in-and-by the discursive move of bringing said cases together as variant instances of the same thing (one of which is the case to hand for adjudication or review). Here, under the Williams Rule applicable in Florida criminal cases regarding admissible evidence about a defendant, the abductive move is not so much focused on criminal cases as tokens, but on matters of biographical fact. If a prosecutor can assemble a set or series of instances of defendant's intent to engage in behavior like that figuring in the current trial, as an extractable "pattern of criminality or *modus operandi*," a type of conduct instantiated consistently, then that pattern of behavior is admissible as evidence in the current trial.

So the prosecutor's task is to present such a pattern, that is, to show that the defendant repeatedly and intentionally engaged in date- or acquaintance-rape over a lengthy period, culminating in the incident for which he is being tried. And she does so by discursively tracing the cumulative similarity across testimony of three women who came forth after the charges against Dr. Smith in this trial had been made public. But not only does she convey the information that all these incidents are tokens of the same intentional and behavioral type, sudden and violent sexual assault by the current defendant, she uses a densely metricalized form of repetition that itself is a picture—an *icon*—of precisely what she is portraying. Matoesian's transcript material emphasizes three uniformities in the incidents that aim to establish the type-level pattern of criminality, *the defendant's plan to meet unescorted young women at some kind of social gathering, to lure them to his house under false pretenses, and once there to make a violent, swift, sudden attack.* And each segment narrates the story in the same order of victimhood, presumably a historical series from earliest to current to drive home the point of continuity over time.

First, we learn of the Dr.-Jeckyll-Mr.-Hyde transformation of the initially *charming, quiet, attractive, well-dressed ... gentleman* of *nice demeanor* in public, who transformed into the *ferocious, almost animal-like* predator who grabbed and tackled his victims and then, after sexual intercourse, *apologized*, was *composed afterwards*, even *very indifferent* to them. The descriptors of Dr. Smith from each of the four depositions roll out in precisely parallel poetic form, effectively to stress the uniform "change in personality" as the *modus operandi*.

Second, the charming Dr. Jeckyll/Smith, the prosecutor generalizes, uniformly *enticed the victims into his territory—his family home—with false pretenses*. Here, each one of the "enticements" was a positive, friendly gesture indexing good-heartedness, as described serially for each incident in turn: *a place to stay in the guest room of his family's home*; an invitation to *a party at his house when in reality there was no party; a place to stay for the night* to someone too drunk to drive; an invitation *in to see the Kennedy estate and then to walk onto the beach*. All *got to his house by false pretenses*, the prosecutor reiterates in concluding this segment of denotational, if not precisely syntactic, parallels across the incidents.

Third, and most complexly in Matoesian's reading of both verbal and gestural transcripts of the prosecutorial discourse, the fact that uniformly *the defendant fostered trust in his victims* is a generalization built up through a complex combination of description of the victims' respective social relations with the defendant, and an *indirect free style* (taking on the verbal characteristics of a first-person voice within a third-person segment describing someone else). The prosecutor in effect transposes their voices/thoughts so as to re-present the very cognition and affect of each as it would have earlier been verbalized, and as well voices are duplicated in the stance, gaze, and gestural accompaniments of the verbal channel. In this remarkable segment of the prosecutor's account, as revealed in the still photographs excerpted from a video, she creates a triangular rhetorical space with three vertices: herself, the (female) judge, and—in front and to the right of the judge; in front and to her left—a large display on an easel of the names of the victims. In effect standing in for each of the victims by a bodily gesture of looking or pointing to each name, selecting it, and bringing it into the triangular interactional space, the prosecutor voices the sense of "trust" in each. We can emphasize this dramatization by italicizing the indirect free style segments of the transcript, where the prosecuting attorney re-uses the language and thought of a third person in descriptive characterization of them:

> *<Looking at judge:>* "Lisa trusted [the defendant]; *<Looking at easel:>* he was a cousin of her boyfriend. *<Looking at judge:>* No reason not to trust him.

The first of the italicized segments reproduces Lisa's consciousness of her identity vis-à-vis the defendant, as though thinking "He is my boyfriend's cousin"; the second, Lisa's ingenuous affective sense of not being in any danger of having to fend off sexual advances. The prosecutor in effect inhabits Lisa as she re-animates the latter's "trust" for—and to—the judge.

Lynn. *<Open-(left-)palmed gesture of "reason(ableness)" in the direction of the easel:>* *He was a fellow medical student*. *<Full-palm point to easel; Looking at judge:>* *No reason not to trust him* *<Palm raised to "Stop!" gesture:>* *as compared to some stranger on the street* *<Hands return to neutral:>* *that would come up and ask you out*.

This intense choreography has a whole rhetoric of gesture that animates the state of mind of the victim Lynn. The open palm signaling reason—and reasonableness—of one's situation, almost like saying "After all, ..."; the reminder of whom the prosecutor is voicing by the palm-point to the easel; segueing to the raised flat palm gesture of "Halt!" or "Stop right there!" when confronting a stranger who "come[s] up" (note the deictic directionality of a perceiving consciousness) bent on taking liberties by "ask[ing] you out" (and note the wonderful second-person generic).

The third sub-segment in the series, on Michelle, is less animated, but still follows precisely the pattern of voicing, with the victim's *No reason not to **trust** him* also delivered with a simultaneous look in the direction of the judge.

And the final segment, with perhaps the most elaborate basis for "trust"— the consultative relationship between a worried parent of an ill child and a physician, no less—emphasizes that the complainant *completely trusted [the defendant] as a physician and as a person*, once again animating the interior mental act of reflexively allaying any suspicion of what was to come:

<Looking at judge:> *There was no reason not to* [*sc.*, "*completely trust him*"].

Note that in this elaborate serial quasi-reenactment of the women's feelings of "trust," the prosecutor actually has presented no evidence that the defendant intentionally and deliberately "fostered trust in his victims" as part of a strategy aforethought to lull them into false security, and so, perhaps, she has focused on the victims' state of mind in the circumstances of encounter.

4.3 Social Persons as Characters and Participants in Rituals of Representation

4A.3 The overt (or denotational) content of trials is generally composed of a competing set of present-time accounts about past events. A crucial part of those accounts is the link created in discourse between present and past, connecting some of the current actors (defendants, for example) with their own and others' prior actions, words, and selves (as narrated in court, creating an interdiscursive link between now and then). These connections are inevitably accomplished through the use of indexical language that points to aspects of speech contexts, including temporal dimensions. In the case of Gruber's defendants performing apologies to the court, the speakers must use their allocutions to establish a discontinuity between their former and current selves. Their use of *I'm sorry* or *I apologize* formats has to convey effectively that the current speaker is different from the prior self who performed criminal actions—that she or he has changed in a fundamental way, and as a true penitent will not commit similar bad acts in the future. By contrast, the prosecutor in Matoesian's example has to establish a continuity across people and actions, showing that the defendant behaved in very similar ways across different times, places, and victims (and presumably thereby showing that he is prone to a pattern of conduct that is an ongoing feature of his present self). Gruber and Matoesian's examples are similar, however, in that voicing—the way a current narrator positions her- or himself vis-à-vis people in the narrated event—is a crucial (although often hidden) part of the decisions made in court, because it is through voicing that advocates and witnesses can persuade the judge or jury that past behaviors are or are not likely to continue into the future.

Although trials are focally future-oriented in the sense of having consequences as a function of acts of judgment—Gruber's defendants receive sentences they must then serve; Matoesian's prosecutor will or will not be able to introduce Williams Rule evidence as the main arguments of the trial unfold—much of trial proceduralism as an unfolding interaction consists of the discursive presentation, exemplification, and analysis of matters that one or another party wishes to establish as fact. Such representations generally take the form of details, sequentially focused upon, contributing to a narrative, organized according to a "theory of the case," that is, a legally consequential structuration and interpretation of doings and sayings of narrated characters, and of the past circumstances and contexts locating the narrated characters—many of whom are as well role-inhabiting individuals in the courtroom itself, such as defendants, witnesses, plaintiffs, etc.

This indexical continuity across time and space—characters about whom narratives are constructed in court showing up in the here-and-now of trial as flesh-and-blood individuals—is key to understanding the voicing we see in transcript material. *Voicing*, signaling one's alignment as a narrator in the here-and-now with the perspective of an actual or stereotypic character in some narrated universe, is thus central to the adversarial interests of principals in trials, since even while agreeing on various aspects of narratives involving currently present individuals (for example, a defendant), the question before a deciding party such as a judge or jury member involves as well projectable continuity of the narrated character in an account of a possible crime-as-committed across space-time to the very here-and-now individual about whom must be determined the consequences of whatever is procedurally established as the narrative.

This is abundantly clear in Gruber's guilty-party allocutions. As noted above, these are supplications preceding an act of judgment by an interlocutory authority, requiring of the convicted individuals the actualization not of characterological continuity across the space-time of narrated world to the courtroom here-and-now, so much as radical change. The trial or even the narrative presumed by a guilty plea involves a character of some criminality of intent, action, demeanor; speaking now in his or her own behalf, the individual who has been, up to this point, that very heinous character, is called upon and given the opportunity to reveal transformation. The "I" of discourse must perform a coming-to-grips with that "me" who is no longer me, as it were. And so, the role-relational schema of the *apology*, as Goffman pointed out, becomes a convenient—and conventional—interactional ready-made with which to sunder the once-more moral and law-abiding current "I" in the here-and-now of allocution from that calculating, perhaps opportunistic, law-breaking "me" of the narrated there-and-then. Hence, it is not so much the literal *apology* that is to the point, as the establishment of an "I" in the state of here-and-now "being sorry," in the instance reflexively predicated by 29 of the 52 defendants in Gruber's set of allocutions. (Others did use the *I apologize* formula, or a synonym of *be- sorry* that predicates an equivalent inner moral intension, perhaps in a slightly more ceremonial register, such as *be- repentant, regret-*, etc.)

But there is generally much more than the recitation of the formula for apologizing in these defendant's allocutions, all of which must be read—imaginatively listened to—in terms of performed discontinuity of character. There is a distancing of the current self from "what I have done," generally denoted with this or another notably semantically bleached phrase. At first, one might wonder if such semantic bleaching is most prevalent after a full trial, rather than after a guilty plea, so as strategically to admit nothing in case of appeal (perhaps on the instruction of defense counsel); yet this does not seem to be the case. I think this notable feature of allocutions is better understood in terms of the discontinuity of selfhood. The ritual requirements are for a self-"cleansing" from the "pollution" of crime, and, like so many denoting terms and expressions for socially unacceptable areas of experience—think of sexuality in its aggressively vulgar aspects, for starters—the specifics of the crime for which the speaker is guilty are, as we say with a ready metapragmatic term, "unspeakable." Not only does the merest allusion to the wrongdoing, verbally avoiding it, metaphorically put the guilty party, the speaking "I," on the side of proper society now, it indexes a current intentional orientation toward propriety in so (not) doing, a hesitancy to go back to the prior state of lawlessness for which a punishment is about to be exacted. In several of the allocutions, in fact, the current "I" is narratively restored to a *status quo ante* the commission of the crime (that previous self portrayed as clearly a state of exception now unfathomable to the speaking "I").

Observe, for example, Gruber's second numbered transcript on p. 37, by defendant Y1, reproduced after Table 4.1 explaining transcription conventions below:

TABLE 4.1
Meaning of transcription symbols (largely following Du Bois 2006)

Transcription Symbol	Meaning
:::	indicates sound prolongation
#	Unintelligible; one per syllable
#word	transcribed word is uncertain
(1.2)	intra-sentence pause duration in seconds and tenths of seconds
..	intra-sentence pause lasting less than one second
<	beginning of wavery/unsteady voice
>	end of wavery/unsteady voice
> <	encloses speech produced at a faster delivery
<<	beginning of crying-while-talking
>>	end of crying-while-talking
Word	boldface indicates emphasis via loudness or contrastive pitch

2. Y1: 1 (1.5) (COUGH) <I'm sorry that> .. I have any part in
the situation,

2 and I regret <u>it</u> to the fullest extent.

3 From the bottom of my heart, .. I'm sorry.

4 That would be it. [end of allocution]

Note that Y1, a 28-year-old white male charged with selling a controlled substance, twice uses the *I'm sorry* self-descriptor and once, in between the two, the *I regret* one. In the first line, he tells what he is sorry for; after a noticeable pause, . . . *that [he had] any part in the situation*, that is, "the situation" of selling drugs (and perhaps being caught doing so). One should note here the phrase *any part*: as contrasted with just *a part*, which would certainly do grammatically, Y1 uses a negative polarity endpoint measure, indexing affective involvement from the point of view of someone for whom no "part in the situation" would be the presumed one. Again, in the next line, Y1 states that he *regret[s] it*, viz., *[his] part in the situation, to the fullest extent*, i.e., completely and utterly. And he lays on a phrase of ingenuousness and sincerity, from the *bottom of my heart* before pausing and repeating *I'm sorry*, then announcing metapragmatically in line 4 that he has concluded: *That would be it*. Each of the lines 1 through 3 must be read in the parallelistic sequence in which they build to a crescendo of performed self-distancing as the speaking "I" from the earlier "me" of "the situation." Now Y1 can speak *from the bottom of [his] heart*.

But actual apologies—note line 5 below, in response to the judge's suggestion—do, as well, occur in the course of supplication. Consider the example of defendant Z21, a 29-year-old African-American woman convicted of

conspiracy to distribute a controlled substance. Her allocution, reproduced as
Gruber's no. 10 on p. 39, starts with a vernacular metapragmatic expression, *I
just wanna say that* ... , and continues, with the judge's assistance, in a double
mode, all the while crying (<<...>>), as shown:

10.   Z21:   1   (SNIFF) (SOB) ## (6.1) (SNIFF) <<I just wanna say
              that I apologize to

         2   the USA for my #waywardness, (1.0)

         3   and I would like to apologize to my family and friends,
              (SNIFF)

         4   <Judge Z:> There, there, why don't you turn around
              and apologize to them ...

         5   ((defendant turns to family)) (1.0) I'm sorry.

              ...

         8   (SNIFF) and I'm sorry.>> [end of allocution]

Ms. Z21 embeds within the initial metapragmatic frame (*I just wanna say*) an
apology *to the USA*—the entity, after all, in the court of which she now stands
convicted of a crime—*for [her] waywardness*. Observe the retrospective ethical-
moral stance of the individual "I" so designating her earlier "me" avatar,[3] a
"wayward" person in the collective estimation of the United States of America.
After a pause, she uses the vernacular formal construction, the conditional
would like to [speech act verb] [= *will-* + PAST *like-* [*to* infinitive phrase]] to issue
a parallel apology *to [her] family and friends*. Judge Z apparently takes this
literally as an expression of perhaps frustrated desire (noting the defendent's
sniffing, perhaps) literally to apologize to them, who are sitting in the courtroom behind the defendant. So the judge suggests to/instructs the defendant
that she *turn around and apologize to them*, whereupon, turning to them so that
now as her addressees they fulfill the conditions for an actual Recipient of an
apology, Ms. Z21 uses the unmarked formula for one, *I'm sorry*. And, turning
back to the judge, now back in supplicational mode, she adds a coordinated
and identical formula, *And I'm sorry*, completing her allocution.

   In Matoesian's transcribed excerpts from narratives bolstering the prosecutor's request to invoke the Williams Rule at trial, the one character continuous
across each recounted incident is, of course, the defendant, Dr. Smith. But as
Matoesian describes the physical set-up of the courtroom at this point in pre-
trial, and as can be seen in the still clips from the video recording, the several
would-be complainants to charges of criminal sexual assault, according to the
prosecuting attorney's narrative, in addition to the actual one, Ms. Bowman,
are in a sense also present in the court synecdochically through the inscriptions

of their names on a list up on the easel facing the judge.[4] Thus is it that the prosecutor gestures again and again with an open-palmed "Behold!" motion toward that easel as she begins each of the sad tales in which Dr. Smith is the villain taking advantage of an unsuspecting and ingenuous young woman.

In the prosecutorial theory of the current case, there is not only continuity of the character, Dr. Smith, serially manifesting the same crime as the one for which he is, at last, on trial. In addition, each of the named victims, made vividly present in the courtroom, is an avatar of the same victimized status in respect of Dr. Smith's hatched plan of gaining the victim's trust the better, once in private, suddenly to pounce and rape and then, in postcoital recovery from the seeming seizure of lustful criminality, to resume a mild-mannered and respectable sociality. It is that continuity of victimhood that the prosecutor makes speak to the court, as noted above. Each account brings the interchangeable victim by name and gesturally to the fore, and lays out the details of the respective incident in phraseology that, through parallelism across incidents, demonstrates the sameness of plotline, only the villain remaining actually the same.

In the first segment, about Dr. Smith's "change in personality," the prosecuting attorney literally quotes from the four women's earlier depositions, emphasizing the suddenness of his transformation once in the privacy of the surroundings, both into and back from the animalistic aggressor that is the constant across all four incidents. Each of the quotations is repeated from the victims as they recalled, while being deposed, their earlier terrifying encounter with the defendant. So it is their actual verbalized memories of the events at the time of deposition, complete with vivid current descriptions of the earlier alleged doings of Dr. Smith, that constitute the doubled temporality with which is presented what is captured in the transcripts. That these memories were so vivid at the time of deposition, as well as so similarly articulated in terms of phrasal synonyms that can be quoted, licenses the prosecuting attorney to repeat them one after another as though all four women were already present in the courtroom as witnesses/complainants.

The second segment, alleging that "[t]he defendant enti:::ced the victims into his territory with false pretenses," is directly addressed to the judge by title. In each one of the four narratives, Dr. Smith is verbally rendered the agentive, volitional subject of a verb of goal-directed communication, a metapragmatic descriptor that makes him the initiating character in a necessarily two-party interaction.[5] Thus: *He offered Lisa a place to stay*, the *offer* a first interactional move to which Lisa could respond either to *accept* or *decline. He told Lynn there was a party . . . he invited her . . .* , the *invitation* a first interactional move to which Lynn could as well respond to *accept* or *decline* the invitation. *[H]e told [Michelle] "I'll give you a place to stay for the night". . . .* , another spontaneous *offer* of safety justified by the victim's having drunk too much. And, in the presenting instance that brought Dr. Smith to court, *he told [Patricia that] he needed a ride home and . . . he invited her in . . .* , a dependent sequence of first moves. The first is an indirect *request* for transport, with which Ms. Bowman could *comply* or, if *declining*, for which she would be obligated to *offer an excuse*; the second, again an *invitation*, which she could *accept* or *decline*.

These paired first and second interactional moves constitute what have been termed *cooperative illocutionary acts*, tightly correlated and in each case strongly asymmetric in expectations: to *decline* an invitation, to *deny* a request for assistance, in each instance requires much interactional work in the way of excuse-making in American social norms. The prosecuting attorney unfortunately emphasizes the "false pretenses" of each of Dr. Smith's narrated first moves, rather than the compelling and socially constraining aggressiveness of the demand for "cooperation" in his alleged intentional plan, which is much more to the point.

The third prosecutorial segment offers a series of parallel narrative elements claiming that Dr. Smith *fostered trust in his victims*, again ascribing a kind of volitional agentivity to the protagonist. Yet, in each one of the narratives, the prosecutor describes some social circumstance involving Dr. Smith and the victim, and then animates for each victim a plausible inference about her affective orientation of "trust" of the alleged rapist. Perhaps it is, indeed, because of the difficulty of establishing volitionally agentive *foster[ing of] trust in his victims* through bland verbal utterance that, as Matoesian describes this segment, the prosecuting attorney seems to move into multi-channel channeling of each of the victim's affect and thought, bringing the characters at the time of the alleged assaults right into the courtroom before the judge. Indirect free style, as described above, adds vividness to the ventriloquated voices of the women, using phraseology that "re-presents"—rather than just represents—their thoughts as characters in the narratives, similar thoughts animated in parallel phraseology so as to actualize the uniformity of reaction of the four women to Dr. Smith's seemingly benign and well-intentioned self-presentation.[6]

4.4 The Transposition of Cultural Values into Courtrooms

4A.4 Silverstein concludes by examining how ritual spaces and times (like a trial in a courtroom) are always working with everyday semiotic materials (that is, the stuff of which everyday signaling is made—the way that we convey meaning in ordinary circumstances). At the same time, those everyday materials are also transformed during rituals, so that they mean somewhat different things now in this special setting (although perhaps not as completely different as is conventionally thought). The "specialness" of communication within ritual settings is created in large part by a sense that ritual communication is bounded off, in a sort of envelope, from the everyday. This envelope's form and capacity depend on particular arrangements of many kinds of signals, verbal and nonverbal, which are distributed in relationship to one another along lines that differ from everyday practices (hence establishing themselves as ritually distinct through a kind of poetic structuring of segments of communication). Thus, for example, particular arm motions and spoken words (perhaps while raising a particular cup of wine), when undertaken in relation to each other in a church at a time specified for Easter Mass, take on special significance. Silverstein proceeds to show how the special ritual protections surrounding trials do not prevent the "everyday" value of privileged members of US society (whether bourgeois or male) from leaking into crucial legal decision-making processes. Attention to meta-level linguistic structures and ideologies reveals this leakage, but it is clear that the legal system is not structured to take account of this metalinguistic level. These leads to some pessimism as to whether law is capable of adequate translation of alternative frameworks for understanding the evidence presented in courts.

As noted at the outset, all ritual develops its semiotic material, the signs that are the media of its consequentiality, in relation to the semiosis[7] of the everyday, in the process of transposition into the ritual space-time frequently transforming that everyday material in multiple kinds of "trans-" relationships. What looks like ordinary biscuit and wine outside the Christian ritual of the Eucharist becomes, when properly brought into the ritual space-time by a duly empowered officiant, "transubstantiated" in essence—cf. alchemy—into Christ's body and blood (or at least, in Protestant traditions, sacralized emblems—conventional indexical icons—of them, the Host).[8] The power of what goes on in ritual space-time depends on fashioning this as an autonomous semiotic realm, necessitating the "trans-"ness of re-definition, as we might term it, derived from establishing boundaries across which whatever comes from outside this space-time is re-purposed within it. Generally, as well, ritual space-time attempts to be self-bounding, in the sense that its form and thus its capaciousness as an envelope of semiosis is established by mutual distribution of its elements (of whatever kind), actualized in event-segments, a poetics of "doing things" not only with words but with bodily actions, manipulations of things, placement of selves mutually and in space-time frameworks, and so forth. Whatever stipulative and con-sequential authority ritual (if we may say) "seeks to have" depends on an aura of autonomous authority, emergent in-and-at the ritual space-time as it is aligned with the extra-ordinary and non-everyday. (Note, for example, how the Eucharistic service announces at the outset, by quoting the Gospel, its (*iconic*) identicalness to and (*indexical*) continuity with what transpired at the Last Supper.)

Adversarial legal trial, organized around event-segments of using what is, after all, denotational language in a hyper-proceduralized ritual of determining "truth and its consequences," thus has a decided "trans-"problem in relation to space-time autonomy, as these papers demonstrate, each in its particular way.

In Gruber's material excerpted from defendant allocutions, we see various kinds of cultural and linguistic defaults at work, on the part of both defendants and judges. In American society, who cannot recall a childhood scene (or many of them) where one has said or done something offensive to someone else, and either that offended other or, more likely in childhood, an intervening parental figure, then demands an *apology* to make things right—or at least as right as they can immediately be in consequence? In fact, while the illocutionary act is an *apology*, the stage directions, the metapragmatic imperative issued by such a parental figure, especially as addressed in simplest vernacular to a young child, involves "Say[ing] you're sorry!" "Sorry!" the unrepentant offender blurts out. To which, of course, the parental figure responds with an evaluation of the insufficiency of intension/affect and a corrective in the form of trying to coax out a more elaborate profession of remorse: "You don't *sound* like you're sorry! Say what you're sorry for, and really mean it this time!" "Oh, all right! I'm sorry that you got hurt." "No! That's not what you're sorry for! Say what you're sorry for doing to [X]!" Note that the parental figure immediately sees that the offender has not directly responded to the request that he/she express being *sorry for* him-/herself having done something offensive and apology-worthy, and has expressed, rather, regret that the consequences of the dastardly act have come to pass. The back-and-forth continues until, with an uttered formula, the offender gives off demeanor indexes of both inner intensional affect—"sounding sorry"—and new moral-ethical stance as someone sorry for the offending act of the earlier "me" are manifest: "I'm (really) sorry for tripping you and making you fall," or "I'm (really) sorry that I tripped you and made you fall." The point is that there is a primordial little everyday ritual of interpersonal *apology* so deeply ingrained in members socialized to this culture as to have its folk vernacular formulaic expression a universal experience even of childhood. To apologize truly and sincerely is to utter such a full formula. (Note that the *OED* glosses[9] the phrase *to say sorry* "to apologize (with or without implication that the word sorry is actually spoken).")

Yet, it is also clear to linguistic analysis that any such formula built around the simplex word *sorry* has an internal syntactic organization, such that variant construction types employing the term have their own semantic (denotational) and pragmatic (indexical/contextual) valences. Consider the difference between the lexical form *sorry-* used as an attributive adjective along with a nominal and the predicating use of (*be-*) *sorry-* such as in one of the accepted first-person formulae for *apology* or some other illocutionary act. When we encounter and designate something or someone "a sorry specimen," say, "of humanity," or experience "a sorry state of things (affairs)," note the intensionality and stance of uttering one of these phrases. It is one of regretfully negative evaluation of—having been caused intensional *sorrow* by—whatever is, as opposed to what might be in the way of specimen or situation. Such an expression is even frequently used in an act of commiseration with someone else who, having encountered or experienced the "sorry" thing or state, reports it to us. We can see the transition, perhaps, to predicating of oneself that "I'm a sorry specimen (of . . .)," where the currently uttering speaker has, regretfully, a negative evaluation of his or her own self, along whatever evaluative dimensions.

Shifting now to the use of the predicate *be- sorry*, a predicate of wide use as a *verbum sentiendi* describing intensionality, note that there are three kinds of complement constructions in which it occurs, each with its own range of denotational and interactional effect. One can *be- sorry that* [+*a clause describing some circumstance*], as in "He was sorry that it was raining, which meant the picnic would be canceled." When used in the present with first-person subject, note that it is a rather neutral speech act expressing the speaker's regretfully negative evaluation of some state of affairs; only if the complement clause explicitly describes the *delict* in the first person might this count as an apology. In our fantasized childhood memory above, note, when the miscreant child says he/she is "sorry that you got hurt," the complement clause assiduously avoids involving the speaker in the outcome, and hence the parental figure finds it insufficient as an *apology. Be- sorry about/at/for* [+*a participle or nominalization of action describing some circumstance (or a noun adjunct negatively impacted by such circumstance)*], as in, "We were all sorry for his suffering (or ... his bad luck)," or, presuming upon such (non-denoted) suffering or bad luck, "We were all sorry for him." When this is used in first person, with a participle or nominalization describing the speaker's offense, it definitely counts as an *apology* for whatever is so described, as in "I am sorry for stealing [or: having stolen] your cookies" [note that with the same subject in the complement clause, no possessor is required; contrast "I am sorry for John's stealing/having stolen your cookies"]. (And note that "I'm sorry for me" is just too ambiguous to be of much use as an act of *apology*.) Finally, *be- sorry* to [+*infinitive clause*], as in "He will be sorry to have left Memphis after such a short stay." Here, the infinitive clause generally describes an event subsequent to the state of being sorry, or at least no earlier than it. Hence, in the first person it is a formulaic mode of prior *excuse* for some undertaking on the part of the speaker that may negatively impact the addressee's person or interests.

Hence, to say *I'm sorry for* ... completing it with a description of one's own earlier action, is the fullest and most explicit use of this formula for *apology*; it unambiguously puts the actions of the earlier "me" under the scope of the regretfully negative evaluation of the speaking "I." And this is what Gruber's Judge X, acting in a sense *in loco parentis* in relation to the inevitably infantilized defendant Mr. X20 before her, is seeking, a "full" *I'm sorry* apology in the way of a supplication, as someone now sorrowful/full of sorrow for what he has done, for mercy in sentencing:

[P]eople come into the court and say "Ah, now I'm really sorry" and it's often hard to distinguish between "I'm really sorry I ever did this and I understand the harm it caused" and the "I'm really sorry I did this and got caught—and have to come to court and take the consequences of my actions." I hope that your remorse is the former kind, that you understand just how much harm you have caused....

To the judge's native speaker focus on words and on formulas, "saying the magic words" is seemingly the only thing that counts as the sought-after ritual act; the rest of the discursive context, no matter how revelatory of precisely the stance sought by the court, can be ignored—to the detriment of those sentenced, to be sure.

Matoesian's prosecutorial discourse, too, shows the bind in which ritual participants in trials operate as they trans-port scenes from people's sayings and doings into adversarial argument, sometimes descriptively characterizing the scene, as we have seen, and sometimes attempting to re-animate it by various tropes of inhabitance by which they align with characters now absent or present in the courtroom. The prosecutor's focus in the hearing on her pre-trial motion for admissibility of evidence is, of course, both the individual relationships between the defendant, Dr. Smith, and each of four young women, and what might be concluded to have been a general characteristic of his intentionality across all four narrated encounters—what the prosecution's theory of the case takes to be a criminal intent to sexual assault.

It is interesting, then, that in the sequence of excerpts Matoesian analyzes, the prosecuting attorney shifts the very modes of description of the particular aspects of the uniform narrative. In the first segment, she quotes from each of the victim's depositions, bringing to the fore their recall at the time of being deposed of Dr. Smith's manner on the earlier occasion of the encounter. In the second segment, she describes the speech acts of Dr. Smith on those occasions of encounter as indirect discourse, moving through the exact wording of the depositions as through a transparent lens, and even purporting to quote Dr. Smith's words to Michelle in one of the encounters. In the third segment, she moves directly into the reactive intensional states of each of the victims, as though at a point when they are about to agree to Dr. Smith's proffered assistance or act of friendly goodwill toward them. Moving back in the temporal series from current courtroom context to the time of deposition of these would-be witnesses/complainants to the assaults they claim to have experienced, moving inward to the psychological state, the intensionality of each, there is a culminating vividness in the modalities through which the prosecutor makes her claim for the kind of consistency that triggers the Williams Rule.

And yet. And yet, as Matoesian points out: in summing up the prosecuting attorney seems to overplay her hand. Anxious to create the image of four serially "perfect" victims of the unprovoked sexual assailant who tricked and trapped them, she asserts *Judge there was absolutely no sexual innuendos exchanged between any of these victims and the defendant at any ti::me…. absolutely no sexual innuendo beforehand.* Here the prosecuting attorney seems to have indexed one of the key things one would want to know about such claims of victimhood of sexual assault under American bourgeois cultural norms about sexual mores. It is such cultural norms that have suddenly clouded the picture, what Matoesian has termed "the patriarchal logic of sexual rationality ... an interpret[at]ive template for assessing the victim and [the] offender's actions during the rape event, a representational logic of power based on male standards of sexual preference...." Matoesian suggests that each of the pieces of prosecutorial evidence in these stories can be aligned in a very different way under this intrusive cultural ideology: how could all these young unmarried women, some drunk, but all partying in a heterosexual environment, not be interested in being objects of male desire? Why do so many of the stories take place in and around bedrooms, ideologically default places of sexuality? Why do all of these stories of victimhood take place in the wee hours of, again, ideologically default erotic hanky-panky? Trying to suppress whatever actual narrative evidence there may have been—and in the case of the trial to hand, there was much, as Matoesian's other accounts reveal—that these incidents occurred as a monstrously, even criminally transfigured version of the normal heterosexual engagement of the "dating" scene of young but sexually active unmarrieds, the prosecutor seems, to Matoesian, to have tripped the wire of an undercurrent of relevant cultural ideologies that, flooding into the courtroom, argue against the prosecutorial theory of the case.

In many ways, we are confronted with a perhaps inherent dilemma. On the one hand, ritual efficacy depends on the institutional grounding of its procedures as autonomous: language, etc., strictly distinct from the everyday and the "poetics" of its unfolding in and over ritual space-time the basis of its power to effectuate consequences in the everyday world. On the other hand, all rituals "leak" inasmuch as they are constituted of language, etc., that draws on and indeed enacts the everyday as a condition of its selective re-presentation of it. Rituals of "fact" and "truth," such as adversarial courtroom trials in which representation of the everyday is central to establishing a "true" version of it, present a particularly acute dilemma in this respect.

Notes

1. In this kind of linguistic analysis, the *poetics* evident in all kinds of essentially metricalized speech consist of rhythmic, repetitive, and/or even rhyming patterns that contribute to a sense of cohesion in a message—or that can, through an unconscious sense of "fit" created by that patterning, actually make what is being spoken seem "natural" or correct.

2. In other words, *performative* language accomplishes (or appears to accomplish) what it describes just in and by the speaking itself. Classic examples include *I promise*, or *I bequeath*. In a larger sense, legal language is often performative in that it accomplishes many social goals in and by the performance of the speech itself. This can be said to be constantly occurring at a grander scale, as legal proceedings of all sorts perform "justice" through a ritually (in this case procedurally) structured linguistic event (a trial, a hearing—and see Burns, this volume, for more on this idea). But it is also occurring at smaller and quite technical levels, as in the fitting of token events within precedent-based types (Matoesian), or

the attempt to successfully perform an apology that fits within the court's unstated framework for "genuine" allocutions.

3. By *avatar*, I allude to Hindu usage denoting one of the many personified forms a god could take, so here indicating an embodied, contextual instance or token of a general social characterological or type or persona.

4. *Synecdoche* refers to the representation of the whole by a part, or vice versa. Here the victims' names stand for the whole person, brought into court and physically represented through the written names on the page resting on the easel.

5. In other words, Smith is represented as willingly taking action as the subject of verbs like *offer* and *invite*, which indicate him as the speaker as having goals specifically aimed at initiating further contact with the victims. As Silverstein points out, these verbs are *metapragmatic*: they are language about language (*meta*) and they are directed at the social contextual aspect of language (*pragmatic*). (This contrasts, for example, with *metasemantic* language, which is aimed at the denotational or semantic content of language— as, for example, with dictionary definitions that describe words in terms of their semantic meanings apart from any particular socially specific usage.)

6. Recall that in indirect free style, the speaker shifts between third-person, descriptive language (*Lisa trusted [the defendant]*) to in essence speaking for the person being described, standing within their thoughts: *No reason not to trust him.*

7. As noted in the text, *semiotics* is the study of signaling behavior in general (as opposed to linguistics, aimed more specifically at studying language). It follows, then, that *semiosis* is the process of signaling in general—including everything from human language to a street sign or a monkey pointing at something.

8. In the terminology of semiotics, these are conventional *indexical icons*—i.e., they are signs that mirror and point to the phenomenon they are signaling (and they are habitually defined within a particular set of cultural conventions, ergo "conventional").

9. *Oxford English Dictionary*. Online at http://www.oed.com/view/Entry/184948?redire ctedFrom=to+say+sorry#eid238563282. Accessed February 15, 2016.

PART TWO

System-Level Challenges

WHEN COURTS TRANSLATE SOCIAL SCIENCE

5

The Law and Science of Video Game Violence

WHO LOST MORE IN TRANSLATION?

William K. Ford

5.1 Introduction

Are legislatures or courts better at understanding evidence based on social science research? Most legislators and judges lack social science training. The few who have relevant background or training will usually lack the time needed to understand a particular area of the social sciences to the same extent as the people who produce the knowledge in that field. Research in the social sciences is typically communicated through publications and conference presentations intended for other specialists, not for policymakers. Authors assume that readers of specialist publications already possess substantial background knowledge and are familiar with the concepts and jargon of the field (Weiss 1978, 51). For the nonspecialists who make legislative and judicial decisions to use social science evidence effectively, it must be translated.[1]

Legislators and judges operate in different institutional environments, and it seems unlikely that legislatures and courts are equally adept at generating good translations of social science research. A "good" translation is not necessarily comprehensive, one that might turn policymakers into experts, but one that is sufficient to support sensible decisions about public policy. Any more than this would probably be a poor use of limited legislative and judicial resources and would further contribute to the "information overload" of decision makers (Hird 2005, 154). Even if courts turn out to be better at generating good translations, we might ordinarily prefer legislatures to make broad policy decisions out of a commitment to democratic principles. When policies implicate constitutional rights, however, we might plausibly choose to be less deferential to the judgment of elected officials, unless we are *especially* confident in the ability of legislatures to understand the relevant evidence.

Together with an earlier article on the judiciary (Ford 2013), this chapter addresses the narrow question of whether legislatures or courts are better at translating social science evidence into something potentially useful for decision-making. As with that earlier article, this chapter is a case study in social science translation in the policymaking sphere, one that considers the long-running legislative efforts to respond to video game violence and the federal courts' repeated resistance to these efforts, resistance that culminated in the US Supreme Court's decision in *Brown v. Entertainment Merchants Association* (2011).

In *Brown*, the Supreme Court held that California's attempt to restrict minors' access to certain violent video games was unconstitutional. The California state legislature's judgment was ostensibly based on extensive social science evidence about the negative effects of video game violence on minors, but the Court considered the evidence insufficient to justify the state's restriction on minors' First Amendment rights. In a dissent, Justice Breyer said that the Court should have deferred to the state legislature's judgment. He noted the existence of many studies supporting the legislature's decision to restrict minors' access to violent video games, but he also noted the disagreement among experts in the scientific literature. He acknowledged his own lack of social science expertise and the lack of expertise among judges generally. Given the conflicting technical evidence, Breyer said the Court owed the elected legislature "some degree of deference" with regard to the legislative facts at issue in the case (*Brown v. Entertainment Merchants Association* 2011, 2768–2770). Breyer's position in *Brown* was consistent with his general belief that legislatures are "better equipped" to find facts and make judgments based on these facts (Breyer 2010, 168). Unlike Breyer, Justice Alito concurred in the outcome in *Brown*, but he revealed some sympathy for Breyer's position. Alito cautioned that the Court "should not hastily dismiss the judgment of legislators, who *may* be in a better position than we are to assess the implications of new technology" (*Brown v. Entertainment Merchants Association* 2011, 2742 (emphasis added)). As the justices might have predicted, an analysis of the performance of the courts in the video game violence cases shows that the courts struggled to translate the social science evidence (Ford 2013). Justice Alito thought that the legislatures *might* have done better than the courts. Justice Breyer assumed that the legislatures *did* do better. So did the legislatures do better than the courts?

While the courts struggled with the translation process, my conclusion in this chapter is that the courts, on the whole, still did a better job than the state legislatures of translating the social science evidence about the relationship between video game violence and real-world aggression. If Justice Breyer and others assume that legislative decisions that jeopardize constitutional rights deserve deference because of the superior translation skills of legislatures relative to courts, then this chapter serves as a cautionary example: legislative skill with the social sciences cannot be assumed. Indeed, this study suggests a significant lack of skill. Whether legislatures ever effectively translate this type of evidence is a question this chapter cannot answer. I would expect that sometimes legislatures do better than they did in the present study. Here, however, the legislatures did poorly, and they demonstrated little aptitude for doing well.

5.2 Legislatures versus Courts: Theory

The present study focuses on the use by legislatures and courts of what legal scholars refer to as "legislative facts." Legislative facts are facts with relevance beyond a particular case, the ones relevant to setting policy. Legislative facts stand in contrast to adjudicative facts, which refer to the details of a particular case, i.e., "who did what, where, when, how, and with what motive or intent" (Davis 1955, 952). The lines between the two categories of facts can be hazy (McGinnis and Mulaney 2008, 75), but a fairly clear example in the legislative fact category is the topic of this chapter: the social science evidence about the effects of video game violence on players in general. Both legislators and judges get their knowledge about these facts through, as Justice Cardozo said, "experience and study and reflection" (Cardozo 1921, 113), but legislatures and courts have their own institutional procedures, norms, and incentives that may work for or against translating social science evidence.

"A courtroom," as Justice Breyer noted, "is not a scientific laboratory" (Breyer 1998, 25), but neither is a legislature. The methods of the social sciences are likely to be somewhat foreign to both legislators and judges. Judge Richard Posner's reference to "a widespread, and increasingly troublesome, discomfort among lawyers and judges confronted by a scientific or other technological issue" should apply to legislators too (*Jackson v. Pollion* 2013, 787). Even if particular legislators or judges possess some background or experience in the social sciences, the literature in specific fields of study is still likely to be unfamiliar. Generally speaking, legislatures and courts both need assistance with identifying and understanding—that is, translating—the social science evidence relevant to particular policies or disputes. Scholars and others disagree about whether legislatures or courts are better at finding legislative facts, but as discussed below, the dominant view is probably that legislatures are better than courts at translating social science evidence (Faigman 2004, 364; Hill 2007, 333; McGinnis and Mulaney 2008, 94; Rebell and Block 1982, 11–14). So far, whether legislatures really have the advantage commonly attributed to them is a question answered more on the basis of theories and hypotheses rather than systematic evidence.

The basic advantage of legislatures is supposed to be their "more flexible mechanisms for factfinding" (*Washington v. Glucksberg* 1997, 788). In terms of specific mechanisms for finding facts, legislatures can hold hearings with expert witnesses and often have the ability to call upon legislative research services for assistance (Faigman 2008, 132–133; Hird 2005, 86–88). Legislatures can draw upon the expertise of their members by matching them to bills and committees based on their individual interests and backgrounds (O. Kerr 2005, 784). Because legislatures are not required to resolve a dispute between particular parties, they can also better reframe or adapt the questions of interest as they acquire more information (Faigman 2008, 132–133; O. Kerr 2005, 784).

While in theory legislatures may have some structural advantages over courts, the question remains as to whether legislatures have the necessary incentives to make use of these advantages (McGinnis and Mulaney 2008, 94; Meazell 2009, 259). Professor Douglas Laycock doubts that legislators regularly have these incentives:

> Legislators *can* do serious investigations, but they rarely do. The typical Congressional hearing consists of witnesses reading prepared five-minute statements in panels of three or four. Many committee members do not attend and those who do often wander in and out. Each member gets to make an opening statement and to ask five minutes of questions to each panel, that is, one to two minutes of questions and answers per witness. Most members read questions prepared by staff, and hardly any member is prepared to ask probing follow-up questions. (Laycock 2007, 1174–1175 (emphasis in original))

Consistent with Laycock's view, a leading scholar on the use of policy-related research in congressional decision-making concluded that the value of research is primarily to support the preexisting positions of legislators. One committee staffer said, "Information is used to make a case rather than to help people make up their minds" (Weiss 1989, 425).

To be sure, the judicial process also presents some challenges to producing good social science translations. At the trial level, expert witnesses are essentially paid to take a particular position, which undoubtedly biases (or corrupts) at least some expert witnesses. Trial courts are not limited to the experts selected by the parties (Fed. R. Evid. R. 706; *Reilly v. United States* 1988, 154–156), but in practice, trial courts usually rely on the parties' experts (Deason 1998, 78–79; Ginsburg 2010, 309). At the appellate level, the judges do not interact with experts at all and must depend on lawyers to translate the social science for them. At both the trial and appellate levels, each side emphasizes the arguments and evidence best suited for winning its case, which may not be the best ones for accurately understanding the social science. Attorneys are not likely to highlight the weaknesses in their arguments. Social scientists, unlike lawyers, are expected to do so (Scheppele 2003, 364–365), but even social scientists are not likely to call attention to the weaknesses in their arguments when they are involved in litigation. When serving as expert witnesses, social scientists' paychecks often depend on their unwavering certainty about the correctness of their conclusions.

Despite these potential limitations in the courts, the judicial process may still have some significant advantages over the legislative process. The adversarial structure of litigation creates a professional responsibility for someone to challenge the other side's evidence. No legislator is similarly responsible for challenging the other side's evidence. Courts may also have a particularly strong advantage when a trial occurs. A trial represents "an intense encounter with the evidence" (Burns 1999, 34; Burns 2009, 9), something that does not necessarily occur in state legislatures or even in appellate courts. For this reason, we might expect the trial process to produce a better translation of scientific evidence than the legislative process. The problem with trials, however, is that they are very rare (Galanter 2004).

While the present case study, which involves a single topic of legislation in a limited number of states, cannot resolve disagreements about the relative abilities of legislatures and courts to translate social science evidence, it can contribute to a resolution. This case study may not be representative or typical of the use of social science in the legislatures and courts, but what makes this case study particularly interesting is that it involves the efforts of multiple legislatures and courts in a situation where the various actors knew that they needed to make an assessment of the social science evidence. Most legislators probably voted in favor of the restrictions on violent video games for reasons only weakly related to the social science evidence, if at all. Some expressed simple offense at the idea of children seeing certain content, but others had a "gut feeling" that violent video games are harmful.[2] Some wanted to "send a message" either to parents about the content of games or to the industry about the need to enforce age restrictions.[3] Some wanted to avoid criticism in the next election. Nevertheless, legislators knew that the violent video game legislation would be challenged in court, and they assumed (correctly) that courts would be interested in the social science evidence. Similarly, lower court judges assumed (again correctly) that higher court judges would be interested in the social science.

5.3 Background on Video Game Violence

Games are a medium of expression. While some games, such as poker or *Pong* (Atari Inc. 1972), have little or nothing to say, games have the capacity to communicate information and ideas, including controversial ones. Until the 1970s, game-related controversies in the United States appear to have been tied mostly to concerns about gambling rather than content (Daniels 2005, 178; *Homiletic Review* 1903, 474–476; Mather 1693, 10–11; Mather 1820, 262; *Presbyterian Banner* 1903, 5–6). Pinball, for example, triggered gambling-related controversies after its debut in the 1930s, and some jurisdictions banned pinball (*Cossack v. Los Angeles* 1974; Githens 1942; Lester 2002, 305–310; Lubell 1939, 38;

Sharpe 1977, 63; *Thamart v. Moline* 1945; Weinstein 1957, 6; *WNEK Vending & Amusements Co. v. Buffalo* 1980, 616–617). Early board games sold in the United States often contained educational or moral themes, but most of these themes were probably uncontroversial when originally published, even though some would be more controversial today (Morris-Friedman and Schädler 2003, 47). Some later nineteenth-century games did contain elements of social criticism, such as the stock market game *Bulls and Bears* (Hofer 2003, 81–82), but if *Bulls and Bears* or other older games stirred any significant controversies in the United States due to their subject matter or content, I am not aware of them.[4]

The gaming medium advanced substantially in the 1970s, creating more possibilities for communication and therefore more possibilities for controversy (Ford 2012, 2–3; Ford and Liebler 2012, 48–54, 56–58). Many new games appeared in the 1970s, including two new forms of commercial games: video games, starting with the release of *Computer Space* in 1971 (Nutting Associates 1971), and role-playing games, starting with the release of *Dungeons & Dragons* in 1974 (Gygax and Arneson 1974). After a *Dungeons & Dragons* player supposedly disappeared into the tunnels beneath Michigan State University in 1979 (Dear 1984), the game received substantial media attention and became one of the most controversial games of all time, partly because of its purported ties to the occult and partly because of its violent content (Chick 1984; Jones 1988, 95–105; Larson 1989, 48–54; Pulling and Cawthon 1989, 77–102; Robie 1991). Other non-electronic games occasionally generate modest controversies because of their content, such as the board game *Ghettopoly* (Chang 2002), which was criticized for its use of racial and ethnic stereotypes (Austin 2003; Fears 2003), or the historical wargame *King Philip's War* (Poniske 2010), which was criticized for trivializing or misstating the history of the seventeenth-century war of the same name (Ford and Liebler 2012, 68–69). It's the enormous popularity of video games, however, that fuels the controversies that most interest legislators.

The controversy over violent video games dates back to the mid-1970s, when Exidy released *Death Race* (Exidy 1976), a driving game where the goal is for one or two players to run down as many stick-figure "gremlins" as possible before the time runs out. Each success generates a shriek from the gremlin and a cross to mark its grave. The National Safety Council published an article describing *Death Race* as "a popular new electronic game that actually teaches a motorist how to kill a pedestrian" (National Safety Council 1976, 8). In the article, a behavioral scientist with the National Safety Council's Research Department criticized *Death Race* for its participatory violence (in contrast to the passive violence on TV) and for promoting a "'war and killing' mentality" and "disrespect for life" (National Safety Council 1976, 9). Other media picked up the story, including *Newsweek*, and some arcades refused to carry the game (*Newsweek* 1977; Roberts 1977; Schiff 1976; Young 1976).

In the early 1980s, at the height of the popularity of video game arcades (Donovan 2010, 81), the dominant concern about games was that they caused truancy and delinquency by attracting children to poorly supervised, unsavory environments at all hours of the day. Local jurisdictions responded to grass roots pressure by restricting access to arcades during school hours or by refusing to issue additional permits for new arcades (P. Kerr 1982). The violent content of video games remained a concern even in these early years of the industry, however. A leading organizer against arcades in the early 1980s, a local PTA president named Ronnie Lamm, worried about the potential effects of exposing children to violent games, though she sometimes acknowledged her uncertainty about what those effects might be (Fitzpatrick 1982; MacNeil/Lehrer 1982; Sito 2013, 112). Some critics in the early 1980s were more confident about the negative effects of video games. Rabbi Steven Fink said, "Video games are dangerous." Pointing to examples like *Space Invaders* (Midway Manufacturing 1978), *Asteroids* (Atari 1979), and *Pac-Man* (Midway Manufacturing 1980), Rabbi Fink said the lesson of these games is "kill or be killed" and that they "teach children to objectify people"; for video game players, "[p]eople become just another blip on the screen to be destroyed" (Fink 1982, 13-A).

In the early 1990s, the controversy over video game violence heated up, reaching a critical point at the end of 1993. On December 9, 1993, Senator Joseph Lieberman and Senator Herb Kohl presided over hearings in the US Senate about video game violence. The game probably most responsible for the hearings was Midway's *Mortal Kombat* (1992), a very popular fighting game that incorporated digital versions of real actors and brutal finishing moves for killing opponents (Donovan 2010, 226–299). The committee also focused on two Sega-CD games for the Sega Genesis home console: *Lethal Enforcers* (Konami 1993), a game about "cleaning up the streets in the baddest parts of Chicago" with a gun-shaped controller called "The Justifer," and *Night Trap* (Digital Pictures 1992), a game with full motion video about trying to protect young women at a slumber party from vampiric attackers (National Cable Satellite 1993).[5]

The primary message of Senators Lieberman and Kohl to the members of the video game industry was that they had better engage in some self-regulation or else the senators would pursue legislation to do it for them. Within a few months, the video game industry formed the Entertainment Software Rating Board (ESRB), an organization charged with rating the games submitted to it by publishers (Donovan 2010, 233–234). The ESRB ratings have changed somewhat over time, but the current ratings are "EC" (Early Childhood), "E" (Everyone), "E10+" (Everyone 10+), "T" (Teen), "M" (Mature, for ages 17 and up), and "AO" (Adults Only, for ages 18 and up).[6] In addition to the ratings, the ESRB also assigns content descriptors to the games to highlight potentially objectionable content. The current descriptors associated with violence include "Animated Blood," "Blood," "Blood and Gore," "Cartoon Violence," "Fantasy

Violence," "Intense Violence," "Sexual Violence," "Violence," and "Violent References." Other descriptors are related to alcohol or drug use, profanity, gambling, and sex (ESRB 2015). These ratings and content descriptors appear on the outside packaging of retail games. As one relevant example, the ESRB assigned *Grand Theft Auto: Vice City* (Rockstar 2003a) an M rating and the following content descriptors: "Blood and Gore," "Violence," "Strong Language," and "Strong Sexual Content."[7]

Self-regulation through the ESRB meant ratings, not content restrictions, but the major console manufacturers will not authorize AO-rated games for their consoles and many retailers will not sell AO-rated games (Snider 2007a). The consequence of console and retailer resistance to AO-rated games likely affects sexual content more than violent content. As with films rated by the Motion Picture Association of America (MPAA), violent content does not easily trigger the highest rating.[8] As a result, the formation of the ESRB did not end the controversy over violent video games.

During the legislative discussions about violent video games covered in this chapter, the games that received the most attention by politicians were *Grand Theft Auto III* (Rockstar 2001), *Postal 2* (RWS 2002), *Grand Theft Auto: Vice City* (Rockstar 2003a), and *Grand Theft Auto: San Andreas* (Rockstar 2004).[9] While these games stand out in the legislative proceedings, a relatively small number of other violent games were briefly viewed or referenced during the events included in this study, such as *Duke Nukem 3D* (GT Interactive 1996),[10] *Mortal Kombat 4* (Midway Games 1997),[11] *Clock Tower 3* (Capcom 2003), and *Manhunt* (Rockstar 2003b).[12] Legislators were concerned that minors could easily purchase these and other games in stores due to the lax enforcement of the ratings at retail.[13] Some legislators were also concerned about a connection between violent games and shootings in places like West Paducah, Kentucky (December 1, 1997); Jonesboro, Arkansas (March 24, 1998); and Columbine High School in Littleton, Colorado (April 20, 1999).[14]

In response to the violence and the inconsistent retail enforcement of the ratings, seven state legislatures enacted restriction on minors' access to some categories of violent video games. Table 5.1 lists the states and the bills they enacted. In at least some of these states, the efforts were led by a legislator who was especially interested in the issue, including Representative Mary Lou Dickerson in Washington, then-Assembly Member Leland Yee in California, and Senator Sandra Pappas in Minnesota.[15] Some city or county governments also enacted restrictions on minors' access to violent games, but activities at the local level are beyond the scope of this chapter.

The states defined the relevant class of violent games to be restricted in different ways, but with the possible exception of Washington, all of these laws directly or indirectly focused on games likely to include graphic violence. Washington defined the narrowest class of restricted games. It defined violent video games as ones with "realistic or photographic-like depictions of

TABLE 5.1
Enacted bills

State	Bill	Chamber	Date	Yeas	Nays
California	A.B. 1179	Senate	September 8, 2005	22	9
		Assembly	September 8, 2005	66	7
		Totals		88	16
Illinois	H.B. 4023	Senate	May 19, 2005	52	5
		House	May 28, 2005	106	6
		Totals		158	11
Louisiana	H.B. 1381	House	May 16, 2006	102	0
		Senate	June 6, 2006	35	0
		Totals		137	0
Michigan	S.B. 416	Senate	September 7, 2005	35	2
		House	September 8, 2005	101	5
		Totals		136	7
Minnesota	S.F. 785	Senate	May 20, 2006	56	6
		House	May 20, 2006	98	33
		Totals		154	39
Oklahoma	H.B. 3004	Senate	April 24, 2006	47	0
		House	May 24, 2006	98	0
		Totals		145	0
Washington	H.B. 1009	House	March 18, 2003	81	16
		Senate	April 17, 2003	42	7
		Totals		123	23

aggressive conflict in which the player kills, injures, or otherwise causes physical harm to a human form in the game who is depicted, by dress or other recognizable symbols, as a public law enforcement officer" (Washington H.B. 1009). This focus on law enforcement eliminated most games from the statute's coverage. Representative Dickerson, the primary sponsor of the bill, thought a narrow definition of the relevant games was more likely to satisfy the constitutional standard applied by the courts. She also thought that because retailers would have no practical way of knowing which games contained violence against police officers, retailers would be effectively forced into restricting minors' access to all M- and AO-rated games (Washington 2003a, 2003d). It's not obvious, however, why only M- and AO-rated games would be covered by the statute's language. The statute did not require the violence in a restricted game to be graphic (*Video Software Dealers Association v. Maleng* 2004, 1189–1190), which would make a game more likely to receive an M or AO rating. Representative Dickerson apparently assumed that games below an M rating would not contain "realistic or photographic-like depictions" of violence directed against police officers, but games below an M rating can include this type of content.[16]

Of the seven states, Minnesota defined the broadest class of restricted games. It avoided Representative Dickerson's circuitous approach to restricting access to M- and AO-rated games by explicitly defining the restricted games as ones rated M or AO by the ESRB (Minnesota S.F. 785). Although games can receive an M or AO rating for reasons other than graphic violence, games rated M or AO are more likely to contain graphic violence. The remaining five states defined a class of games somewhat narrower than Minnesota but much broader than Washington.

In effect, the definitions in Illinois, California, Louisiana, Michigan, and Oklahoma covered only a subset of M- and AO-rated games, ones with violence likely to offend members of the public. Illinois' definition of violence started broad but was narrowed by an affirmative defense. In part, Illinois' statute defined the relevant violent games as ones with "human-on-human violence in which the player kills ... another human" (Illinois H.B. 4023). As this definition was not limited to graphic violence, this definition should have covered many T-rated games and maybe even some rated below Teen, which would have made Illinois' statute the broadest by far. However, the statute included an affirmative defense for games rated EC, E, E10+, or T. Illinois in effect targeted only M- and AO-rated games, but unlike in Minnesota, Illinois' statute was restricted only to M- and AO-rated games with human-on-human violence.

As a practical matter, California, Louisiana, Michigan, and Oklahoma all defined violent video games in terms of graphic violence. Louisiana omitted a definition of violence, but drawing on Supreme Court precedent, its statute prohibited the sale or rental of a game to a minor if a trier of fact found it appeals to a minor's "morbid interest in violence" under "contemporary community standards"; contains violence that is "patently offensive to prevailing standards" of what content is "suitable for minors"; and "lacks serious literary, artistic, political, or scientific value for minors" (Louisiana H.B. 1381). While the remaining states further elaborated on the meaning of violence, California, Michigan, and Oklahoma each included enough of this same language to insure that only graphic violence would be covered by the statute (California A.B. 1179; Michigan S.B. 416; Oklahoma H.B. 3004).

The language in these statutes referenced violence that is offensive according to community standards, which is likely to be violence that is more graphic in nature. Sanitized violence, such as the bloodless violence in many children's programs, is less likely to register as violent with the public, yet even this type of violence is of concern to media violence researchers (Potter 1999, 73–77). For media violence researchers, the traditional Saturday morning cartoons, such as *Bugs Bunny* or *Tom and Jerry*, are considered quite violent (Potter 1999, 73–76), and they classify many E-rated games as violent (Anderson 2002, 103; Haninger, Ryan, and Thompson 2004; Thompson and Haninger 2001). There are multiple factors that affect the public's perceptions of violence in media. For example, the realism of the setting—how similar it is to "everyday reality"—is a relevant factor (Gunter 1985, 245). But the degree of graphicness is also an important factor for determining whether particular depictions of violence will stand out to viewers and be perceived as shocking or offensive to members of the public (Gunter, Harrison, and Wykes 2003, 173, 174; Howitt and Cumberbatch 1975, 127; Potter 1999, 73–77; Riddle et al. 2006, 281–282). As politicians are likely to share the public's perception of media violence, it is not surprising that at least six of the seven state legislatures targeted graphic violence rather than violence generally, even though the media violence literature offers little support for making this distinction (Ford 2013, 321–324; Shibuya et al. 2008, 528).

As can be seen in Table 5.1, all of these bills enjoyed broad support, but not surprisingly, legislators offered different reasons for supporting the bills. At one extreme was a pure electoral calculation. Senator Mike Jacobs of Illinois admitted that he was voting for the Illinois bill even though it would be "killed by the courts" and potentially cost the state as much as a half million dollars, but he thought if he voted against the bill, "it's going to end up on a mail piece that I'm somehow for violent and crazy video games, and seniors don't get that" (Illinois 2005c, 126–127). In contrast to Senator Jacobs' naked appeal to politics, most legislators, as would be expected, described their support or opposition to these bills in terms of public policy. Despite the good politics involved in supporting these bills, many politicians also care about good policy (Fenno 1995, 1),[17] however they define it, and some legislators seemed to genuinely believe that these laws could protect minors from harmful games.

5.4 The Constitutional Standards

Legislators knew that laws restricting minors' access to violent video games would trigger litigation, but until the Supreme Court decided the *Brown* case in 2011, it was not clear what legal standard or test courts would use to evaluate these laws. There were four basic possibilities, but not all were equally plausible. Under the more plausible standards, the social science about the effects of video game violence would be relevant to the constitutional analysis.

One unlikely possibility was that video games would be denied First Amendment protection, leaving the states free to regulate them as they saw fit. On multiple occasions in the 1980s, courts held that video games are not entitled to First Amendment protection because they supposedly lacked the necessary communicative elements to qualify as speech (Saunders 2003b, 93–97). These early cases were based on arcade classics like *Space Invaders* (Midway Manufacturing 1978), *Ms. Pac-Man* (Midway Manufacturing 1981), *Tron* (Bally-Midway 1982), and *Donkey Kong* (Nintendo of America 1981; see *Marshfield Family Skateland, Inc. v. Marshfield* 1983, 609 n.5; *Caswell v. Licensing Commission for Brockton* 1983, 926). Many years after these decisions involving early arcade games, in April 2002, the US District Court for the Eastern District of Missouri accepted the argument that games do not qualify for First Amendment protection (*Interactive Digital Software Association v. St. Louis County* 2002, 1132–1135), but this decision was not very persuasive.

In the Washington legislature, Representative Mary Lou Dickerson noted her agreement with these decisions denying First Amendment protection to video games (Washington 2003a), but the odds that courts would continue to deny protection to video games probably appeared low even before the Eighth Circuit reversed the April 2002 decision of the Eastern District of Missouri (*Interactive Digital Software Association v. St. Louis County* 2003). Whether or not *Space Invaders* and other early arcade games deserve First Amendment protection, it's simply not plausible to rule out protection for the entire medium. Modern games can accommodate far more content than the arcade classics, not just in the form of higher-resolution graphics, but also in the form of extensive dialogue. Books are now devoted to writing stories and scripts for video games (Dille and Platten 2007). Games like *Grand Theft Auto: Vice City* include not just elaborate plots, but also elements of social and political criticism (Garrelts 2006).[18] One commentator called *Vice City* the "smartest, savviest, and most politically astute" game in the *Grand Theft Auto* series (Redmond 2006, 109), an assessment not easily applied to the much simpler arcade games of the 70s and early 80s that courts found unworthy of constitutional protection.

A more plausible constitutional standard for reviewing restrictions on minors' access to violent video games was the variable obscenity standard recognized by the Supreme Court in *Ginsberg v. New York*, a case about what the court referred to as "girlie" magazines (1968, 631, 634). The Court upheld a New York statute that prohibited the sale of sexual materials to minors that "(i) predominantly appeals to the prurient, shameful or morbid interest of minors, and (ii) is patently offensive to prevailing standards in the adult community as a whole with respect to what is suitable material for minors, and (iii) is utterly without redeeming social importance for minors" (1968, 633). The material at issue in *Ginsberg* was not obscene for adults to view, but the Court said it could be obscene for minors.

Two things about the Supreme Court's decision in *Ginsberg* were unclear. First, did the rule in *Ginsberg* apply only to sexual material or could it also apply to violence? The Court was ambiguous on this point, but in 2001, the Seventh Circuit accepted at least the possibility that violent material could be obscene for minors (*American Amusement Machine Association v. Kendrick* 2001, 579). Second, did the rule require a legislature to rely on at least some social science evidence showing the material causes harm? In *Ginsberg* the Court said commentators viewed the social science evidence as ambiguous (1968, 642). Under one plausible reading of *Ginsberg*, some social science evidence is needed, but the state can make a judgment call in the face of ambiguous evidence. Thus, *Ginsberg* potentially empowered states to regulate minors' access to even violent material, provided the state relied upon at least some credible social science evidence of harm.

The third possibility for the applicable constitutional standard was strict scrutiny. This standard requires that a restriction on speech be "narrowly tailored to serve compelling state interests" (*R.A.V. v. St. Paul* 1992, 395). Unlike in *Ginsberg*, the state is not free to make a judgment call based on ambiguous evidence. The burden of proof is instead on the government to justify the restriction (*United States v. Playboy Entertainment Group* 2000, 816–817). Social science evidence would be essential under this standard. This is the standard that was ultimately adopted by the Supreme Court in 2011 (*Brown v. Entertainment Merchants Association* 2011, 2738).

A fourth and final possibility was the standard applied by the Supreme Court in *Brandenburg v. Ohio* (1969). Under *Brandenburg*, video game violence would need to be seen as advocating violence. To proscribe this advocacy, the state would have to show that statements by the producers of violent video games are "directed to inciting or producing imminent lawless action" and are "likely to incite or produce such action" (1969, 447). Even if the social science demonstrated that some players become violent after playing video games, the states had no plausible chance of satisfying this standard. They did not identify evidence that *any* producers of violent video games were trying to incite violence among their players, let alone evidence that the typical producer was trying to incite violence.

While the social science evidence is effectively irrelevant to the legal analysis under the first and fourth standards—the states simply win under the first standard and lose under the fourth—the likelihood that courts would instead apply the second or third standard made the social science important in the legislative process. Additionally, the first "modern" case in the series leading up to *Brown* increased the likelihood that other courts would apply the third standard, i.e., the strict scrutiny standard.

This modern case involved not a state restriction, but a local one. The City-County Council of Indianapolis and Marion County, Indiana enacted an ordinance in 2000 requiring arcade operators to label and to restrict minors' access to certain graphically violent video arcade games. The industry challenged the restriction in *American Amusement Machine Association v. Kendrick* (2000) and sought a preliminary injunction in the Southern District of Indiana. The district court applied the *Ginsberg* standard and denied the injunction (2000, 946). In applying *Ginsberg*, the district court held that the city needed a "reasonable basis" for concluding that violent video games cause harm and found that the city's social science evidence was adequate (2000, 962–963).

On appeal, the Seventh Circuit reversed (*American Amusement Machine Association v. Kendrick* 2001). In an opinion written by Judge Posner, the court held that the city could not plausibly show that the particular games in the record were offensive, because they were too cartoonish; therefore, the city could not defend the ordinance as a regulation of obscenity, which made *Ginsberg*'s lower standard of review of little help to the city. The city could have successfully defended the ordinance if it could have shown that violent video games cause harm to children or to public safety, but the city could not support this defense based on mere assertions or common sense. The court said, "The City rightly does not rest on 'what everyone knows' about the harm inflicted by violent video games.... The City instead appeals to social science to establish that games such as 'The House of the Dead' and 'Ultimate Mortal Kombat 3,'... are dangerous to public safety" (2001, 578). The government did not, however, convince the court that the social science was on its side.

While the Seventh Circuit allowed for the possibility that the government might be able to restrict access to some games under *Ginsberg* because of their offensiveness, this aspect of the *Kendrick* ruling offered little help to state legislatures. The court said that games that "used actors and simulated real death and mutilation convincingly" or games that are "merely animated shooting galleries" with no story might be subject to less First Amendment protection (2001, 579), but games in the *Grand Theft Auto* series, i.e., the ones of particular interest to state legislators, could not plausibly qualify as offensive under this standard. The violence in *Grand Theft Auto III, Grand Theft Auto: Vice City*, and *Grand Theft Auto: San Andreas* is not convincing, and there are in fact storylines in each of these games. While *Kendrick* was binding in only the Seventh Circuit, i.e., Illinois, Indiana, and Wisconsin, it reinforced the conclusion that state legislatures needed to anchor their legislation in the social science to improve their odds of prevailing in the courts.

5.5 Looking for Translations in the State Legislatures

Justice Breyer was not specific in *Brown* about what type of legislative performance he thought would justify judicial deference to a state's decision to restrict minors' access to some class of violent video games, but he clearly thought that legislatures are capable of doing a better job of assessing social science evidence than "most judges," including himself (*Brown* 2011, 2769, 2770). He made this point about legislative competence in *Brown* and earlier in his book, *Making Our Democracy Work* (Breyer 2010, 168). A starting point for thinking about the sort of state legislative performance he had in mind in *Brown* is Breyer's own dissenting opinion, which he clearly thought was inferior to what the legislatures could do. In his dissent, Breyer provided an overview of the literature, including citations to eleven studies. With the help of the Supreme Court's library, he also identified a total of 149 peer-reviewed academic articles about the effects of violent video games.

He determined that 115 of these studies support the conclusion that violent video games are harmful and 34 do not (*Brown* 2011, 2772–2779). After noting his lack of expertise to assess the conflicting social science, he said, "I would find sufficient grounds in these studies and expert opinions for this Court to defer to an elected legislature's conclusion that the video games in question are particularly likely to harm children" (2011, 2770). But what sort of assessment of the literature would Breyer have expected the California legislature or another legislative body to have undertaken?

The quality of any legislative assessment of the social science cannot plausibly be measured just by the number of studies in the legislative record. The mere appearance of a study in the record doesn't mean that any legislators actually read it. The Illinois legislature included only 17 studies in its record and only ones that supported the legislature's conclusion that video games cause harm (*Entertainment Software Association v. Blagojevich* Oct. 7, 2005, 7–9; *Entertainment Software Association v. Blagojevich* Dec. 2, 2005, 1058, 1063). The Michigan legislature included more studies in its record, probably about 45 or 55,[19] but to the extent a list of studies can be considered meaningful, Justice Breyer did a better job than both Illinois and Michigan—and probably all of the other states. Unlike Illinois and Michigan, he subdivided his list of studies into two separate categories, one for studies that found evidence of harm from video game violence and one for studies that did not.

The quality of the state legislatures' assessments of the social science must be measured by something more than counting the number of studies on a list or the number of photocopies in a file. At a minimum, there should be an indication that at least some legislators understood the studies well enough to have made a reasonable judgment based upon them. Presumably, Justice Breyer would not expect that all or even most members of a state legislature labored through the 149 studies he listed in his dissent. Such an expectation would be totally unrealistic. There isn't time for every member in the legislature to become an expert on every subject that comes before the legislature (Dodson, Brownson, and Weiss 2012, 445; Polsby 1973; Wald 2003, 357; Weiss 1989, 429), let alone topics like video game violence that occupy such a small part of the legislative agenda. A more reasonable expectation would be that the legislature delegated the assessment to a committee: "Freed from the very great inconvenience of numbers," said former Speaker of the House Thomas Reed, a committee "can study a question, obtain full information, and put the proposed action into proper shape for final decision" (Reed 1894, 53). Speaker Reed's expectation of "full" information may be unrealistic, even for a committee. *Sufficient* information is a more realistic one.

As a reasonable estimate of Breyer's position, perhaps he would expect that the members of one committee, in at least one house of a bicameral legislature, would have acquired sufficient information to make a reasonable assessment of the social science literature about the effects of video game violence.

In the present context, this would have required committees to consider a variety of issues related to the video game violence literature: how media violence researchers define and operationalize both violence and aggression; the effects of violence on players; the effects of particular types of violent content on players, such as graphic violence versus non-graphic violence, realistic settings versus unrealistic settings, justified versus unjustified violence, the role of humor, etc.; the effects of violence on different age groups; and the likely effectiveness of government restrictions on reducing minors' exposure to harmful content (Ford 2013, 356; Shibuya and Sakamoto 2005).

Much of the translation process depends upon communicating to policymakers the results of the social science literature in general, in the form of either narrative literature reviews or quantitative meta-analyses, but legislators probably should consider at least a few individual studies too. Some researchers argue against translating individual studies to policymakers because individual studies are usually insufficient on their own for making policy decisions. Any particular study may not be representative of the studies in the field (Grimshaw et al. 2012, 2–3). Literature reviews and meta-analyses have drawbacks too, however. Some are clearly written for an audience with a background in the literature, such as Professor Craig Anderson's often-cited 2004 meta-analysis of the social science literature on video game violence (Anderson 2004; Ford 2013, 327–328). While more detailed reviews *might* be sufficient for policymakers, depending on their level of detail, it's not clear that policymakers could really come to a fair assessment of the media violence literature without considering in more depth some of the typical research designs employed by researchers. Engaging with at least a few individual studies, in addition to systematic reviews, could make clear what the authors of literature reviews and meta-analyses assume readers already know.

Putting what legislators ought to have known about the social science in these detailed terms already sounds somewhat idealistic, even when confined only to the members of a single committee, but once we have some idea of what legislators ought to have known, how do we determine what they really did know? My approach in this study is to rely primarily on the oral statements of legislators, not the written material filed in the legislative record. These statements come from the available floor sessions, committee meetings, and one press conference. Focusing on oral communication is consistent with the literature on Congress. Congress is recognized for its strong oral tradition. Members of Congress "take pride in their ability to 'read people' rather than read reports" (Weiss 1989, 414). According to Professor Bruce Bimber, the tradition of oral communication "demands face-to-face contacts between experts and politicians" (Bimber 1996, 96). As social science articles are not usually written with particular legislation in mind, face-to-face interactions are opportunities for legislators to ask researchers questions related to the fit between the research and the proposed legislation.

Floor debates can involve substantive exchanges (Mucciaroni and Quirk 2006, 197), but floor debates alone are inadequate to determine the quality of the translation of the social science evidence in the state legislatures. Committee discussions in Congress are usually more detailed and thorough than floor debates (Mucciaroni and Quirk 2006, 5; Quirk 2005, 330). It's reasonable to assume that state legislatures operate in a similar way. The primary rationale for committees, after all, is to divide up the work. As a state senator in Michigan explained, "[T]hat's what the whole committee process is all about, is to build a record and to put together a package of information that we can use to support our position when we go talk to our caucuses and when we debate this issue on, on the floor" (Michigan 2005a, Tape 2, Side A).[20] During the floor debates on the video game violence bills, some legislators emphasized the importance of what they learned about the social science during the committee hearings, but they did so without offering much detail. A senator in Washington referred to "some testimony in committee that was very compelling" with very little elaboration as to *why* it was compelling (Washington 2003f).[21] Figuring out how well the legislatures did in translating the social science requires looking to the committee meetings, which, unlike floor sessions, involve that very important face-to-face contact between legislators and experts.

While floor sessions and especially committee events are important opportunities for legislators to acquire information, they are not the only ones. Some legislators could have learned about the social science on video game violence through interactions outside of official legislative activities. Legislators are not subject to the same rules about *ex parte* communications as judges. Compared to judges, legislators can more easily acquire information through informal contacts (Colker and Brudney 2001, 117). In Illinois, for example, Governor Rod Blagojevich created a task force ostensibly charged with researching "the effects of violent and sexually explicit video games on the psychological well being of children under 18" (Blagojevich 2004, 3). Although the task force's formal activities were limited, the sponsor of H.B. 4023 in Illinois briefly acknowledged it at one committee meeting ("thank you to the task force that worked on this so diligently"), indicating that she could have acquired information about the social science from task force members (Illinois 2005a).[22] There is no feasible way to determine what was said at unrecorded events, either inside or outside the legislature, but my assumption is that members who invested substantial time in learning about the social science would have been likely to say something demonstrating their knowledge or expertise during those events that are available in recorded form.

Table 5.2 contains a list of the recorded events that are the focus of this study. The list is not limited to legislative events strictly about the bills listed in Table 5.1, i.e., the bills that were enacted and challenged in court; however, the list is inevitably incomplete. Researching legislative activities associated with the translation of the social science evidence is more difficult than researching

TABLE 5.2

Pre-enactment legislative events

State	Date	Event	Length (Minutes/Pages)	Source Formats	Source ID	Citation
California	April 13, 2004	Assembly Committee on Arts, Entertainment, Sports, Tourism, and Internet Media	118 minutes	DVD	04-0413C1	California 2004
	May 3, 2005	Assembly Committee on Arts, Entertainment, Sports, Tourism, and Internet Media	83 minutes	DVD	05-0503C2	California 2005a
	September 8, 2005	Senate floor session	6 minutes	DVD (disc 3 of 5)	305	California 2005b
	September 8, 2005	Assembly floor session	22 minutes	DVD (disc 6 of 7)	05-0908FS	California 2005c
Illinois	March 9, 2005	House Judiciary I—Civil Law Committee	68 minutes	audio file	N/A	Illinois 2005a
	March 16, 2005	House floor session	67 pages	transcript	09400031	Illinois 2005b
	May 19, 2005	Senate floor session	13 pages	transcript	09400044	Illinois 2005c
	May 24, 2005	House Judiciary I—Civil Law Committee	29 minutes	audio file	N/A	Illinois 2005d
	May 25, 2005	House Judiciary I—Civil Law Committee	< 1 minute	audio file	N/A	Illinois 2005e
	May 28, 2005	House floor session	17 pages	transcript	09400060	Illinois 2005f
Louisiana	May 16, 2006	House floor session	20 minutes	website	N/A	Louisiana 2006a
	May 30, 2006	Senate Judiciary A Committee	53 minutes	audio file	N/A	Louisiana 2006b
Michigan	April 26, 2005	Senate Judiciary Committee	89 minutes	audio cassette tape	N/A	Michigan 2005a
	May 10, 2005	Senate Judiciary Committee	118 minutes	audio cassette tape	N/A	Michigan 2005b
	May 12, 2005	Senate floor session	28 minutes	DVD	MGO2251	Michigan 2005c
	August 31, 2005	House floor session	5 minutes	DVD	MGO2319	Michigan 2005d
	September 7, 2005	Senate floor session	6 minutes	DVD	MGO2317	Michigan 2005e
	September 8, 2005	House floor session	3 minutes	DVD	MGO2318	Michigan 2005f

State	Date	Event	Length	Format	Source ID	Event ID
Minnesota	March 5, 2003	Senate Commerce and Utilities	65 minutes	website	N/A	Minnesota 2003
	March 8, 2005	Senate Crime Prevention and Public Safety	47 minutes	website	N/A	Minnesota 2005a
	May 23, 2005	Senate floor session	15 minutes	website	N/A	Minnesota 2005b
	April 4, 2006	House Public Safety Policy and Finance	34 minutes	website (audio only)	N/A	Minnesota 2006a
	May 18, 2006	House floor session	98 minutes	DVD (disc 2 of 3), website	N/A	Minnesota 2006b
	May 20, 2006	Senate floor session	2 minutes	website	N/A	Minnesota 2006c
	May 20, 2006	House floor session	6 minutes	website	N/A	Minnesota 2006d
Oklahoma	March 16, 2006	House floor session	6 minutes	website (audio only)	N/A	Oklahoma 2006a
	May 24, 2006	House floor session	4 minutes	website (audio only)	N/A	Oklahoma 2006b
Washington	February 10, 1999a	House Democratic Press Conference	26 minutes	DVD, website	1999020095	Washington 1999a
	February 10, 1999b	House Criminal Justice and Corrections Committee	72 minutes	DVD, website	1999020096	Washington 1999b
	February 12, 1999	House Criminal Justice and Corrections Committee	8 minutes	DVD, website	1999020085	Washington 1999c
	January 24, 2002	House Juvenile Justice and Family Law Committee	60 minutes	DVD, website	2002010115	Washington 2002
	January 22, 2003	House Juvenile Justice and Family Law Committee	91 minutes	DVD, website (audio only)	2003010099	Washington 2003a
	January 30, 2003	House Juvenile Justice and Family Law Committee	8 minutes	website (audio only)	2003011894	Washington 2003b
	March 18, 2003	House floor session	37 minutes	DVD, website (audio only)	2003030116B	Washington 2003c
	April 1, 2003	Senate Children and Family Services and Corrections Committee	84 minutes	website (audio only)	2003042377	Washington 2003d
	April 4, 2003	Senate Children and Family Services and Corrections Committee	5 minutes	DVD, website (audio only)	2003040041	Washington 2003e
	April 17, 2003	Senate floor session	53 minutes	DVD, website	2003040100A	Washington 2003f

Note: These events all took place prior to the enactment of the legislation listed in Table 5.1, on a state-by-state basis. Not all of these events were specifically about the legislation listed in Table 5.1, however. Some of these events were about earlier or related bills involving violent video games, but these other bills were still an opportunity to learn about the subject of the bills eventually enacted. Length refers to the approximate length of time spent on the video game issue(s), not to the length of the entire recorded event. The total time for the May 12, 2005 Michigan Senate floor session, which was broadcast on June 3, 2005, is based not only on Senate Bill 416, the bill listed on Table 5.1, but also on three other bills and resolutions that resulted in relevant references to video games and violence: Senate Bill 249 (2005), Senate Resolution 32 (2005), and Senate Resolution 33 (2005). The relevant portion of the August 31, 2005 Michigan floor session was broadcast by Michigan TV on September 9, 2005. "Source ID" refers to the catalog number (California), tracking number (Illinois), transcript number (Michigan), or event number (Washington) assigned to the recordings by their sources. The event IDs used by TVW, the source of the Washington recordings, come in two slightly different forms. The numbers in this table appear on the website in the same form. On the DVDs, these same numbers appear with a hyphen in place of the 7th digit. For example, the number 1999020095 on the TVW website is 199902-095 on a TVW DVD.

judicial activities. The items most relevant to assessing the judiciary's efforts are listed on easily found docket sheets and usually available in written form, such as transcripts, briefs, or opinions. While it's possible that judges acquired factual information about the social science evidence from sources outside the litigation process and then did not reference these sources in their written decisions, it's even more likely that legislators acquired relevant factual information during activities related to different bills than the ones ultimately enacted and litigated. Legislators can reintroduce the same or similar bills across multiple sessions, making testimony at earlier sessions relevant to the consideration of bills at later sessions. Legislators can also introduce multiple bills on the same subject during the same session. Although legislatures offer online bill tracking, there is no legislative "docket sheet" that lists all of the events relevant to legislators learning about the social science evidence. The bill tracking information available for those bills known to be relevant doesn't necessarily provide detailed information about the committee meetings related to the bills, such as whether the meetings included testimony by expert witnesses. And not all relevant legislative events are available in recorded form. Therefore, Table 5.2 does not include the complete universe of relevant events, but it goes beyond events formally about the bills that were enacted and litigated.

Table 5.2, then, is essentially a convenience sample of those legislative events I could identify as related to video game violence and could obtain in recorded form, which usually meant a video or audio recording or occasionally a transcript. The generalizations in this study about what occurred in the legislatures are based on these events. Some of the events in Table 5.2 did not include any discussion of the social science. Some relevant and apparently recorded events that could have involved discussions of the social science are missing from Table 5.2. For example, I was not able to obtain a recording of a meeting of the California Assembly's Judiciary Committee in April 2005 that was related to A.B. 1179.[23] Despite the unavailability of some recordings, the events that are available for most states should be adequate to determine how well the states translated the social science evidence, with the possible exception of Oklahoma.[24]

5.6 Translating the Gaming Medium

Although the focus of this chapter is on the translation of social science evidence in both legislatures and courts, there was an additional translation problem associated with the efforts to restrict minors' access to violent video games, that of translating the gaming medium. This may sound somewhat odd. After all, video games are sold in large quantities to a mass market. They are played by people of all ages. Formal study and training are not required to play and understand video games. A video game player listening to any random portion of the hearings or floor debates, however, would almost immediately find some of the language slightly off. Many participants referred not to "video games," but to "videos."[25] Some participants also referred to "watching" the games rather than to "playing" them.[26] Most video game players are not likely to talk in this way. By itself, these word choices are not particularly significant, but they suggest that many of the participants in the legislative process were quite unfamiliar with the medium they sought to regulate. Other evidence confirms legislators' poor understanding of the medium, even legislators on the committees tasked with studying the issue. The fact that the committees did so poorly with the gaming medium does not bode well for its handling of the more difficult social science evidence.

One might expect that at least some of the committee meetings included witnesses demonstrating the play of various games or maybe even legislators trying the games themselves. Neither of these two things happened. Neither the witnesses nor the committee members played any games at these meetings. At least one sponsor of a video game bill considered playing a game for a committee. At the March 5, 2003 meeting in Minnesota, Senator Sandra Pappas said she thought about demonstrating *Grand Theft Auto: Vice City* (Rockstar 2003a) on a PlayStation 2 console, but she decided it would take too long. She instead asked a relative of an intern to testify about the contents of *Vice City*.[27] He spent about four minutes doing so (Minnesota 2003).

At most, legislators watched very brief prerecorded clips from a small number of games on videotapes (or possibly DVDs in some cases). These clips focused on violent or sexual content without any context for the events in the games. They did not watch these clips during the floor sessions,[28] but they did at some committee meetings. The clips ranged in length from about one-and-a-half minutes to not quite five minutes.[29] As some examples, the committee in Washington on February 10, 1999 watched a two-minute tape that included scenes from two games (Washington 1999b).[30] At the January 22, 2003 meeting in Washington, the committee watched two sets of clips totaling about four minutes and 41 seconds (Washington 2003a). At the April 13, 2004 committee hearing in California, the committee chairperson allowed the sponsor of the bill, Leland Yee, to show one minute from a videotape. When the video ran about 30 seconds over, the chairperson had had enough and directed the staff person to turn it off (California 2004). At the March 8, 2005 Minnesota meeting, the committee watched about four minutes of video, part of which included clips from games and part of which included some brief remarks by Dr. David Walsh and Senator Joseph Lieberman, two critics of video game violence (Minnesota 2005a).[31] At the March 9, 2005 Illinois meeting, the committee watched about two minutes of footage (Illinois 2005a). At the May 3,

2005 committee meeting in California, the same chairperson as the previous year did not allow any clips to be shown (California 2005a).[32]

Some legislators did view clips outside of the committee meetings[33] and a few individuals acknowledged more significant game playing experience,[34] but the typical members of the relevant committees appear to have had little exposure to video games. Other members of the legislature likely had even less exposure.[35] One legislator who spoke in favor of restricting violent games on the floor of the Washington Senate acknowledged that he had never seen the examples of the games mentioned by others.[36] A couple of members noted that they avoided looking at the available clips because they did not want to see the violent content.[37]

While actually playing video games might not have changed the outcomes in the committees or the legislatures, there is some evidence that playing controversial games can change people's perceptions of them. One small study included 20 parents playing *Grand Theft Auto IV* for about an hour. All of the participants found the game more enjoyable than they thought it would be (Schott 2011, 227–230, 234). Some participants had thought the game would be a "simple murder simulator" (2011, 238). Instead, "many of the participants recognized the irony and social satire operating within the game more generally" (2011, 236). One study is hardly conclusive, but even without this limited evidence about the value of actually playing the games, it should be disconcerting that legislators were so unfamiliar with the targets of their legislative activities. One Illinois senator said, "[W]hat has been fundamentally misunderstood is that video games are not art or media, they are simulations" (Illinois 2005c, 119). Whether or not video games should be labeled art, they clearly are a form of media, and legislators with so little exposure to this particular medium are not in a very good position to make judgments about it or to compare games to other forms of media.[38]

Assorted comments made about games during the hearings or floor sessions reveal multiple misconceptions about the medium. One indicator of higher-quality policy debates is when inaccurate claims are rebutted (Mucciaroni and Quirk 2006, 50), but questionable generalizations often went unchallenged during these sessions. At a committee meeting in Washington, one witness wondered whether any films, like some games, include scenes of decapitation, though he conceded some films might. Some films, in fact, do (Prince 2000, 1–2). He then compared the violence in video games to the sex in pornographic films: "In these videos, violence is the plot. There is no plot except violence" (Washington 2003a).[39] While some games can fairly be said to lack plots, such as *Pong* (Atari 1972) or *Breakout* (Atari 1976), or to contain only very thin plots, such as *Pac-Man* (Midway Manufacturing 1980) or *Donkey Kong* (Nintendo 1981), this witness' statement was not accurate about games in general or even M-rated games in particular, not even in 2003. Games routinely have plots beyond violence (Dille and Platten 2007).

While the comment about video games lacking plots might be dismissed as an inaccurate statement by one poorly informed witness, multiple legislators and witnesses suggested that rape is a common feature in video games.[40] These speakers provided no specific examples of games where a player can commit rape, but at least a few speakers seemed to think that some version or versions of *Grand Theft Auto* include this feature.[41] While there may be an event in *Grand Theft Auto V* (Rockstar 2013) involving rape,[42] there are no examples of rape in the earlier *Grand Theft Auto* games available during the events listed in Table 5.2.[43] Some games rated by the ESRB and sold in retail stores in the United States do depict rape in some way, but despite the suggestions of some legislators or witnesses to the contrary, rape is not common in mainstream games.[44]

Another belief expressed by legislators and witnesses on multiple occasions, at least in Washington, was that games commonly conceal the more violent content for higher levels of the game or for parts of the game that can only be accessed with secret codes.[45] The implication was that parents might purchase a game that appears appropriate for children and perhaps even see a child play the early levels, but parents will not realize that the child can later access inappropriate content. Perhaps it would be an E- or T-rated game with hidden violence appropriate only for an M-rated game. No legislator or witness named a specific game that is set up in this way, yet no one challenged these claims. One committee member asked a video game industry representative if the industry is willing to make parents aware of these secret codes. Without confirming or denying the premise of the question or even asking for an example of a relevant game, the representative simply said he would get back to the committee member (Washington 2003a).[46] While there may very well be one or more games that fit this description—there are many thousands of games and not all of them are rated—hiding content to manipulate a game rated by the ESRB is inconsistent with the ESRB's requirements, a point made clear when hidden sexual content in *Grand Theft Auto: San Andreas* (Rockstar Games 2004) was revealed in June 2005. The ESRB treated this as a serious breach of the publisher's obligation to disclose content relevant to the ratings process.[47] While legislators seemed to think this type of situation with *San Andreas* was routine, video game journalist David Kushner described the situation as unprecedented (Kushner 2012, 208).

In sum, while a small number of legislators outside the committees demonstrated some greater knowledge or experience with video games, the members of the committees showed no significant familiarity with the medium, perhaps beyond playing some of the classic arcade titles like *Pac-Man*. The committee meetings could do little to increase their knowledge. In no way did the committees engage in any serious study of the content of video games generally or even the content of the few games repeatedly referenced, such as *Grand Theft Auto: Vice City*—or, as one bill's sponsor frequently referred to it, "*Grand Theft Auto: City Vice*."[48]

5.7 Translating the Science in the Legislature

Legislators may not be very good at assessing the content of video games, but perhaps they might still be good at assessing the social science evidence related to the effects of video game violence. Assessing scientific work may not be easy, but it is probably a task closer to ordinary legislative activities than studying (or playing) video games. As it turns out, however, there were also serious problems with the legislatures' efforts to assess the social science. This assessment takes time, and the legislators had a lot of ground to cover at the committee meetings. The social science was only one of several topics related to the proposed bills. In addition to the social science evidence, the other topics commonly discussed at these committee meetings included the structure of the ESRB ratings system, retail enforcement of the ESRB ratings, the practical ability of retailers to comply with the proposed laws, and the constitutional standards for reviewing the laws during the expected legal challenges.

There were at least four specific problems with the legislative discussions of the social science. First, committee members were not prepared for a serious discussion about the social science. Only rarely was there any reason to think members had read or discussed anything beyond a general summary of the video game violence research, assuming they had read anything at all. Second, they did not devote enough time to interact with the experts, i.e., to listen to their presentations and then to ask them follow-up questions. At one committee meeting, a lawyer for the video game industry said, "I'm not really going to touch on the research. Reasonable minds agree to disagree on the research, and I think if we were to start debating the research, it would, it could go on for hours, so I'm just going to jump ahead to the unconstitutionality."[49] She was right. A serious discussion or debate about this topic *would* take hours, but legislators thought of the topic in terms of minutes. Third, legislators did not hear from enough experts to provide a range of viewpoints. Lastly, some of the "experts" were not really experts on the social science literature, despite suggestions to the contrary by legislators.

My focus in this section is primarily on legislators' interactions with four witnesses at five different committee hearings: Lt. Colonel (ret.) Dave Grossman in Washington in 1999; attorney Jack Thompson in Washington in 2003; Dr. Michael Rich in Illinois in 2005; Professor Craig Anderson in Michigan in 2005; and Jack Thompson again, this time in Louisiana in 2006. Legislators introduced all four of these witnesses as experts on the effects of media or video game violence. Presumably for this reason, the committees allowed these witnesses to speak for more than the customary five or fewer minutes granted to most other speakers. These examples, discussed in chronological order, therefore represent the legislatures' "best" efforts at translating the social science evidence. California, the state whose efforts were actually before the Supreme Court in *Brown*, is missing from this group because of the very limited time given to witnesses to speak at the available committee hearings (Ford 2013, 349–355).

Lt. Colonel Dave Grossman was a popular speaker early in the video game violence debates leading up to *Brown*. He spoke before several state legislatures, including Washington in 1999, Minnesota in 2000, and Oklahoma in 2001. (Unfortunately, I could not locate recordings of the latter two events.[50]) Grossman is a retired Army Ranger with an M.Ed. in Counseling Psychology. He is also a former professor in the Department of Behavioral Sciences and Leadership at West Point and the Department of Military Science at Arkansas State University. He is a prolific author of articles and several books, including *On Killing* (1995), and he is the coauthor of *Stop Teaching Our Kids to Kill: A Call to Action against TV, Movie & Video Game Violence* (1999).[51] Senator Sandra Pappas, the primary sponsor of S.F. 785 (2006) in Minnesota, said she became concerned about video game violence after her husband read *Stop Teaching Our Kids to Kill* (Dormer 2006). Grossman is an engaging speaker, and he avoids the hedging and qualifications typical of social scientists. He speaks more like the "policy entrepreneurs" who offer "unambiguous diagnoses" so appealing to politicians seeking clear and definite answers (Krugman 1994, 10–13).

Grossman spoke at two events in Washington listed in Table 5.2, a House Democratic press conference and a meeting of the House Criminal Justice and Corrections Committee. Both events were on February 10, 1999, several years before the Washington legislature enacted H.B. 1009 in 2003. The events in 1999 were about a bill directing the Washington Department of Health to prepare a report about violent video games and to obtain a "definitive scientific study" on the effects of violent video games on juvenile aggression (Washington House of Representatives 1999). At both events, Representative Mary Lou Dickerson, the primary sponsor of H.B. 1009 in 2003, described Grossman as a leading expert on human aggression (Washington 1999a, 1999b). At the committee meeting, she also introduced him as "this country's leading expert on the area of video game violence" (Washington 1999b). Grossman spoke about both the effects of media violence and the potential liability of the video game industry for acts of violence committed by video game players. His presentation at the press conference lasted about eight minutes. This presentation was essentially an abbreviated version of his committee presentation. The committee presentation lasted about 25 minutes, followed by about 23 minutes for questions and answers.

Grossman's argument about the effects of media violence began with the claim that humans and other species share a "powerful resistance" to killing one another, even in life-threatening situations (Washington 1999b). In order for humans to kill other humans this natural resistance must somehow be overcome. In World War II, Grossman said only 15–20% of soldiers fired on enemy soldiers in combat (a statistic he repeated twice), making most soldiers ineffective in combat. In the 1960s, he said the FBI determined that the "vast majority" of law enforcement officers similarly would not fire, even when firing was necessary to save their lives (1999b). According to Grossman, the military made a simple change in training to break down this resistance to killing. Specifically, the military switched from the bull's-eye targets used during training in World War II to human silhouette targets that drop when hit. He said law enforcement organizations made similar changes to their training programs. The result for people trained with these post–World War II targets is that they become *conditioned* to kill when necessary. Grossman claimed this form of training is incredibly effective, improving the rate of fire from 15–20% in World War II to over 90% in later conflicts.[52]

According to Grossman, media violence, much like firing on silhouette-shaped targets, can break down a person's resistance to killing, but media violence does so without the discipline associated with military and law-enforcement training: "Visual violence results in real-world violence. We know it. It has been happening around the world. Anywhere in the world that television appears, with very few exceptions, fifteen years later the murder rate doubles: direct cause and effect relationship" (Washington 1999b). As compared to passive media like television, Grossman said video games are even more effective, particularly when the games involve controllers shaped like firearms. He described some common arcade games like *Operation Wolf* (Taito America 1987) and *Lethal Enforcers* (Konami 1992) as "military and law enforcement quality trainers" (Washington 1999b). But Grossman said these games teach more than marksmanship. He said they also condition children to kill. Grossman offered the examples of the shooting of a clerk in a convenience store in South Carolina and the shooting of multiple students at a high school in Paducah, Kentucky. Both shooters, he said, trained on video games.[53]

Grossman's presentation was mostly theory and conclusions with minimal explanations for how he confirmed his theory. No experts presented alternative views. The committee members were not particularly inquisitive, despite Grossman making some remarkable claims. For example, no one followed up on his statement about the dramatic effects of television on the murder rate.[54] Nevertheless, at least one member of the committee was not fully persuaded by Grossman's presentation. Representative Jack Cairnes, a veteran of the Vietnam War, accepted that soldiers can improve their marksmanship skills by practicing on a firing range, but he questioned Grossman's claim about how training affects a soldier's willingness to kill. He also questioned Grossman's claim that "videos" (presumably meaning video games) could make a child willing to kill. Cairnes said he was skeptical, a "tough sell," but he was not prepared to critically assess Grossman's claims (Washington 1999b).

Grossman's argument, both in 1999 and today, depends in substantial part on several contestable claims, none of which were subject to any serious scrutiny by the committee. These contestable claims include at least the following:

(1) that only a small percentage of military personnel were willing to fire their weapons at the enemy in World War II; (2) that their unwillingness to fire reflected a resistance to killing; (3) that changing the targets used in training can overcome this resistance to killing and can account for the increases in firing rates after World War II; and (4) that video games mimic the effects of firing on silhouettes but without the safeguards of military discipline.

Grossman's statistics for the rate of fire in World War II and his explanation for these surprisingly low percentages come from Brigadier General S. L. A. Marshall's influential book *Men against Fire*, first published in 1947. The most controversial part of the book involved Marshall's claim that the average rate of fire among soldiers in World War II was 15%, with an upper bound of 20–25%. He attributed these low rates of fire to a resistance to killing (S. L. A. Marshall 2000, 50–63, 78–79). Missing from the committee discussion was the fact that these figures are widely doubted (Chambers 2003; Engen 2011; Glenn 2000a, 134–136; Glenn 2000b 4–6; Spiller 1988). They were doubted even in 1999. One of the early challenges to these numbers was published by Marshall's son in 1993. Acutely aware of the controversy over his father's figures, Marshall's son discussed "that damn statistic" (specifically referring to the 25% upper bound) with a historian who worked with Marshall during World War II. The historian said that Marshall wanted to emphasize the need for improved training and simply picked a figure to help make his point (J. D. Marshall 1993, 186–187). But even if the figures were correct, Marshall's explanation for the low rates of fire is still open to question. Perhaps many soldiers in World War II were unwilling to kill, but there are other explanations that must be considered. Perhaps the soldiers who failed to fire in a particular battle were instead afraid or exhausted or perhaps they lacked targets. Marshall's explanation was just one of several plausible ones (Engen 2011, 42–43).

In print, Grossman continues to defend Marshall's figures, but unlike his earlier testimony in Washington, he sometimes hedges. Many years after his committee presentation, he wrote that whatever the actual percentages in World War II, Marshall was really just claiming that "some" soldiers do not fire and that "more realistic targets" will improve the rate of fire (Grossman 2009a, xviii; Grossman 2009b). But no one could doubt that "some" soldiers did not fire in World War II. What made Grossman's presentation in Washington so striking was the supposedly dramatic increase in the rate of fire after World War II due to something as simple as changing the targets used during military training. Even more recently, in 2014, Grossman combined a slight hedge with the same dramatic conclusion. He said that the introduction of silhouette targets "*appears* to have been sufficient to increase the firing rate manifold," but then in the very next sentence asserted that the switch in targets was "*undeniably* responsible for increasing the firing rate from 15 to 20 percent in World War II to 95 percent in Vietnam" (Grossman and DeGaetano 2014, 93) (emphasis added).

The problem here is only partly with Marshall. Grossman is the one putting so much weight on the change to silhouette targets, but military doctrine and training have changed in other ways besides just changes in the targets used at firing ranges (Glenn 2000a, 51–52). Marshall himself recommended several changes in military practices, such as better communication on the battlefield and more realistic training, including marksmanship training with both human silhouette targets and nonhuman targets (Williams 1990, 47–51, 79).[55] In his study of the Korean War, Marshall referred to different causes for increased firing rates. Leaders, for example, better monitored their men by moving among them during combat to insure they were participating in the fighting (S. L. A. Marshall 1953, 4–5). Grossman singles out a change in targets as the critical one in the evolution of military training and doctrine, but he does not provide any data isolating the effects of this particular change from the effects of any other change.[56] Regardless of whether Grossman is ultimately correct or not, the main problem in Washington was that his claims were open to serious questions, yet there was a serious failure to critically engage them.

In addition, there was also a lack of discussion about the implications of Grossman's claims for concerns about graphic violence in video games and for the ratings system. Games using a first-person perspective and even games using gun-shaped controllers are not necessarily graphically violent or rated M.[57] On Grossman's account, the classic Nintendo Entertainment System game *Hogan's Alley* (Nintendo 1985b) should be more of a concern than any *Grand Theft Auto* title.[58] *Hogan's Alley* is a first-person shooter that uses a light gun. Players are supposed to quickly shoot cartoonish gangsters that look like cardboard targets, while avoiding the bystanders, either a lady, a professor, or a police officer. Nintendo published *Hogan's Alley* prior to the formation of the ESRB, but it is plausible that it would be rated E or E10+ if published today.[59] The *Grand Theft Auto* games, which were the focus of discussion in many state legislatures, are third-person games (meaning, the player's character is visible on the screen). They are also played with standard controllers, not light guns.[60] Grossman himself states in his book that games used for military training may be no more sophisticated than modified versions of *Duck Hunt* (Nintendo 1985a) (Grossman and DeGaetano 1999, 74), a target shooting game played on the same console and with the same light gun as *Hogan's Alley*. If Grossman is correct, then the focus on *graphically* violent video games in Washington and elsewhere was a mistake. This failure to think about the relationship between graphic violence and the social science was a recurring problem in the state legislatures.

Like Dave Grossman, Jack Thompson has been a very public critic of the video game industry.[61] Until the Florida Supreme Court permanently disbarred him in 2008 (*Florida Bar v. Thompson* 2008), Thompson represented plaintiffs in multiple suits against video game publishers, including the case resulting from the shooting in West Paducah, Kentucky (*James v. Meow Media, Inc.* 2000, 799).

He testified at an April 1, 2003 committee meeting in Washington (and later in Louisiana in 2006). While Thompson is not a social scientist, he was still treated as an expert on the effects of video game violence.

At the April 1, 2003 hearing on H.B. 1009 before the Senate Children and Family Services and Corrections Committee in Washington, Senator Val Stevens referred to Jack Thompson as an expert witness and Representative Mary Lou Dickerson introduced him as having "assembled an incredible body of knowledge about the impact of violent video games" (Washington 2003d). Thompson spoke for about 18 minutes, followed by about eight minutes for follow-up questions. He said his experience in medical malpractice cases over a period of 22 years gave him the experience and expertise to understand the literature on the effects of video game violence. He said video games cannot alone cause a child to kill, but they can increase the risk that a child will kill.

During his testimony, Thompson mentioned three sources. Two of these sources were studies, one he attributed to Harvard University and the other he attributed to Iowa State Medical School (even though Iowa State does not have a medical school). He did not name the actual authors of either study. Here is what Thompson said about the Harvard study:

> In June of 1998, months before Columbine, Harvard University hooked up adults and adolescents to magnetic resonance imaging devices—MRIs—and showed the two groups violent images. Harvard found that adults by virtue of where the blood flow was occurring processed these images in the forebrain, where reasoning occurs and where one can differentiate between reality and fantasy. But Harvard found that the adolescents processed those same violent images in the amygdala, which is the seat of emotions of the brain.
>
> Harvard, not I, concluded that that is why teens who see violent and emotion-laden images are more likely to copycat the entertainment they consume because the images are then wedded structurally to the part of the brain that controls emotion controlled or uncontrolled behaviors [sic]. And therefore, is [sic] there is a structural, neurobiological hard-science reason why parents intuitively know—and why this bill reflects that intuition—that your child should not be exposed to violence because he or she—more likely he—will copycat it, and Harvard has proven why. (Washington 2003d)

In addition to the Harvard study, Thompson offered two other sources. He briefly summarized the "Iowa State Medical School" study. Thompson claimed this study proves that violent video games alter the brains of adolescents at a cellular level and "can predispose a child to violence" (Washington 2003d), but I remain unsure of what study Thompson was attempting to summarize. Thompson also referred to an *ABC World News Tonight* piece in which Thompson himself appeared. According to Thompson, another participant in the same broadcast "explained that when a child plays a video game and performs a killing task hundreds of times, he grows neural pathways called dendrites that literally re-hardwire the brain of that child and thus pre-dispose it structurally to perform that killing task as if it were a player piano, hard-wired, predisposed to play a particular tune, in this case killing individuals" (Washington 2003d).[62] As far as the social science was concerned, this was the substantive part of Thompson's testimony.

While these studies or theories were certainly relevant to the proceedings, Thompson's presentation was extremely thin. He was not clear about the sources of the studies, vaguely attributing them to institutions rather than to the actual authors. He provided few details on the methodology of the studies beyond what is contained in the quoted material. The committee members asked him no questions about these studies, such as the number or types of participants. They did not ask him about the nature of the violent images used in the study Thompson attributed to Harvard. They did not ask him if the studies were peer-reviewed or even published or if the results had been replicated by others in the field.

As the "Harvard" study constituted the bulk of Thompson's presentation of the social science evidence, it's worth trying to figure out exactly what he was talking about. In a 2000 discussion on *CNN Talkback Live*, Thompson also discussed a study he attributed to Harvard University, but on that occasion, he said the study was conducted by Professor Deborah Yurgelun-Todd and released in June 1998 (Cable News Network 2000). In his 2005 book, Thompson again mentioned the "Harvard" study and Yurgelun-Todd. The book has endnotes, but they do not clearly identify the likely source of his information at the April 2003 committee meeting. One endnote refers to an interview with Professor Yurgelun-Todd on *Frontline* (Thompson 2005, 233). The second endnote says, in its entirety, "Based on a 1999 Harvard study at McLean Pediatric Hospital/ University of Massachusetts" (Thompson 2005, 233). The third endnote cites a paper called "Studying Functional Differences in the Adolescent Brain May Prove [sic] Evidence that the Nervous System Is Responsible for Behavior" (Thompson 2005, 233). This source, which has a promising title, turns out to be a paper posted online by a student as part of an undergraduate biology class at Bryn Mawr College (Powell 2004). A broken link in that paper refers to the work of Yurgelun-Todd (Powell 2004). So it's fairly clear that Thompson was relying on Yurgelun-Todd's research during his testimony in Washington.

Thompson's knowledge of Professor Yurgelun-Todd's study may have been limited to journalistic accounts, and these accounts may be all that are available about these particular experiments. Either way, they do not support Thompson's description of her study or the conclusions he drew from it. The "violent images" mentioned by Thompson were more likely images of faces expressing fear. Yurgelun-Todd's research questions were whether adolescent and adult participants could accurately identify the particular emotions represented in pictures of faces and what parts of the participants' brains would be activated by this task. The results showed differences in brain activity between adolescents (*n*=16) and adults (*n*=24). The adolescents were also less accurate in correctly identifying the emotions (Hotz 1998, B2; Landau 2000).[63] Yurgelun-Todd's conclusion was not that she had found proof that violent images in video games or any other forms of media become hardwired in adolescent brains. Her conclusion was far more modest. According to Yurgelun-Todd, her "results suggest that adolescents are more prone to react with 'gut instinct' when they process emotions, but as they mature into early adulthood, they are able to temper their instinctive 'gut reaction' response with rational, reasoned responses" (Hotz 1998, B2).

No one on the committee gave any indication of knowing anything about Yurgelun-Todd's study or Thompson's other two sources, beyond what Thompson said at the hearing. Thompson's comments might have prompted the committee to invite experts on brain activity to testify, but there is no indication that the committee did so. On one of the critical questions before the legislature, the members of the committee were willing to accept descriptions of these studies from an attorney specializing in lawsuits against the video game industry, and these descriptions were less detailed than what one would expect from a typical abstract in a journal article.

Although Representative Dickerson did not rely on Thompson's claims when she explained H.B. 1009 in the Washington House, Thompson's testimony about the Harvard study constituted the bulk of the scientific evidence discussed on the floor of the Washington Senate. On April 17, 2003, the Senate spent about 53 minutes on the bill. The proceedings began with a reading of Section 1 of the bill, which referred to a finding on the part of the legislature "that there has been an increase in studies showing a correlation between exposure to violent video and computer games and various forms of hostile and antisocial behavior" (Washington 2003f). There was only one other explicit reference to the scientific research during the proceedings. After spending a little under 40 minutes on several proposed amendments, the Senate turned to the final discussion of the bill. Senator Jim Hargrove, who was a member of the committee that heard Thompson's testimony, spoke first. Senator Hargrove said,

> We had some testimony in committee that was very compelling. Not only does seeing some of these video games really strike you, but we had some testimony about a research study at Harvard University that suggested that adolescents process these violent images in a different part of their brain than adults do, and that in fact, it can have a significant impact on how, we, these kids perceive that violence and how maybe they act that violence out. (Washington 2003f)

Hearing this, a person unfamiliar with the earlier proceedings might think the committee carefully assessed this study. In reality, the committee knew about as much as the full Senate. Indeed, the full Senate may have been better informed than the committee because Senator Hargrove omitted Thompson's unwarranted conclusions about the study. In this case, hearing less about the social science was probably better than hearing more.

Unlike the Washington legislature, the Illinois legislature heard testimony from someone with significantly more expertise in the social science literature, Dr. Michael Rich. At the time, he was the director of the Center on Media and Child Health, a practitioner at Children's Hospital Boston, and a faculty member at Harvard Medical School. On March 9, 2005, the Illinois House Judiciary I—Civil Law Committee heard testimony related to H.B. 4023 from several witnesses. The committee allotted 15 minutes for each side followed by 30 minutes for questions. Dr. Rich received the full 15 minutes allotted for the supporters of H.B. 4023, and he read from prepared remarks until his time ran out. While he provided what was probably the most detailed overview of the media violence literature presented at any of the events in Table 5.2, he still provided only an overview, one equivalent to a very short literature review. He explained, "Hundreds of studies have nearly unanimously shown that simply watching violent behaviors can cause increased anxiety and fear, desensitization to violence, and aggressive thoughts and behaviors in viewers" (Illinois 2005a). He referenced one of the common ways of operationalizing aggression in media violence experiments, that of subjects punishing opponents in a competitive task, but he did not explain this method and it seems unlikely the committee members were familiar with it. He also briefly explained the use of functional MRI (fMRI) brain scans to study the effects of violent media on the brain by a colleague from the Center on Media and Child Health, Children's Hospital Boston, and Harvard Medical School. As Rich ran short on time, he had to skip some of his prepared remarks, including his comment about E- and T-rated games containing violence (Illinois 2005a; Rich 2005, 5).

Dr. Rich's discussion of the fMRI study was a noteworthy part of his testimony because it came up later on the House floor. His comments were a simplification of a study published a year after the hearing (Murray et al. 2006). He explained the study as follows:

> Pilot data—and we have handouts for you if you'd like on this—indicate that unique areas of a child's brain are activated with violence—primitive areas on the right side of the brain which is focused on processing negative material. When viewing violence, the amygdala, our "fight or flight" center . . . and motor planning are activated. To our surprise and our concern, what was also activated was the posterior cingulate, which is the brain area that is activated in post-traumatic stress disorder survivors when they relive their traumas. This is an area of long-term, permanent memory encoding, the "survivor's ROM" if you will, and this explains why we see increasing aggressiveness as a cumulative effect of to [sic] increased exposure to violence in media. (Illinois 2005(a); cf. Rich 2005, 3–4)

During the debate on the Illinois House floor, Representative Linda Chapa LaVia mentioned a "Harvard" study and was asked by another representative about the study's findings (Illinois 2005b, 21, 42). It's not completely clear what study Chapa LaVia was referring to because she did not mention any publication details, including the author or authors. As in the Washington legislature, any association whatsoever between a study and Harvard is apparently sufficient to make Harvard the institutional author of the study, but it is very likely she was referring to the study summarized by Rich.

With the assumption that Representative Chapa LaVia was referring to the study discussed by Dr. Rich, as appears to be the case, her summary of Rich's summary was as follows:

> On the findings that they had done from twel . . . 2- to 17-year olds, it showed that their pattom. . . pattern of aggressive behavior when watching video games went up. It showed the detection of the different colors of the brainwaves when they were taking in this information. And it . . . it indicated three areas. It indicated like I said earlier, flight or fight, the . . . the adrenaline rush. And then third, which really worries me, because being a Army officer and going through programs that I'm trained to kill, take people into war, bring 'em back but know the difference between right and wrong as opposed to these under 18 individuals which. . . which might not because their brain is still developing. But it showed that there was post-trauma effect on the brain. The children would keep on reliving these games as if they were playing them. And they've been playing them constantly. So, the . . . the stats showed how long the length of time they were playing the games, how it affected the brain and a . . . a great deal of data. (Illinois 2005b, 42–43)[64]

Dr. Rich's translation simplified the study for the committee. Representative Chapa LaVia's translation did not simplify it for the Illinois House. Her summary was almost incomprehensible, unless one reads it right alongside Rich's comments above. One thing she did make clear is that the study supported her bill, but she failed to note that the study was based on pilot or preliminary data. The representative who asked Chapa LaVia about the study's findings did not ask her to clarify her muddled summary of the research, but as another example of floor discussions suggesting deference to the more detailed work purportedly done elsewhere, he did ask Chapa LaVia if she and her staff reviewed the study when drafting the bill and if the study affected the language of the bill. She answered "yes" to both questions without elaborating (Illinois 2005b, 43).

While Dr. Rich provided a much better introduction to the media violence literature than Grossman and Thompson, it was largely uncritical. He "confess[ed]" a problem with "research designs that have lagged behind the advancements in game technology" and said that early video game studies "met with wide ranging criticism and conclusions of some scholars that their findings may be un—inconclusive [sic]" (Illinois 2005a; cf. Rich 2005, 3), but he did not

offer details about these problems or how the problems were potentially overcome. Despite Dr. Rich's very general introduction to the topic, there were few
questions after his presentation. These questions did not probe the details of the
media violence literature, but there was no time for that anyway. Representative
John Fritchey, the committee chair, asked the only questions, such as whether
adults are affected in the same way as children and whether video games are
related to suicide. He also asked for copies of any data or studies supporting
Rich's testimony. At the very end of the hearing, after all of the witnesses had
testified, Fritchey added that it was "imperative" to get copies of these materials into the record, stating that it could be the "underpinning" for the bill to
survive a legal challenge (Illinois 2005a). Fritchey didn't say whether he would
read them, but it seems unlikely. Plus, the person who could have assisted the
committee members with understanding the studies was already done testifying.
As in other states, legislators were interested in conclusions from authoritative
sources that could be added to the record, not explanations of how these sources
reached their conclusions. Of the 17 items in the "scholarship" category of the
legislature's record (*Entertainment Software Association v. Blagojevich* Oct. 7,
2005, 7–8), it is plausible that no member of the legislature read any of them.

In contrast to the committees in Washington and Illinois, the committee
in Michigan initially appeared like it would seriously engage the social science
literature. On April 26, 2005, the Senate Judiciary Committee held a hearing on S.B. 416 (2005) and other bills. The committee first heard testimony
from Professor Kevin Saunders of Michigan State University College of Law.
Professor Saunders has written extensively on the topic of media violence and
the law (e.g., Saunders 1996, 2003a), and the chair of the committee introduced
him as an expert. Saunders spent about 18 minutes reading from a prepared
statement that provided an overview of the legal issues and an overview of the
social science research on media violence generally and on video game violence
specifically. At the start of his discussion of the social science, Saunders said
that he was providing only a starting point for the committee (Michigan 2005a,
Tape 1, Side A). In the comments that follow, the non-italicized text matches
his prepared remarks (with only two trivial exceptions), and the italicized text
represents his ad-libbed additions. He said:

> There is a long history of research on the effects of violent media on chil-
> dren. I'm not a social scientist but I have studied the results and as a former
> teacher of statistics do have some understanding of the field. *As I told
> majority counsel, I'm not a social scientist, but I play one before legislative
> committees.* I will try to discuss the results with the aim of providing direc-
> tion for you in developing a record to justify your proposed statute. *That
> is, you don't rely on me for what I say, but go to those studies, and I'll give you
> guidance in terms of what studies to look for.* (Michigan 2005a, Tape 1, Side
> A; Saunders 2005, 3–4)

The ad-libbed comments show Saunders' emphasis on the additional work the committee needed to do.

After offering the caveat about not being a social scientist, Saunders provided a summary of the findings of media violence researchers, including the finding that there is a causal link between media violence and real-world aggression and violence. He also briefly addressed a problem that occurred in both legislatures and courts, specifically, misunderstanding the relationship between correlational evidence and causal evidence and misunderstanding the nature of the causal claim made by media violence researchers. Researchers do not claim that *everyone* exposed to media violence will behave aggressively any more than researchers claim that everyone who smokes will get lung cancer. They instead claim media violence may cause aggression, just as smoking may cause cancer. Saunders also referenced two studies coauthored by Professor Craig Anderson, including a meta-analysis (Bushman and Anderson 2001), and he summarized Dave Grossman's argument. Lastly, he summarized the constitutional challenges the bill would face (Michigan 2005a, Tape 1, Side A).

As Saunders himself said, his testimony was only a starting point. Much more could have been said about several points he made. For example, he referenced claims about the link between media violence and real-world violence, but this claim requires extensive elaboration. As Joanne Savage explained in an academic article the year before the Michigan hearings, few studies look at criminal aggression (Savage 2004, 101). Even media violence researchers who question Savage's analysis concede that "although we believe that exposure to violence does cause increases in crime, the overall conclusion that it is unproven to date is probably fair" (Huesmann and Kirwil 2007, 555). Additionally, Saunders did not address how media violence researchers define and operationalize violence and aggression, a critical point for assessing the literature.

The Q&A after Saunders' presentation lasted about an additional 18 minutes. Part of the discussion was about how the committee should proceed to build the legislative record. Senator Mark Schauer began by stating that Saunders had "made the case that we can't wait" to enact legislation (Michigan 2005a, Tape 1, Side A). Senator Alan Sanborn said Saunders gave him "the data to prove what I knew all along when it comes to kids: garbage in, garbage out" (Michigan 2005a, Tape 1, Side B). However, Senator Alan Cropsey, the chair of the committee, was particularly concerned about laying a foundation for legislative action. He asked Saunders about what legislative "groundwork" was needed to make the legislation more likely to survive a constitutional challenge (Michigan 2005a, Tape 1, Side B). Saunders responded that the legislature needed to make findings of fact and suggested putting citations to studies into the record. The problem, as already indicated, is that lists of citations, without more, are no more than a legislative formality. Saunders initially emphasized the greater importance of building a trial record when the litigation occurs, but he also recommended that the committee contact the leading social scientist in the area, presumably referring to Professor Craig Anderson (Michigan 2005a, Tape 1, Side B). Senator Cropsey responded by emphasizing the importance of the legislative record:

> Whenever we work with First Amendment issues, it seems like having a legislative record is extremely important—or can be extremely important—to make sure that not only are we doing the right thing as far as the legislature is concerned, but then laying the legal groundwork and framework for when it's challenged in court, that the courts understood that the legislature made some, made some consideration of the current social studies findings into these areas and that therefore they were, they were grounded in fact or in science as best we can determine at that time. (Michigan 2005a, Tape 1, Side B)

Saunders agreed with this assessment.

After completing the Q&A with Professor Saunders, Senator Cropsey noted that he had scheduled a second meeting to consider the social science, but not all the committee members thought it necessary. Cropsey believed that the committee should have some studies in its possession before passing the bill out of committee. He suggested at one point that maybe only the committee staff needed to look at the studies, but he left this particular question unresolved. While Senator Schauer was open to the legislature hearing additional testimony, perhaps on the House side, he did not think that he personally needed to hear any additional testimony. He had seen clips of some games on videotape, and he mentioned *Grand Theft Auto: San Andreas* by name. He described the games as "disgusting" and "very realistic" in their violence (Michigan 2005a, Tape 1, Side B). Other committee members, however, wanted more information, and they wanted the committee to build a more detailed record. More than one committee member noted that Professor Saunders had urged them to do so.[65] After hearing from two more witnesses, a representative of the Michigan Family Forum in support of the bill and a game developer in opposition to it, the committee voted to hold the bill over for a second hearing (Michigan 2005a, Tape 2, Side A).

On May 10, 2005, the Senate Judiciary Committee held its second hearing on video game violence, again including S.B. 416 and some related bills. As with other hearings, the committee's discussion was not confined only to the social science. Over the course of about two hours, the committee heard testimony from five witnesses, the president of the Interactive Entertainment Merchants Association, a sheriff representing the Michigan Sheriff's Association, a representative of the Entertainment Software Association, an attorney from Jenner & Block representing the Entertainment Software Association, and finally, Professor Craig Anderson of Iowa State University.

Prior to Anderson's testimony, some witnesses made general comments about the social science research, including Hal Halpin, the president of the

Interactive Entertainment Merchants Association. During a testy exchange with an exasperated Senator Cropsey, Halpin claimed that the social science was inconclusive about the effects of violent video games on children, but none of his comments were specific enough to confidently say Halpin had ever read any studies. What follows is the end of their exchange:

> Senator Cropsey: "You know, I have got study after study after study after article after article after article talking about violent videos and they're coming to the, the conclusion is that violent videos show aggression in children and that the causal link is there now—that it's just, it's just overwhelming as far as violence in the media, violence in videos, violence on TV. And what you're saying is, you're saying, no, just throw those studies away, but yet you cannot cite me one study that says otherwise."
>
> Halpin: "I believe that there are studies that say things both ways and that we would welcome seeing a study where, you know, it was comprehensive and objective on a nationwide basis in order to, to have an, the answer to that question." (Michigan 2005b, Tape 1, Side A)

Setting aside whether Cropsey or Halpin was correct about what conclusion to draw from the literature, the takeaway from this exchange is that it is not productive to have these discussions with people who have not read the studies and who therefore cannot explain with any specificity why the studies support one conclusion or another. While Halpin was qualified to speak to some relevant issues before the committee, such as whether retailers were enforcing the ratings at the point of sale, he was not qualified to speak about the social science. The committee needed to hear from people knowledgeable about the research, preferably representing a range of views. While the committee did not hear from experts with a range of views, it did hear from one expert very qualified to speak on the topic.

Professor Craig Anderson of the Psychology Department at Iowa State University has published extensively on the effects of video game violence (e.g., Anderson, Gentile, and Buckley 2007), and as Senator Cropsey correctly noted, Anderson is one of the most prominent researchers on the effects of video game violence. Anderson was the last person to testify at the hearing, but he was not physically present, instead participating by speaker phone. Senator Cropsey asked Anderson to provide a "brief" background on himself and his work on media violence (Michigan 2005b, Tape 2, Side A). After providing some background, Anderson read, with some minor deviations, the first paragraph from the summary of a 2003 literature review he coauthored:

> Research on violent television and films, video game[s], and music reveals unequivocal evidence that media violence increases the likelihood of aggressive and violent behavior in both immediate and long-term contexts.

The effects appear larger for milder than for more severe forms of aggression, but the effects on severe forms of violence are also substantial when compared with effects of other violence risk factors or medical effects deemed important by the medical community (for example, the effect of aspirin on heart attacks). The research base is large; diverse in methods, samples, and media genres; and consistent in overall findings. The evidence is clearest within the most extensively researched domain, television and film violence. The growing body of video-game research yields essentially the same conclusions. (Michigan 2005b, Tape 2, Side A; Anderson et al. 2003, 81)[66]

This summary of the literature did not go much further than the overviews of the literature offered by others at various times in other states,[67] but it was the brief summary requested by the committee. Anderson then asked what "more detailed information" the committee wanted (Michigan 2005b, Tape 2, Side A).

The committee members asked only three follow-up questions of Anderson. Senator Cropsey asked two; Senator Schauer asked one. Cropsey, who said he had read one or more studies, asked if the relationship between media violence is correlational or causal. Anderson explained the confusion that often results over this question among people with different backgrounds. Like Professor Saunders, Anderson briefly explained that media violence researchers are making a claim similar to the one made about smoking. He said, "The evidence is that, in general, exposure to violent media causes an increase in the likelihood of aggressive behavior in a future situation" (Michigan 2005b, Tape 2, Side A). Anderson also volunteered some information about the relationship of the media violence literature generally to the video game violence literature. He noted that while there were longitudinal studies on the effects of television violence, there was a lack of published longitudinal studies at the time on video game violence. However, he mentioned the existence of laboratory experiments and correlational studies about video game violence effects. In response to a follow-up question from Senator Cropsey, he explained that media violence researchers are basically in agreement about their conclusions and explained the value of meta-analyses for establishing the meaning of a large number of studies. Senator Schauer also asked one question about whether brain studies show that children are more likely to be affected by media violence than adults. Anderson responded that he was not an expert in brain development and was reluctant to make claims in this area, but he did note that there was some research suggesting modest age differences (Michigan 2005b, Tape 2, Side A).

Anderson's short presentation and Q&A with the committee involved relevant information, but Anderson was largely clarifying some of the basic *conclusions* of the media violence literature. The committee did not get into the details necessary to make a serious assessment of the literature, including how media violence researchers define and operationalize both violence and aggression.

For example, the Michigan bill targeted "ultra-violent explicit video games," defined in such a way that even many M-rated games probably would not qualify (*Entertainment Software Association v. Granholm* 2006, 648–649). No one on the committee explained the bill's definition of violent games to Anderson or asked him if the bill's approach to violent games matched the social science literature's approach to violent games. Graphicness is only one of several contextual features of violence that could increase or decrease the potential effects of violence (Potter 2003, 140–152), and as Anderson explained during his testimony before the Northern District of Illinois in November 2005 (more on this below), the research findings about the effects of various contextual features on players are weaker than the "basic findings" in the literature (*Entertainment Software Association v. Blagojevich* November 15, 2005, 348). Perhaps the primary basic finding is that "media violence (broadly defined) causes aggression (broadly defined)" (Ford 2013, 324), but as recently as 2008, one article noted, "Researchers have not yet answered a simple question: What *kinds* of violent video games are problematic for children?" (Shibuya et al. 2008, 528 (emphasis added)).

Anderson participated in the hearing for only about 15 minutes, hardly enough time to get into any details. The fault was not with Anderson. There was no evidence that the committee members would have participated in a multi-hour symposium on the topic. The fault was with the committee who thought they could make a "finding of fact" about the substantial social science literature in 15 minutes (or slightly longer if the time Saunders spent discussing the social science is added to Anderson's time). A single meeting of a graduate-level seminar would involve a more detailed and critical analysis of the literature than what occurred at this committee meeting. Furthermore, no one knowledgeable offered any alternative viewpoints. The presence of multiple experts explaining areas of agreement and disagreement could have at least alerted the committee to how little they knew. Of course, whether the committee would have had an incentive to act on their lack of knowledge, if confronted with it, is another question. Toward the end of the hearing, Senator Elizabeth Brater suggested that she was still unsure or confused about the causal relationship between media violence and aggression and that more testimony was needed. Notably, she said she appreciated *how much* time had been devoted to the topic, but she said she still could not vote in favor of S.B. 416 without more testimony. The committee did not schedule additional time for more testimony, however. The committee was done. It approved the bill (Michigan 2005b, Tape 2, Side A).

Two days after the committee hearing, on May 12, 2005, Senator Cropsey offered his description of the committee's efforts and a summary of the social science on the floor of the Michigan Senate. He recognized that the legislature needed to "lay the basis for this legislation" for it to satisfy the courts, and he claimed the committee had done the necessary investigation into the social science: "As promised, the Judiciary Committee has done its homework. We have exercised due diligence" (Michigan 2005c). He said he had personally read many peer-reviewed studies and brought at least 40 to the chamber for other legislators to examine, should they care to do so. He spent about 15 minutes summarizing the media violence and video game violence literature, but he did so in very general terms. He did not explain how the various studies defined or operationalized violence or whether the studies supported the definitions used in S.B. 416.[68] While Senator Brater offered a brief explanation for her vote against the bill, claiming that it was a content-based restriction on speech that would be struck down by the courts, there was no debate about the social science (Michigan 2005c). A casual observer of the floor session might be concerned about the lack of debate,[69] but based on the statements of Senator Cropsey, he or she might still conclude that the Senate Judiciary Committee had engaged in a serious study of the social science. The casual observer would probably not think the committee had heard from only one media violence researcher and for only about 15 minutes.

As the last example with the four major witnesses, Jack Thompson testified in Louisiana in support of H.B. 1381, about three years after his appearance in Washington. According to the primary author of the bill, Thompson assisted with the drafting of the bill (Louisiana 2006a). Thompson apparently testified before committees in both the Louisiana House and Senate, with one member of the House subsequently describing him as a "top expert in the country" on the House floor (Louisiana 2006a).[70] While I could not locate a recording of a committee hearing in the House, I was able to obtain the Senate hearing in audio form. Thompson testified before the Senate committee on May 30, 2006, speaking and taking questions for about 15 minutes (Louisiana 2006b).

Between the time of his testimony in Washington and the time of his testimony in Louisiana, Thompson apparently changed his mind about some things. In Washington, Thompson said there was no constitutional problem with H.B. 1009. He called it a "wonderful, brilliant bill" (Washington 2003d). By the time he testified in Louisiana, the courts in Washington, Illinois, California, and Michigan had either preliminarily or permanently enjoined the enforcement of these states' laws restricting minors' access to violent video games (*Video Software Dealers Association v. Maleng* 2004; *Entertainment Software Association v. Blagojevich* Dec. 2, 2005; *Video Software Dealers Association v. Schwarzenegger* 2005; *Entertainment Software Association v. Granholm* 2006). During his testimony before the Senate committee in Louisiana, Thompson was more critical of the other states' laws. He said, "There is a simple reason why they've been struck down: they've been unconstitutional" (Louisiana 2006b).

Thompson identified three problems with the laws in these other states. One was how they defined the restricted class of violent video games. Thompson said it was a mistake to try and define violence. The other two problems were with how the state attorneys general and the state legislatures dealt with the scientific evidence. He said the attorneys general had "not done their home-work" and had made a poor showing of the evidence to the courts (Louisiana 2006b). As for the legislatures, he said they failed to create a proper and thorough record of the scientific evidence of the harm caused by video games: "The evidence is there, but the legislatures have not considered it" (2006b).

After criticizing the legislatures in other states for their poor assessment of the social science, he proceeded to read from the July 26, 2000 Joint Statement issued by several medical organizations, which said that over 1000 studies show a causal link between media violence and aggression in children (American Academy of Pediatrics et al. 2000). He also mentioned a resolution of the American Psychological Association from 2005 that violent video games can cause aggression in children (American Psychological Association 2005). He very briefly mentioned a Stanford study (it's not clear which one) and brain studies from several universities, including one from Harvard. The committee chair interrupted Thompson more than once as Thompson tried to state the conclusions (though not the details) of these studies. The chair said time was short and the committee needed to move on to testimony from the bill's opponents. Although he had little time to even mention the studies during his testimony, Thompson seemed to think that adding some written materials to the official record would suffice to improve on what the legislatures in the other states had done.

Steve Duke of the Entertainment Software Association, one of the speakers opposing the bill in Louisiana, spent a few minutes responding to Thompson, even though he gave no evidence of having any background in the social sciences. Although no one—not even Jack Thompson—claimed video games are the sole cause of violence among children or anyone else, Duke argued that crime rates have not increased at the same rate as the increase in game sales; therefore, video games must not contribute to violent crime. Like opposition speakers at committee hearings in other states, Duke also ran through a list of several organizations that claimed the social science evidence does not warrant legislation restricting minors' access to violent video games or that point to other causes of violence among youth as more serious concerns than video games.[71] He also claimed that the courts reviewing legislation in other states had spent more time looking at the social science evidence than the committee in Louisiana, yet the courts were still not persuaded by it. At the end of the meeting, despite Duke's quite correct suggestion that the committee had spent too little time looking at the evidence, the chairperson said that the committee had held a "full hearing" and then took a vote, which went in favor of the bill (Louisiana 2006b).

As noted throughout the discussion, these five examples with Grossman, Thompson, Rich, and Anderson are not the only ones where someone referenced the social science, but with the exception of Kevin Saunders, the other witnesses offered very short and conclusory statements. Other than Saunders, few other witnesses exhibited any real qualifications to discuss the social science anyway. A possible exception is Mike Males, now a senior research fellow at the Center on Juvenile and Criminal Justice in San Francisco. He spoke against the legislation in California on April 13, 2004, but like the other three witnesses at that hearing, he was allotted only five minutes to speak, hardly enough time to say anything in detail about the social science literature (California 2004). Sherwin Cotler, a clinical psychologist who spoke in Washington on January 22, 2003, seemed to have some relevant background, but he spoke for only about six minutes and probably was not closely following the media violence research beyond what could be found in popular summaries of the literature. He recommended two books to the committee meeting, a book he studied in graduate school in the 1960s by Albert Bandura and *On Killing* by Dave Grossman (Washington 2003a).

5.8 Legislatures versus Courts Revisited

Professor Laycock's dim view of legislative fact-finding is largely applicable to the video game violence legislation. The legislatures did not perform well in translating the social science, but did they still do relatively better than the courts, as Justice Breyer thought they would? The judicial decisions dealing with the social science include some confusion about significant issues. The Eighth Circuit, for example, conflated the concepts of causation and certainty, assuming that talk of causation is only appropriate when the evidence of causation is certain (Ford 2013, 333–337). The Supreme Court's opinion also has some shortcomings in its approach to causal evidence, defining causal evidence much more narrowly than most scientists (Ford 2013, 344–347). And while the courts discussed specific studies more often the legislators, they were not particularly thorough: "One could easily skim over the citations to this literature in the lower courts' opinions and conclude that there are only a handful of media violence studies worth reading" (Ford 2013, 325). Nevertheless, the courts were more seriously engaged with the social science.

The trial before the US District Court for the Northern District of Illinois provides a striking contrast with the efforts of state legislatures. Judge Matthew Kennelly, the district court judge, was not particularly engaged with the video games *as games*—he found the games submitted to the court very difficult to play and instead relied on screenshots of the games (*Entertainment Software Association v. Blagojevich* November 16, 2006, 447)—but he was much more engaged with the social science evidence than any of the state legislators. Judge Kennelly spent parts of three days on a trial that was mainly about whether the social science was sufficient to justify Illinois' restriction on violent video games. The full transcript runs 489 pages. Critically, there were witnesses on both sides prepared to talk in detail about the social science, including Professor Craig Anderson, and someone was responsible for making sure that the other side's evidence was challenged. In the legislatures, no one had this obligation. As a result, the discussions before Judge Kennelly were far more detailed than any of the discussions with the witnesses at the legislative hearings, and Judge Kennelly interjected with additional questions as needed. The Senate Judiciary Committee in Michigan spent 15 minutes talking to Professor Anderson. Judge Kennelly likely spent well over two hours with him (as measured by the approximately 120 transcript pages devoted to Anderson's direct and cross-examination).

One could imagine improvements in the trial in Illinois, such as some additional experts and perhaps demonstrations of the research methods used by researchers, but the trial was in the ballpark as "an intense encounter with the evidence" (Burns 1999, 34; Burns 2009, 9). Nothing in the legislatures came close to an "intense encounter" with anything, much less the social science. The typical approach of legislators was to focus on the very general conclusions of the social science and to ignore the methodological issues. Legislators asked experts to translate the bottom line and not much more. Without serious attentiveness to the methodological issues, which require more time and greater assistance from the experts to understand, legislatures were at best counting studies. They were not seriously assessing the conclusions of the literature or the literature's relationship to proposed bills. And even if the goal was just to count studies, it turns out Justice Breyer was better at even this limited approach to the evidence.

Even without the benefit of a trial, at least some courts were attentive to basic issues the legislatures missed. The district court in Washington, for example, took note of the mismatch between the social science and the state's ostensible goal of preventing access only to video games featuring violence against law enforcement. No social science research addresses this particular context for violence.[72] The Supreme Court in *Brown* similarly identified a severe mismatch between California's narrow definition of violence and the social science literature's broad definition (Ford 2013, 347–348). An evaluation of the match between the definitions of violence in the social science research with the definitions in the legislation was almost entirely missing in the state legislatures.[73]

5.9 Conclusion

Legislatures may be capable of serious work, but little serious work occurred in the states that enacted restrictions on minors' access to violent video games. Professor Emily Hammond Meazell suggests that at least in some situations, "a court might consider whether, *and the extent to which*, a legislature actually considered the scientific issue" (Meazell 2009, 283) (emphasis added). To the extent it matters to a court how well a legislature considered the social science evidence when passing a law, this chapter suggests courts should not assume a legislature was careful and thorough. Admittedly, whether the present example is typical awaits future research. The video game violence bills passed in each of the seven state legislatures with substantial majorities. This fact may have deterred the opponents in the legislature from putting more effort into the process. However, supporters had a clear incentive to prepare a legislative record that would support the expected lawsuits, yet these records appear to be mostly bibliographies of unread articles—and not particularly good bibliographies at that.[74] Contrary to Justice Breyer's assertions (and to a lesser extent Justice Alito's), second-guessing the legislature appears to be quite justified, at least when constitutional rights are at stake. While courts, like legislatures, face serious challenges in dealing with social science evidence (and scientific evidence generally), courts may have an edge over the legislatures in fact-finding based on social science evidence. Courts may be hit-and-miss when it comes to dealing with social science evidence, especially in the absence of a trial, but in the present study, the legislatures were all misses and no hits.

Notes

1. In the healthcare field, "knowledge translation" may refer both to the communication of knowledge *and* to its implementation. What I am calling "translation" might instead be called "knowledge exchange" in that literature because I am focusing more on communication than implementation (Rabin & Brownson 2012, 28). I note this because researchers in the healthcare field appear to have thought about the problem of translating science into policy more than researchers in other fields.

2. Senator Linda Scheid of Minnesota used this particular phrase about a "gut feeling" (Minnesota 2003), but other legislators expressed this sentiment in different words, such as Assembly Member Paul Koretz of California. Koretz said, "[E]ven if there aren't the studies yet, I think it's, it's very clear, it's very intuitive" that violent video games lead to violence (California 2005a).

3. Representative Jeff Johnson, the primary sponsor of S.F. 785 in the Minnesota House of Representatives, said he didn't think anyone would actually be fined under the Minnesota law, but he thought the signs in the stores threatening enforcement would cause "some of the painfully oblivious parents in this state" to more carefully evaluate the games they allow their children to play (Minnesota 2006b). Senator Dan Swecker of Washington is an example of someone who wanted to "send a serious message" to the industry to "get its act together" (Washington 2003f).

4. A candidate for a pre-1970s game that surely could have provoked controversy is the explicitly anti-Semitic board game *Juden Raus!*, which was published in Germany in 1938 (Morris-Friedman & Schädler 2003). This obscure game may not have been known in the United States at the time, however.

5. Senator Byron Dorgan incorrectly described *Night Trap* as a game in which the players are trying to trap and kill the women at the slumber party (National Cable Satellite 1993). The goal of the game is to *save* the women.

6. Although there is no industry ratings system for board games, some do include mature or adult content. An example is *Spartacus: A Game of Blood and Treachery* (Kovaleski, Sweigart, and Dill 2012), which is based on the television series of the same name. The box top warns of "Mature Content" and further says, "Recommended for Ages 17+."

7. The accuracy of the ratings was one of several subjects discussed in the state legislatures, but the quality of the discussion was poor. For example, after briefly describing some of the violent possibilities in *Grand Theft Auto: Vice City*, Cristal Downing, a witness at the January 22, 2003 committee meeting in Washington, said: "The labels on the back of the box seem to be sugar-coated on just how graphic the violence really is. They misrepresent to parents what the game is really about, so that parents in all reality don't know what type of game that they are buying for their kids" (Washington 2003a). She did not elaborate on just what appears on the *Vice City* packaging and no one at the committee meeting asked her to elaborate on this or any other example, but her comments are not consistent with the information contained on the three versions of *Vice City* I examined. The content descriptors Blood and Gore, Violence, Strong Language, and Strong Sexual Content are included on the case for the PlayStation 2 version of *Vice City* and on the box for the PC version. The Xbox version of *Vice City* is missing the content descriptors on the case itself, but this version came in a two-game double-pack along with *Grand Theft Auto III*, and the same four descriptors appeared on the exterior box that originally held both games when sold at retail. Representative Jim McIntire of Washington, a supporter of H.B. 1009, mentioned on the House floor that he had purchased M-rated games for his teenage children and that the descriptors on the box provide useful information (Washington 2003c), but he did not discuss specific examples.

8. The most prominent example of a game earning an AO rating for violence is *Manhunt 2* (Rockstar 2007). Rockstar subsequently revised the *PlayStation 2* version of the game to earn an M rating (Snider 2007a, 2007b).

9. References to games in the *Grand Theft Auto* series are frequent, but it's not always clear which particular game in the series someone was referring to.

10. *Duke Nukem 3D* is visible on the videotape played during two hearings and was also mentioned by Representative Dickerson (Washington 1999a, 1999b).

11. *Mortal Kombat 4* is visible on the videotape played during two hearings (Washington 1999a, 1999b).

12. Representative Jeff Johnson mentioned *Clock Tower 3* and *Manhunt* during the April 4, 2006 hearing in Minnesota (Minnesota 2006a). As noted by one reviewer, *Clock Tower 3* includes "[w]atching (yes, watching) a 15-year-old girl get killed with a sledgehammer" (Dudlak 2003, 74).

13. Regarding the enforcement of the ratings at retail, Hal Halpin, the President of the Interactive Entertainment Merchants Association (IEMA), said that the members of his organization took "very seriously" the need to prevent minors from purchasing M-rated games. Yet over half of the IEMA's members had only just started carding purchasers of M-rated games in December 2004, a decade after the formation of the ESRB. Moreover, Halpin said that by preventing underage purchasers from buying or renting M-rated games only 66% of the time, these retailers had "seen and met their social obligations" (Michigan 2005b).

14. When introducing her bill on the House floor in Washington, for example, Representative Mary Lou Dickerson said, "Alarm bells were raised about the effects of video game violence when children were involved as the shooters in school killings in Columbine, Jonesboro, and Paducah. We knew then that these games were bad news for some of our children" (Washington 2003c).

15. Representative Dickerson not only worked on the issue for several years, but she also raised money to print 100,000 copies of a booklet to educate parents about video

games (Washington 2003d). Assembly Member Yee was described in *The New York Times* as someone "who has long called for legislation to curb the sales of video games to children" (Lohr 2005, C3). On the day the Minnesota legislature passed S.F. 785, Senator Sandra Pappas said she had been trying to get a bill passed for six years (Minnesota 2006c).

16. *Infamous 2* (Sony Computer Entertainment America 2011), for example, is a T-rated game in which the player can attack and kill law enforcement officers. (The earliest opportunity to do this probably occurs after the completion of the "Good Samaritan" side mission. The three officers who are present after the completion of this mission do not fight back, but a player can attack and kill them, despite it serving no purpose in the game to do so.) But is the violence in *Infamous 2* "realistic" as required by the statute? The problem is that the meaning of "realistic" could refer to the realism of the illustration of a human or to the realism of the situation. The graphics in *Infamous 2* are more realistic than the graphics in *Grand Theft Auto: Vice City*, a game that Dickerson was clearly targeting with her bill, but the storyline in *Infamous 2*, which involves a super-powered human, is less realistic. Even E-rated games could have been a problem under the statute. For example, players can attack the police with Godzilla-like monsters in the E-rated game *Rampage: Total Destruction* (Midway Amusement Games 2006). Despite the unrealistic premise and the need to illustrate the police and other humans as very small relative to the size of the screen (to make more room for the monsters), the police are still realistic in their appearance. Retailers might have had to worry about games of every rating.

17. Senator Alan Sanborn described the Michigan bill as "fantastic politic[s]," though he added that he wanted it to be "fantastic policy" too (Michigan 2005a, Tape 1, Side B).

18. At the same hearing where Representative Dickerson said video games deserve no First Amendment protection, the Executive Director of the Washington Council of Police and Sheriffs challenged the message of some unnamed game or games, calling them "an affront to every police officer who ever gave their life for their profession" (Washington 2003a). Presumably, he was thinking of the *Grand Theft Auto* series because of the well-known ability to attack police officers in that game. This description of a message, even one of disrespect for the police, supports the games' claim for First Amendment protection, yet Representative Dickerson did not challenge this particular description.

19. The May 10, 2005 minutes of the Michigan Senate Judiciary Committee list 45 studies put into the record by Senator Alan Cropsey (Michigan Senate Judiciary Committee 2005, 1–4). The number 55, however, is reported in one of the case filings (*Entertainment Software Association v. Granholm*, Defendants' Motion in Opposition to Plaintiffs' Motion for Summary Judgment and Defendants' Cross Motion for Summary Judgment 2006, 18). This same filing also refers to "hundred [sic] of meta-studies" in the record. Presumably, the meaning is that other studies beyond the 55 are represented through the inclusion of the meta-studies.

20. Senator Michael Bishop of Michigan made this comment.

21. This comment by Senator Jim Hargrove is discussed at greater length in the section below about Jack Thompson's testimony before the Washington Senate.

22. There are minutes for a meeting of the Illinois Task Force that would be useful for the present discussion, but I was not able to obtain a copy.

23. One of the speakers at this committee meeting in California was Professor Kevin Saunders, a key speaker at the Michigan Senate Judiciary Committee meeting on April 26, 2005 (Michigan 2005a).

24. The extent of Oklahoma's engagement with the social science is not clear. I found recordings of floor sessions for Oklahoma, but not committee meetings. Little was said on the floor about the social science. According to the US District Court for the Western District of Oklahoma, which found Oklahoma's law unconstitutional, there was "a complete dearth of legislative findings, scientific studies, or other rationale in the record to support the passage of the Act." The court said Oklahoma instead relied on "common sense" (*Entertainment Merchants Association v. Henry* 2007, 17), yet during a floor session, a member of the Oklahoma House of Representatives referenced an "interim study" and a doctor providing some testimony (Oklahoma 2006a). (The doctor referenced during the floor session was probably Eric Dlugokinski. According to Dlugokinski, he testified before the Health and Human Services Committee in the Oklahoma House (Dlugokinski 2006). Also, a purported expert on video game violence named Dave Grossman, who receives more attention below, spoke to Oklahoma legislators in 2001. Oklahoma apparently tried to do *something* with the social science evidence, but based on what little was said on the floor and especially what the district court said, whatever was done in Oklahoma apparently did not make much of a mark on the legislative process.

25. Referring to video games as "videos" is common throughout the various legislative events. Louisiana Representative Kay Katz even called games "films" (Louisiana 2006a). Representative Terry Parke used the term "game" at first but then switched to calling them films: "I'm looking at a sheet having game ratings and decipher . . . decipher (sic–descriptor) guide. How does these ratings get put on these films?" (Illinois 2005f, 68).

26. Senator Val Stevens asked witness Tom Paine, who testified on behalf of the Video Software Dealers Association, "Do you watch these games?" (Washington 2003d). Senator Kathleen Wojcik of Illinois said she "was rather horrified to realize that young people were watching these [games]" (Illinois 2005c, 127).

27. Similarly, a high school student with some game-playing experience testified in Washington. Apparently, she had not played the games in the *Grand Theft Auto* series, but based on what she had heard from friends, she briefly talked about the content of these games. Afterwards, the chair thanked her for sharing her "first-hand knowledge" (Washington 2003d).

28. During the floor session in the California Senate, Senator Sheila James Kuehl said, "[W]e don't have the facilities, nor do I want to take your time to show you one or two of these video games, but they include decapitation, dismemberment, all kinds of mayhem, rape, and of course murder" (California 2005b).

29. The recording of the March 5, 2003 committee meeting in Minnesota starts with the meeting already in progress and with the video game clips already playing. The length of this particular viewing is therefore not clear, but only about 30 seconds appear in the recording, including some time devoted to Senator Lieberman speaking (Minnesota 2003).

30. The games appear to be *Quake 2* (Id Software 1997) and *Mortal Kombat 4* (Midway Games 1997).

31. As the TV was facing away from the camera, only the audio can be heard in the recording. The video clips sound like ones assembled by the National Institute on Media and Family and available on a DVD entitled *Sex, Murder, and Video Games* (National Institute on Media and Family 2003).

32. This point about not being allowed to play a videotape with clips was made during the testimony of James Steyer, the CEO of Common Sense Media (California 2005a). During a subsequent discussion on the floor of the California Assembly, Assembly Member

Dave Jones implied that the Assembly Judiciary Committee viewed (at least) ten minutes of game footage (California 2005c), which, if correct, would make it the longest of the legislative viewings described here.

33. Representative Mary Lou Dickerson said she showed clips to some senators the day before the April 1, 2003 committee meeting (Washington 2003d). Representative Linda Chapa LaVia said that she e-mailed clips from five games to other members on the morning of the Illinois House floor session (Illinois 2005b, 81). Assembly Member Rick Keene said on the floor of the California Assembly, "We, in this body, have had the chance to look at the data, to look, to sit there, to look what's really on some of these things" (California 2005c).

34. Representative Anthony Sertich of Minnesota, for example, described himself as being in the target market for video games, something he thought other members might not realize. He also mentioned that he was carded when he last purchased a violent video game (Minnesota 2006b). Representative Chapin Rose of Illinois said he played games in the *Madden* series throughout college (Illinois 2005b, 65).

35. Representative Jim Clements predicted on the Washington House floor that the "debate would have ended tonight if we'd locked this place down and made everybody watch one of, watch two or three of those videos on the screen, and you would not have anything to discuss because they're disgusting" (Washington 2003c). Representative Linda Chapa LaVia said on the Illinois House floor that members needed to watch the clips she circulated because "a lot of us have never ... haven't picked up a video game since *Pac Man*" (Illinois 2005b, 81). Representative Monique Davis said she saw some games at a press conference with Governor Rod Blagojevich, but speculated on the Illinois House floor that most other members had not seen relevant examples of games: "But I think what most of us in here are not aware of is what some of these games contain" (Illinois 2005f, 71).

36. Senator Stephen Johnson said, "Many of the examples given of these games, which I have never seen by the way, involve violence not just with law enforcement officers but with women, children, all sorts of gruesome things" (Washington 2003f).

37. Senator Mady Reiter of Minnesota said she did not watch "most" of what was shown at the committee meeting (Minnesota March 5, 2003). Senator Rosa Franklin of Washington said on the Senate floor, "You've seen them, but I would not look at them" (Washington 2003f).

38. Representative Jeff Johnson offered a surprising comparison between video games and slasher films: "We're not talking about R-rated slasher movies here. We're not talking about cops and robbers. We're talking about absolutely disgusting stuff, in at least in some of these games" (Minnesota 2006b). Contrary to Johnson's suggestion, the slasher genre of films is extremely violent, and to the extent the discussion about violent video games emphasized violence against women, his comparison is particularly odd. While the killers in slasher films often leave behind a trail of both male and female victims, there is often an emphasis on the female ones. As Professor Stephen Prince explains, "The imagery of victims dismembered by spikes, axes, chain saws, or power drills, or run through meat grinders evoked a swift and stern backlash from critics, especially feminist scholars, who pointed out that a basic slasher film premise was a male killer stalking and slaughtering female victims" (Prince 2000, 16).

39. Larry Pederson was the witness who made these comments. He identified himself as the Advocacy Coordinator for the State Coalition of Community Public Health and Safety Networks (Washington 2003a).

40. As examples, Senator Sandra Pappas of Minnesota suggested rape is common. She referred to "many images of blood, guts, gore, *rape*, and the physical effects of beatings" (Minnesota 2005a (emphasis added)). Lonnie Johns-Brown of the Washington Coalition of Sexual Assault Programs and the Washington chapter of the National Organization of Women, a witness at a Washington committee meeting, said, "Seventeen years ago people weren't being rewarded in video games for raping and murdering women or shooting and killing police officers" (Washington 2003a). On the Washington Senate floor, Senator Dale Brandlund referred to rape and the murder of prostitutes (Washington 2003f). On the Michigan Senate floor, during a discussion of S.B. 249 (2005), a bill related to the one primarily of interest in this study (S.B. 416 (2005)), Senator Hansen Clarke referred to a game (probably *Grand Theft Auto: San Andreas*) where the player "interactively solicits prostitutes, rapes them, and then murders them" (Michigan 2005c). On the California Senate floor, Senator Sheila James Kuehl of California said, "Recent Gallup Polls show that over 70% of teenage boys are regularly playing video games that glorify and reward players for virtually performing criminal acts against women as a form of entertainment: maiming, *raping*, killing, dismembering" (California 2005b (emphasis mine)). Similarly, Assembly Member Dennis Mountjoy of California referred on the Assembly floor to games that depict and glorify rape (California 2005c).

41. Representative Karen Clark of Minnesota referred to "raping prostitutes and killing them" in a game (Minnesota 2006b), which is likely a reference to one or more of the *Grand Theft Auto* games.

42. In a random event in *Grand Theft Auto V*, two computer-controlled men are, in the words of the official strategy guide, "harassing a lady on the side of the road," and one of the men has the woman pinned down (Bogenn and Barba 2013, 287). Some players have interpreted this scene as an attempted rape, but Rockstar claims the scene instead depicts attempted cannibalism (Matyszczyk 2013). The men are indeed members of a cult of cannibals called the Altruist Cult, but the intent of the men in this particular scene remains ambiguous. Either way, the player does not commit an act of rape or even cannibalism. The game even encourages players to help the woman because she rewards players who rescue her and drive her to safety by paying them $80. Players are not always encouraged to stop the cannibals from committing crimes, however. Other random events involve the player delivering hitchhikers to the cultists for rewards (Bogenn and Barba 2013, 282–284, 287).

43. Games in the *Grand Theft Auto* series do allow players to have sex with prostitutes, kill them, and then recover their payments to the prostitutes (Finn 2006, 36–39). Some speakers, such as Representative Jeff Johnson of Minnesota, noted this feature in the *Grand Theft Auto* series without adding inaccurate statements about rape (Minnesota 2006b).

44. Examples of games available in the United States that depict rape include *Silent Hill 2* (Konami 2001) and *Phantasmagoria* (Sierra On-Line 1995) (Rusch 2009, 248–249; Perron 2008, 133). *Silent Hill 2* includes a scene in which the player is hidden in a closet and observes a murderous entity called Pyramid Head raping two mannequin creatures. The scene is relevant to the psychological theme of the game. Professor Doris Rusch suggests Pyramid Head represents "some deeply buried fear" of the main character (Rusch 2009, 243). Games that feature rape are more common in the Japanese market (*Daily Yomiuri* 2009).

45. At the committee meeting in the Washington House on February 10, 1999, witness Larry Shannon of the Washington State Trial Lawyers Association claimed that his son and a friend used secret codes to "escalate the level of graphic depiction of violence in

this game," but he did not identify the game or its ESRB rating (Washington 1999b). At the committee meeting in the Washington House on January 22, 2003, several speakers made a similar point. Representative Mary Lou Dickerson said, "They don't get to do this often right off the bat in the lower levels of the games. They are rewarded for their expertise in violence by this further violence, so they have to progress through the levels of the game to get to some of these higher levels of violence." Witness Larry Pederson similarly said games "have built in protection from parents. Kids have to acquire a certain level of skill to access the most violent parts." Witness Cristal Downing said, "Unless you have the playing skills of your child, the extent of violence can be hidden from parents." Witness Lonnie Johns-Brown referred to "secret messages" in the games (Washington 2003a). On the Washington House Floor on March 18, 2003, Representative Dickerson repeated the point she made at the earlier committee hearing: "As players gain expertise, they enter higher and higher levels of violence" (Washington 2003c). In the Washington Senate on April 17, 2003, Senator Rosemary McAuliffe said that she probably would have unknowingly allowed her grandchildren to play inappropriate games because she cannot reach the levels where the violence against women and children occurs. Later at the same session, Senator Rosa Franklin said, "I was introduced to these video games when my grandson was 3, and he could get to levels at the age of 3 and 4 that I never even thought of, that I can't even get to the first level" (Washington 2003f).

46. The question was asked by Representative Eric Pettigrew. At one point, he referred to "secret codes ... communicated through some sort of underground" (Washington 2003a).

47. A modder in the Netherlands discovered and publicized the hidden sexual content, what came to be known as the "Hot Coffee mod." The result was an unprecedented problem for the ESRB. The ESRB had rated the game M, but this additional content arguably warranted an AO rating. Eventually, the ESRB did re-rate the game (Kushner 2012, 186–221). As it's hard to imagine the exact same footage projected onto a movie screen as receiving more than an R rating, the hidden content is plausibly viewed as additional M-level content in an already M-rated game, but according to video game journalist David Kushner, "M-rated games couldn't get away with the same kind of content one would see in an R-rated film" because games were (and maybe still are) seen as products for children (Kushner 2012, 172).

48. Anyone, even an expert on a topic, can misspeak, but Representative Mary Lou Dickerson, the lead sponsor of H.B. 1009 in Washington, referred to the game as "Grand Theft Auto: City Vice" or just "City Vice" three times during one committee meeting and then later on the House floor while reading from prepared remarks (Washington 2003a, 2003c).

49. The lawyer was Jennifer Byron (Minnesota 2003).

50. Grossman lists these events on his curriculum vitae, which is available at www.killogy.com. Grossman also lists presentations in several other states, both before legislative bodies and other government bodies. Among them, he lists a presentation before the Louisiana Attorney General's Violence Prevention Task Force in 1999 and two presentations at the Oklahoma Governor's State Violence Prevention Conference, one in 2000 and one in 2001. These events could have influenced legislators in these states. He also lists a presentation before the Minnesota legislature on March 2, 2000. Representative Karen Clark made a reference on the Minnesota House floor in 2006 to a speaker from the military talking about desensitization, which might have been a reference to Grossman.

Representative Clark's comment suggested the event was more recent than March 2000, but she may have just misstated how recent it was (Minnesota 2006b).

51. During the committee meeting, Grossman referred to *Stop Teaching Our Kids to Kill* (1999) as not yet published (Washington 1999b), so committee members would not have had access to the published version. Grossman mentioned distributing a chronology of media violence findings and statements. This chronology can be found in the book (Grossman and DeGaetano 1999, 132–136).

52. Grossman's post–World War II example during the committee meeting was the Falkland Islands War. He claimed the Argentine military fired at a 10–15% rate but the British military fired at over a 90% rate (Washington 1999b).

53. Grossman said the Paducah, Kentucky shooting was also evidence that video games provide highly effective marksmanship training. In a book published several years after his Washington testimony, Grossman said, "There can be no doubt that video games can teach marksmanship skills" (Grossman and Christensen 2008, 88). While it is certainly plausible that video games teach marksmanship skills, just as Grossman said in 1999, there appears to be a lack of systematic research on this question. Grossman offered only one study in the 2008 book in support of this claim, a study done by the Center for Successful Parenting (or CSP). Grossman asked the CSP to undertake the study because he wondered whether the marksmanship skills of the Paducah shooter could be attributed to the playing of video games. The CSP study involved an experiment with 40 boys, all without firearms experience. Of the 40 boys, 20 had little experience with first-person shooter video games and 20 had extensive experience. At a pistol range with human silhouette targets, the group with extensive first-person shooter experience was much more accurate. The CSP study explicitly states that Grossman was convinced by the results of the study, *but the CSP was not*. The study said that "the CSP recognizes that this experiment can only be regarded as a *pilot study*" and called for additional research (Center for Successful Parenting 2002, 11–12 (emphasis added)).

54. Grossman's source for this claim was clearly the work of Brandon Centerwall (Centerwall 1989, 1992, 1993). Grossman's awareness of Centerwall's work is confirmed by a brief (and uncritical) discussion of Centerwall (1992) in his book (Grossman and DeGaetano 1999, 31–32). Criticisms of Centerwall's analysis and conclusions can be found in Savage (2004, 107–108).

55. While Marshall was concerned about offering realistic training to soldiers (Williams 1990, 49), the most extensive analysis of Marshall's influence on the army describes Marshall's views about target training in different terms than Grossman: "To overcome the soldier's learned reluctance to kill, Marshall urged a new approach to marksmanship training. Soldiers should be trained to fire at *non-personnel targets such as bushes and windows rather than solely the traditional bulls-eyes*" (Williams 1990, 50 (emphasis added)). Williams does not explain the theoretical reasons for why firing at non-personnel targets would affect a soldier's reluctance to kill.

56. In print, Grossman claims the "scientific data supporting realistic training is so powerful" that the decision of the Tenth Circuit in *Oklahoma v. Tuttle* (1984) requires firearms training of police to be realistic and "include stress, decision-making, and shoot-don't shoot training" (Grossman 2009a, xix; Grossman and Christensen 2008, 79). This decision, which is not cited very often (probably because the Supreme Court reversed the Tenth Circuit), did speak of a "lack of training to cope with robberies," but it did not refer to

"shoot-don't shoot" training, and the court said nothing at all about the scientific evidence related to training.

57. *Operation Wolf*, a game mentioned by Grossman, predates the ESRB rating system, but it is included with the compilation of classic arcade games for the Xbox and PlayStation 2 entitled *Taito Legends* (Sega 2005). This compilation is rated T for Teen with a descriptor for Mild Violence.

58. Grossman mentioned "Hogan's Alley" during his testimony, but he was probably referring to the "Hogan's Alley" facility at the FBI's Training Academy in Quantico, Virginia, rather than the Nintendo game of the same name.

59. A version of *Hogan's Alley* is included as a "mini-game" in *WarioWare, Inc. Mega Party Game$!* (Nintendo 2004), which is an E-rated collection of games. This version of *Hogan's Alley* is played with a standard GameCube controller, not a light gun. The ESRB did not use the E10+rating until 2005, so a re-release of *Hogan's Alley* today with a light gun controller might receive the E10+rating instead of an E rating. Anything higher than E10+ seems unlikely.

60. In their book, Grossman and DeGaetano claim that even games played with a mouse rather than a light gun can promote "the will to kill by repeatedly rehearsing the act until it feels natural" (Grossman and DeGaetano 1999, 77). They make this claim as part of a discussion of games they consider particularly gruesome, but it's not clear what role graphic violence is playing in Grossman's theory. Silhouette targets do not include blood and gore, yet according to Grossman, the introduction of these bloodless targets almost completely solved the military's problem of soldiers who would not fire on the enemy. It's therefore unclear what more could be accomplished by adding graphic violence.

61. For example, Thompson appeared on *60 Minutes* in a March 6, 2005 piece on *Grand Theft Auto* (CBS Video 2005).

62. Thompson named this person, but I am unsure of who exactly he was referring to. Perhaps he mispronounced the person's last name. As best I can tell from the audio recording, Thompson referred to "Dr. Robert Greenway" of the University of Illinois, but I cannot identify any information about this person, even after various searches in Google and the ABC News transcripts in LEXIS.

63. There are some minor discrepancies between Hotz's (1998) and Landau's (2000) accounts of Yurgelun-Todd's study, such as the ages of the adolescent participants (ages 9 to 17 versus 11 to 17), but the two articles are clearly discussing the same experiment or series of experiments.

64. Unlike most of the legislative events discussed in this chapter, the Illinois floor sessions are available in transcript form. I've rendered this quotation as it appears in the original transcript. The ellipses appear in this transcript and clearly represent faltering or broken speech, not omissions.

65. Senator Bruce Patterson, for example, commented on the need to build a factual record and how building this record required testimony from experts and scientific studies (Michigan 2005a, Tape 2, Side A).

66. The only substantive deviation from the published version is that the published version includes correlation coefficients for the relationship between media violence and aggressive behavior (Anderson et al. 2003, 81). Anderson did not read these coefficients to the committee (Michigan 2005b, Tape 2, Side A).

67. As examples, Anderson's initial overview is roughly comparable to the overviews offered by Jo Seavy-Hultquist and Senator Sandra Pappas (California 2005a, 2005b), in

the sense that each one is a summary of some basic findings in the literature. Senator Pappas also referenced Dave Grossman's views. Although Saunders mentioned Grossman's argument to the committee at the previous meeting, the committee members did not ask Anderson about Grossman, and Anderson did not bring him up.

68. Senator Cropsey concluded his comments with a specific example of the harm supposedly caused by violent video games, one drawn from the committee testimony of a sheriff, but his example further demonstrated a lack of engagement with both the social science evidence and the video game medium. He described a fatal automobile accident that occurred after a 16-year-old driver played a violent video game. According to the sheriff, speaking at one of the earlier committee hearings, the game was *Grand Theft Auto* (Michigan 2005b, Tape 1, Side A). According to Cropsey, who said he was relying on the police report, it was *True Crime: Streets of LA* (Activision 2003), an M-rated game with descriptors for "Blood and Gore" and "Violence." Quoting from the report, Cropsey attributed the accident to the driver imitating how he drove his car in the game (Michigan 2005c), but to the extent the real-world imitation of reckless driving in video games is a concern, Cropsey did not explain whether the social science provides evidence that video game violence causes this type of imitative behavior. He did not even discuss whether minors' access to games depicting reckless driving would necessarily be restricted by his bill. Most, if not all, driving games at least *allow* players to drive recklessly. Games like *Burnout* (Acclaim Entertainment 2001) and *Burnout 2: Point of Impact* (Acclaim Entertainment 2002), which are both E-rated and carry a descriptor for "Mild Violence," actually encourage and reward automotive mayhem, at least within the games. Senator Cropsey's bill applied to games depicting violence against humans, and many driving games, including *Burnout* and *Burnout 2*, depict automobiles without showing the drivers and would therefore not be covered by the bill's language (Michigan S.B. 416; Michigan Senate Fiscal Agency 2005, 1).

69. At a later session, according to the *Journal of the House of Representatives*, Representative Leon Drolet explained his vote against the bill with references to three studies questioning the link between video game violence and real-world aggression (Michigan House of Representatives 2005, 1255–1256). Substantive rebuttals are an important part of informed legislative debates (Mucciaroni and Quirk 2006, 47), but this one was very brief. Although the *House Journal* reports that Drolet offered the rebuttal shortly after the vote, which would reduce its value as a contribution to a debate, the video recording reveals that he did not actually make a statement on the House floor (Michigan 2005d). As for the later floor sessions, there was no discussion of the social science evidence at the approximately six-minute September 7th Senate floor session (Michigan 2005e) or at the approximately three-minute September 8th House floor session (Michigan 2005f).

70. During an exchange on the House floor between Representative Roy Burrell, the primary author of H.B. 1381, and Representative A. G. Crowe, a secondary author, Crowe offered this flattering description of Thompson, and Burrell agreed with it. The two of them also referred to Thompson's earlier appearance before a committee (Louisiana 2006a). This discussion on the House floor predates the committee hearing in the Senate.

71. A frequently noted point made by the opposition to the bills in Table 5.1 is the conclusion of the Washington State Department of Health that "current research evidence is not supportive of a major public concern that violent video games lead to real-life violence" (Bensley and Van Eeenwyk 2000, Executive Summary). The authors repeated this same point in a version of the report published in a journal (Bensley and Van Eenwyk 2001, 256).

72. Of course, a complication for this example was the expectation of at least some legislators in Washington that explicitly targeting games with violence against police officers effectively targets violent games generally, something that legislators thought could not be done directly. The district court did not call shenanigans on this legislative ploy.

73. Senator Don Betzold of Minnesota did raise a relevant question about the definition of violence, but nothing came of it. He asked, "You know, it may be appropriate to talk in terms about violence and exposure, but I don't know always how to classify it. If a child is watching Wile E. Coyote drop a boulder on the Road Runner, and it bounces back and lands on him, is that, is that violence? If. . . if Bugs Bunny hands Yosemite Sam a stick of dynamite and it blows up, is that violence? I mean where—at what level, do we say, you know, this is violence and that is not violence? I don't know" (Minnesota 2005a). In her response, Senator Pappas seemed to think he was asking about how her legislation defined violence, but Senator Betzold may have been asking about how the social science defines violence. Betzold did not clarify his question or otherwise follow up.

74. As an additional deficiency, the list of studies in the Michigan Senate Judiciary Committee's May 10, 2005 minutes includes only the authors and article titles. The names of the publications and the years of publication are missing (Michigan Senate Judiciary Committee 2005, 1–4).

References

Acclaim Entertainment, Inc. 2001. *Burnout*. Glen Cove, NY.

Acclaim Entertainment, Inc. 2002. *Burnout 2: Point of Impact*. Glen Cove, NY.

Activision, Inc. 2003. *True Crime: Streets of LA*. Los Angeles, CA.

American Academy of Pediatrics, American Academy of Child & Adolescent Psychiatry, American Psychological Association, American Medical Association, and American Academy of Family Physicians. 2000 (July 26). "Joint Statement on the Impact of Entertainment Violence on Children." Available at http://www2.aap.org/advocacy/releases/jstmtevc.htm.

American Psychological Association. 2005 (August 19). "Review of Research Shows That Playing Violent Video Games Can Heighten Aggression." Available at http://www.apa.org/news/press/releases/2005/08/violent-video.aspx.

Anderson, Craig A. 2002. "Violent Video Games and Aggressive Thoughts, Feelings, and Behaviors." In *Children in the Digital Age*, edited by Sandra L. Calvert, Amy B, Jordan, and Rodney R. Cocking, 101–119. Westport: Praeger.

Anderson, Craig A. 2004. "An Update on the Effects of Playing Violent Video Games." *Journal of Adolescence* 27: 113–122.

Anderson, Craig A., Leonard Berkowitz, Edward Donnerstein, L. Rowell Huesmann, James D. Johnson, Daniel Linz, Neil M. Malamuth, and Ellen Wartella. 2003. "The Influence of Media Violence on Youth." *Psychological Science in the Public Interest* 4(3): 81–110.

Anderson, Craig A., Douglas A. Gentile, and Katherine E. Buckley. 2007. *Violent Video Game Effects on Children and Adolescents*. New York: Oxford University Press.

Atari, Inc. 1972. *Pong*. Santa Clara, CA.

Atari, Inc. 1976. *Breakout*. Sunnyvale, CA.

Atari, Inc. 1979. *Asteroids*. Sunnyvale, CA.

Austin, Elizabeth. 2003 (October 26). "Turning a Profit from Stereotypes." *Chicago Tribune* Perspective 1.

Bally-Midway Mfg. Co. 1982. *Tron*. Franklin Park, IL.

Bensley, Lillian, and Juliet Van Eenwyk. 2000. "Video Games and Real Life Aggression: A Review of the Literature." Olympia: Washington State Department of Health Office of Epidemiology.

Bensley, Lillian, and Juliet Van Eenwyk. 2001. "Video Games and Real Life Aggression." *Journal of Adolescent Health* 29: 244–257.

Bimber, Bruce. 1996. *The Politics of Expertise in Congress*. Albany: State University of New York Press.

Blagojevich, Rod. 2004. "Executive Order Creating the Safe Games Illinois Task Force on Violent and Sexually Explicit Video Games."

Bogenn, Tim, and Rick Barba. 2013. *Grand Theft Auto V: Limited Edition Strategy Guide*. Indianapolis: DK/BradyGames.

Breyer, Stephen. 1998 (July-August). "The Interdependence of Science and Law." *Judicature* 82: 24–27.

Breyer, Stephen. 2010. *Making Our Democracy Work*. New York: Alfred A. Knopf.

Burns, Robert P. 1999. *A Theory of the Trial*. Princeton: Princeton University Press.

Burns, Robert P. 2009. *The Death of the American Trial*. Chicago: University of Chicago Press.

Bushman, Brad J., and Craig A. Anderson. 2001. "Media Violence and the American Public." *American Psychologist* 56: 477–489.

Cable News Network. 2000 (July 20). *CNN Talkback Live*. Transcript #00072000V14.

Cardozo, Benjamin N. 1921. *The Nature of the Judicial Process*. New Haven: Yale University Press.

Capcom Entertainment, Inc. 2003. *Clock Tower 3*. Sunnyvale, CA.

CBS Video. 2005 (March 6). "Grand Theft Auto" (VHS).

Center for Successful Parenting. 2002. "Do Video Games Improve Violent Skills?" News from ICCVOS 2: 11–12.

Centerwall, Brandon. 1989. "Exposure to Television as a Cause of Violence." In 2 *Public Communication and Behavior*, edited by George Comstock, 1–58. San Diego: Academic Press, Inc.

Centerwall, Brandon. 1992. "Television and Violence: The Scale of the Problem and Where to Go from Here." *Journal of the American Medical Association* 267: 3059–3063.

Centerwall, Brandon. 1993 (Spring). "Television and Violent Crime." *The Public Interest* 56–71.

Chambers, John Whiteclay II. 2003 (Autumn). "S. L. A. Marshall's *Men against Fire*: New Evidence Regarding Fire Ratios." *Parameters* 113–121.

Chang, David T. 2002. *Ghettopoly*. Saint Marys, PA: Ghettopoly.com, Inc.

Chick, Jack T. 1984. *Dark Dungeons*. Chino, CA: Chick Publications.

Colker, Ruth, and James J. Brudney. 2001. "Dissing Congress." *Michigan Law Review* 100: 80–144.

Daily Yomiuri. 2009 (May 16). "Rape Video Games Still on Sale." Tokyo, Japan. 4.

Daniels, Bruce C. 2005. *Puritans at Play: Leisure and Recreation in Colonial New England* (10th Anniversary Edition). New York: Palgrave Macmillan.

Davis, Kenneth Culp. 1955. "Judicial Notice." *Columbia Law Review* 55: 945–984.

Dear, William. 1984. *The Dungeon Master: The Disappearance of James Dallas Egbert III*. Boston: Houghton Mifflin Co.

Deason, Ellen E. 1998. "Court-Appointed Expert Witnesses: Scientific Positivism Meets Bias and Deference." *Oregon Law Review* 77: 59–156.

Digital Pictures, Inc. 1992. *Night Trap*. San Mateo, CA.

Dille, Flint, and John Zurr Platten. 2007. *The Ultimate Guide to Video Game Writing and Design*. New York: Long Eagle Publishing.

Dlugokinski, Eric. 2006. "Video Games and Violence Explored." Available at http://newsok.com/video-games-and-violence-explored/article/2930488.

Dodson, Elizabeth A., Ross C. Brownson, and Stephen M. Weiss. 2012. "Policy Dissemination Research." In *Dissemination and Implementation Research in Health: Translating Science to Practice*, edited by Ross C. Brownson, Graham A. Colditz, and Enola K. Proctor, 437–458. New York: Oxford University Press.

Donovan, Tristan. 2010. *Replay: The History of Video Games*. East Sussex, Great Britain: Yellow Ant.

Dormer, Dan. 2006 (June 5). "Minnesota Video Game Bill Sponsor Talks to 1UP." Available at http://www.1up.com/news/minnesota-video-game-bill-sponsor.

Dudlak, Jonathan. 2003 (April). "Clock Tower 3." *Electronic Gaming Monthly* 74.

Engen, Robert. 2011. "S.L.A. Marshall and the Ratio of Fire: History, Interpretation, and the Canadian Experience." *Canadian Military History* 20: 39–48.

Entertainment Software Rating Board. 2015. "ESRB Ratings Guide." New York. Available at http://www.esrb.org/ratings/ratings_guide.jsp.

Exidy, Inc. 1976. *Death Race*. Sunnyvale, CA.

Faigman, David L. 2004. *Laboratory of Justice*. New York: Times Books.

Faigman, David L. 2008. *Constitutional Fictions: A Unified Theory of Constitutional Facts*. New York: Oxford University Press.

Fears, Darryl. 2003 (October 12). "'Ghettopoly' Provokes Protests." *Washington Post* A3.

Federal Rules of Evidence. 2012. Washington, DC: US Government Printing Office.

Fenno, Richard F., Jr. 1995 [1973]. *Congressmen in Committees*. Berkeley: Institute of Governmental Studies.

Fink, Steven M. 1982 (October 20). "The Real Threat of Pac-Man." *The Philadelphia Inquirer* 13-A.

Finn, Mark. 2006. "Political Interface: The Banning of *GTA3* in Australia." In *The Meaning and Culture of* Grand Theft Auto, edited by Nate Garrelts, 35–48. Jefferson, NC: McFarland & Company.

Fitzpatrick, Denise. 1982 (October 27). "Fun and Games: Psychologist Says Pac-Man Poses Few Behavorial [sic] Pitfalls." *Daily News* (Bowing Green, KY) 2A.

Ford, William K. 2012. "Copy Game for High Score: The First Video Game Lawsuit." *Journal of Intellectual Property* 20: 1–41.

Ford, William K. 2013. "The Law and Science of Video Game Violence: What Was Lost in Translation?" *Cardozo Arts & Entertainment Law Journal* 31: 297–356.

Ford, William K., and Raizel Liebler. 2012. "Games Are Not Coffee Mugs: Games and the Right of Publicity." *Santa Clara Computer & High Technology Law Journal* 29: 1–98.

Galanter, Marc. 2004. "The Vanishing Trial: An Examination of Trials and Related Matters in Federal and State Courts." *Journal of Empirical Legal Studies* 1: 459–570.

Garrelts, Nate, ed. 2006. *The Meaning and Culture of Grand Theft Auto.* Jefferson, NC: McFarland & Company.

Gentile, Douglas A., Muniba Saleem, and Craig A. Anderson. 2007. "Public Policy and the Effects of Media Violence on Children." *Social Science and Policy Review* 1: 15–61.

Ginsburg, Douglas H. 2010. "Appellate Courts and Independent Experts." *Case Western Law Review* 60: 303–324.

Githens, Perry. 1942 (June). "Pin-Money Plungers." *Reader's Digest* 18–20.

Glenn, Russell W. 2000a. *Reading Athena's Dance Card.* Annapolis: Naval Institute Press.

Glenn, Russell W. 2000b. "Introduction." In S. L. A. Marshall, *Men against Fire*, 1–8. Norman: University of Oklahoma Press.

Grimshaw, Jeremy M., Martin P. Eccles, John N. Lavis, Sophie J. Hill, and Janet E. Squires. 2012. "Knowledge Translation of Research Findings." *Implementation Science* 7 (50): 1–17.

Grossman, Dave. 1995. *On Killing.* Boston: Little, Brown and Co.

Grossman, Dave. 2009a. *On Killing* (rev. ed.). New York: Back Bay Books.

Grossman, Dave. 2009b. "S.L.A. Marshall Revisited . . . ?" *Canadian Military Journal* 9: 112–113.

Grossman, Dave, with Loren W. Christensen. 2004. *On Combat.* PPCT Research Publications.

Grossman, Dave, with Loren W. Christensen. 2008. *On Combat*, 3rd ed. Warrior Science Publications.

Grossman, Dave, and Gloria DeGaetano. 1999. *Stop Teaching Our Kids to Kill: A Call to Action against TV, Movie & Video Game Violence.* New York: Crown Publishers.

Grossman, Dave, and Gloria DeGaetano. 2014. *Stop Teaching Our Kids to Kill: A Call to Action against TV, Movie & Video Game Violence* (revised and updated edition). New York: Harmony Books.

GT Interactive. 1996. *Duke Nukem 3D.* New York.

Gunter, Barrie, Jackie Harrison, and Maggie Wykes. 2003. *Violence on Television: Distribution, Form, Context, and Themes.* Mahwah: Lawrence Erlbaum Associates.

Gygax, Gary, and Dave Arneson. 1974. *Dungeons & Dragons.* Lake Geneva, WI: Tactical Studies Rules.

Haninger, Kevin, M. Seamus Ryan, and Kimberly M. Thompson. 2004. "Violence in Teen-Rated Video Games." *Medscape General Medicine* 6(1). Available at http://www.ncbi.nlm.nih.gov/pmc/articles/PMC1140725/.

Hill, Jessie. 2007. "The Constitutional Right to Make Medical Treatment Decisions: A Tale of Two Doctrines." *Texas Law Review* 86: 331–431.

Hird, John A. 2005. *Power, Knowledge, and Politics: Policy Analysis in the States.* Washington: Georgetown University Press.

Hofer, Margaret K. 2003. *The Games We Played.* New York: Princeton Architectural Press.

The Homiletic Review. 1903 (May). "Editorial Notes: 'A Growing Social Evil.'" Edited by I. K. Funk and D. S. Gregory, 474–476. New York: Funk and Wagnalls Co.

Hotz, Robert Lee. 1998 (June 25). "Studies with Adolescents' Brains Find Possible Physiological Basis for Turbulent Teenage Emotions." *Los Angeles Times* B2.

Howitt, Dennis, and Guy Cumberbatch. 1975. *Mass Media Violence and Society*. London: Paul Elek Ltd.

Huesmann, L. Rowell, and Lucyna Kirwill. 2007. "Why Observing Violence Increases the Risk of Violent Behavior by the Observer." In *The Cambridge Handbook of Violent Behavior and Aggression*, edited by Daniel J. Flannery, Alexander T. Vazsonyi, and Irwin D. Waldman, 545–570. New York: Cambridge University Press.

Id Software, Inc. 1997. *Quake 2*. Mesquite, TX.

Jones, Rick. 1988. *Stairway to Hell: Rescuing Teens from Their Well-Planned Destruction*. Chino, CA: Chick Publications.

Kerr, Orin S. 2005. "Congress, the Courts, and New Technologies: A Response to Professor Solve." *Fordham Law Review* 74: 779–790.

Kerr, Peter. 1982 (June 3). "Should Video Games Be Restricted By Law?" *The New York Times* C1.

Konami Inc. 1992. *Lethal Enforcers* (arcade edition). Buffalo Grove, IL.

Konami Inc. 1993. *Lethal Enforcers* (Sega-CD edition). Buffalo Grove, IL.

Konami of America. 2001. *Silent Hill 2*. Redwood City, CA.

Kovaleski, John, Sean Sweigart, and Aaron Dill. 2012. *Spartacus: A Game of Blood and Treachery*. Earlysville, VA: Gale Force Nine LLC.

Krugman, Paul. 1994. *Peddling Prosperity*. New York: W.W. Norton and Co.

Kushner, David. 2012. *Jacked: The Outlaw Story of Grand Theft Auto*. Hoboken: John Wiley & Sons.

Landau, Misia. 2000 (April 7). "Deciphering the Adolescent Brain." *Focus: News from Harvard Medical, Dental, & Public Health Schools*. Available at http://archives.focus.hms.harvard.edu/2000/Apr21_2000/psychiatry.html.

Larson, Bob. 1989. *Satanism: The Seduction of America's Youth*. Nashville: Thomas Nelson.

Laycock, Douglas. 2007. "A Syllabus of Errors." *Michigan Law Review* 105: 1169–1187.

Lester, Brian. 2002. "The Free Replay Feature in Pinball Machines: A Fresh Look at the Elements of Gambling and a Revised Method of Analysis." *Brandeis Law Journal* 41: 297–332.

Lohr, Steve. 2005 (July 11). "In Video Game, a Download Unlocks Hidden Sex Scenes." *The New York Times* C3.

Lubell, Samuel. 1939 (May 13). "Ten Billion Nickels." *The Saturday Evening Post* 12–13, 38–43.

MacNeil/Lehrer Productions. 1982 (December 29). "The McNeil-Lehrer Report: PacMan Perils" (DVD).

Marshall, John Douglas. 1993. *Reconciliation Road*. Syracuse: Syracuse University Press.

Marshall, S. L. A. 1953. *Commentary on Infantry Operations and Weapons Usage in Korea*. Chevy Chase: Operations Research Office of the Johns Hopkins University Press.

Marshall, S. L. A. 2000. *Men against Fire*. Norman: University of Oklahoma Press.

Mather, Cotton. 1693. *Winter Meditations: Directions How to Employ the Leisure of Winter for the Glory of God*. Boston: Benjamin Harris.

Mather, Cotton. 1820. *Magnalia Christi Americana or The Ecclesiastical History of New England*, vol. 1. Hartford: Silas Andrus.

Matyszczyk, Chris. 2013. "GTA V: That Rape Scene? No, That's Just Cannibalism." CNET. Available at http://news.cnet.com/8301-17852_3-57603790-71/gta-v-that-rape-scene-no-thats-just-cannibalism/.

McGinnis, John O., and Charles W. Mulaney. 2008. "Judging Facts Like Law." *Constitutional Commentary* 25: 69–130.

McLoughlin Brothers. c. 1883. *Bulls and Bears: The Great Wall St. Game*. McLoughlin Brothers: New York, NY.

Meazell, Emily Hammond. 2009. "Scientific Avoidance: Toward a More Principled Judicial Review of Legislative Science." *Indiana Law Journal* 84: 239–283.

Michigan House of Representatives. 2005 (August 31). *Journal of the House of Representatives*. Lansing.

Michigan Senate Fiscal Agency. 2005 (May 9). "Bill Analysis: Senate Bill 416 (Substitute S-1)." Lansing.

Michigan Senate Judiciary Committee. 2005 (May 10). "Minutes of the Committee on Judiciary." Lansing.

Midway Amusement Games, LLC. 2006. *Rampage: Total Destruction*. Chicago, IL.

Midway Games, Inc. 1997. *Mortal Kombat 4*. Chicago, IL.

Midway Manufacturing Co. 1978. *Space Invaders*. Franklin Park, IL.

Midway Manufacturing Co. 1980. *Pac-Man*. Franklin Park, IL.

Midway Manufacturing Co. 1981. *Ms. Pac-Man*. Franklin Park, IL.

Midway Manufacturing Co. 1992. *Mortal Kombat*. Chicago, IL.

Morris-Friedman, Andrew, and Ulrich Schädler. 2003. "'Juden Raus!' (Jews Out!)—History's Most Infamous Board Game." *Board Game Studies* 6: 47–58.

Mucciaroni, Gary, and Paul J. Quirk. 2006. *Deliberative Choices*. Chicago: University of Chicago Press.

Murray, John P., Mario Liotti, Paul T. Ingmundson, Helen S. Mayberg, Yonglin Pu, Frank Zamarripa, Yijun Liu, Marty G. Waldorff, Jia-Hong Gao, and Peter T. Fox. 2006. "Children's Brain Activations While Viewing Televised Violence Revealed by fMRI." *Media Psychology* 8: 25–27.

National Cable Satellite Corporation (C-Span). 1993. "Hearing on Video Game Violence." Program ID 52848-1.

National Institute on Media and Family. 2003. *Sex, Murder, and Video Games* (DVD).

National Safety Council. 1976–1977 (Winter). "The Name of the Game Is Death Race." *Family Safety* 35(4): 8–9.

Newsweek. 1977 (January 10). "Sick, Sick, Sick." 54.

Nintendo of America, Inc. 1981. *Donkey Kong*. Seattle, WA.

Nintendo of America, Inc. 1985a. *Duck Hunt*. Seattle, WA.

Nintendo of America, Inc. 1985b. *Hogan's Alley*. Seattle, WA.

Nintendo of America, Inc. 2004. *WarioWare, Inc. Mega Party Game$!* Redmond, WA.

Nutting Associates, Inc. 1971. *Computer Space*. Mountain View, CA.

Perron, Bernard. 2008. "Genre Profile: Interactive Movies." In *The Video Game Explosion: A History from* PONG *to PlayStation and Beyond*, edited by Mark J. P. Wolf, 127–133. Westport: Greenwood Press.

Polsby, Nelson W. 1973. "Does Congress Know Enough to Legislate for the Nation?" In *The Role of Congress: A Study of the Legislative Branch*. New York: Time, Inc.

Poniske, John. 2010. *King Philip's War*. Millersville, MD: Multi-Man Publishing.

Potter, W. James. 1999. *On Media Violence*. Thousand Oaks: Sage.

Potter, W. James. 2003. *The 11 Myths of Media Violence*. Thousand Oaks: Sage.

Powell, Elizabeth. 2004. "Studying Functional Differences in the Adolescent Brain may Provide Evidence That the Nervous System is Responsible for Behavior." Available at http://serendip.brynmawr.edu/bb/neuro/neuro04/web1/epowell.html.

Presbyterian Banner. 1903 (February 12). "A Growing Social Evil." Pittsburgh. 5–6.

Prince, Stephen. 2000. "Graphic Violence in the Cinema: Origins, Aesthetic Design, and Social Effects." In *Screening Violence*, edited by Stephen Prince, 1–44. New Brunswick: Rutgers.

Pulling, Pat, with Kathy Cawthon. 1989. *The Devil's Web*. Lafayette: Huntington House, Inc.

Quirk, Paul J. 2005. "Deliberation and Decision Making." In *The Legislative Branch*, edited by Paul J. Quirk and Sarah A. Binder, 314–348. New York: Oxford University Press.

Rabin, Borsika A., and Ross C. Brownson. 2012. "Developing the Terminology for Dissemination and Implementation Research." In *Dissemination and Implementation Research in Health: Translating Science to Practice*, edited by Ross C. Brownson, Graham A. Colditz, and Enola K. Proctor, 23–51. New York: Oxford University Press.

Rebell, Michael A., and Arthur R. Block. 1982. *Educational Policymaking and the Courts: An Empirical Study of Judicial Activism*. Chicago: University of Chicago Press.

Redmond, Dennis. 2006. "Grand Theft Video: Running and Gunning for the U.S. Empire." In *The Meaning and Culture of* Grand Theft Auto, edited by Nate Garrelts, 104–114. Jefferson, NC: McFarland & Company.

Reed, Thomas B. 1894. *Reed's Rules: A Manual of General Parliamentary Law*. Chicago: Rand, McNally & Co.

Rich, Michael. 2005 (March 9). "Testimony of Michael Rich, MD, MPH, Center on Media and Child Health, Children's Hospital Boston/Harvard Medical School, Before the Illinois House Judicial Committee."

Riddle, Karyn, Keren Eyal, Chad Mahood, and W. James Potter. 2006. "Judging the Degree of Violence in Media Portrayals: A Cross-Genre Comparison." *Journal of Broadcasting & Electronic Media* 50: 270–286.

Roberts, Jack. 1977 (January 5). "Sick Game Makes You a Killer." *The Miami News* 5A.

Robie, Joan Hake. 1991. *The Truth about* Dungeons & Dragons. Lancaster: Starburst Publishers.

Rockstar Games. 2001. *Grand Theft Auto III*. New York, NY.

Rockstar Games. 2003a. *Grand Theft Auto: Vice City*. New York, NY.

Rockstar Games. 2003b. *Manhunt*. New York, NY.

Rockstar Games. 2004. *Grand Theft Auto: San Andreas*. New York, NY.

Rockstar Games. 2007. *Manhunt 2*. New York, NY.

Rockstar Games. 2013. *Grand Theft Auto V*. New York, NY.

RWS, Inc. 2002. *Postal 2*. Tuscon, AZ.

Rusch, Doris C. 2009. "Staring into the Abyss—A Close Reading of Silent Hill 2." In *Well Played 1.0*, edited by Drew Davidson, 234–253. Pittsburgh: ETC Press.

Saunders, Kevin W. 1996. *Violence as Obscenity*. Durham: Duke University Press.

Saunders, Kevin W. 2003a. *Saving Our Children from the First Amendment*. New York: New York University Press.

Saunders, Kevin W. 2003b. "Regulating Youth Access to Violent Video Games: Three Responses to First Amendment Concerns." *Law Review of Michigan State University Detroit College of Law* 1: 51–114.

Saunders, Kevin W. 2005 (April 25). "Statement of Kevin W. Sanders." (testimony before the Michigan State Senate Judiciary Committee).

Savage, Joanne. 2004. "Does Viewing Violent Media Really Cause Criminal Violence? A Methodological Review." *Aggression and Violent Behavior* 10: 99–128.

Scheppele, Kim Lane. 2003. "Cultures of Facts." *Perspectives on Politics* 1: 363–368.

Schiff, Martha. 1976 (December 31). "Electronic 'Killer' Game Spurned by Area Parlors." *The Evening News* (Newburgh, NY) 3A.

Schott, Gareth. 2011. "Grand Theft Auto IV (The Not So Terrible): The Result of Asking Parents to Play Games." In *Vice City Virtue: Moral Issues in Digital Game Play*, edited by Karolien Poels and Steven Malliet, 223–244. Leuven, Belgium: Acco Academic.

Sega of America. 2005. *Taito Legends*. San Francisco, CA.

Sharpe, Roger C. 1977. *Pinball!* New York: E.P. Dutton.

Shibuya, Akiko, and Akira Sakamoto. 2005. "Quantity and Context of Video Game Violence in Japan: Toward Creating an Ethical Standard." In *Gaming, Simulations, and Society*, edited by Rei Shiratori, Kiyoshi Arai, and Fumitoshi Kato, 111–120. New York: Springer.

Shibuya, Akiko, Akira Sakamoto, Nobuko Ihori, and Shintaro Yukawa. 2008. "The Effects of the Presence and Contexts of Video Game Violence on Children: A Longitudinal Study in Japan." *Simulation & Gaming* 39: 528–539.

Sierra On-Line, Inc. 1995. *Phantasmagoria*. Bellevue, WA.

Sito, Tom. 2013. *Moving Innovation: A History of Computer Animation*. Cambridge, MA: The MIT Press.

Snider, Mike. 2007a (June 26). "Game's Violence Stirs Debate: 'Manhunt 2' Gets Adults Only Rating." *USA Today* 6D.

Snider, Mike. 2007b. (October 2). "'Manhunt 2' Bloodied . . . But Unbowed as Game Earns M Rating." *USA Today* 6D.

Sony Computer Entertainment America LLC. 2011. *Infamous 2*. Foster City, CA.

Spiller, Roger J. 1988 (Winter). "S.L.A. Marshall and the Ratio of Fire." *RUSI Journal* 133: 63–71.

Taito America Corporation. 1987. *Operation Wolf*. Wheeling, IL.

Thompson, Jack. 2005. *Out of Harm's Way*. Carol Stream: Tyndale House Publishers.

Thompson, Kimberly M., and Kevin Haninger. 2001. "Violence in E-Rated Video Games." *Journal of the American Medical Association* 286: 591–598.

Wald, Patricia M. 2003. "Scholars in the Arena: Some Thoughts on Bridge Building." *Perspectives on Politics* 1: 355–362.

Washington House of Representatives. 1999. House Bill 1315.

Weinstein, George. 1957 (October). "The Pinball Business Isn't Child's Play." *Better Homes and Gardens* 6, 139–140, 142. Des Moines, IA: Meredith Publishing Co.

Weiss, Carol H. 1978. "Improving the Linkage between Social Research and Public Policy." In *Knowledge and Policy: The Uncertain Connection*, edited by Laurence E. Lynn, Jr., 23–81. Washington: National Academy of Science.

Weiss, Carol H. 1989. "Congressional Committees as Users of Analysis." *Journal of Policy Analysis* 8: 411–431.

Williams, F.D.G. 1990. *SLAM: The Influence of S.L.A. Marshall on the United States Army*. Fort Monroe: Office of the Command Historian, United States Army Training and Doctrine Command.

Young, Larry. 1976 (December 29). "Local Safety Authorities Denounce Game." *The Spokesman-Review* 10.

Cases and Case Filings Cited

American Amusement Machine Association v. Kendrick, 115 F. Supp. 2d 943 (S.D. Ind. 2000).

American Amusement Machine Association v. Kendrick, 244 F.3d 572 (7th Cir. 2001).

Brandenburg v. Ohio, 395 U.S. 444 (1969).

Brown v. Entertainment Merchants Association, 131 Sup. Ct. Rep. 2729 (2011).

Caswell v. Licensing Commission for Brockton, 444 N.E.2d 922 (Mass. 1983).

Cossack v. Los Angeles, 523 P.2d 260 (Cal. 1974).

Entertainment Merchants Association v. Henry, No. 06-0675, 2007 U.S. Dist. LEXIS 69139 (W.D. Okla. September 17, 2007).

Entertainment Software Association v. Blagojevich, No. 05-4265 (N.D. Ill. Oct. 7, 2005) (Defendant Governor Blagojevich's Local Rule 56.1(a) Statement).

Entertainment Software Association v. Blagojevich, No. 05-4265 (N.D. Ill. Nov. 14–16, 2005) (Transcript of Proceedings).

Entertainment Software Association v. Blagojevich, 404 F. Supp. 2d 1051 (N.D. Ill. Dec. 2, 2005), *aff'd* 469 F.3d 641 (7th Cir. 2006).

Entertainment Software Association v. Granholm, 426 F. Supp. 2d 646 (E.D. Mich. 2006).

Florida Bar v. Thompson, 994 So.2d 306 (Fla. 2008).

Ginsberg v. New York, 390 U.S. 629 (1968).

Interactive Digital Software Association v. St. Louis County, 200 F. Supp. 2d 1126 (E.D. Mo. 2002).

Interactive Digital Software Association v. St. Louis County, 329 F.3d 954 (8th Cir. 2003).

Jackson v. Pollion, 733 F.3d 786 (7th Cir. 2013).

James v. Meow Media, Inc., 90 F. Supp. 2d 798 (W.D. Ky. 2000), *aff'd* 300 F.3d 683 (6th Cir. 2002).

Marshfield Family Skateland, Inc. v. Marshfield, 450 N.E.2d 605 (Mass. 1983).

Oklahoma v. Tuttle, 728 F.2d 456 (10th Cir. 1984), *rev'd* 471 U.S. 808 (1985).

R.A.V. v. St. Paul, 505 U.S. 377 (1992).

Reilly v. United States, 863 F.2d 149 (1st Cir. 1988).

Thamart v. Moline, 156 P.2d 187 (Idaho 1945).

United States v. Playboy Entertainment Group, 529 U.S. 803 (2000).

Video Software Dealers Association v. Maleng, 325 F. Supp. 2d 1180 (W.D. Wash. 2004).

Video Software Dealers Association v. Schwarzenegger, 401 F. Supp. 2d 1034 (N.D. Cal. 2005).

Washington v. Glucksberg, 521 U.S. 702 (1997).

WNEK Vending & Amusements Co. v. Buffalo, 434 N.Y.S.2d 608 (1980).

6

Being Human

NEGOTIATING RELIGION, LAW, AND SCIENCE
IN THE CLASSROOM AND THE COURTROOM

Winnifred Fallers Sullivan

> ... contemporary societies have to reanalyze their own differences
> without referring to either the over-rapid unity of nature or the over-easy
> diversity of cultures.
> —Latour 2010, 246

6.1 Law, Religion, and Science

The languages of law, religion, and science are three of the dominant modes of discourse today for comprehending the human.[1] While at times they appear to function independently, they are, in fact, deeply dependent one on the other, both historically/genealogically and structurally/phenomenologically. This essay will reflect on the challenge of translating among the languages of law, religion, and science, using the contemporary US science classroom as the focus. The exemplary case will be that of the high school biology teacher now required by law in many states to teach evolution as "the organizing principle of life science" to students who claim a religious—and a constitutional—right to reject such teaching (Harmon 2008).

In the paradigmatic case, a student, often prompted and primed by family or by church leaders, raises her hand during a class on evolutionary biology and asks, "What about Genesis?" or "What about God?" What should the teacher say at that very moment? And who decides? Can law, science, or religion, or some combination, provide the teacher with a satisfactory response? Or, is it just a matter of populist politics? There is no obvious answer to these questions in the United States, in part because, notwithstanding periodic efforts at establishing a constitutional hierarchy, all three discourses claim to occupy the entire space, resisting subordination to any of the others. All three claim to "cover the earth," as the old Sherwin-Williams advertisement boasted, notwithstanding a conventional politics of separation. What distinguishes the human? How did we become human? In what ways do the answers to these questions impinge on how we live together? Talking about Charles Darwin and his legacy has proved to be a potent location for sharp debates on these topics.

The public school is also a primary site for Americans to work out their identities. Not just with respect to the teaching of biology. We are at odds over the teaching of history and reading, as well as over moral and physical education. The administration of American education is also distinctively local so that municipal governance, regional, religious, and ethnic differences, and economic disparities, as well as unresolved tensions with respect to the proper functioning of federalism, also affect the classroom. But there is a particular poignancy when it comes to teaching evolution. Discussing human origins rings the changes on so many aspects of American cultural divides.

Approaches to teaching evolution have lurched radically from place to place and year to year over the last century. Some states and local school boards have tried simply ignoring evolution in their science curriculums, hesitant to deal with the loud opposition. Some states and school boards have tried insisting on equal time for the teaching of creation science or Intelligent Design (ID). But most states today follow national science teaching standards in requiring the teaching of the theory of evolution as the foundation of modern biology, leaving to individual school districts any explicit attention to popular anxiety about the theory and its implications.[2] For the purposes of this essay, I will assume that the best up-to-date science teaching is generally regarded as a worthy goal of primary and secondary education in the United States by most children and parents and educators and politicians.[3] But I will also assume that simply ruling a child's religious beliefs out of order is also regarded by most of those same people as bad pedagogy and bad politics. How to accommodate these two *desiderata*? What *specifically* do we in the United States want the science teacher to say in answer to a child's question about God? Should the curriculum be adapted to acknowledge and accommodate epistemological diversity? Do such conversations belong in a different class or do they not belong in school at all?

If simple-minded separationism is rejected as displaying a lack of respect and a lack of realism, how then can one talk about science and religion in the same space and time? It has been done for centuries, of course, but how might one do that today, given assumptions both about the autonomy and status of science and of our commitments to religious freedom? The theoretical and practical challenges presented by the adoption of new science teaching standards in Florida in 2007 illustrate the complexities of any effort to reconcile the competing claims of law, science, and religion. The standards announced that "[t]he scientific theory of evolution is the fundamental concept underlying all of biology" (Ralston 2009).[4] While efforts were made in the Florida legislature to ensure that, in addition to the teaching of evolution, religious perspectives on human origins would also be permitted in the classroom, no laws have been enacted.[5] National organizations on science teaching have provided definitions of science, and carefully distinguished scientific and religious theories, but the persistent problem of addressing student and parent worries about the compatibility of science and religion has been mostly left to teachers. Florida teachers, like most science teachers in the United States, are largely on their own today with respect to handling the issues in their own classrooms—with the ever-present possibility of a lawsuit lurking in the background.

An article in *The New York Times*, published shortly after the adoption of the new Florida standards, profiled Florida biology teacher David Campbell, a self-described churchgoing Episcopalian, who told the reporter that his goal as a teacher is to persuade his skeptical Christian students to love science as much as he does (Harmon 2008). His approach, he says, is founded in his conviction that "science and religion just ask different questions" (Harmon 2008). *The New York Times* reporter described Campbell's interaction with students in the classroom:

> [Mr. Campbell] bounced a pink rubber Spalding ball on the classroom's hard linoleum floor. "Gravity," he said. "I can do this until the end of the semester, and I can only assume that it will work the same way each time."
>
> He looked around the room. "Bryce, what is it called when natural laws are suspended? What do you call it when water changes into wine?" "Miracle?" Bryce supplied. Mr. Campbell nodded.
>
> The ball hit the floor again. "Science explores nature by testing and gathering data," he said. "It can't tell you what's right and wrong. It doesn't address ethics. But it is not anti-religion. Science and religion just ask different questions." (Harmon 2008)

Campbell's teaching would be the conventional position of many would be peacemakers. "We're doing something different here" (Harmon 2008). Instead of returning to gravity, however, leaving miracles for another place and time, Campbell took a risk:

> He grabbed the ball and held it still. "Can anybody think of a question science can't answer?" "Is there a God?" shot back a boy near the window. "Good," said Mr. Campbell.... "Can't test it. Can't prove it, can't disprove it. It's not a question for science." (Harmon 2008)

The two are still comfortably separate. But Bryce is not satisfied:

> Bryce raised his hand. "But there is scientific proof that there is a God," he said. "Over in Turkey there's a piece of wood from Noah's ark that came out of a glacier."
>
> Mr. Campbell chose his words carefully. "If I could prove, tomorrow, that that chunk of wood is not from the ark, is not even 500 years old and not even from the right kind of tree—would that damage your religious faith at all?"

Bryce thought for a moment. "No," he said. The room was unusually quiet.

"Faith is not based on science," Mr. Campbell said. "And science is not based on faith. I don't expect you to 'believe' the scientific explanation of evolution that we're going to talk about over the next few weeks." "But I do," he added, "expect you to understand it." (Harmon 2008)

Mr. Campbell's choice, given what he thought he knew about his students, was to deliberately introduce Christian theology into his classroom. Doing that could be understood as an effort to make a safe and tolerant space for such avowals—but the confession was also prelude to an effort to convert Bryce to a new theological position. Using a carefully coded challenge to the strength of Bryce's religious position, he had skillfully elicited a confession of faith from Bryce, a young man already known to him as a committed Christian, in part by selecting relevant "facts"—the age and kind of the wood—facts whose very relevance depends on a shared religious acceptance of the authority of the text—and then bullied him into accepting his own separationist understanding of the relationship of religion and science. The article does not record whether Bryce was satisfied with Mr. Campbell's sleight-of-hand attempt to erase the Ark from that Turkish mountaintop and from Bryce's imagination—or with his assertion that faith is not based on science, that is, that it does not "explore nature by testing and gathering data" (Harmon 2008). Maybe Bryce was convinced. But it is not at all clear from the article how exactly Bryce is supposed to regard the building of the Ark, a story which has now decisively been made unavailable as proof of God's concern about the lives of humans.

Mr. Campbell confidently teaches that properly understood there is no conflict between science and religion. Religion is about faith and ethics. It is not a subject for proof and "understanding," like science. What counts in religion is that you believe, not that you see the wood of the Ark. "Blessed are those who have not seen and yet have believed," Jesus tells the apostle Thomas (John 20:29 (NRSV)). Science and religion are compatible because they are about different things. No problem. What kind of text the Bible is and how it has been and might be understood as a source of truth about how we should live our lives is left unclear, and probably cannot constitutionally or politically be discussed in the public school classroom in the United States. Revelation—religious evidence—has a murky status in these conversations. The Bible is accepted as authoritative because a fideist biblical Christianity is the dominant form of Christianity in the United States but the basis on which a person's convictions rest is not closely examined. And what about the miracles? Must Bryce cut them out of his Bible as Thomas Jefferson did?[6]

As for Mr. Campbell, his bifurcated solution is a common discursive strategy for scientists and others who believe that it solves their conflicting desires both to live in a modern scientific world and yet to make a space for religion.

Stephen Jay Gould (1999), the well-known American paleontologist, in his *Rocks of Ages: Science and Religion in the Fullness of Life*, characterized the relationship of religion and science according to what he called his NOMA (Non-overlapping Magisteria) principle:

> NOMA is a simple, humane, rational, and altogether conventional argument for mutual respect, based on non-overlapping subject matter, between two components of wisdom in a full human life: our drive to understand the factual character of nature (the magisterium of science), and our need to define meaning in our lives and a moral basis for our actions (the magisterium of religion). (Gould 1999, 175)

The National Academy of Sciences (NAS) has a slightly different articulation of the difference between religion and science:

> Science and religion are based on different aspects of human experience. In science, explanations must be based on evidence drawn from examining the natural world. Scientifically based observations or experiments that conflict with an explanation eventually must lead to modification or even abandonment of that explanation. Religious faith, in contrast, does not depend *only* on empirical evidence, is not *necessarily* modified in the face of conflicting evidence, and *typically* involves supernatural forces or entities. Because they are not a part of nature, supernatural entities cannot be investigated by science. In this sense, science and religion are separate and address aspects of human understanding in different ways. Attempts to pit science and religion against each other create controversy where none needs to exist. (National Academy of Sciences and Institute of Medicine 2008 (emphasis added))

For Gould, religion is about meaning and morality, a "different component of wisdom" from science. For the NAS, religion is about the supernatural. The supernatural is, by definition, not part of nature. Both assert that reasonable people can see that religion and science are in different businesses. To speak of them together is simply to stir up trouble where "none needs to exist" (National Academy of Sciences and Institute of Medicine 2008). And yet, how can it be that humans are able to access these two different components of wisdom unless religion is located somewhere in the human experience, somewhere that science seeks to explain—and unless science is understood to operate in a historical context with certain cultural assumptions? Many religious folks would claim that their "faith" is true because rooted in experience. Many scientists do in fact claim that meaning and morality can be derived from observation of the natural world.

It might seem to many in the mainstream legal academy as if Gould and the NAS and Campbell have the better of the argument. Perhaps most might even agree that such a solution is constitutionally required in the classroom whether it can be rationally defended or not. But Bryce, the student who asked the question about the Ark, also speaks out of a long American tradition, one of several in which there is significant overlap between religion and science. As American religious historian E. Brooks Holifield (2004) explains, the perennial concern in the United States about the conjunction of religion and science has a history. Many American Protestant theologians in the late eighteenth and nineteenth centuries employed a particular reading of Francis Bacon's natural philosophy, which came to them by way of their reading of the philosophers of the Scottish enlightenment, to explain the apparent contradictions between emerging modern scientific discoveries and their reading of the Bible.

The first big battle was about geology, not biology. How could the accepted biblical timeline of 6,000 to 10,000 years be reconciled with the increasingly well-documented story of geological time? Many American Protestant theologians were convinced that Bacon's inductive philosophy provided a solution, one which, in their search for doctrinal certainty, had always enabled them to find confirmation of the biblical account in nature. As Holifield says, "Most American theologians in the mid-nineteenth century turned to geology as a normative authority for interpreting scripture" (2004, 5). Relying on that authority, they accommodated their reading of Genesis in various ways. One strategy was to expand the six days into eons. This already well-practiced accommodation with respect to geology was then extended to Darwin, again adapting the biblical account to science.[7]

But other American theologians read Bacon differently, as Holifield explains:

> In 1874 Charles Hodge, who defended Calvinist orthodoxy at Princeton Seminary, published *What Is Darwinism?* He concluded that Darwinism was atheism. Hodge conceded that some form of evolutionary theory might be consistent with conservative theology, but he objected to Darwin on the grounds that the idea of natural selection permitted no reference to teleology. To bolster his case, he appealed to the Baconian view of science. The aim of natural science, he said, should be to "arrange and systematize the facts of the external world." The theologian could not dispute any "scientific fact." "Theories," however, were another matter. Darwin's explanations were no more than speculative theories. (Holifeld 2004, 6)[8]

The solution, as Hodge saw it, was to distinguish between facts and theories. Theories were a realm in which theologians could compete and a realm in which they had always had competed with natural philosophers and scientists. Hodge's criticism of Darwin was that his theories were too speculative.

But, whether you read Bacon one way or the other, the assumption of many nineteenth-century American theologians was that theology and science could and should work together. They were committed to both. Indeed, the prestige of modern science and the naïve positivism of American theology arguably together produced in the United States a distinctive way of engaging all important issues. It is a style that historian Mark Noll (1994) has described as "supernatural rationality," one that we continue to live with today. It is both pragmatic and magical at the same time. It is also intensely democratic and populist, deferring neither to clerical nor to academic authority. "Intent on preserving a religious vision of the world, the scientific creationists—like the antebellum Baconians—have in effect agreed that religious claims must be, in some sense, 'scientific' or else they are meaningless" (Holifield 2004, 10). And so also with ID, the newest creation of those who would reconcile biblical Christianity and the evidence for evolution. Both creationists and proponents of ID have arguably largely acceded to the superior authority and prestige of modern science, just as Bryce has. It is the discoveries of science that drive the story. In contrast to Gould's NOMA principle, however, these thinkers assert that truth is one, however awkward and evolving one's accommodation, and they will not have the Bible banished from the conversation.[9]

Where does/should law come into this debate? What is law's position on the proper relationship between science and religion? Between fact and theory? Between fact and meaning? Does it have one? Does law align itself with religion, or with science? Or, does law also just ask different questions? Is it also subject to the NOMA principle? Different positions have been taken on law. For some, law is simply the rational deployment of force. For some, law is—or should—be scientific. For others, law is rather an art—or a humanities discipline—continuous with other forms of moral discourse, including those of religious communities. The normative force of law, however, arguably always depends always on either implicit or explicit theories and narratives of the human and on what might be broadly termed religious anthropologies and cosmologies.[10]

The First Amendment to the US Constitution provides that "Congress shall make no law respecting an establishment of religion or prohibiting the free exercise thereof" (US Const. Amend. I). Known as the religion clauses, the Establishment Clause and the Free Exercise Clause, these words are understood today to mean, in the school setting, that students are free to practice their religion in school, outside the classroom, or silently inside the classroom, but that religion cannot be promoted by teachers or administrators or taught in American classrooms (although it is formally permitted to teach "about" religion in history or comparative religions classes[11]). Religion clause jurisprudence has largely agreed with Gould and Campbell that religion does not belong in science classes. That is the separationist position in both the legal and the epistemological sense.

One could argue then that, speaking more broadly, both in its religion clause jurisprudence and in its regulatory institutions over the last half-century or so, American law has developed a theory of science and a theory of religion. Briefly put, that jurisprudence understands science to be unitary and to be based in the scientific method and religion to be diverse and to be about meaning and morality. But this jurisprudence has failed to persuade many. Most religious people do not practice a religion that is either entirely about meaning and morality, or that is entirely non-empirical. And many would argue that science cannot be defined simply by the scientific method.[12] Science has its faith-filled promoters as well.

Religion is neither just about morality, as Gould would wish it, nor just about the supernatural, as the NAS would have it. One reason for the persistence of religion may indeed lie in its capacity to hold these sometimes disparate aspects of human experience together, not just in codes of morality, but in narrative and ritual, as well. The history of religion would suggest, in fact, that religion asks—and answers—many of the same questions as law and science and that law and science are profoundly embedded in religious understandings of the world. Certainly in the United States, as Holifield and Noll suggest, the strength of scientific positivism in all three fields and the depth of cultural Biblicism binds them together and gives them a shared history in which each discourse colonizes the other. The intertwining of discourses and the slippery nature of distinctions made by law are reflected in many recent court cases, particularly those concerning marriage and reproductive rights, but here I will focus on the teaching of evolution.

6.2 Reading the Cases

The American science classroom is now governed explicitly by law, constitutional law, statutory law, and administrative law, as is much of the rest of American life, and Christians are not the only ones complaining of exclusion. The self-proclaimed protectors of other major religious traditions have joined with some Christians to protest school curricula and the activity of science teachers. Conservative Muslims and Jews join with conservative Christians to protect their children from teaching that seems to them un-scriptural.[13] Native Americans argue that the way in which western science is taught in schools is erasing their cultural heritage.[14] And many who do not object on their own accounts are sympathetic to these worries. Reluctant to define religion, courts have responded by examining the motives of legislators and by defining science. It sometimes seems as if anything that is not science in a narrow sense, as lawyers and judges understand it, must be religion, and therefore be forbidden.

From after the Scopes trial in the 1920s until the 1960s, successful lobbying with textbook companies limited the teaching of evolution in many public schools (Greenawalt 2005; Harding, 2000, 210ff). Beginning in the 1960s, however, spurred partly by Cold War–era perceptions of a need to compete with the Soviet Union, efforts were made to strengthen science teaching. Science textbooks were revised to include evolutionary biology, spurring a concomitant return of laws prohibiting the teaching of evolution. Following on the Supreme Court's mid-century incorporation of the religion clauses into the Fourteenth Amendment and their application to the states,[15] the Supreme Court began to weigh in on the constitutionality of laws limiting the teaching of evolution with its 1968 decision in *Epperson v. Arkansas* (1968). In its decision in the *Epperson* case, the Supreme Court struck down an Arkansas law making it unlawful "to teach the theory or doctrine that mankind ascended or descended from a lower order of animals" (Initiated Act No. 1, Ark. Acts 1929; Ark. Stat. Ann. §§ 80–1627 as cited in *Epperson v. Arkansas* 1968, 98–99 n. 3). No positive teaching concerning human origins was required by the Arkansas statute. Justice Fortas' opinion for the majority found the Arkansas statute to violate the First Amendment Establishment Clause because "there can be no doubt that Arkansas has sought to prevent its teachers from discussing the theory of evolution because it is contrary to the belief of some that the Book of Genesis must be the exclusive source of doctrine as to the origin of man" (1968, 107). He added that "No suggestion has been made that Arkansas' law may be justified by considerations of state policy other than the religious views of some of its citizens" (1968, 107). The problem with the Arkansas law, according to the Court, was that the Court believed that it was improperly motivated.[16]

Some twenty years later, in *Edwards v. Aguillard* (1987), the Court held that a Louisiana requirement that public schools teach "creation science" along with evolution, a requirement which was defended as furthering "academic freedom," rather than as advancing religion, also violated the Establishment Clause, again because the Louisiana legislature was found to be motivated by a desire to advance religion. Justice Brennan, writing for the majority, and employing the newly adopted *Lemon* test, emphasized that the apparently religion-neutral language of the statute was not sufficient to pass constitutional muster:

> ... the Creationism Act is designed *either* to promote the theory of creation science which embodies a particular religious tenet by requiring that creation science be taught whenever evolution is taught *or* to prohibit the teaching of a scientific theory disfavored by certain religious sects by forbidding the teaching of evolution when creation science is not also taught. (*Edwards v. Aguillard* 1987, 593)

Again the concern was with an assumed legislative motivation. While the opponents of the teaching of evolution said that they sought to cause the teaching of science to be less imperialist, the proponents and their legal allies sought to cast the defenders of the legislation as members of a sly religious conspiracy plotting to take over the schools.

Justice Scalia wrote a lengthy dissent in the *Edwards* case, arguing that legislative motivation was an improper test of constitutionality:

> It is important to stress that the purpose forbidden by *Lemon* is the purpose to "advance religion." Our cases in no way imply that the Establishment Clause forbids legislators merely to act upon their religious convictions. We surely would not strike down a law providing money to feed the hungry or shelter the homeless if it could be demonstrated that, but for the religious beliefs of the legislators, the funds would not have been approved. Also, political activism by the religiously motivated is part of our heritage. Notwithstanding the majority's implication to the contrary, we do not presume that the sole purpose of a law is to advance religion merely because it was supported strongly by organized religions or by adherents of particular faiths. To do so would deprive religious men and women of their right to participate in the political process. Today's religious activism may give us the Balanced Treatment Act, but yesterday's resulted in the abolition of slavery, and tomorrow's may bring relief for famine victims ... Similarly, we will not presume that a law's purpose is to advance religion merely because it "happens to coincide or harmonize with the tenets of some or all religions," or because it benefits religion, even substantially. [citations omitted] (*Edwards v. Aguillard* 1987, 614–615)

Scalia also argued that there was insufficient evidence, in any event, to determine such intent, given the formal assertion in the legislative record that its object was the teaching of the scientific basis of creation, not the teaching of religion.

Edwards did not end efforts by anti-evolutionists to convince school boards and legislatures and courts that their concern was with how science is taught, not a desire to spread religion. For the most part, conservative American Christians and others want to teach religion at home or in church. And they believe in religious freedom. Indeed they believe that they invented it.[17] These issues were again rehearsed in the widely reported *Kitzmiller v. Dover Area School District* (2005),[18] a federal district court case challenging the efforts of a local school board in Pennsylvania to bring ID theory to the attention of local students. After a lengthy trial, John E. Jones III, the judge in *Kitzmiller*, found that ID is not science but religion because science is defined by methodological naturalism and ID lacks an empirical foundation in the scientific method. Since it wasn't science, it must be religion—or, as he implied—superstition. Ironically appearing as a latter-day Baconian himself, Jones announced that science is about facts while religion is about theory. Furthermore, while ID presented itself as nonreligious, lacking any explicit references to God or the Bible, its history, he said, showed it to be covertly and mendaciously religious in intention.

"Intelligent design," in its most simple semantic reference, denotes the conviction that the beauty and complexity of the natural world is itself evidence of an intelligent designer and has, at various times in history, been offered as one proof for the existence of God. Intelligent Design as a political movement came into being in the United States in response to the politics of the teaching of evolution and the failures of earlier anti-evolution efforts. As a movement, it refrains from identifying a designer, but dedicates itself rather to showing the failure of Darwinian theories to account for what it terms "gaps" in the fossil record. ID is a product, one might say, of the failure of the public discourse about religion and science teaching in the United States.

Judicial opinions on the constitutionality of various statutory efforts to limit the teaching of evolution exhibit marked confidence that religion and science are different things and belong in different spaces.[19] It is just a matter of sniffing out the impostors, or, as the ID movement is sometimes accused of, the effort to insert a "Trojan horse" into American schools.[20] But, interestingly, in *Kitzmiller*, the court also turned for the first time to a sustained effort at defining science, rather than simply looking for improper legislative motives. In addition to finding the Dover School Board's actions tainted by association with what all of the courts have derisively termed "fundamentalist religion,"[21] as in *Epperson* and *Edwards*, law, in the shape of the resolutions of the Dover school board, is further found in *Kitzmiller* to have failed in its understanding of the nature of science.[22] While the judge focused in his own opinion largely on the alleged conspiracy by ID proponents and on his own effort to define science, the expert testimony in the *Kitzmiller* decision is also sadly instructive as to ongoing misreadings of American religion by both law and science.

On October 18, 2004, the *Kitzmiller* defendants, the Dover Area School Board of Directors,[23] passed the following resolution by a 6-3 vote:

> Students will be made aware of gaps/problems in Darwin's theory and of other theories of evolution including, but not limited to, intelligent design. Note: Origins of Life is not taught. (2004, 1)

A month later, it announced that, beginning in January 2005, teachers would be required to read the following statement to students in the ninth-grade biology class at Dover High School:

> The Pennsylvania Academic Standards require students to learn about Darwin's Theory of Evolution and eventually to take a standardized test of which evolution is a part.
>
> Because Darwin's Theory is a theory, it continues to be tested as new evidence is discovered. The Theory is not a fact. Gaps in the Theory exist for which there is no evidence. A theory is defined as a well-tested explanation that unifies a broad range of observations. Intelligent Design is an explanation of the origin of life that differs from Darwin's view. The reference book, *Of Pandas and People*, is available for students who might be interested in gaining an understanding of what Intelligent Design

actually involves. With respect to any theory, *students are encouraged to keep an open mind*. The school leaves the discussion of the Origins of Life to individual students and their families. As a Standards-driven district, class instruction focuses upon preparing students to achieve proficiency on Standards-based assessments. (*Kitzmiller v. Dover Area School District* 2005, 1–2 (emphasis added))

While the School Board's statement was ridiculed in the press and by academics, the statement seems a genuine, if somewhat untutored, effort, to explain to students how science education works and how the Board intends to handle dissent in the community. It appears to be an effort to accomplish yet one more tidy two-step between Bible-believing Christianity and modern science.[24] There is no explicit mention of religion in the statement, but the confining of discussions of the origins of life to the family is a clear note that the school board wished to convey to parents their understanding that this subject matter concerns what Gould would term meaning and morals. It is, in a sense, sympathetically read, in my view, as a lay attempt at separation through a distinction between public school- and family-based education, an attempt to conform religious concerns to scientistic education policy by suggesting how students might put the two together, while keeping an "open mind."

The plaintiffs in the *Kitzmiller* case were a group of parents challenging the school board's required statement as an unconstitutional establishment of religion similar to those essayed by the legislative authorities on trial in *Epperson* and *Edwards*. The plaintiffs argued that ID, while presented by the school board as simply another scientific theory explaining the known facts about the fossil record, was in fact a religious program strategically masked as a scientific one. Among the experts supporting their theory about the essentially religious and nonscientific nature of the school board's actions, and of the unambiguous distinction between religion and science, were actual NOMA spokespersons: one of the authors of the high school biology textbook used in the Dover Area School District, Kenneth Miller, a Brown University professor, and John Haught, a professor of theology at Georgetown University (Miller and Levine 2000).

Both Miller and Haught are veterans of the evolution wars. With accomplished condescension, they meticulously noted, in their reports and in their testimony at the trial, the errors of understanding—scientific and theological—in the school board's statements and in those of the proponents of ID. Any intelligent person, they implied, ought to be able to see that religion and science are up to different projects. For example, in his expert report, Kenneth Miller carefully straightened out the difference between *scientific* fact and theory:

> The Board statement tells students that "The theory is not a fact," and that "it continues to be tested as new evidence is discovered." Both of these statements are clearly designed to mislead students about evolution. The

Board's emphasis that evolution is not a fact might be appropriate if they had pointed out instead that *no scientific theory* is a fact, and that *all scientific theories* continued to be tested in the light of new scientific discoveries. Instead, their claim that evolution "is not a fact" is clearly designed to undermine the scientific standing of evolution by implying that if science were certain of the validity of evolutionary theory, it might some day be regarded as a fact. The important point to be made is that scientific theories don't ever become facts; rather, scientific theories explain facts. (Miller [expert statement] 2005, 8–9)

Having both impugned their integrity and instructed the school board members that they do not understand the difference between a theory and a fact, Miller went on to explain why ID falls into the realm of theology and therefore does not qualify as a fact or a theory:

Joseph Levine [his co-author] and I did not include "design" theory in our textbook because it has not won acceptance from a significant portion of the scientific community ... Since the "design" explanation is not testable, it falls outside the realm of science, and places it in the realm of theology, where non-natural explanations are an accepted part of the explanatory landscape. (Miller [expert statement] 2005, 11)

"Acceptance from a significant portion of the scientific community" and "testability" are characteristics of science, not religion.

Miller did not deny either the reality or the truth of religion. Indeed, he went out of his way, in his written report, to confess his own faith:[25] "Theological explanations may be correct, of course (as when I believe that a loving God hears my prayers and acts in my life to answer them), but they cannot be tested by the methods of science—and therefore they are not science" (Miller [expert statement] 2005, 11). Although he further explained his religious views on cross-examination, he was not asked in court how he knows that God answers his prayers and acts in his life, or about what methods he uses to test such convictions. (Such scientific testing of religion is, of course, commonplace today, with respect to the effect of prayer and other spiritual practices on healing.)

Miller, a self-described Roman Catholic who cited John Paul II's encyclical *Fides et Ratio* in his testimony, further explained his religious position when he was cross-examined, affirming a belief in a God who "has a plan," quoting directly from the Catholic liturgy, and sounding in many ways at times as if he believes in something very much like ID:

Q .... you believe that the universe was created by God?

A. I believe that God is the author of all things seen and unseen.[26] So the answer to that, sir, is yes.

....

Q. And you believe that God coined the laws of physics and chemistry?

A. Well, I have to say that I'm not on the stand as you pointed out your-self, sir, as an expert witness in theology. I can certainly tell you what I believe. And that is as I said before, God is the author of all things seen and unseen, and that would certainly include the laws of physics and chemistry.

Q. And you believe that evolution is a way in which God can bring about His divine plan in this universe?

A. I certainly believe that evolution is a natural process that occurs in our universe, and as such it and all other natural processes fall in—again I don't want to pretend to be a theologian, but I think it would fall under the purview of what a theologian would call divine providence.

Q. But in terms of your personal beliefs you believe that that is consistent with God's overall plan the way evolution operates?

A. I believe that God is the author of nature, and therefore I believe that things that happen in nature are consistent with God's overall plan, and evolution is a natural process. (*Kitzmiller v. Dover School District* [transcript, Sept. 27, 2005, morning session] 2005, 62–63)

He then distinguished his position from one of philosophical naturalism, affirming instead a belief in what he called the "spiritual" correctness of the biblical account:

Q. So you don't ascribe to philosophical naturalism, correct?

A. As I understand philosophical naturalism, it is a doctrine that says that the physical world is all there is, and the only way we have of learning anything about the nature of existence is the scientific way, and if that is what philosophical naturalism means, no, sir, I am not a philosophical naturalist.

Q. Now, when you read the Book of Genesis, you take that to be a spiri-tually correct account of the origins of our species, correct?

A. I take all of the Bible, including the Book of Job, the Book of Psalms, New Testament, and Genesis to be spiritually correct.

Q. And you find repeatedly verses that say that God commanded the waters of the earth and the soil of the earth to bring forth life, and from an evolutionary point of view you believe that's exactly what happened?

A. Well, I just don't find them. They're there. And the way in which I look at Genesis is that Genesis as I read it, and unfortunately I don't read Hebrew, my co-author does, and he's frequently discussed Genesis with me, but as I read English translations of Genesis I see a series of commands of the Creator to the earth and its waters to bring forth life and, you know, without requiring, my church certainly doesn't, without requiring Genesis to be a literal history, you know, that's pretty much what happens, which is that the earth and its waters and so forth brought forth life.

Q. And that's consistent with evolutionary theory?

A. In the broad figurative poetic sense it is consistent with natural history, which underlies evolutionary theory. (*Kitzmiller v. Dover School District* [transcript, Sept. 27, 2005, morning session] 2005, 66–67)

Thus the biology professor, in a series of contradictory claims, explained that his own belief in divine providence was consistent with evolutionary theory. Denying that science was the only way of learning about "the nature of existence," he affirmed that he believes that God hears and answers his prayers but that belief is not scientific. Religion, he finally says, is poetic.[27]

Miller was then reminded by the cross-examining attorney of his testimony in another case:

Q. [referring to document] And starting at line 3 the question was asked, "When you were writing material on evolution, did you add any information on creationism?" And then your answer begins at line 5. Would you please read your answer from line 5 down to line 24, please?

A. Okay. "Answer: No, we did not, and the reason that once again is that there is no scientific evidence that supports the idea of creationism. Now, it's very important to define what one means by creationism. I'm a Roman Catholic for example, so I believe the universe was created, and you could always say that means you're a creationist. But in the modern usage of that language in the United States the word creationist means something quite different, other than a person who simply believes in a supreme being and thinks that there is meaning and order and purpose to the universe. In the current usage in the United States creationist is taken to mean someone who thinks that the earth is six to ten thousand years old, that all living organisms were simultaneously created during a very brief period of time, perhaps six days, and that the entire geologic record is an illusion, a column of flood deposition from the single forty day flood that has been misinterpreted for 250 years by the geological sciences as a series, a system of 16 geological ages." (*Kitzmiller v. Dover School District* [transcript, Sept. 27, 2005, morning session] 2005, 68–69)

Miller is here distinguishing between two theological positions on the Creation, his own Catholic one that understands God as creator but understands the evolutionary story to describe God's actions, and one that also believes that

God is the Creator but sees the description of God's actions in the Bible as being a description of historical events, skeptical of a scientific explanation that does not admit of the primacy of revelation. The *Kitzmiller* defendants' error is apparently to be a certain kind of Protestant, rather than a certain kind of Catholic.[28] They employ different biblical hermeneutics.

It is not at all clear why Professor Miller's personal theology is relevant to any of the facts at issue in the case, or why any of the testimony of the other expert on religion, John Haught, professor of theology at Georgetown University, was admissible. Haught testified for the plaintiffs concerning the distinctions between science and religion. He expressed the view that ID is "an essentially religious idea."[29] In his report (Haught 2005), having first refuted defendants' arguments that ID is not religion by explaining that ID can be traced genealogically to a line of Christian theology beginning with Aquinas, Haught concluded:

> ID tries to squeeze what is undeniably a supernatural cause, intelligent design, into an explanatory slot where only natural causes are methodolog-ically permissible ... Throughout the modern period scientific method has refused to use categories such as purpose, God, intelligence, value, mean-ing, importance, etc., and has attempted to understand all phenomena in a very limited impersonal and indeed physical, way ... *Theologically*, more-over, major traditions maintain that if God influences and interacts with the created world it cannot be in the same way that physical causes operate. From the point of view of the most prominent theologians, therefore, not only is ID poor science, it is also appalling theology. (*Kitzmiller v. Dover School District* [expert witness] 2005, 6)

Haught agreed with Miller that religion and science are compatible but differ-ent because science concerns natural causes while religion concerns ultimate explanations, although he was less persuaded than Miller about the likelihood of God's intervention in the natural world. "Major" traditions and "the most prominent" theologians have worked out a "modern" theology. No "good sci-entist" would indulge in professional speculations on ultimate causes. That is reserved for what he refers to as their "private moments." Sophisticated thinkers thus get to eat their cake and have it too. The rest, including the ID movement, are, Haught concludes, engaged in "poor science" and "appalling theology." He speaks as a theologian, that is, he speaks as a Christian thinker propounding orthodox Christian doctrine, not as an academic scholar of religion describing the vast range of Christian religious positions with respect to science.

What Haught describes as "appalling theology" is the theology of many Americans. Many Americans, including Kenneth Miller, believe that God inter-venes in discernible ways in human life. How and whether they try to explain the actual mechanism of that intervention are tremendously varied. And what role they understand the Bible to play differs. But most of them believe that the morality of Americans derives from something called the Judeo-Christian tradition, a morality that is confirmed in the natural world, in the institution of marriage, for example. To portray these Americans as primitive "fundamentalists" posing a threat to human progress is deeply problematic—descriptively, politically, and constitutionally speaking. It is thought by many, and reiterated in court opinions, that people called fundamentalists espouse something called biblical literalism, meaning that they believe the account of human origins in the book of Genesis to describe events that occurred in historical time. In fact, scholarship on conservative Christians in the United States demonstrates that they, like other groups of Christians in the United States, have a wide range of hermeneutical approaches to the biblical texts.[30] Different books of the Bible are understood to communicate in different ways and to demand different kinds of reading. But all demand fidelity, as Miller affirmed in his testimony.

The judge in the *Kitzmiller* case, John E. Jones III, now a minor celebrity on the liberal left, wrote a 140-page opinion, mostly focused on the history of ID and what he saw to be its efforts to conceal its religious genealogy, paralleling similar concerns reflected in the opinions in *Epperson* and *Edwards*. But he also extensively considered the nature of science and concluded that, as a matter of law, ID is not science, whatever its history:

> After this searching and careful review of ID as espoused by its proponents, as elaborated upon in submissions to the Court, and as scrutinized over a six week trial, we find that ID is not science and cannot be adjudged a valid, accepted scientific theory as it has failed to publish in peer-reviewed journals, engage in research and testing, and gain acceptance in the scientific community. ID, as noted, is grounded in theology, not science. (*Kitzmiller v. Dover School District* 2005, 88–89)

The judges and the experts seem to agree. Religion is religion; science is science. They know the difference. Science is published in peer-reviewed journals, the result of research and testing and accepted in the scientific community and belongs in the classroom while religion lacks these markers so does not. But their tautological definitions and certainty do not really solve the political, epistemological, or pedagogical problem.

The overlap remains. The sociological evidence concerning attitudes toward trial testimony by experts, and indeed about the culture more generally, suggests that experts are often regarded with skepticism in the United States; and that religious explanations have a persistent and stubborn salience. The *Kitzmiller* case could be seen to illustrate the tragic failure of First Amendment jurisprudence, possessed as it is by its "moral grandeur," to deal with what Bruno Latour in *We Have Never Been Modern* calls "the triage of circumstances and cases" (1993, 46). Supported by expert witnesses for the *Kitzmiller* plaintiffs who each use the modernist division of science from religion to mock the proponents of ID and to accuse them of bad faith, the court performs just the modern doubling that Latour describes; Jones says he is concerned with immanence while he trumpets the transcendence of nature and denies the hybrid nature of the situation before him. What he does could also be described as an establishment of religion, giving government sanction to one theological position among many.

6.3 Being Human Today

Bruno Latour (1993) argues in *We Have Never Been Modern* that the separation of nature and culture, and of immanence and transcendence, what he calls "the bracketing of God," is what most characterizes the modern, a strategy of separation that necessarily ignores the fact that hybrids continue to multiply. Elaborating on the thesis of Steven Shapin and Simon Schaffer (1985) in their book about Boyle and Hobbes, Latour outlines the "constitution" of the modern as being inescapably bound to the invention of nonhuman things, of "facts," in the seventeenth century. It was Robert Boyle's use of the vacuum pump that first established science as being based in practice, rather than ideas. Important as this moment is for understanding modern science, Latour insists that Thomas Hobbes' contemporaneous reinvention of politics, and the subsequent acceptance of Hobbes' analysis of power, is as important for understanding our modern predicament. In his lengthy and powerful essay, Latour explains the power of the modern as being in its capacity to wield the power of science and politics independently:

> They are going to be able to make Nature intervene at every point in the fabrication of their societies while they go right on attributing to Nature its radical transcendence; they are going to be able to become the only actors in their own political destiny, while they go right on making their society hold together by mobilizing Nature. On the one hand, the transcendence of Nature will not prevent its social immanence; on the other, the immanence of the social will not prevent the Leviathan from remaining transcendent. We must admit that this is a rather neat construction that makes it possible to do everything without being limited to anything. (Latour 1993, 32)

"They"—those Latour calls the "invincible moderns"—can control everything with their manifold separation and doubling:

> You think that thunder is a divinity? The modern critique will show that it is generated by mere physical mechanisms that have no influence over the progress of human affairs. You are stuck in a traditional economy? The modern critique will show you that physical mechanisms can upset the progress of human affairs by mobilizing huge productive forces. You think that spirits of the ancestors hold you forever hostage to their laws?

The modern critique will show you that you are hostage to yourselves and that the spiritual world is your own human—too—human construction. You then think that you can do everything and develop your societies as you see fit? The modern critique will show you that the iron laws of society and economics are much more inflexible that those of your ancestors. You are indignant that the world is being mechanized? The modern critique will tell you about the creator God to whom everything belongs and who gave man everything. You are indignant that society is secular? The modern critique will show you that spirituality is thereby liberated, and that a wholly spiritual religion is far superior. You call yourself religious? The modern critique will have a hearty laugh at your expense! (Latour 1993, 38)

Jones, Campbell, Gould, Miller, and Haught, are all modern adepts in Latour's sense. But so are Bible-believing Christians. So are we all.

Another Christian effort to reconcile science and Christianity is espoused by Francis Collins, geneticist, appointed to be Director of the National Institutes of Health by President Obama. In addition to his importance as a geneticist and leader of the genome project, Collins is the author of *The Language of God: A Scientist Presents Evidence for Belief* (2006). Collins is also founder of the BioLogos Foundation which describes its mission as follows: "BioLogos represents the harmony of science and faith. It addresses the central themes of science and religion and emphasizes the compatibility of Christian faith with scientific discoveries about the origins of the universe and life."[31] In numerous publications and public presentations, Collins has spoken of the compatibility of science and religion. He dismisses Gould's NOMA theory as overly simplistic, positing rather an open-ended interaction of science and religion, understanding them to be overlapping in many ways. Collins has described his own conversion to Christianity to be the result of his experiences as a doctor with dying patients and his encounter with the apologetical writings of C. S. Lewis.[32]

How should American courts choose between these various religious positions—and many others? It is important to note that they are all religious positions. However one chooses to locate religion in relation to law and science, one is taking a position with respect to the nature and status of religion. There is no neutral non-theological materialist position on these matters. A massive intellectual effort to rethink the secular assumptions of modernity is currently underway by philosophers, anthropologists, sociologists, and historians.[33] The secular is increasingly seen to have a history and to form itself in relation to the religious, even to invent the religious. The relevance of this debate for law is readily apparent in the evolution cases. It is becoming more and more difficult to locate the secular or to find a basis on which to do so, given the thoroughly intertwined nature of law, science, and religion.

One of the puzzling aspects of law's interactions with religion in US courts, from the perspective of the academic study of religion, is the tendency of lawyers, judges, and legal scholars to regard theology (usually Christian), rather than comparative religious studies, as the appropriate conversation partner for law.[34] On the one hand, given the normative pretensions of law and legal scholarship, theology seems a natural partner for law. Theology, like most American law, academic and otherwise, operates within certain doctrinal presumptions. Law and theology can recognize each other in some ways more easily than can law and social science. On the other hand, given critiques of the pretensions of secularism and an increased acknowledgment of religious diversity, social scientific perspectives on the history and phenomenology of religion can claim a perspective on religion that might be more useful to both legal policymakers and academic lawyers interested in understanding the bewildering array of religious ideas and practices now present everywhere in the world, within as well as outside Christianity. Christian theology, for social scientific scholars of religion, is largely regarded as a part of the data, facts not theory, at its most positivist, as law is for social scientific students of law.

Religion in many modern states is assigned the task of promoting morality through the training of citizens. The academic study of religion, on the other hand, occupies an often ambiguous space with respect to this project, understanding itself as disinterested interdisciplinary research into religion as a social and cultural phenomenon across space and time (even by some of its practitioners as science!), an effort whose relativism tends to erode any special political status for religion. The academic study of religion understands itself to be valuable for law because it can help lawyers to think about the structural relationship between religious and political institutions, the religio-political aspects of education policy, and the religious aspects of multiculturalism, among many other public issues. The comparative perspective that is foundational to the academic study of religion can, in theory, help to focus on and expand understanding of the political and legal challenges of religious, legal, and epistemological pluralism. In this context, the practical public policy implications of teaching evolution might be more successful if the public conversation was structured less by the clichéd binaries of the culture wars and more by a historical contextualization of those positions.

Legal and scientistic readings of religion often beg persistent epistemological issues raised in the academic study of religion, including the indeterminacy of definitions, recent re-examinations of the assumptions about secularization, as well as evidence of the migration, dispersal, and continued reinvention of the sacred in the modern period. Incorporating the academic study of religion into the social scientific community that is in conversation with law can illuminate what is distinctive about religion as well as what law—and science— can be understood to share with religion, historically and phenomenologically. Religion can then be seen as an ongoing source of anthropologies and cosmologies for both law and science at the same time as religion is shaped by both legal and scientific epistemologies.

One persistent misreading of religion in the American context, by lawyers and others, then, from the perspective of the comparative study of religion, reflects its protestant (small "p") bias. Taking its understanding of religion largely from an American Christian evangelical/pietist emphasis on religion as an internal phenomenon—a matter of individual belief—American law tends to regularly shortchange religion as enacted in ritual and embedded in everyday practices. The academic study of religion can fill out the nature of religion as a historical human activity for legislators and judges, for the purposes of the regulation of religious activity, the protection of religious rights, meaningful implementation of the cultural defense, etc. The neat mental compartmentalization of religion and science performed by scientists and lawyers (and by the "new" atheists) is more difficult when religion, too, is understood to be immanent.

Increasingly, the common intellectual genealogies of critical legal studies and critical religious studies—and, potentially of science studies—both broadly understood to incorporate a range of philosophical and social-scientific perspectives, are providing a space for communication among them. The deconstruction of religio-legal assumptions implied in academic law—and the academic study of religion—allows religion both to critique law and to be critiqued by it. The boom in interest in political theology is providing another point of contact. The two might be allies in calling for a more nuanced and critical understanding of the regulation of science teaching in the United States. In all of these areas, the reintegration of the academic study of religion into legal studies might enable a fuller understanding of past and present. The separationist model has assigned religion the task of ethics and personal morality. But law thinks it is in charge of ethics too. Meanwhile, religious notions and institutions of community, ritual, aesthetics, and metaphysics reside uneasily on the margins of both. The gap created by what is often conceived to be the Enlightenment legal settlement with respect to religion leaves unfinished business for the accommodation between religion, law, and science.

The academic study of religion is, of course, itself a product of this history. As with other academic fields, there is little consensus among its practitioners about the appropriate object of its study or the theories and methodologies to be employed in such studies (although most would agree that the United States word "faith" is an imperfect synonym for religion, favoring as it does a protestant Christian understanding of what it means to be religious, as well as facilitating a particular legal and political arrangement with respect to religion). The academic study of religion moves between two poles with respect to the nature of its project: the first, that religion is properly understood to be an object of study (and regulation) that is studied (and regulated) using the same social scientific tools as any other human production and without regard to the views of its practitioners; and, the second, that religion is properly understood as a unique object requiring special academic tools for its study, one that inhabits a special relationship to law and science; both law and science, on this understanding, should acknowledge its *sui generis* quality and respect the experiences and views of its practitioners.

Religious studies is a growth field. And the study of religion by people outside of religious studies is booming. This is so for obvious reasons: religious revival and increased diversity resulting from global migration and reactions to scientism and hyper modernity, as well as the politics of fear. It is also so for less obvious reasons: the decline of top-down religious authority, the fissiparous nature of religious communities, an increase of hybrid religious identities, and the decline of seminaries and doctrinal theology. These changes mean that religious practitioners and others look to religious studies as a location to think about their own traditions and those of others. The fragmentary nature of religious studies as a field reflects its subject matter and provides both an opportunity and a challenge for law.

Religion is studied by anthropologists (as culture), sociologists (as forms of social organization), historians (as motivations for historical actors), literary scholars (as texts), psychologists (as forms of experience), philosophers (as systems of explanation), political scientists (as sources of legitimation of political motivation and action), etc. The growth of cognitive science has led to an increased interest among scholars of religion in the potential for understanding religion as a function of brain activity.[35] All of this (scientific?) work arguably produces knowledge about religion that can be useful to law. What do theologians do? What do ministers and rabbis and priests and monks and nuns do? Do they have expertise that is relevant to law or is their expertise relevant only to their members? Can there be legally recognized expertise in religion? Or is that in itself establishmentarian in a US constitutional sense? Is religious studies as to theology as sociolegal studies is to law? Dangers abound for religious studies though, as with all academic disciplines that are enlisted descriptively to support normative legal projects.[36]

Law, science, and religion each, at its most ambitious, claims a space as a self-sufficient discourse and practice that aspires to occupy the entire field of human life. Modern law claims for itself the capacity to regulate all of human existence. Modern science claims for itself the capacity to explain all of that exists. Modern religion, that is, the religion of practitioners, claims for itself the right to mediate the human experience. Healthy humans are understood to govern themselves according to norms, to be continuous with the rest of the material world, and to inhabit a world structured by narratives and rituals.

What should a biology teacher do? Should she refuse to talk about religion, announcing that religion and science are different subjects? Should she attempt to harmonize religion and science, employing one of the many theologies that are on offer to accomplish such an operation? Should she make it personal, using her own religious commitments to either align herself with the student or convert the child to a different religious position? Each of these choices reflects an accommodation among the three discourses that has both a history and a present instantiation in popular religion and science as well as in academic contexts. From the standpoint of the academic study of religion, each reflects a theory of religion and a position on the interrelationship of law, religion, and science, an array of positions that cannot be resolved into one by the academic study of religion. If religion and/or law is an attempt to preserve a space for the human and other sentient beings, as not reducible to scientistic naturalism, a critical project in a time of global climate change, then the academic study of religion can help to fill out the religious field so that the religion that is represented in classrooms and courtrooms is less cartoonish. But ordinary politics will have to decide what a teacher should do. Law will be improved if we stop deferring to male clerical authority and pretending that religion is not an inescapable part of being human.

Notes

1. I would like to thank Richard Nance, Ann Taves, Mateo Taussig-Rubbo, and Robert A. Yelle for helpful conversations on the issues presented in this essay.

2. In honor of the two hundredth anniversary of Charles Darwin's birth, the NAS developed a special website dedicated to issues around the teaching of evolution. http://www.nationalacademies.org/evolution/index.html (accessed November 30, 2012). See the website of the American Geological Institute for a state-by-state analysis of education policy. http://www.agiweb.org/gap/evolution/ (accessed November 30, 2012).

3. Awareness of global competition is science education is once more a concern in the United States, as during the period after the Soviet launching of Sputnik. Many studies suggest that the United States is falling behind in science education.

4. "Scientific" was added to the standards on the insistence of Christian lobbyists.

5. In response, across the country, legislators supported by The Discovery Institute (a project of the proponents of ID) sponsored "academic freedom" bills to promote the teaching of critical perspectives on evolution. www.discovery.org/a/4537 (accessed November 30, 2012).

6. In 1820, Thomas Jefferson cut and pasted an edited version of the gospels, omitting the miracles, to create a volume he called "The Life and Morals of Jesus of Nazareth." Reprinted versions are widely available.

7. For an intellectual history of the early anti-Darwinists, see Moore (1979).

8. For one introduction to Francis Bacon's own views of the relation of religion and science, see McKnight (2006).

9. An insistence on reconciling religion and science is not a strategy only of conservative religious thinkers or only of Christians. Religious scientism is manifested in various other universalisms, shading toward mysticism and New Age spirituality as well. See Bender (2010). There are also evolutionary biologists who try to explain religion as an adaptive product of evolution. See, for example, the description of "evolutionary religious studies" at http://evolution.binghamton.edu/religion/. On reconciling Buddhism and science, see Lopez, Jr. (2010) for a discussion of a nineteenth-century effort to integrate modern astronomy into Islamic science and Stolz (2012).

10. For an introduction to the relationship of law and religion, see Sullivan and Yelle (2005). See also Sullivan, Yelle, and Taussig-Rubbo (2011). See also Cover (1982).

11. *Abington School District v. Schempp*, 374 U.S. 203 (1963). For a discussion of the problematic use of the *Schempp* decision as an origin story in the field of religious studies, see Imhoff (2016). For a discussion of the present law with respect to religion in US public schools, see Greenawalt (2005). As a practical political matter in the United States, unlike most other liberal democracies, comparative religions classes have been impossible in many school districts because of objections from the right and the left. Teaching about religion has become a more pressing matter in many countries since 9/11. In November 2007, for example, the Organization of Security and Cooperation in Europe published its "Toledo Guiding Principles on Teaching about Religion and Beliefs in Public Schools."

12. Philosopher Susan Haack (2010) asserts that there is no accepted definition of science.

13. For an excellent discussion of American Jewish teaching and attitudes with respect to evolution and ID, see Robinson (2007).

14. See for example, Deloria (1995). For a discussion of the unintended consequences of the epistemological pluralism built into NAGPRA (The Native American Grave Protection and Repatriation Act) see Johnson (2007).

15. *Cantwell v. Connecticut*, 310 U.S. 296 (1940); *Everson v. Board of Education*, 330 U.S. 1 (1947).

16. Whether religious motivation irreparably taints legislation is a matter of ongoing debate among the justices and among First Amendment scholars. Anti-evolution laws might be motivated by a desire to avoid conflict in the classroom or to privatize the teaching of human origins, as is sexuality in many districts. Arguably, legislative motivation should be irrelevant to the constitutionality of a statute. Focusing on motivation, according to critics, misreads the Establishment Clause, produces impossible evidentiary demands, depends on a completely unrealistic understanding of how legislation is produced, and arguably deflects attention from the actual effect of the statute. It also can lead, and has, at times, led, to the strategic reframing of legislation. See dissent by Justice Scalia in *Edwards v. Aguillard* (1987), discussed below.

17. Sociologist Christian Smith (2000) has convincingly documented the ongoing commitment of conservative Christians in the United States to individual religious freedom. Religious freedom, American style, is increasingly understood to have a tangled genealogy, one with important contingent political roots in the political history of British colonialism and more recently in the twentieth-century politics of the Cold War, among other motivating factors, modern political protection for religious freedom, particularly in its US iteration, finds its origins in large part in the political theories of the radical reformation, the protestant separatists who withdrew from and criticized the state churches of Europe in the seventeenth and eighteenth centuries. Evan Haefli, "Toleration and Empire" in the *Cambridge History of the British Empire*; Sullivan et al. (2015).

18. Documents from the trial are posted at the website of the National Council for Science Education. http://ncse.com/creationism/legal/kitzmiller-trial-transcripts (accessed November 30, 2012).

19. The scientism of US courts could be traced in other areas as well, including in those concerning reproductive health, family law, and sodomy, among many others. For a critique of the cases concerning reproductive health, see Bridges (2011).

20. One of the decisive expert witnesses in the *Kitzmiller* case, Barbara Forrest, presented an extensive analysis of two different editions of the book on ID recommended by the Dover School Board, purporting to show how a formerly creationist text had been purged of references to creation. One could, of course, read this as an effort to conform to the law, rather than as an effort to subvert the law.

21. Fundamentalist religion is typically defined in US judicial opinions, as is common with respect to religious matters, simply by citations to prior judicial opinions without engagement with the voluminous scholarly literature questioning the descriptive accuracy of the word "fundamentalist" and detailing the enormous diversity of opinions and religious practices among American Christians.

22. Although Judge Jones does not mention the decision, his anxiety about getting science right might perhaps be explained in part by the intervening landmark decision in *Daubert v. Merrell Dow Pharmaceuticals, Inc.*, 509 U.S. 579 (1993), redefining science for the purpose of the Federal Rules of Evidence. Concern about the scientific basis for forensic evidence in criminal cases and expert testimony in plaintiffs' personal injury cases has led to reconsideration of the standards generally for the presentation of scientific evidence in the courtroom and worry about the capacity of judges and jurors to evaluate such evidence. For a philosophical exploration of tensions between law and science, see Haack (2009).

23. The Dover Area School District encompasses an area around York, Pennsylvania, west of Philadelphia.

24. See Harding (2000), chapter 8, "The Creation Museum," for a subtle cultural reading of contemporary creationism.

25. Miller is also the author of *Finding Darwin's God: A Scientist's Search for Common Ground between God and Evolution* (1999).

26. Miller is here quoting from the Nicene Creed, the summation of Christian faith as recited by Catholics during Mass.

27. For an account of recent quantitative sociological research on the religious attitudes of scientists, see Ecklund and Scheitle (2007). Ecklund and Scheitle discuss the difficulty of generalizing from their findings about the reasons for the religiosity of a substantial proportion of American scientists. While significantly lower than the general population, roughly 50% of American scientists report religious commitments. The clearest predictor of adult religious commitment among scientists is that they come from a religiously committed childhood home.

28. Miller also displays a lack of knowledge of American Catholic history. There was a time when the shoe was on the other foot, so to speak, when Protestants excluded Catholics from public spaces because of their theology.

29. Most academic scholars of religion today would be skeptical of the notion that there are any ideas that are "essentially" religious, believing rather that what counts as religion depends on the context.

30. See, for example, Bartkowski (1996).

31. BioLogos is funded by the Templeton Foundation. www.biologos.org (accessed November 4, 2009).

32. Clive Staples Lewis, best known in the United States as the author of the *Narnia* children's book series, was a noted Cambridge University medievalist and Christian apologist. While his fantasy fiction and apologetic works are read across contemporary Christian churches, he is a towering figure in the evangelical community in particular

today. According to evangelical historian Roger Olson, "Lewis is probably quoted more often than any other single person after Jesus Christ and the writers of Scripture" because "[h]e presented an example of an intellectual engaged in the life of a major secular university holding high his Christian identity and vigorously criticizing the excesses of secular culture" (2004, 119–121). Olson adds that "It is doubtful that Lewis himself [an orthodox Anglican] ever understood his passionate embrace by North American postfundamentalists" (2004, 119–121). Or that North American fans of Lewis really understand Lewis, loyal to the end to the Church of England, an established church. For further discussion of evangelical Christianity in the United States and its politics, see Sullivan (2009).

33. Key texts in this discussion include Asad (2003), Casanova (1994), Chakrabarty (2000), and Taylor (2007). For a summary and critique of this conversation, see McLennan (2010). For a reconsideration of secularism and law, see Sullivan, Yelle, and Taussig-Rubbo (2011).

34. In another evolution case, *McLean v. Arkansas*, the well-known liberal Protestant theologian, Langdon Gilkey, served as an expert witness against the creation science statute in Arkansas. He used the Protestant Christian theology of Paul Tillich to define religion and to critique creation science. Gilkey wrote a book about his experiences in *Creationism on Trial: Evolution and God at Little Rock* (1985).

35. Empirical studies of the effects of a range of religious activities including prayer, meditation, and other forms of bodily discipline are proliferating, many funded by the Templeton Foundation.

36. Those dangers have been explored by James Clifford and Lawrence Rosen, among others. And also by this author in *The Impossibility of Religious Freedom* (2005).

References

Asad, Talal. 2003. *Formations of the Secular: Christianity, Islam, Modernity*. Palo Alto: Stanford University Press.

Bartkowski, John. 1996. "Beyond Biblical Literalism and Inerrancy: Conservative Protestants and the Hermeneutic Interpretation of Scripture." *Sociology of Religion* 57(3): 259–272.

Bender, Courtney. 2010. *The New Metaphysicals*. Chicago: University of Chicago Press.

Bridges, Khiara. 2011. *Reproducing Race: An Ethnography of Pregnancy as a Site of Racialization*. Berkeley: University of California Press.

Casanova, José. 1994. *Public Religion in the Modern World*. Chicago: University of Chicago Press.

Chakrabarty, Dipesh. 2000. *Provincializing Europe: Postcolonial Thought and Historical Difference*. Princeton: Princeton University Press.

Collins, Francis. 2006. *The Language of God: A Scientist Presents Evidence for Belief*. New York: Free Press.

Cover, Robert M. 1983. "The Supreme Court, 1982 Term-Foreword: *Nomos* and Narrative." *Harvard Law Review* 97(4): 4–67.

Deloria, Vine. 1995. *Red Earth, White Lies: Native Americans and the Myth of Scientific Fact*. New York: Scribner.

Ecklund, Elaine Howard, and Christopher P. Scheitle. 2007. "Religion among Academic Scientists: Distinctions, Disciplines, and Demographics." *Social Problems* 54: 289–307.

Gilkey, Langdon. 1985. *Creationism on Trial: Evolution and God at Little Rock*. Charlottesville: University of Virginia Press.

Gould, Stephen Jay. 1999. *Rocks of Ages: Science and Religion in the Fullness of Life*. New York: Ballantine Books.

Greenawalt, Kent. 2005. *Does God Belong in Public Schools?* Princeton: Princeton University Press.

Haack, Susan. 2009. "Irreconcilable Differences? The Troubled Marriage of Science and Law." *Law and Contemporary Problems* 72: 1–22.

Haack, Susan. 2010. "Cracks in the Wall, A Bulge under the Carpet: The Singular Story of Religion, Evolution, and the U.S. Constitution," lecture presented at the International Association for the History of Religion, XX World Congress, Toronto, August 20, 2010. (Unpublished, cited with permission of author.)

Harding, Susan Friend. 2000. *The Book of Jerry Falwell: Fundamentalist Language and Politics*. Princeton: Princeton University Press.

Harmon, Amy. 2008 (August 8). "A Teacher on the Front Line as Faith and Science Clash." *The New York Times*. www.nytimes.com/2008/08/24/education/24evolution.html. Accessed August 8, 2010.

Haught, John. 2005 (April 1). Expert Statement filed with *Kitzmiller v. Dover Area School District*, 400 F. Supp. 2d 707. Available at http://ncse.com/creationism/legal/expert-witnesses. Accessed July 8, 2013.

Holifield, E. Brooks. 2004. "The Odd Couple: Theology and Science in the American Tradition." The Ninth Distinguished Faculty Lecture. March 25, 2004. Emory University. (Privately published, on file with author).

Imhoff, Sarah. 2016. "The Creation Story of Religious Studies, or How We Learned to Stop Worrying and Love Schempp." *Journal of the American Academy of Religion* (forthcoming, March 2016).

Johnson, Greg. 2007. *Sacred Claims*. Charlottesville: University Press of Virginia.

Latour, Bruno. 1993. *We Have Never Been Modern* (trans. Catherine Porter). Cambridge, MA: Harvard University Press.

Latour, Bruno. 2010. *The Making of Law: An Ethnography of the Conseil d'État* (trans. Marina Brilman and Alain Pottage). Cambridge: Polity.

Lopez, Jr., Donald S. 2010. *Buddhism and Science: A Guide for the Perplexed*. Chicago: University of Chicago Press.

McKnight, Stephen A. 2006. *The Religious Foundations of Francis Bacon's Thought*. Columbia: University of Missouri Press.

McLennan, Gregor. 2010. "The Postsecular Turn." *Theory Culture Society* 27: 3.

Miller, Kenneth. 1999. *Finding Darwin's God: A Scientist's Search for Common Ground between God and Evolution*. New York: Cliff Street Books.

Miller, Kenneth. 2005 (March 30). Expert Statement filed with *Kitzmiller v. Dover Area School District*, 400 F. Supp. 2d 707. Available at http://ncse.com/creationism/legal/expert-witnesses. Accessed January 16, 2013.

Miller, Kenneth R., and Joe Levine. 2000. *Biology: The Living Science*. Upper Saddle River: Prentice Hall.

Moore, James R. 1979. *The Post-Darwinian Controversies: A Study of the Protestant Struggle to Come to Terms with Darwin in Great Britain and America 1870–1900*. Cambridge: Cambridge University Press.

National Academy of Sciences and Institute of Medicine. 2008. "Compatibility of Science and Religion." (From Science, Evolution, and Creationism). Available at www.nas.edu/evolution/Compatibility.html. Accessed July 8, 2013.

Noll, Mark A. 1994. *The Scandal of the Evangelical Mind*. Grand Rapids, MI: Eerdmans.

Olson, Roger E. 2004. "C. S. Lewis." In *The Westminster Handbook to Evangelical Theology*. Louisville: Westminster John Knox Press.

Ralston, Michelle. 2009 (February 4). "Fighting over Darwin, State by State." *Pew Forum on Religion & Public Life*. Available at http://pewforum.org/Science-and-Bioethics/Fighting-Over-Darwin-State-by-State.aspx. Accessed November 30, 2012.

Robinson, Ira. 2007. "American Jewish Views of Evolution and Intelligent Design." *Modern Judaism* 27(2): 173–192.

Shapin, Steven, and Simon Schaffer. 1985. *Leviathan and the Air-Pump: Hobbes, Boyle and the Experimental Life*. Princeton: Princeton University Press.

Smith, Christian. 2000. *Christian America? What Evangelicals Really Want*. Berkeley: University of California Press.

Stolz, Daniel. 2012. "'By Virtue of Your Knowledge': Scientific Materialism and the *Fatwās* of Rashīd Ridā." *Bulletin of the School of Oriental and African Studies* 75: 223–247.

Sullivan, Winnifred Fallers. 2009. *Prison Religion: Faith-Based Reform and the Constitution*. Princeton: Princeton University Press.

Sullivan, Winnifred Fallers. 2005. *The Impossibility of Religious Freedom*. Princeton: Princeton University Press.

Sullivan, Winnifred Fallers, and Robert A. Yelle. 2005. "Law and Religion." In *Encyclopedia of Religion*, 2nd ed. New York: Macmillan.

Sullivan, Winnifred Fallers, Robert A. Yelle and Mateo Taussig-Rubbo, eds. 2011. *After Secular Law*. Palo Alto: Stanford University Press.

Sullivan, Winnifred Fallers, Elizabeth Shakman Hurd, Saba Mahmood, and Peter Danchin, eds. 2015. *Politics of Religious Freedom*. Chicago: University of Chicago Press.

Taylor, Charles. 2007. *A Secular Age*. Cambridge, MA: Harvard University Press.

Cases Cited

Abington School District v. Schempp, 374 U.S. 203 (1963).

Cantwell v. Connecticut, 310 U.S. 296 (1940).

Daubert v. Merrell Dow Pharmaceuticals, Inc., 509 U.S. 579 (1993).

Edwards v. Aguillard, 482 U.S. 578 (1987).

Epperson v. Arkansas, 393 U.S. 97 (1968).

Everson v. Board of Education, 330 U.S. 1 (1947).

Kitzmiller v. Dover Area School District, 400 F. Supp. 2d 707 (2005).

7

Social Science and the Ways of the Trial Court

POSSIBILITIES OF TRANSLATION

Robert P. Burns

7.1 Introduction

This essay identifies in broad strokes some of the issues to be resolved if deft translations between the "central institution of law as we know it," the trial, and social scientific evidence is to be possible (J. B. White 1999, 108). That is a vast subject. It is addressed in detail in the many cases, few of which are reported, in which trial judges decide, with more or less doctrinal elaboration, whether or not a particular bit of social scientific evidence will "assist the trier of fact." Here I will try to identify some of the philosophical quandaries that lay beneath these particular decisions. I argue that a "craving for generality" will likely do more harm than good. I am thus in the paradoxical situation of offering general observations that urge sensitivity to context and particularity. I conclude that more sophisticated understandings of both the trial and the social sciences offer new possibilities of translation and of fruitful relationships even where translation is not possible or desirable. Throughout, I am concerned not with the social scientific treatment of the trial, surely an important topic, but with the trial's treatment of the social sciences.

The languages and rules that prevail in the contemporary American trial court are, in their detail, products of the relatively recent past, arising well after the rise of modern science. On the other hand trial practices took their contemporary shape during roughly the same period of time, the last one hundred fifty years, in which *social* science was rising and taking its contemporary form. Nonetheless, the ways of the trial court and those of contemporary social science seem to exist in different language regions, to use a term Wittgenstein often employed (Pitkin 1972, 140–149). An understanding of the possibilities of translation from each to the other is complicated by basic controversies relating to the grammar of each region. First, disputes exist concerning the range of norms that may legitimately be invoked at trial. One view, characterized below as the "received view" of the trial, is consistent with legal positivism and bears a family resemblance to philosophical neo-positivism ("logical empiricism") in the sciences. This view insists that the only norms to be deployed at trial are those embodied in the substantive legal rules and that the jury's task is to be "fact-finder," to discover the accurate "underlying" value-free factual narrative to which the legal norms are to be applied to decide the case. Other positions, more plausible in my view, suggest that the trial is a fundamentally interpretative enterprise and that its power stems from its invoking a large range of life-world norms embedded in narrative and refined by the trial's linguistic devices (Burns 1999, 155–182). Disputes exist as well on the "factual" side of the trial's functioning, including arguments about the usefulness of the law of evidence generally and particular disputes about the range of situations in which social scientific evidence will prove "helpful" to the judge or the jury.

Likewise, within the social scientific community and the philosophy of the social sciences there have long existed important controversies about whether the social sciences should emulate the methods of the physical sciences and the validity, to use a deliberately vague word, of distinctively "interpretive" methods discontinuous with those of the natural sciences (Bernstein 1976, 1–55; Turner and Roth 2003). (The "mainstream" self-understandings of the various social sciences seem to vary fairly dramatically on this question.) And these questions are themselves complicated by contemporary controversies with a lineage back to Kuhn addressing both descriptive questions concerning how the natural sciences have historically proceeded and philosophical questions about how they ought to proceed (if any such questions remain after the descriptive questions are answered) and what science achieves (e.g., the question of "scientific realism"), specifically whether natural science achieves truth in the sense of correspondence with reality or only in the sense of a wholly instrumental prediction and control (Psillos 2008; Suppe 1977, 617–730). These complexities within both language regions suggest that any translation from one to the other will involve a kind of highly contextualized prudential judgment far removed from simple deduction or categorization. After all, there are very different sorts of trials and very different sorts of social sciences.

I suggest that the oppositions between the ways of knowing that prevail in the trial court and those that prevail in the social sciences should be rethought. In particular, I suggest that the sharp oppositions between the practices are often a product of understandings or "philosophies" of each that fail to appreciate the actual practices that prevail at both trial and in the social sciences. Second, I want to follow Wittgenstein and be on guard against that "craving for generality" which demands uniform treatment of differing social scientific material in differing legal contexts. With so much controversy in both language regions, how is that likely to be possible? Once again, I find that our canonical pronouncements in the legal and in the social scientific contexts to be misleading, and a poor guide *either* to a description of our actual practice or to "finding our way around" deftly in the practices in which we are engaged.

7.2 The Received View of the Trial

The received view of the American trial understands it to be the institutional device necessary to effect the rule of law in situations where there are, unfortunately within this vision's point of view, disputes of fact. The operative understanding of the rule of law here is familiar: publicly announced rules expressing categories within which actual actions can be located and to which legal consequences are attached. In short, the rule of law is understood "as a law of rules," as Justice Scalia likes to put it and, ideally, and despite the warning by Justice Holmes, general rules *do* decide particular cases (Scalia 1989, 1). The "fairness" which a judge shows in locating a particular fact pattern within a legal category is most akin to accuracy. (Chief Justice Roberts said, recently and notoriously during his confirmation hearings, that judging was like umpiring, simply calling balls and strikes.) As we have recently been reminded by the confirmation hearings of Justice Sotomayor, the notion that a court may reach a decision by simply "following the law" is deeply engrained in our public culture. When not advanced in an extreme and deeply unrealistic form, it reflects important values in a liberal regime: the immunity of the citizen from official intrusion into his zone of freedom save under rules announced ahead of time and control of official discretion to injure or benefit arbitrarily (Hart 1968).

But in order for general rules—the "semantic content" of rules—to decide[1] particular cases, there must be a method by which the facts of those particular cases are determined accurately *and* in a form that will be utterly plastic to the content of those general rules. Those two exigencies explain the deep structure of the law of evidence and trial procedure as it has evolved in the United States (and also explain why that structure is a poor guide to what actually happens at trial, a kind of "misplaced concreteness"). The law of evidence excludes unreliable evidence by insisting that physical and documentary evidence be "authenticated," that the contents of documents be proven by the originals of the documents, and that hearsay evidence be generally excluded. The hearsay rule requires that all human statements on whose truth the jury may rely be made in court subject to the protections of the oath, the jury's assessment of the "demeanor" of the witness, and cross-examination, thought to be "the greatest legal engine ever invented for the discovery of truth" (Wigmore 1974, 32). More subtly, the hearsay rule requires that statements on whose truth the jury will rely must be made in a particular *form* which is so "artificial," so discontinuous with the way we usually speak, that it can only be imposed in court. In the jargon of evidence law, those in-court statements must be made based on "personal knowledge," that is, *perceptual knowledge*, and reported to the jury *in the language of perception.* For testimony given in court is subject to the "non-opinion rule" which excludes a large range of speech acts other than the present reporting of a past perception: no (or only unavoidable) opinions, conclusions, interpretations, recommendations, requests, imperatives, and so forth.

The requirement that testimony be in the language of perception connects up with both of the goals of the received view of the trial. Our empiricist temper has convinced us that perceptions are *generally* more reliable, less affected by our delusions and self-interest than are our opinions and evaluations. By contrast, our opinions are, as Federalist No. 10 teaches, the objects to which our self-love attaches itself. True, we can "see what we want to see," but we can also see what surprises and disappoints us.[2] Testimony in the language of perception, however, not only advances the interests of the law of rules by promoting accuracy. It also seeks to advance the liberal values embedded in the rule of law by assuring that the norms by which the jury will decide the case are the norms embedded in the jury instructions, not the values embraced by witnesses and surreptitiously injected into their accounts through styles of speech more obviously theory or value laden.

This all comes together in the received view's understanding of the evidentiary doctrine of legal relevance, one of the basic conditions of the admissibility of evidence. Relevance has two aspects, materiality and logical relevance.[3] Materiality requires that the fact any bit of evidence is offered to prove have significance *given the legal rule established by the substantive law and provided in the jury instructions.* For example, the traditional legal rule of "independent covenants" in landlord-tenant law required the tenant to pay his or her rent regardless of the (sometimes deplorable) condition of the dwelling. Thus evidence of the latter conditions (e.g., photographs of the apartment) would be "immaterial" in an eviction action and would be excluded from the trial. Material facts may be either elements of the crime or claim or episodes in a party's "theory of the case," the narrative, usually told in the opening statement, that brings the case within all the legal elements of the claim, crime, or defense or, for the defendant, places the case outside at least one of the elements. Logical relevance requires that the evidence offered have some logical force in changing the probability of a material fact. Within the received view of the trial which shapes the vision embedded in evidence law, logical relevance is a *relationship* between proffered evidence and material facts. The link between evidence and material fact is an empirical generalization. Typically, that generalization is provided by common sense and has the form, "Generally and for the most part, (e.g.) rejection by an important romantic interest creates strong feelings." (Common sense also provides an open-ended set of debatable exceptions to these generalizations, ". . . but not where (e.g.) the individual has another partner in whom he or she has a greater interest and who is requiting his or her affection.") Common sense is here understood as a thesaurus of empirical generalizations, our "web of belief," ideally without normative valence. (Normative valence would endanger the jury instructions and so the substantive law as the exclusive source of norms for decision.)

7.3 How Scientific Questions Are Translated into the Language of Evidence Law within the Received View of the Trial

Putting aside for the moment any discontinuity between the natural and social sciences, what place does science have within the vision of the trial embedded in the law of evidence? In the paradigm case, science provides an alternative link between evidence offered and some material fact. Science is thus understood to be value-free, and its deployment within the trial does not threaten the hegemony of the norms found in the substantive law. What it does is provide an alternative link to common-sense empirical generalizations between bits of evidence and material facts. A scientific generalization, sometimes a "law," replaces a common-sense generalization as the relationship between perceptual judgments and material facts. The perceptual judgments may be simply observed by a lay or expert witness or, sometimes be generated by practices distinctive to the science. The latter may include laboratory techniques with samples of physical evidence, more subjective analyses by fingerprint or ballistics technicians ("forensic evidence"), or clinical interviews by psychologists or psychiatrists. In each case, the received view of the trial would (aspire to) limit the admissibility of the "opinion testimony" that derived from the observation or the procedure to those that were "of consequence" to the issues defined by the substantive legal rule. Scientific testimony is usually[4] "opinion testimony" because the witness himself typically draws the conclusion (or reports the result of a device or procedure) concerning the material fact based on a scientific generalization, which paradigmatically has a law-like quality, known to the "expert," but outside the ken of the laymen on the jury or to the generalist judge. (Indeed, one of the usual requirements for the admissibility of expert testimony is that the jury does *not* have knowledge of these scientifically determined relationships between observations and material facts.) Difficult questions arise, on which there has been no truly principled resolution, about whether it makes sense to offer expert testimony about scientifically determined relationships between specific perceptions and material facts *without* also providing true "opinion testimony" in which *the expert himself* offers an ultimate judgment about the particular case, whether *this bridge* collapsed because of metal fatigue, or *this eyewitness* identification was inaccurate or *this defendant* could not distinguish right from wrong or has confessed falsely. After all, an expert may have developed a sort of "clinical" judgment about the understanding of a particular case against the background of his specialized theoretical knowledge and it may be nonsensical to expect a jury to make that sort of judgment itself. But in either case, the expert is offering testimony that is not limited to "personal knowledge," in the technical evidentiary sense of a report of perceptual knowledge. Instead, he or she is supplementing, perhaps contradicting, the common-sense beliefs that normally provide the links between perceptual judgments of witnesses and material facts.

The *Daubert* (1993) vision of expert testimony is of a piece with the received view of the trial. In the case of non-expert evidence, the judge is expected to do a very light policing of the relationship between proffered evidence and material facts under the rubric of "logical relevance." Here the judge is given the power to determine whether there exists in common sense an empirical generalization linking the evidence offered with the material fact which is sufficiently germane and powerful to change the probability of the material fact being true. (This would seem to be a matter of pure assessment of probabilities, but for the additional power the judge has to take into account a number of pragmatic "trial concerns," such as "unfair prejudice" or "confusing the jury" or "waste of time.") Generally, this determination is not a matter of legal doctrine at all, but a kind of meta-assessment of common sense, though accretions of various legal doctrines serve to qualify that statement. (For example, appellate cases may render generally authoritative the link between certain types of evidentiary material and the material facts, ultimately the elements of the claims or defenses, important to the case, thus "legalizing" the link.) In the contrasting case of expert testimony, *Daubert* requires the judge to perform an analogous role, though with important qualifications.

Scientific evidence is assessed using analogues to the familiar materiality and logical relevance standards. Determinations of relevancy take common sense as a source of empirical generalizations whose validity is not subject to question. When scientific evidence is offered, under a rubric usually called "fit," the judge makes a determination analogous to the usual materiality judgment, as to whether the testimony connects up, to use another deliberately vague term, to one of the elements in the claim or crime, and, on the negative side and more delicately, whether it implicitly invokes some norm of decision, embedded in the principles and methods of the science, discontinuous with the norm embedded in the instruction.[5] Under the rubric of "reliability," the judge also makes determinations analogous to the usual logical relevance determination. Oddly enough, given that they usually have no scientific training, judges are empowered to assess whether the science itself comprises "reliable principles and methods," an assessment that would never occur with regard to common sense. (Indeed, it probably *could* never occur except at the margins, given that our common sense is a function of the pre-theoretical world or forms of life into which we are always already inserted.) The judge also assesses whether the opinion is based on "sufficient facts or data," a judgment that seems akin to the ordinary determination as to whether a lay witness has perceptual knowledge, save that here the judge's determination must inevitably *itself* be based on standards developed by the relevant discipline. The judge also determines whether the expert "has applied the principles and methods reliably to the facts in the case." Here too, the court must depend on the standards implicit in the discipline, though the *Daubert* court seemed (overly) willing to generalize from Karl Popper's philosophy of science to provide a list of unweighted factors, now helpfully summarized in the Advisory Committee's Notes to Rule 702. (The *Daubert* majority was unconvinced by Justice Rehnquist's argument in dissent that it was institutionally incompetent to make judgments in the philosophy of science with apparent legal effect.)

Since *Daubert*, the Supreme Court ruled in the *Kumho Tire* case that the sort of analysis just described applies outside physical sciences and lower courts have struggled to identify how this kind of analysis, now embedded in Federal Rule of Evidence 702, could possibly apply to the range of "specialized knowledge" that includes forensic "sciences" such as fingerprint and ballistics analysis, each of which involves a subjective judgment as to whether there is a match (and with virtually no rigorous empirical validation of their methods or results) and "experiential" testimony by businessmen about industry custom and by policemen about the ways of drug dealers. They have struggled, also without consistent effect, with the applicability of these standards of "reliability" to social scientific evidence. The cumulative effect of *Daubert* on actual practice has thus been rather slight. Mostly, courts have adhered to their own relatively unexamined traditions with regard to the sorts of expert witness testimony—psychological, "forensic," and social scientific—that they have historically embraced, relying on their own rules of thumb, driven more by outcome-related concerns rather than principle. These have included maxims which have never been considered in a comprehensive way, like, "Expert testimony with regard to credibility invades the province of the jury" (Mueller and Kirkpatrick 1999, 627).

The received view of the trial and the logical empiricist (or "neo-positivist" (Suppe 1977, 619–632)) view of science have certain parallels. Positivism in science fits well with positivism in law. This is in part true because great evidence treatise writers, Wigmore, Bentham, and Thayer, broadly reflected dominant understandings of science. They were children of their age, aspiring to be men of science and to make the common-law trial broadly more "scientific." Their views shaped "the rationalist tradition in evidence scholarship" (Twining 1990, 71–76). They largely accepted the preeminence of science and the ability of science to supplement if not supplant common sense, the sharp distinction between fact and value, and that science was value-free and could advance our knowledge of issues of fact without supplanting the authoritative norms that a positivist understanding of law embraced. Both logical empiricism and the traditional non-opinion rule in evidence law were committed to the notion that perceptions were not theory and/or value laden, and so could provide the foundational bedrock basis for inferential knowledge. This rationalist tradition in evidence law would have little place for truly *interpretive* social science, just as it actually has rather little room for interpretation in its understanding of the trial, as an important aspect of the cognitive operations that take place at trial.

The received view of the trial has always been an ideal type, some would say caricature, of the actual trial as we have it. It is nonetheless important, because it animates one aspect of the trial, evidence law, and guides a good deal of actual decision-making at trial. In particular, it continues to animate decisions concerning the admissibility of evidence, including social scientific evidence. It represents only a partial view of the trial, one that reflects the values embedded in the liberal vision of the rule of law as a law of rules.

7.4 A Fuller Understanding of the Trial

Space does not permit anything close to a full account of the consciously structured hybrid of languages and practices that the contemporary trial comprises and which creates the many tensions that give it such power (Burns 1999, 2009). I can provide only a sketch most immediately relevant to the many issues of translation that arise once we have a more concrete grasp of the nature of the trial *and* of the social sciences themselves.

The trial is a set of practices designed to converge on a fair interpretation of past events and their fair evaluation in light of a set of often competing moral sources (Taylor 1992). It proceeds through the construction and deconstruction of competing and legally constrained narratives. When successful, these narratives rely on inspired simplifications that assign competing meanings to a human action to make a judgment of relative importance. They are usually rooted in the highly contextual common-sense morality of the life-world, mirror the structure of corrective justice, and place the judge or the jury within the unfolding stories; they thus reinforce that practical or moral role (Burns 1999, 171–172). The competing nature of the narratives of opening statement present contrasting "as-structures" for the case and presents an issue of practical theory choice which, like all hermeneutical issues, cannot simply be answered by comparing "the evidence" to the competing narratives. The choice between narratives is a practical choice, determined in part by moral, political, as well as legal sources. Narrative "is a demand ... for moral meaning, a demand that sequences of events be assessed as to their significance as elements of a moral drama" (H. White 1981, 1). In the trial setting, it has a public significance as well and trial decision-making is an act of political self-definition. To quote de Tocqueville's classic words, "By obliging men to turn their attention to other affairs than their own, it rubs off that private selfishness which is the rust of society" (Tocqueville 1945, I, 295).

But the narrative attempt in opening statements to subsume the events at trial to broadly accepted norms is placed in sharp tension with the obsessive concern with detailed narrative accounts presented as strictly as possible in the language of perception in the direct examination of witnesses. Without ever formulating an ever more refined rule, the jury can see the limitations of the common-sense generalizations of opening. The trial's languages thus create a "justice that is conflict" (Hamsphire 2000) and provide an internal critique of both common sense and legal rule. "[O]nly by entertaining multiple and mutually limiting points of view, building up a composite picture, can we approach the real richness of the world" (Rhodes 1992, § 7). One such tension is between "the more powerful norm" (Bennett and Feldman 1981, 5) and truth in the sense an accurate account of "the brutally elemental data" (Arendt 1954, 239) revealed in witness examination and the presentation of documentary evidence.

These tensions are enacted within a highly time-compressed dramatic event where the performances of the participants will inevitably provide metaphors and lenses by and through which to understand the underlying events: the better the case, the more coherent and convincing the performances. Even the semiotics of the physical courtroom—the spoken word at formal distances—encourage both sympathy and detachment and so good judgment. And good judgment under the "discipline of the evidence" seems to be precisely what the most thorough of social scientific investigators find when they study the trial (Burns 1999, 144–154). Philosophers have given plausible accounts of this sort of integrative judgment under the rubrics of reflective judgment, practical wisdom, and interpretive understanding (Burns 1999, 211–219).

I have noted before that this account shares with the Realists the view "that doctrine obscured more than it explained about why a court decided as it did," and who argued that "judges react primarily to the underlying facts of the case, rather than to applicable legal rules and reasons (the latter figuring primarily as ways of providing post-hoc rationales for decisions reached on other grounds" (Burns 2001, 224–225, quoting Leiter 1999, 148). My emphasis is, however, on the ways in which all generalizations, including the generalizations of common-sense "intuitive" morality, are subjected to both refinement and critique by the devices of the trial in a way that honors a literally unique synthesis of particular facts and incommensurable norms. That emphasis does not mean that there are no recurrent situations whose general characteristics are consistently judged more important than the many specific details of particular cases. However, I do suspect that at least some of the Realists' search for fairly general "situation types" in adjudicated cases may be a transposition of a craving for generality from legal formalism into the idiom of social science; it often happens that one is partially determined by what one negates.

7.5 The Social Sciences on Trial

The vision of the legal trial just sketched out understands it as a set of linguistic practices that make a normative judgment with practical import possible. Further, every trial focuses ultimately on the evaluation of and practical response to a human *action*. Now, there is a line of philosophical criticism of the very possibility of a social *science* addressing human action. Pitkin summarizes the arguments of a diverse group of thinkers in the following terms:

> In brief summary, the common structure of their arguments runs something like this: The subject matter of social and political study is actions—something unique to human beings, involving freedom, choice, and responsibility, meaning and sense, conventions, norms, and rules. Though other, animal aspects of human conduct can perhaps be studied scientifically, actions cannot. This is because the language of actions being used and shaped in the course of action by the actors, actions can only be identified in the actors' concepts and according to the actors' norms. This means, first, that detached, objective, scientific observation of actions is impossible; and second, that the explanation of actions must necessarily be in terms of the actors' intentions, motives, reasons, purposes—never in scientific, causal terms. (Pitkin 1972, 242)

Similarly, A. R. Louch writes that "ethics and the study of human action are one" (1966, 235). We "identify and describe" action "by means of terms of appraisal." "Consequently, 'there are not two stages, an identification of properties and qualities in nature and then an assessment of them, stages of which could then become the business of different experts. There is only one stage, the delineation and description of occurrences in value terms'" (Louch 1966, 56, quoted at Pitkin 1972, 253–254). Thus '[t]he idea of a science of man or society is untenable' because its method and its conception of science are "borrowed from physics," while its conception of its subject matter is "borrowed from moral action" (Louch 1966, 235, quoted at Pitkin 1972, 252).

This line of philosophical criticism of the possibility of a social science of human action has affinities with the fuller notion of the trial sketched out above. Each of the hybrid languages of the trial is in some way evaluative. Because the practical is primary and we are primarily practical creatures, the multiple languages of the trial allow for an understanding of a human act that is unsurpassed by any more theoretically or scientifically driven perspective. If disciplined social studies could achieve reliable results, they could at most allow for predictions or reconstructions of perceivable events, but never determine the human action that lay at the center of the trial. It would seem then that a social scientific account of human action would not add anything to the central enterprise at trial. Indeed, it would bring an alien and literally immaterial perspective founded on causal explanation rather than on moral judgment. It would displace the appropriate set of languages with misleading causal explanation. (This is precisely the criticism made of psychiatric testimony in criminal trials (Slobogin 2007, 21–38).) But things are a bit more complex, in ways that raise our questions of translation.

Pitkin rejects the propositions, associated with Winch, that actions must "necessarily be identified in the actors' concepts" and that "action concepts are logically incompatible with causal explanation" (Pitkin 1972, 254). With regard to the former proposition, it is not true that the individual's own conception defines his action, or that "the concepts and norms of (all the actors in) a given language region or human enterprise" (such as a political unit from which a judge or jury is drawn) exhaustively "define actions in that region" or "cross-culturally, that the norms and concepts of (the actors in) a given culture define their actions" (Pitkin 1972, 254). The *extent* to which each of them is true will vary widely with the kind of example that is chosen to illustrate the thesis: again, the craving for generality must be resisted.

Nor is it true that the various language regions which may characterize a human act—of morality, of law, of causal social science, of interpretive social science—are absolutely self-contained and universally resist translation. Consider Winch's example of a man embellishing a church with jewels. It is not true that the only way to understand his action is from within his own concepts, which may see the action as an act of prayer. "A man's way of worshipping may well also be a form of art and an action of economic exchange or saving. The economist or anthropologist is wrong only in stating his views as exclusive alternatives to the man's own. . . . And even if a nonreligious discipline, like law, undertakes to decide what constitutes prayer, we cannot conclude with Winch that it must accept a religious definition of the activity" (Pitkin 1972, 257–258).

The trial, of course, recognizes that the explanation by a party-witness of what he was doing when he acted is not absolute. *His* account, in which he was loaning money, not giving a gift; or defending himself, not gaining revenge; or engaging in an objective investigation, not coercing a confession; or independently setting competitive prices, not acting pursuant to an implicit price-fixing agreement, is important but not definitive. His actions can be and are evaluated by other actors in the same "language region," the members of the jury using the devices of the trial sketched out above. But are the disciples of economics, sociology, psychology, or anthropology—to mention disciplines whose practitioners have in fact offered expert testimony on one or other of those questions—possibly *relevant* to the normative trial determination of "what his action was"? I think there can be no one answer.

It may be true that "accounts of what the men are doing, from rival disciplines or language regions, need not be mutually incompatible; they can coexist" (Pitkin 1972, 257). An anthropologist, to choose one of the more interpretive disciplines, may say of a tribe member engaged in a traditional dance that he is reaffirming tribal norms or respecting elders when the member says he is making rain.[6] The anthropologist cannot remain true to his or her discipline and simply repeat the tribe member's account; anything the anthropologist says "has implications"; anything he says will at least imply an evaluation of the tribe member's claim, at least for some purposes (Pitkin 1972, 258–259). They will not be purely value-free. The question in our context, though, seems to be whether they can coexist *in mutually enlightening ways*, whether accounts from different language regions are relevant to each other for purposes of the kind of practical determinations made at trial. Indeed, it seems to me that much of the "chaos" surrounding the evidentiary rules for the reception of social scientific evidence at trial reflects these translation problems (Slobigin 2007, 38).

In one special context the answer seems clearly affirmative. It is *possible* that the assertions made within the language region of one or other of the social sciences may, as a result of legal developments in the substantive and procedural law, have even *more* relevance to the determination of an action than the life-world norms that dominate the trial as we have it. It is possible that the "law of rules" may at least attempt to legitimate ideals implicit in a social science that are discontinuous with those norms. Various theorists have argued that large segments of the "systems world" in modern society are, for better or worse, constituted by social scientific methods. The thrust of the *Twombley* case, which rendered summary dispositions without trial more available in antitrust cases, seems to be that the methods and conclusions of the science of economics render unnecessary, or at least economically unjustified (!), a full trial on the merits of the claim. Economics could define the act which lay at the center of the dispute without any need for the kind of trial described above.

In an antitrust case that actually goes to trial, the jury would be asked to engage in an act of "theory choice" between understanding an act within the language region of common-sense evaluation or the conclusions of applied economic science, where each perspective may "see" the act differently. Likewise, in a case involving a violent crime, where the law retains a (qualified) commitment to traditional notions of moral responsibility, the jury may be asked to choose between understanding an act through common-sense evaluation or the causal categories of psychiatry (Burns 1999, 103–123). Although the trial has a kind of procedural primacy in the legal order, the "central institution of law as we know it," it is possible that legal devices may assimilate social scientific understandings that are discontinuous with its genius. We would then have fewer trials (and we do) (Burns 2009).

Again, the narrative and argumentative language games that constitute the trial and social scientific accounts "can coexist" peacefully and mutual relevance is the real issue (Pitkin 1972, 257). We can have a conflict of interpretations where we are "essentially helpless," where the persons studied "have a different distribution of concepts altogether, a different conceptual system than ours..." (Pitkin 1972, 260). This possibility for conflict is itself rooted in the nature of human action:

> ... Here again, as within a single culture or society, action is ultimately dual, consisting *both* of what the outside observer can see *and* of the

actor's understanding of what they are doing. The duality, not the latter feature alone, is what distinguishes action. The duality, and not intentionality alone, sets the problem for social science. That problem is not, as Winch and the others argue, our inability to observe actions objectively or to identify them without consulting the actors. Instead, the problem is twofold: conceptual puzzlement when social science attempts to generalize about actions, and the necessity of commitment and judgment.

Action concepts, developed largely in the course of action, are significantly shaped by signaling or quasi-performative language games, so that their grammar is rich in potentially contradictory implications. They work well in context, in particular cases; but anyone attempting to articulate broad, general abstract principles about the nature of promises, obedience, voting, and the like will encounter conceptual puzzlement and paradox. Anyone attempting to study such phenomena scientifically, through empirical observation, will be troubled by the problem of just what phenomena count as instances of promise, obedience, voting, roughly in the way that Thrasymachus and Socrates are at odds over what counts as an instance of justice. (Pitkin 1972, 261)

And so the views of the critics of social scientific accounts of human action and their claims that the understanding of social events can only be normative are "still in the grip of the dichotomization between fact and value, ... [whereas] action concepts are not purely labels nor purely performatives...." (Pitkin 1972, 262):

An action, as Chisholm says, "is both imputative and descriptive. When we say of a man that he *did* something, we may be declaring, by way of imputation, that the man is to be held responsible for making a certain thing happen; that is to say, we may be pronouncing a verdict, notifying our hearers that forthwith we are holding this man responsible. But we are also making a descriptive statement; we are saying that the man was a causal factor in making something happen, or in keeping something from happening." And of course the two are inextricably interrelated: we ascribe responsibility *because* he *did* the action, and part of what it means for him to have done the action is that he is responsible for it. Our saying that he acted [in a certain way] goes beyond the labeling of observed motions into imputation, but not arbitrarily so. (Pitkin 1972, 262–263, quoting Chisholm 1966, 28)

Of course the practices of the trial richly reflect and comprise both description and evaluation and, indeed, *enact* the close relationship between description and evaluation. It is because the trial pays an almost obsessive attention to description and then redescription, breaking through its various forms of narrative, that its evaluation can be so refined. As we will see shortly, there is no categorical reason why social scientific evidence may not contribute to this enterprise. Its contribution may be different depending on whether the empirical science is descriptive or interpretive or quantitative-causal. In the former two cases, the evidence may simply be continuous with the trial's general effort to determine the appropriate reach of competing general norms. In the latter case, social scientific evidence may be relevant to the question of whether we are considering a human act at all.

Pitkin's reflections on these questions of translation are based on Wittgenstein's later philosophy. A key development was his rejection of the positivist notion that more complex propositions could be translated without remainder into more basic propositions about perceptions or even sense data (Pitkin 1972, 28–29). One reason why his later philosophy came to emphasize the multiplicity of "language games" rooted in different "forms of life" was to reject the positivist notion that the central function of language is to make claims about what is the case. Wittgenstein never provided a complete inventory of these language games or language regions.

> He uses "language game" as more or less synonymous with "way of operating with language in action," and no one would be tempted to catalogue all the ways that we may do that. He uses "forms of life" as more or less synonymous with "coherent pattern of human activity or reaction," and no one would be tempted to classify such patterns exhaustively. For Wittgenstein, the point is that language games and forms of life *exist*, and that they are tremendously *varied* and that whenever we become particularly interested in a particular one we can describe and explore it. (Pitkin 1972, 147)

"Confronted with this multiplicity of language uses, we are less likely to suppose that one or two of them must be privileged cases which define the essence of language and that the others need to be translated into these privileged cases before they can be fully understood" (Pitkin 1972, 42). When a proposition spoken in one language game is analyzed and then reconstituted within another "an aspect of the matter is lost on you" (Wittgenstein 1958, 31e). "It is not that we never refer or describe, never make true or false assertions, never use words as labels. But these functions are not privileged or definitive" (Pitkin 1972, 43). Full translatability in or out of the languages of description, explanation, or evaluation is not to be expected.

But this should not be taken to an extreme. Some later philosophers were given to ontologizing this multiplicity of language games into rigidly defined and separated "regions or strata in our language," a development "likely to foster the illusion of systematic rules, of sharply distinct, fixed subdivisions whose boundaries may not be violated" and among which there no translations (Pitkin 1972, 146). Wittgenstein spoke of language being like an old city, "a maze of little streets and squares, of old and new houses, and of houses with additions from various periods" (Wittgenstein 1958, 8e). This old city of life-world languages has been "surrounded" with the languages of science: "a multitude of new boroughs with straight regular streets and uniform houses" (Wittgenstein 1958, 8e). However, too rigid a separation between the language regions where we describe and evaluate human action in moral terms and those where we bring at least some social scientific approaches to bear places us "in danger of wanting to treat the center of our ancient city as if it consisted of nothing but suburbs" (Pitkin 1972, 146).

> But any subdivisions we distinguish within the main body of our language will be only questionably distinct; the categories will be categories *we* set up because we happened to have concepts available for them: "science," "morality," "religion," and so on.... One may treat mathematics as a language region, but one may also see it as a whole collection of different language regions with different rules. And how much more will this be true in "regions" like "historical discourse," "music-criticism discourse," "accounting discourse," and so on. How many categories are there? And does every possible utterance fit into just one of them? And is each of them internally consistent, or can they have conflicted subdivisions? Here, as elsewhere in the study of language, the borderline will often depend on what we decide to take as a borderline for particular purposes. (Pitkin 1972, 146–147)

And so it is not surprising that there are continuing controversies concerning the degree to which one form of discourse may be translated into another and, in our context, the extent to which one form of discourse may be *relevant* to another. Writers like "Winch, Polanyi, and Oakeshott, maintain that the regions are not mutually reducible, that the terms of one cannot be *exhaustively* [emphasis added] characterized by or translated into the terms of another. H_2O is not just another name for water, and promising is not just another name for physical movements" (Pitkin 1972, 148). There is no complete theoretical reconciliation of language regions because different practical interests define the regions.

> But other writers point out that divisions among language regions are not that sharp; and that the different regions do, after all, form a single language.... What can be said in one context by the use of a certain expression depends for its sense on the uses of that expression in other contexts (different language games). Thus, the idea of language regions is a difficult and perhaps seductive one, the nature, identification, and distinctness of such regions being theoretically troublesome. We must consequently take special care never to use the conception as a pseudo-explanation, as an excuse for our failure to think or our failure to look and see how language is actually used. (Pitkin 1972, 148–149)

In the context of the trial, we should not be too quick to say in categorical terms that perspectives from the social sciences are not relevant to both defining and evaluating a human action.

7.6 Conclusion

The master criterion for the relevance of all expert witness testimony at trial is that it "assist the trier of fact or determine a fact in issue."[7] Helpfulness cannot be reduced to "reliability" understood in the ways in which *Daubert* at least seemed to imply, with its privileging of hypothesis testing, known error rate, and peer review. There is no categorical reason why social scientific perspectives cannot contribute to the interpretive enterprise and the evaluative enterprise as well.

The danger is not a categorical problem about mixed language regions, but a wholly practical one, that the productive tensions of the trial could be dissipated by injection of more theoretical issues and perspectives from the various disciplines in a way that leaves the jury helpless. That is the practical fear that underlies aversion to the trial becoming a battle of the experts. One of the trial's strengths is that it resists the obfuscation of technical language and preserves a "strong truth-bearing everyday language, not marred or corrupted by technical discourse or scientific codes . . . of which we are in need as citizens, and as moral agents" (Murdoch 1992, 162). But in some contexts we may argue that juries are *entitled*, in the exercise of judgments for which they are morally responsible, to the perspectives brought by good social science and which may serve to deepen and elevate the exercise of their common sense in much the way that the devices of the trial themselves do. (I think of the good social scientific studies addressing the limitations of eyewitness identification and the circumstances likely to produce false confessions.) Of course, it is reassuring to remember that the discourse goes both ways. Social scientific judgments themselves, at least as they bear on questions of particular fact, may be elevated and disciplined by the devices of the trial: the requirement of evidentiary foundations as to the adequacy of its data and methods, cross-examination, the presentation of contrary evidence, and final argument (Slobogin 2007, 88–89).

It is important not to overemphasize the discontinuity between the social sciences as we actually have them with the kind of thinking that takes place at trial. After all, they operate within the "manifest image" of man, the perspective that implicitly conceives of persons with intentions acting subject to ethical and logical norms. They sometimes seek to discern and establish correlations and employ an aspect of the scientific method that can be described as "correlational induction" (Bernstein 1976, 122). They do not, however, pose a fundamental challenge to the interpretive perspective employed at trial by invoking "scientific image" that postulates the exhaustive causal power of theoretical entities without human meaning joined by mathematical covering laws (Bernstein 1976, 122).

There is thus considerable continuity between much social scientific work and the elevated and critical common-sense perspectives the trial realizes. Their language regions significantly overlap. Descriptive social science may provide a broader factual context for jury decision-making. Interpretive social science may enrich the jury's understanding of the meaning of the human acts being judged. Although much social science may fail the Popperian tests *Daubert* invoked it may *for that very reason* prove helpful to the judge or jury in refining the common sense through which he or she decides the case. Consider, for example, Alasdair MacIntyre's account of the kind of social science most likely to provide the "best available stock of generalizations about social life":

> It seems probable that they will have three important characteristics. They will be based on a good deal of research, but their inductively-founded character will appear in their failure to approach law-likeness. No matter how well-framed they are the best of them may have to coexist with counter-examples, since the constant creation of counter-examples is a feature of human life. And we shall never be able to say of the best of them precisely what their scope is. It follows of course that they will not entail well-defined sets of counterfactual conditionals. They will be prefaced not by universal quantifiers but by some such phrase as "Characteristically and for the most part. . . ."
>
> But just these, as I pointed out earlier, turned out to be the characteristics of the generalizations which actual empirical social scientists claim with good reason to have discovered. In other words the logical form of those generalizations—or the lack of it—turns out to be rooted in the form—or lack of it—of human life. We should not be surprised or disappointed that the generalizations and maxims of the best social science share certain characteristics of their predecessors—the proverbs of folk societies, the generalizations of jurists, the maxims of Machiavelli. (MacIntyre 1984, 104–105)

This sort of social science may thus be able to provide historical or social context or serve as an important corrective where one or other of the "generally and for the most part" maxims of common sense is skewed, perhaps the result of one of the familiar heuristics of practical reasoning. Even without full translatability, social scientific testimony and, one day, jury instructions rooted in our most reliable and replicated social scientific inquiries may add something to the trial's richness.

Philosophers have argued that we can gain insight through the tensions among perspectives not fully translatable into one another. "We achieve insight by making something appear by juxtaposing images or, even harder to explain, by juxtaposing words. The epiphany comes from between the words or images, as it were, from the force field they set up between them, and not through a central referent which they describe . . ." (Taylor 1992, 465–466). Insight can come from "a juxtaposed rather than integrated cluster of changing elements that resist reduction to a common denominator, essential core, or generative first principle" (Bernstein 1992, 201).

Notes

1. Ideally, the process of subsumption of the particular under the general would be deductive (Steinberger 1993, 91).

2. The non-opinion rule was relaxed, allowing a broader range of opinion testimony, just as an understanding of "the given" truly was "a myth" occurred in the philosophy of science as part of the upending of logical empiricism. In both the law of evidence and the philosophy of science, the partial "theory-ladenness" of perception is now accepted. Federal Rule of Evidence 701.

3. In the scheme of the Federal Rules of Evidence, "relevance" is the master category of which materiality is one aspect: "'Relevant evidence' means evidence having any tendency to make the existence of any fact that is of consequence to the determination of the action more probably or less probable than it would be without the evidence." The notion of materiality is embedded in the language "any fact that is *of consequence* to the determination of the action." The notion of logical relevance is embedded in the words "any tendency to make the existence of any fact . . . more probably or less probably than it would be without the evidence."

4. The Federal Rules of Evidence allow an expert to testify in the form of an opinion "or otherwise."

5. For an argument that this rule is often honored in the breach in the ubiquitous psychiatric testimony in criminal trials, *see* Slobogin 2007.

6. The example is Pitkin's own.

7. Federal Rule of Evidence 702.

References

Arendt, Hannah. 1954. "Truth and Politics." In *Between Past and Future: Eight Exercises in Political Thought*, by Hannah Arendt, 227–264. New York: Penguin Books.

Bennett, W. Lance, and Martha S. Feldman. 1981. *Reconstructing Reality in the Courtroom: Justice and Judgment in American Culture.* New Brunswick: Rutgers University Press.

Bernstein, Richard J. 1976. *The Restructuring of Social and Political Theory*. Philadelphia: The University of Pennsylvania Press.

Bernstein, Richard J. 1992. *The New Constellation: The Ethical-Political Horizons of Modernity/Postmodernity.* Boston: MIT Press.

Burns, Robert P. 1999. *A Theory of the Trial*. Princeton: Princeton University Press.

Burns, Robert P. 2001. "The Lawfulness of the American Trial." *The American Criminal Law Review* 38: 205–231.

Burns, Robert P. 2009. *The Death of the American Trial*. Chicago: University of Chicago Press.

Chisholm, Roderick K. 1966. "Freedom and Action." In *Freedom and Determinism*, edited by Keith Lehrer, 11–44. New York: Random House.

Hampshire, Stuart. 2000. *Justice is Conflict*. Princeton: Princeton University Press.

Hart, HLA. 1968. *Punishment and Responsibility: Essays in the Philosophy of Law*. Oxford: Clarendon Press.

Leiter, Brian. 1999. "Positivism, Formalism, Realism." *Columbia Law Review* 99: 1138–1164.

Louch, A. R. 1966. *Explanation and Human Action*. Berkeley and Los Angeles: University of California Press.

MacIntyre, Alasdair. 1984. *After Virtue*. Notre Dame: Notre Dame University Press.

Mueller, Christopher B., and Laird C. Kirkpatrick. 1999. *Evidence, Second Edition*. New York: Aspen Law and Business.

Murdoch, Iris. 1992. *Metaphysics as a Guide to Morals*. New York: Penguin Books.

Pitkin, Hanna Fenichel. 1972. *Wittgenstein and Justice: On the Significance of Ludwig Wittgenstein for Social and Political Thought*. Berkeley: University of California Press.

Psillos, Stathis. 2008. "The Present State of the Scientific Realism Debate." In *Philosophy of Science Today*, edited by Peter Clark and Katharine Hawley, 59–82. Oxford: Oxford University Press.

Rhodes, Richard. 1992 (Jan. 26). "The Philosopher Physicist," *New York Times* (reviewing Pais, Abraham. *Neils Bohr's Times: In Physics, Philosophy, and Polity*).

Scalia, Antonin. 1989. "The Rule of Law as a Law of Rules." *University of Chicago Law Review* 56: 1175–1188.

Slobogin, Christopher. 2007. *Proving the Unprovable: The Role of Law, Science, and Speculation in Adjudicating Culpability and Dangerousness*. Oxford: Oxford University Press.

Steinberger, Peter J. 1993. *The Concept of Political Judgment*. Chicago: University of Chicago Press.

Suppe, Frederick. 1977. *The Structure of Scientific Theories*. Urbana: University of Illinois Press.

Taylor, Charles. 1992. *Sources of the Self: The Making of the Modern Identity*. Cambridge: Cambridge University Press.

Tocqueville, Alexis de. 1945. *Democracy in America* (Harry Reeve trans.). New York: Vintage Books.

Turner, Stephen P., and Paul A. Roth, eds. 2003. *The Blackwell Guide to the Philosophy of the Social Sciences*. Oxford: Blackwell Publishing.

Twining, William. 1990. *Rethinking Evidence: Exploratory Essays*. Oxford: Basil Blackwell.

White, Hayden. 1981. "The Value of Narrativity in the Representation of Reality." In *On Narrative*, edited by W. J. T. Mitchell, 1–23. Chicago: University of Chicago Press.

White, James Boyd. 1999. *From Expectation to Experience: Essays on Law and Legal Education*. Ann Arbor: University of Michigan Press.

Wigmore, John H. 1974. *Evidence in Trials at Common Law*, vol. 5, sec. 1367, edited by James H. Chadbourn. Boston: Little Brown.

Wittgenstein, Ludwig. 1958. *Philosophical Investigations* (G. E. M. Anscombe trans.). New York: Macmillan.

Cases Cited

Bell Atlantic Corporation v. Twombly, 550 U.S. 544 (2007).

Daubert v. Merrell Dow Pharmaceuticals, 509 U.S. 579 (1993).

Kumho Tire Co. v. Carmichael, 526 U.S. 137 (1999).

8

Part Two Commentary

PROCESSES OF TRANSLATION AND DEMARCATION
IN LEGAL WORLDS

Susan Gal

8.1 Introduction

"Translation" is a fruitful metaphor suggesting a whole family of processes. They purport to change the outward form, social place, or meaning of a text while also, *at the same time*, seeming to keep something about it the same. The change then comes to seem a mere repetition. Most familiarly, translation renders in one language system what has been said or written in another. The usage of *translation* as a term has been extended considerably in recent decades, as in the phrase "the translation of DNA to RNA to protein." But such extension is nothing new. Practices and objects too can be translated. There is a history of diverse uses of the term, indexing different social domains: Removing a bishop from one see to another; conveying a person to heaven without death; imputing linguistic specificity to a gesture such as a smile; rendering academic research available for practical use; imparting motion without rotation to a mechanical object. And most generally: paraphrasing or expressing one thing in terms of something else. All these have been called translation.

Such a disparate list points to the double effect: a similarity between two utterances or practices is coupled with an apparent change or difference. This produces a duality that, for those who take it up, yields the effect of movement ("from-to," hence "trans").[1] Judgments of similarity and difference are centrally at issue. It is therefore important to remember that any two texts (or objects, practices) have innumerable qualities and properties, many of which can be picked out as similar in some way. Thus, similarity and difference are always judgments relative to those who judge and to their roles, situations, and projects (Goodman 1971). We have to ask: In what way is *this* a translation of *that*?

What frames of understanding—what priorities, situations, metadiscourses, ideologies, presumptions—enable us to see a bishop as the same before and after taking up his new post, while at other times or for other purposes we see instead the ways he is different. How and for what purposes is a smile the same as a description of it? By invoking the meta-term *translation*, both similarity and difference seem to be acknowledged: Same-yet-different. But, in what respects? This turns out to be a question for any instance of language use.

Indeed, it is a truism in the social study of language that *texts*—defined as coherent chunks of ongoing real-time, discursive practice—may be endlessly cited, recited, imitated, parodied, quoted, and otherwise reported and repeated in whole or in part. Each such citation is an *entextualization*, constructing the textual form itself, as well as its reframing and *recontextualization*. Any quotation is simultaneously imitative and novel. Considered semiotically, objects and practices are also recontextualizable in this way, when they are reframed by metacommunicative signals. It is ideologies of language—or semiotic ideologies generally—that constrain what properties are in focus; in what ways a practice, an "object" or text is seen to be (partly) stable, a repetition—or to be regimented now by some different social and institutional context; perhaps seen as *token* of a different *type* (Silverstein and Urban 1996).

Recontextualizations, as discussed in the informative chapters by Ford, Sullivan, and Burns, are not simply quotations of talk from one scene in another ("As I said yesterday: read that book"). Nor are they translations from one standard language to another. Rather, they are utterances within one standard language (English), repeated (or quoted, imitated, reframed) in a saliently different, ritually central, and highly consequential social scene: the American courtroom and legislature.

In these chapters, analyses of video game violence published in social science journals are discussed and cited in courts and legislatures; avowals of religious faith usually made in church are restated in court; definitions of science—by scientists—are heard by the court; diagnoses by psychiatrists from their case-notes are displayed in court. The types of analyses, avowals, definitions described here are text-types with specific discursive features, each arising through its own conventional practices of making knowledge. Each indexes stereotyped personae, social roles, values, and epistemological assumptions. So does the court, via its own special linguistic practices. Bakhtin (1981) would call all these *social languages*. Sociolinguists call them *registers*. With different emphases Wittgenstein wrote about *language regions*, anthropology usually calls them *discourses*, and this volume is aptly calling them *disciplinary languages*. The chapters focus on contextually specific intertwinings of disciplinary languages. The questions are not simply about "social science" in "law," nor "translation" in the usual cross-language sense. Rather, we have evidence about several specific ways social actors in legal contexts take up, recontextualize, and repurpose varied social scientific texts.

What insights does a linguistic anthropological approach offer for understanding the semiotic and communicative processes discussed in these chapters? I would like to elaborate on three points the chapters raise. First, what dominant *language ideology*—i.e., metacommunicative assumption—plays a role in all the institutional contexts discussed here? Since language ideologies render some aspects of linguistic practice obvious to participants while erasing others, what suppositions about language exist in these examples, but remain hidden (Gal and Irvine 1995; Irvine and Gal 2000)?

Second, considered in the light of language ideologies, semiotic devices that create equivalence-in-difference (*translation*) are not all alike. I focus on two. The first of these finds or creates pragmatic analogies between texts or practices in different disciplinary languages (*transduction*). It creates authority for one set of practices by modeling them on another. The second *subsumes* the practices and texts of one disciplinary language by reframing them as also, and more consequentially, instantiations (*tokens*) of categories (*types*) defined by another (*voicing/polyphony*). These two mechanisms have quite different social results (Gal 2015). Expert testimony at trials—mentioned in all three chapters—is an illustration of translation-as-voicing. It helps in understanding how the credibility of social science testimony is locally achieved or denied.

Finally, the papers discuss the way law takes up the demand to draw boundaries between discourses, distinguishing "religion," "science," "law," even though these disciplinary languages have been closely intertwined in US history. Pushing this observation a step further, I argue that the disciplinary languages are not only intertwined but historically co-produced through competitive transductions. This is one way new categories of social life are created. To be sure, it is often courts that accomplish the separations. But equally important, I suggest, are the actions of social movements and activists that appeal to legal process for the authorization of the novel categories and distinctions the movements create.[2] Those distinctions themselves—of knowledge forms, identities, social practices, psychopathologies—are often part of *looping effects* (Hacking 1999) derived from and with impact on social science. Many apparent "translations" of social science categories to legal contexts are mediated in this way by social movements. Law adds to its own legitimation in the process, first by deciding its jurisdiction over new categories, and also by taking up the call to ratify or deny distinctions among discourses.

8.2 Language Ideologies/Metacommunicative Assumptions

To illustrate disciplinary languages and their multiple relations to language ideologies, let us consider two brief examples. The point is to show that an overarching and very powerful language ideology of Euro-American communicative practice focuses attention on *denotation* and often on single words (Bauman and Briggs 2003). That is, the ideology limits our view to word-as-labels, eschewing attention to contextual meaning (*pragmatics, indexicality*). It narrows our curiosity to one question: whether or not the word-label accurately corresponds to some item in what is assumed to be a separately available real world. The "facts" of the world can, on this view, be separated from the value placed on them by a speaker who describes them. The possibilities of interpretation are thereby limited to two: under the aegis of this ideology, the world can be described *either* truthfully and accurately *or* unreliably, erroneously, and duplicitously. It is this ideology that subtends what Burns identifies as the positivist or "received" view of the trial. Yet, as Burns rightly argues, there are other ways of analyzing the language of trials. Indeed, participants themselves invoke other ways of interpreting. Two examples illustrate this.

The first, from Sullivan's chapter, was part of an exchange at trial. Mr. Miller, a self-described scientist and practicing Roman Catholic, testified as a scientific expert witness in a trial concerning policy in the handling of Intelligent Design in a public school. Although not a religious expert, he was nevertheless cross-examined by the opposing attorney about his religious views:

Q: . . . you believe that the universe was created by God?

A: I believe that God is the author of all things seen and unseen. So the answer to that, sir, is yes.

The attorney was perhaps trying to undermine Mr. Miller's testimony by catching him (a scientist!) in an inconsistency by getting him to admit to a view that, as Sullivan points out, pretty much matches denotationally the one proposed by Intelligent Design. But Mr. Miller's words are not only denotational. They also and inescapably have an indexical dimension that ties them to a set of values. They invoke by quotation a disciplinary language that indexes social roles, epistemologies, institutional locations, and values not present in the immediate social setting of the trial. In the first sentence of his reply, Mr. Miller is quoting with utmost seriousness the Nicene Creed, today taken to be definitional of virtually all forms of Christianity. In this way, he is momentarily inhabiting the social role of Christian believer that is indexed by that disciplinary language. Such quotations are recognizable, even if they are not explicitly marked, because disciplinary languages (like all registers and the textual genres associated with them) have an internal coherence that allows knowledgeable listeners to hear them as instances (tokens) of their type, even outside of their usual social and institutional context.

Mr. Miller, like all social actors, can and does inhabit numerous social roles that are not necessarily entirely consistent with each other. Rather, they each fit a particular institutional context.[3] Mr. Miller's response, far from undermining his scientist's position, could as well be read as making hearable the other institutions in addition to science (and the legal system) in which he participates. Read within an ideology that recognizes indexical meaning, this verbal exchange could stand as a model (an icon) of the relationship between religion and science that Mr. Miller supports: Simultaneous commitment to two different disciplinary languages that admittedly contradict each other as denotation, but are appropriate to and gain their deeper significance in different social institutions. The attempt to undermine his expert credibility fails if the cross-examination is seen to pose a false dichotomy.

There is also a more delicate point here. As commentators on American legal language have noted, the ideology of trials is officially denotational. Denotationally, "created by God" and "God ... the author" might well be taken as equivalents. Mr. Miller can answer "yes" to the question in the explicit ideological frame of the court. He will not be taken to be lying. But, as Mr. Miller himself later explains, the term he chooses is significant. He avoids "created" because it has become associated with (indexical of) a social position, namely "creationism," that he rejects in the legal dispute being adjudicated. Although he is a witness in a courtroom, Mr. Miller is relying on a metadiscursive frame (an ideology) that prioritizes the indexical value over the denotational. For him, in using one term over another in this scene, the issue is not a denotational (truth-value) one of what God did or did not do. It is a political one of which "side" in this dispute Mr. Miller's response is formulated to support. Both ideological frames are in play.

Another example comes from a dialogue in Mertz's analysis of law school classrooms. It shows the general applicability of the insight that different disciplinary languages—and different ideologies—can be operating within the same standard language (here English), and within the same social scene. The class is reading the summary of a personal injury case and the professor starts with a question:

P: ...How did this [case] get to the appellate court?

A: Well, um the the patient was a woman who wanted a –

P: How did this case get to the appellate court?

A: The defendant disagreed with the way the damages were awarded in the trial court.

P: How did this case get to the appellate court? The Supreme Court once a—I think this is true—they asked some guy who'd never argued a case before

the Supreme Court before—they said to him—[...] ah, Counsel, how did you

get here? (Laughter) Well, he said, I came on the Chesapeake and Ohio River (Louder laughter). How did this case get to the supreme judicial court?

A   It was appealed.

P: It was appealed, you say. Did you find that word anywhere except in my problem? (Mertz 1996, 230).

The example displays the difference between the everyday understanding of the phrase "get to" and uptake of it as part of the disciplinary language of the law. As Mertz shows, the legal way of "reading" includes recognizing the procedural history of the case, a matter not explicitly found in the written case summary. Learning this is part of the socialization to the lawyer role. But the students will not stop using the ordinary, non-legal version of this phrase even when they have become seasoned lawyers. As in Mr. Miller's response, so in Mertz's example, different disciplinary practices do different kinds of interactional and institutionally appropriate "work"; several disciplinary languages can coexist even in a single moment of a social scene. As Burns warns, Wittgenstein's term *language regions* would be misinterpreted if we think of disciplinary languages as isolated or separated. On the contrary, the effects we see here—Mr. Miller's carefully formulated position; the student's initial befuddlement—are due to the invocation of several disciplinary languages, simultaneously.

What is true for "get to" and "author" and "creation" is also true for many of the social scientific phrases discussed in Ford's chapter. Each denotes something in the real world, but it does so by its relation to social institutions whose practices of knowledge-making either define or actually create the object named. The practices point to a way of discerning or constituting that "thing in the world" and then they "baptize" or name it.[4] The social institution becomes the authorizer for that type of use of that linguistic form. The American legal system teaches, and through its manifold practices reproduces, the particular relationships among courts of different jurisdictions that are named by this use of "get to" in Mertz's example. The legal system also authorizes this usage.

Similarly, Ford describes the practices by which social scientists who research video games have defined "violence," and the ways social scientists define "causation" and "certainty." The knowledge-practices invariably imply epistemological and ontological commitments, and these are different from the assumptions embedded in legal epistemology. Yet many definitions and commitments no longer need to be mentioned; they are presupposed. Indeed, presupposing the definitional/stipulative practices, the interpretive procedures, the forms of "reading" characteristic of a legal or a research tradition, of a religious community or of other kinds of social grouping, is usually one of the ways to signal membership. It is a way to inhabit the institution's roles in the relevant settings. Thus, even if members were aware—or could be aware—of all such presuppositions, there are likely to be social costs and contextual constraints on making them explicit. This creates difficulties for those who, relying on referentialist ideology, search only for "accuracy" in the way words label supposedly preexisting phenomena.

Close analyses of legal language show that within the institution of American law itself there are several ideologies at play, contrasting ways of regimenting linguistic practices. Different ones apply to different aspects of the legal system, to different roles, or to different understandings of the way the trial operates. In addition to what Burns calls the "received" view of the trial, in which a referentialist, denotation-focused ideology is prominent, there are, as Burns notes, "interpretive" approaches and a whole raft of "hybrid languages of the trial" practiced if not always acknowledged. Many of these other ideologies deny the separation of fact and value that the received (positivist) view affirms. Techniques of persuasion used by advocates are often based on such alternate presumptions. Distinctions in presuppositions about language appear also within subfields. In evidence law, juries and judges are assumed to differ in the way they process what they hear and see (Philips 1993). It has been standard practice to strike from juries those who are knowledgeable in the relevant areas at issue in a trial, in order to maintain the jury's lack of "bias." Yet judges are often expected to know far more than they actually do—as in Ford's (2013) examples in his previous article on this topic—about relevant areas, if they are to be fair-minded.

The logic of legal precedents provides a further example. While a referentialist ideology would presume that texts describing cases have determinate meanings because they label the world, Mertz shows that in US case law, "what a text 'means' only emerges as it is interpreted as precedent in subsequent cases; at the same time . . . any subsequent authoritative interpretation relies in a fundamental way upon the authority of the prior text. In terms of meaning and authority, these legal texts are mutually constitutive" (1996, 235). Yet there are moments when the texts are "fixed" as precedent, only to be "re-fixed" in another case. As Edward Levi noted: "The words used by the legislature or the constitutional convention must come to have new meanings . . ."; the law forum is a mechanism for "a moving classification system" (1949, 4). These interpretive practices change the kinds of facts the words denote; the practices thereby fail to conform to the presumptions of referentialist ideology.

Despite this diversity of ideologies, it is the referentialist, positivist one that is most often avowed in American social life. As Sullivan points out, many US denominations espouse a kind of "religious scientism" and "literalism" so that "the strength of scientific positivism in all three fields [religion, science, law] . . . binds them together . . ." (11). In terms of presumptions about language, then, we have not a "clash of cultures" in these fields, as some have suggested (Haack 2009), but mutually reinforcing dominant suppositions. Crucially, this dominant ideology erases the social processes through which linguistic practices and the social life they name are mutually constituted. It elides or backgrounds the modes of constructing and deconstructing rival narratives at trial. It dulls our awareness of the distinct disciplinary languages that—despite this overarching referentialist ideology—actually populate social life. Erased or veiled are the non-denotational meanings—such as the political implications understood by Mr. Miller to constrain his use of the word *created*—that index opposed positionalities in social interactions and political disputes. Yet these *erasures* (Irvine and Gal 2000)—ironically—allow actors to call on supposedly value-free denotation to authorize their non-denotational practices (e.g., Mr. Miller could rightly claim he was, after all, telling the "truth").

This brings us to linguistic anthropology's guiding perspective, that communicative acts are situationally emergent, unfinalizable, inherently unstable (Bakhtin 1981). The metadiscursive regimentations (ideologies) we have been discussing can be seen as attempts to stabilize communication for the sake of knowledge, justice, or social order. Presuming that denotation is independent of social process, merely a mirror of a separately constituted world, is one way to achieve the effect of stabilization. This mode of stabilization also permits privileging of single perspectives. Stability may also be constructed in other ways, through other cosmologies and values. It need not imply agreement among interactants, only coordination. It is always a delicate achievement, reached through uptake and interactional negotiation. "Translation" as discussed here—the making of what counts as similarities and differences in communicative action—is part of such emergent accomplishment.

For understanding and analyzing translations among disciplinary languages, reliance on an ideology of fixed denotation alone is a poor guide. What are other modes of stabilization and coordination? This invites a different set of questions: What are other kinds of equivalence than the denotational? In the examples we have seen, successful translation was backed by knowledge of specialized practices (e.g., as learned in law school, or church). How are such parallelisms displayed in real-time situations?

8.3 Modes of "Translation"

Much of the philosophical discussion about translation has taken "radical translation" as its problematic: linguists attempting to translate a completely unknown language into their own, when forced to rely solely on the observed behavior of speakers (Quine 1969). Alternatively there is "radical interpretation," a speaker forced to understand others in a condition of radical linguistic and social alterity, without any prior knowledge about others or their mental states (see Povinelli 2002). This is, in many ways, opposite to our problem of disciplinary languages, whose modes of difference are often only implicitly recognized by the uninitiated (they all seem to be "English"). In the relatively new discipline of translation studies (Venuti 2000), on the other hand, the focus is on literary works, even when the writers are linguists. Their key question is whether translation is denotationally "faithful" to the original or relatively "autonomous" from it. This too seems off the mark for our purposes. It ignores the questions of indexicality, metadiscourse, and interpretive and interactional practice that differentiate disciplinary languages from each other. The *processes* of recontextualizing and boundary making, rarely discussed in translation studies, are important here.

To highlight such broadly metadiscursive and cultural questions, Silverstein (2003) proposed the notion of *transduction*. In physics, transduction occurs when one form of organized energy is asymmetrically converted into another kind of energy at a transduction site, thereby harnessing at least some of the energy across "energetic frameworks." An electric motor is a transducer, converting electrical energy into mechanical energy. To achieve a semiotic transduction, Silverstein explained, a scholar would start by identifying a system of indexical signaling, and then find a way of "doing" a signaling of the same kind in another lingua-culture.[5] Taking the example of expressing deference, Silverstein showed the partial parallels across honorific systems in different lingua-cultures. Synchronization of films provides another familiar example. How should an American Southerner talking to Northerners in a Civil War movie sound in French? In Turkish? The identities and relationship between the American North and South, as indexed (and iconized) by their speech forms, would have to be reproduced by finding a different set of stereotyped speech forms, signaling some other—but partially comparable, analogous—relative groupings of French or Turkish speakers. Of course, these are examples among lingua-cultures already closely aligned. But that is not dissimilar to our problematic of disciplinary languages.

I suggest we extend this approach from indexical systems in language to analogies among social practices more generally, and focus on the *creative* aspects: one kind of practice is taken as a model for creating another one, achieving similar effects in a different organizational realm: A transduction of practices, including knowledge practices. An example is the analogy proposed by John Locke in the 1690s. He argued that authority grounded in old writings would never lead to true knowledge. He proposed an experiential warrant for knowledge, based on the legal model of testimony. When knowledge relied on "assent in matters wherein testimony is made use of: . . . ." he suggested that " . . . it may not be amiss to take notice of a rule observed in the law of England . . . though the attested copy of a record be good proof, yet the copy of a copy ever so well attested . . . will not be admitted as proof in judicature." (Locke 1823 [1690], IV xvi 10). For Locke, truth claims had to rely on "original" perception. He proposed dispensing with truth claims that relied on "copies," that is, on the authority of ancient writings. Making the transductive argument from law, Locke based the credibility of science on witnesses' "original" perception of experimental results, in contrast to the claims of old texts.

This was not the only transduction from legal practices to the realm of experimental science. Reliability via witnessing was also used as a model by Locke's colleague Robert Boyle. "If knowledge was to be empirically based, as Boyle and other English experimentalists insisted it should, then its experimental foundations had to be attested to by eye witnesses . . .In natural, as in criminal law, the reliability of testimony depended crucially on multiplicity" (Shapin 1984, 487). Boyle proposed that the workings of his air pump could be taken as "fact" if witnessed by two or more people, as was the case for matters of life and death or estate in criminal law. "The thrust of the legal analogy should not be missed. It was not just that one was multiplying authority by multiplying witnesses (although this was part of the tactic); it was that right action could be taken, and seen to be taken, on the basis of these collective testimonies. The action concerned the positive giving of assent to matters of fact" (1984, 488). Or rather to matters that, once witnessed, would—as in court—gain the status of *fact*, this time natural fact, not social.

These examples of "transducing practices" differ in a number of ways from the cases of deference and synchronization, mentioned earlier. Instead of an outside observer trying to "find" usable pragmatic parallels, Locke, Boyle, and their colleagues were themselves *creating* the authority of independently existing natural fact by drawing the analogy with law. They instituted and *enacted* the public witnessing of experiments. Identifying several key practices of English trials, they appropriated these practices as their own, re-creating them performatively using the semiotic materials of their own disciplinary language (e.g., air pump, gentlemen as witnesses, the front parlor of the Royal Society). Finally, they themselves—and not outside observers—created the metadiscourse that drew attention to the similarities between, indeed the equation of, the two kinds of witnessing, perhaps even erasing what seem to us obvious differences between witnesses at trials and witnesses of experimental phenomena. This broadly interdiscursive logic is a common way in which aspects of disciplinary languages, and practices more generally, are modeled on each other and thereby seem to "spread."[6]

There is a nice historical irony here, one that presumably reflects multiple mutual transductions over centuries: While Locke proposed that the evidentiary practices of English law be adapted to secure scientific knowledge, some recent analysts find the law of evidence in American court trials to be "draw[ing] upon . . . scientific evidentiary concerns with factuality or facticity and proof. . . . [based on] scientific models of evidence . . . [therefore] facts are what is directly experienced" (Philips 1993, 248, 258).

Contemporary examples of transduction from *social* sciences to law are harder to find. Perhaps this is because, as Edward Levi suggested, the effect of social theories on law is generally indirect. In discussing the expansion of the legal category of "things inherently dangerous or evil" Levi notes that the extension happened in a period when government took more and more responsibility for the safety of individuals. Yet: "No one economic or social theory was responsible [for the expansion], although as changes came about in the manner of living, the social theory moved ahead to explain and persuade" (1949, 102). To be sure, there are recent examples of results from social science having more direct effects (e.g., in family law). But Levi's larger point is that social science is most likely to influence legal decisions by changing what counts as "common sense." Sullivan's example of conflicts around Intelligent Design is, arguably, a case of transduction from science to religion that might well be changing American "common sense." I will return to this interesting case in the final section.

If not in these chapters, yet we could perhaps find transductions from social science to law, if we looked farther afield. We might speculate that Kenneth Clark's "doll experiments" were not merely a justification for the Supreme Court's decision in *Brown vs. Board of Education,* nor simply evidence.[7] Perhaps the Court was taking the dismaying responses of some African-American children in a test situation and transducing them, jumping scale and finding their analogue to be damage caused in all of American society by segregated public schools.

Cost-benefit analysis could be another example. Invented in the nineteenth century as an informal mode of accounting for the cost of bridges built by the Army Corps of Engineers, it was routinized in the twentieth century, and incorporated into flood control legislation. Later, the standardization of its calculations gave it what Porter (1995) calls a "mechanical objectivity." That is, it relied on rules of procedure and numbers, so it seemed independent of human will and thus seemed free of political interest. Economists took it up and provided a philosophical ground for it in economic theory. It is now part of virtually all government regulations and their judicial review. One could say that an informal practice of commensuration, created for one quite limited activity and context has been theorized, formalized (entextualized) and transduced (repeatedly analogized, i.e., used as a model), and regimented under the ideology of "objective" decision-making (see Espeland and Stevens 1998). Now, escalated in no small part by the law-and-economics movement, it is ubiquitous in legal contexts where, according to its critics, it replaces other modes of judgment about the legality, harm, or advisability of regulation and legislation, while eliding the values on which it is based (Kysar 2010).

Most examples of "translation" in the three chapters at hand are not transductions at all, however, in the sense illustrated here. The testimony of expert witnesses at trial that the chapters discuss most thoroughly involves another configuration of "sameness-in-difference," another kind of recontextualization. A brief comparison will bring out the contrasts:

In transduction/modeling the participants engineering the imitation (e.g., John Locke, the Supreme Court Justices, the appropriators of Cost Benefit Analysis) locate a model in a distant disciplinary language and *perform* or *enact* some subset of its parts in their own realm, reframing it as their own, thereby transforming their own disciplinary language and practices. A single set of allied actors selects the desired practices; they name and frame the type of activity it is. These same transducers judge whether or not a particular instance is a proper token of the practice. They construct the metadiscourse (ideology) of similarity or equivalence between practices, a similarity that leads to the desired pragmatic equivalence or at least claim: authority created, harm identified, unbiased efficiency secured. It is these same participants whose social scenes and roles are the contexts for the newly modeled practices.

In the second kind of "translation," by contrast, participants (expert witnesses) *represent, describe*, or *voice* the texts of their own discipline, for the benefit or by demand of another. What they *perform* is the role of expert witness. They create a quotation (a recontextualization) of utterances in their own disciplinary language, now reframed as acts defined by another disciplinary language over which they have little control. Not only a diagnosis of a patient, but also at the same time testimony about a diagnosis; not only social scientific report, but testimony about such a report. The linguistic practice (token) of one disciplinary language becomes also a token of another genre in another discipline. The utterance is double-voiced, polyphonic. The scene and social roles are those of the court, not the experts' home discipline. Metadiscourses of equivalence are up for grabs. (Is this testimony the same as other such experts would provide? Are these experts saying the same things here in court as they would say among their peers?) In this second kind of "translation," practices and texts of one disciplinary language are *subsumed* by reframing them (revoicing them) in context as also, and consequentially, instantiations (tokens) of textual/genre categories (types) defined by another discipline.[8]

Much has been written about the role of expert witnesses. There are manuals purporting to teach the reader how to participate as an expert in American trials, with versions targeted at virtually every social science from anthropology to statistics. The manuals understand that witnessing is a performance. From a semiotic perspective, the construction of credibility by any witness, and certainly an expert witness, is a moment-by-moment accomplishment that can be undermined at any time during questioning. A close-up textual analysis of real-time questioning, based on recordings and transcripts, is the best way to get a sense of how this works (e.g., Brannigan and Lynch 1987; Matoesian 2001, this volume).

Such analyses suggest that there is a structural bind in the very definition of expert witness, one that derives from double voicing/polyphony. Claiming and inhabiting any expert role requires an interactional enactment, a conventionalized performance of the role. Simply having the knowledge is not enough to achieve the social fact of credible expertise in interaction (Carr 2010). As I noted earlier, being able to artfully wield the disciplinary language is one sign among peers of really belonging to a particular guild of experts, and often the key to being taken up or understood at all.

Enactment of the expert role for a general audience, however, is necessarily different. While displays among scholarly peers typically conform to mutually understood rules of presentation and argumentation, expert witnesses are performing before audiences who cannot "hear" the same cues in the same way. The very same interactional means—technical terms, hedges, limited claims, unspoken assumptions, embedding data in conceptual lines of argument—can signal refined, careful, and therefore trustworthy procedure to social scientific peers, while sounding obfuscatory, uncertain, or condescending to laypersons. Instead of guild-internal expectations, the role of expert witness requires orienting to stereotypes of expertise or of a particular expert-type, either to play them up or to undermine them. Indeed, the stereotyping between expert and audience is often mutual. This is true even within the academy, across specializations within a single overarching discipline. Experimental physicists, when addressing theoretical physicists, "skip the connecting details by which experimental procedures bind to each other" while theorists, on their side, "reduce the complexity" by "suppressing the ... structure linking theory to theory," when talking to experimentalists (Galison [1997] 1999, 156). We can say that each side tailors or streamlines its own talk to appeal to the imagined interests and expectations of the other. This can be extended to legislatures, when they formulate laws with future audiences in mind, such as courts that will hear challenges to the law the legislators are enacting.

It is hardly surprising that streamlining and stereotypes play a role in what has been called the "theater" of the trial. To be sure, the law of evidence is supposed to filter out sources of information people use in everyday life, but which are believed to be biased, unfair, or unreliable in some way. The aim is to improve reliability of reports by controlling and constraining what can be presented to juries. Yet, what is not controlled for any witness is what lawyers call "demeanor." This includes *how* something is said as much as what is said. The linguistic formulation of testimony and the paralinguistic surround are crucial. As trial lawyers know very well, nonverbal, paralinguistic behavior as well as matters of phrasing are understood by listeners and viewers as indicative of more or less certainty, more or less reliability, among other effects. These are what jurors use—and are supposed to use—to decide whether the truth is being told, or how much to trust the expert (Philips 1993, 257). Courtroom challenges to expertise are often focused on the personal credibility of witnesses, as judged by their demeanor (Philips 1995, 211).

Thus, there are unavoidable, contradictory pressures on discursive production by expert witnesses. Expert reports in court, to be useful, must respond in their formulation to the non-expert scene in which they are displayed. It is the very effort to communicate effectively under trial conditions—or in legislative hearings and investigative committees—that produces the streamlining effect, shaping what can count as "the same" between quite different modes of speaking. The recontextualization of their own peer-oriented voice into that of another sort of person-type, in a different scene, with its own roles and participant framework, takes a great deal of reflexivity on the part of expert witnesses. The problem of evaluating written social scientific reports, as discussed here and in previous work by Ford (2013), is only partly a matter of judicial and lawyerly "ignorance." Reports written for a scholarly community of peers are of a different genre than testimony; they cannot in themselves function as polyphonic expert witnesses.

8.4 Demarcations and Connections

A final point takes us out of courtrooms and into the broader social world governed by law, in keeping with this volume's ambition to think about *Translating the Social World for Law*. As these chapters show, courts are sometimes called upon to decide the limits of disciplinary languages: for instance, the lines between "religion" and "science" in American public schools. As Sullivan notes, it is not easy to discern, after centuries of intertwining, where the border lies between talk identified as one or the other of these discourses, or who counts as an expert to represent each.

The question is broader than this particular dispute. Judges are involved in more frequent, if less momentous, demarcations about expertise. They decide which experts provide relevant testimony. As Ford (2013, 303–304) has shown, they draw the dividing line between appropriate and inappropriate offers of expertise; between "genuine" vs. "fake" social science. Judges also decide whether expertise is necessary at all. For instance, whether special skills are needed for viewing a videotape of the activity at issue, or that it be evaluated by the untutored, common-sense eye (Goodwin 1994).

Yet none of these judgments is merely an assessment of an already existing social reality. Despite the instructions of *Daubert*, it is not enough to apply the "correct" criteria for what is "expertise" in some area. Legitimation of expertise is never entirely separate from the processes of law. Expertise in the legal context is often more the consequence than the cause of demarcation. This is true in the narrow sense of a judge's decisions about what kinds of evidence to admit in a single trial. But it is also true over time, when the expert witnesses who have spoken effectively in one case are therefore called upon in subsequent cases. Such speakers produce tokens of knowledge types. Over time, the types of expertise accepted in courts come to have legitimacy outside the legal system, for the very reason that they have been accepted in courts. In a feedback process that can be tracked historically, what counts as "mainstream science" is co-produced by a community of researchers and the courts that accept them (Jasanoff 1995).[9]

Furthermore, knowledge is sometimes created specifically for the use of courts. For instance, in a discussion of statistical reasoning in a legal setting, the author of one research paper advised potential expert witnesses that for disparate treatment cases in labor law there is as yet no way to decide statistically some of the issues the law raises. He suggested that "statistical methods should be developed" to do so (Gastwirth 1992, 59). More generally, Ford (this volume) suggests that legislatures create records of their investigations—a form of knowledge-making—precisely to convince courts that legislators had engaged in a serious review of the relevant science before acting.

The intertwining of broadly understood disciplinary languages—here: "science" and "religion"—is closely related to legal strategies that have, in turn, changed the social world in which legal decisions about science and religion are made. This feedback is mediated by transduction. Picking just a few moments of a centuries-long dispute, we can glimpse the semiotic processes by which "creationism" became "creation science" in the 1970s and 1980s, and the implications of this for the authority of law.

The *Kitzmiller* case, Sullivan explains, is one of the latest in a long series of disputes about the teaching of evolution in US public schools. Arguably, the complex changes in conservative Protestantism in the 1960s—a relatively apolitical movement became a powerful presence in national politics—were in part triggered by government initiatives in science education. These were driven by fears of Soviet success in space exploration during the Cold War (Nelkin 1982). Federally sponsored curricular reforms of the 1960s and 1970s became occasions for backlash through conflicts around textbooks, school board decisions, and legislation. Much of this social action against the teaching of evolution can be traced to the Institute for Creation Research. By sponsoring research, training, publication, and legislation, the Institute made creationism a political issue. "Bible-believing common sense changed after the 1960s, when a veritable creationist revival displaced [older metaphorical readings of creation] with a new 'strict creationist' position" (Harding 2000, 213).

The Institute adopted communicative modes and practices widely perceived as scientific: hiring research scientists with standard PhDs, staging debates with evolutionary scientists at secular colleges and universities, publishing research reports. It "articulated the case for special creation and the case against evolution within the intellectual apparatus of science—using its language, its evidentiary rhetoric and paraphernalia of overhead projectors displaying charts, diagrams, photos and citations" (Harding 2000, 214, 215). The Institute constructed a museum, filled with fossils, samples, and labels. As Harding's ethnography explains, this Museum of Earth and Life History closely imitated the public practices of a natural history museum, but "transmogrif[ied] . . . secular science['s] origin theories" into Genesis (2000, 222). In short: "Instead of denying evolution its scientific credentials, as Biblical creationists had done for a century, the scientific creationists granted creation and evolution equal scientific standing. Instead of trying to bar evolution from the classroom ... they fought to bring creation into the schoolhouse ... Instead of appealing to the authority of the Bible ... they emphasiz[ed] the scientific aspects of creationism" (Numbers 2006, 269). In this way, they changed not only the common sense of "Bible-believ[ers]" but also the broader common sense within which litigation takes place.

"Creation science," in short, is a striking example of transduction. The semiotic practices of the Institute must be seen together with what it denotationally claimed. Adopting science as a model in many ways, the Institute and its affiliates produced objects, propositions, and assumptions that were recognized by participants as authorized in ways similar to science, yet *not* science. Harding argues that the facts amassed in the museum showed the Bible, not science, makes creation true. The transduction was accomplished in part through a legal move that utilized another semiotic device: *fractal logic* (Irvine and Gal 2000).[10] Subdividing both science and religion, the Institute's staff attorney helped construct the category of "creation science" through a legal argument. "Equal time" for "creation science" and "evolutionary science" in public schools would not violate the First Amendment, he wrote. This is because it would equally exclude two further novel categories: "creationist religion" and "evolutionary religion" (Bird 1982).

Ultimately, the Supreme Court rejected this argument in 1987, holding unconstitutional a law that mandated a "balanced approach" for teaching "creation science" along with evolution in public schools. The logic of the Institute's fractal distinctions enabled the next response: "Some religious fundamentalists ... turn[ed] on its head the argument that 'creation science' was a form of science. They now claimed that 'secular humanism,' the complex of values associated with modern science was really a 'religion' in its own right; teaching these values deprived their children of the freedom to practice their own faith" (Jasanoff 1995, 111). The Supreme Court's decision defined neither science nor religion, and declined to support science's knowledge claims against other claims. Yet, the fact of ruling itself was as important as argumentation. For it reaffirmed the Court's right to police relations among science, religion, and the state.

As Edward Levi noted, transformations in common sense are taken up through the logic of case law. In this mediated way, changes in common sense change the law. But another step deserves more attention. Social reflexivity—self-conscious knowledge of the workings of the legal world—allows social movements and other actors to use the courts to change common sense. Legal battles to get creation science taught in public schools brought unprecedented national publicity for its proponents (Numbers 2006, 316). Litigation helped establish novel cultural categories and to connect those who define and name the categories with those who inhabit them (Gal 2007). Further, the people who study and teach "creation science" were not the only ones who took up the new categories, made familiar by litigation. So have others. In opposition to creation science, they newly recognize themselves as "evolutionary religionists" or "secular humanists" (Pfeffer 1987). As the law-and-society literature has recognized, litigation, even if unsuccessful, is part of the way the social world is changed.

Sullivan ends her chapter on a powerful note by asking, in the light of the continuing science/religion controversies: "What should a biology teacher do?" She responds that despite the many accommodations between science and religion over the last century and despite the rulings of courts: "ordinary politics will have to decide what a teacher should do." I suggest that going to trial about such contested issues is very much a part of "ordinary politics" in the United States, and transductions are a key semiotic device in planning for and performing such struggles.

Notes

1. *Trans* derives from Latin "across," and is directional with respect to an *origo: trans* depicts movement here to there, *cis* depicts movement from there to here.

2. By *social movement* or activism I mean any set of organized groups, citizens' groups or NGOs that are loosely connected and working for what they consider a single direction of social change: Planned Parenthood and other organizations for reproductive rights in the US; or those working for protection of traditional marriage; civic groups that support literacy to adults; groups working for the safeguarding of parks or "the environment" more generally.

3. Austin's long-ago comment comes to mind. In discussing whether the statement "France is hexagonal" is true, he did not reject the question of denotation; he merely noted that "it is true for certain intents and purposes . . .it is suited to some contexts and not others (1962, 142).

4. See Putnam (1975) on the "linguistic division of labor."

5. That is, in another language, as it is used in another cultural context.

6. Foucault's (1977) analysis of the *panopticon*, his tracing of its appearance in one institutional site after another—military, prisons, schools—can be seen as an example of the transduction of practices.

7. In these studies, African-American children in segregated schools seemed to show more self-disparagement than those in integrated schools. These experiments were highly suggestive, though their methodology was flawed. Transduction of their findings seems a more fitting characterization than "generalization" from laboratory results. They did not pretend to rigorous sampling, controls, and other methods that are now routine in psychological research, hence they must have worked more as analogy, metaphor, transduction.

8. The more technical term for this process would be *interdiscursivity* (see Agha and Wortham 2005).

9. Scholars in sociolegal studies have called this process *recursivity*. For instance, they have shown the effects of legal procedures about employment on human resources departments and the subsequent effects of HR departments' actions on court decisions (Edelman et al. 2011). This too changes "common sense." Co-production, of course can involve numerous parties.

10. *Fractal recursivity* is a semiotic process in which a distinction salient at one level of generality is projected onto a more encompassing level or a less encompassing one. The result is similar contrasts at various levels of generality.

References

Agha, Asif, and Stanton Wortham, eds. 2005. "Semiosis across Events. Special Issue." *Journal of Linguistic Anthropology* 15(1).
Austin, John L. 1962. *How to Do Things with Words.* Cambridge, MA: Harvard University Press.
Bakhtin, Mikhail M. 1981. "Discourse in the Novel." In *The Dialogic Imagination*, Mikhail M. Bakhtin, 259–422. Austin: University of Texas Press.
Bauman, Richard, and Charles Briggs. 2003. *Voices of Modernity.* New York: Cambridge University Press.
Bird, Wendell. 1982. "Creation-Science and Evolution-Science in Public Schools: A Constitutional Defense under the First Amendment." *Northern Kentucky Law Review* 9(2):159–248.
Brannigan, Augustine, and Michael Lynch. 1987. "On Bearing False Witness." *Journal of Contemporary Ethnography* 16(2): 115–146.
Carr, E. Summerson. 2010. "Enactments of Expertise." *Annual Review of Anthropology* 39: 17–32.
Edelman, Lauren, Scott Eliason, Virginia Mellema, Linda Krieger, and Catherine Albiston. 2011. "When Organizations Rule: Judicial Deference to Institutionalized Employment Structures." *American Journal of Sociology* 117: 888–954.
Espeland, Wendy, and Mitchell Stevens. 1998. "Commensuration as a Social Process." *Annual Review of Sociology* 24: 313–343.
Ford, William K. 2013. "The Law and Science of Video Game Violence: What Was Lost in Translation?" *Cardozo Arts & Entertainment Law Journal* 31(2): 297–356.
Foucault, M. 1977. *Discipline and Punish: The Birth of the Prison.* New York: Pantheon.
Gal, Susan. 2007. Clasps and Copies: Circulation in the "New" Economy. *Paper presented at the 106th Meeting of the American Anthropological Association, Washington, DC Nov 29–Dec 2.*
Gal, Susan. 2015. "Politics of Translation." *Annual Review of Anthropology* 44: 225–240.
Gal, Susan, and J. T. Irvine. 1995. "The Boundaries of Languages and Disciplines." *Social Research* 62(4): 967–1002.
Galison, Peter. 1999 [1997]. "Trading Zones." In *The Science Studies Reader*, edited by Mario Biagioli, 137–160. New York: Routledge.
Gastwirth, Joseph. 1992. "Statistical Reasoning in the Legal Setting." *The American Statistician* 46(1):55–70.
Goodman, Nelson. 1971. "Seven Strictures on Similarity." In *Problems and Projects*, N. Goodman, 437–447. Indianapolis: Bobbs-Merrill.
Goodwin, Charles. 1994. "Professional Vision." *American Anthropologist* 96(3): 606–633.
Haack, Susan. 2009. "Irreconcilable Differences? The Troubled Marriage of Science and Law." *Law and Contemporary Problems* 72(1): 1–23.
Hacking, Ian. 1999. *The Social Construction of What?* Cambridge, MA: Harvard University Press.

Harding, Susan. 2000. *The Book of Jerry Falwell*. Princeton: Princeton University Press.

Irvine, J. T., and Susan Gal. 2000. "Language Ideology and Linguistic Differentiation." In *Regimes of Language*, edited by P. Kroskrity, 35–84. Santa Fe: SAR Press.

Jasanoff, Sheila. 1995. *Science at the Bar*. Cambridge, MA: Harvard University Press.

Jasanoff, Sheila. 1998. "The Eye of Everyman: Witnessing DNA in the Simpson Trial." *Social Studies of Science* 28(5–6): 713–740.

Kysar, Douglas A. 2010. *Regulating from Nowhere: Environmental Law and the Search for Objectivity*. New Haven: Yale University Press.

Levi, Edward. 1949. *An Introduction to Legal Reasoning*. Chicago: University of Chicago Press.

Locke, John. 1823 [1690]. *Essay on Human Understanding. Book Four*. London: Tho. Bassett.

Matoesian, Gregory. 2001. *Law and the Language of Identity: The Discourse of the WK Smith Rape Trial*. New York: Oxford University Press.

Mertz, Elizabeth. 1996. "Recontextualization as Socialization: Text and Pragmatics in the Law School Classroom." In *Natural Histories of Discourse*, edited by Michael Silverstein and Greg Urban, 229–252. Chicago: University of Chicago Press.

Nelkin, Dorothy. 1982. *The Creation Controversy: Science and Scripture in the Schools*. Boston: Beacon Press.

Numbers, Ronald. 2006. *The Creationists: From Scientific Creationism to Intelligent Design* (Expanded ed.). Cambridge, MA: Harvard University Press.

Pfeffer, Leo. 1987. "The 'Religion' of Secular Humanism." *Journal of Church and State* 29: 495–507.

Philips, Susan. 1993. "Evidentiary Standards for American Trials: Just the Facts." In *Responsibility and Evidence in Oral Discourse*, edited by Jane Hill and Judith Irvine, 248–259. New York: Cambridge University Press.

Philips, Susan. 1995. *Ideology in the Language of Judges*. New York: Oxford University Press.

Porter, Theodore. 1995. *Trust in Numbers: The Pursuit of Objectivity in Science and Public Life*. Princeton: Princeton University Press.

Povinelli, Elizabeth. 2001. "Radical Worlds: The Anthropology of Incommensurability and Inconceivability." *Annual Review of Anthropology* 30: 319–334.

Putnam, Hilary. 1978. "The Meaning of Meaning." In *Meaning and the Moral Sciences*, by Hilary Putnam, 131–193. London: Routledge and Kegan Paul.

Quine, Willard V. 1969. *Ontological Relativity and Other Essays*. New York: Columbia University Press.

Shapin, Steven. 1984. "Pump and Circumstance: Robert Boyle's Literary Technology." *Social Studies of Science* 14(4): 481–520.

Silverstein, Michael. 2003. "Translation, Transduction, Transformation: Skating 'Glossando' on Thin Semiotic Ice." In *Translating Cultures: Perspectives on Translation and Anthropology*, edited by Paula G. Rubel and Abraham Rosman, 75–105. New York: Berg.

Silverstein, Michael, and Greg Urban, eds. 1996. *Natural Histories of Discourse*. Chicago: University of Chicago Press.

Venuti, Lawrence, ed. 2000. *The Translation Studies Reader*. New York: Routledge.

Woolard, Kathryn. 1998. "Language Ideology as a Field of Inquiry." In *Language Ideologies*, edited by Bambi Schieffelin, Kathryn A. Woolard, and Paul V. Kroskrity, 3–50. New York: Oxford University Press.

PART THREE

Toward Improved Translations

RECOGNIZING THE BARRIERS

9

"Can you get there from here?"
Translating Law and Social Science
Elizabeth Mertz

9.1 Introduction

Funding agencies, universities, and many leading scholars have all touted the benefits of interdisciplinary research, and the new millennium continues to bring with it a cascading set of new technologies for scholarly collaboration.[1] Often missed in these bursts of enthusiasm is the question of just what the goal of interdisciplinary work should be—and indeed, whether it is possible for experts from different disciplines to frame their goals in a common language. Not generally mentioned are the quieter studies showing the difficulties of cooperating across disciplines that differ in epistemological assumptions, standards, goals, and ways of using language to express disciplinary knowledge (see, e.g., Strathern 2011). Putting people together to "communicate" via ever-expanding networks may not produce much real communication if important underlying differences have not even been considered—let alone addressed.

In this time when performing interdisciplinary research on law is all the rage, recognizing these pitfalls takes on added importance. How often do scholars from different disciplines come together in conferences or even within their own universities, only to conclude that they have very little to learn from each other? How often do they misunderstand each other, perhaps without even recognizing that misunderstanding? How often do scholars from one field misappropriate methods or findings or materials from another field in ways that can't be intellectually justified? (And is it ever possible to discuss this misappropriation in acceptably collegial and thoughtful ways?) This chapter explores the challenges surrounding interdisciplinary research and communication—with a particular focus on issues that arise in crossing the boundaries between law and social science. For this exploration, I use transcript segments from a 1995 conference that brought linguists and legal scholars together in an effort at cross-disciplinary communication. In addition, I draw on insights from an interdisciplinary working group in Chicago—which formed more than a decade later, and which, at several of its meetings in 2009, wound up discussing a number of transcript segments from the earlier conference.

Work on law and translation has generally focused on the glaring issues that arise when people speaking obviously different languages must navigate the legal system together. For example, scholars have raised questions about the gaps in justice that can accompany gaps in translation between different languages in settings ranging from courtrooms to police interrogations (see, e.g., Berk-Seligson 1990, 2009; Eades 2008; from a legal vantage, see Cunningham 1992). Sociolinguists tend to treat linguistic differences between disciplines as issues more of *register* than of *language*—that is, an English-speaking anthropologist and an English-speaking economist in conversation with one another are merely speaking different *registers* of the "same" language (Trudgill 1983, 100–101). When we think of the situation this way, we may be tempted to minimize the degree to which "real" translation is needed: after all, these two speakers, though they are anthropologist and economist, share a core language—English. Certainly the broad set of academic communities now vigorously engaged in interdisciplinary discussions has not paid a great deal of systematic attention to the translation process involved when they attempt to work together. For this reason, with full deference to the distinction between professional registers and entire languages, I will be talking about "translation" between "disciplinary *languages*" here in order to underscore and insist upon the need for more attention to this kind of process.

I come to this perspective, which highlights the distance to be traveled in interdisciplinary conversations, from several distinct backgrounds. First, as I'll elaborate below, I draw on the field of linguistic anthropology, which has given us a way to conceptualize conversations that cross disciplinary registers as occupying a *continuum of translation practices* which also includes conversations that take place between speakers of distinct languages (see Silverstein 2003). Second, I am guided by a growing literature in the field of science and technology studies (STS), which has demonstrated the significant divisions in epistemology and language that exist even among the "hard" sciences, let alone the messier social sciences (see, e.g., Jasanoff 1995; Knorr Cetina 1999; on social science see Camic, Lamont, and Gross 2011). Third, I build on a sensitivity to language derived from scholarship in translation studies and the law-and-literature tradition.

This chapter applies those combined perspectives to a transcript generated in the spring of 1995, when a group of legal scholars and linguists held a conference called "What Is Meaning in a Legal Text? Northwestern University/ Washington University Law and Linguistics Conference."[2] The primary goal of that conference was to ascertain whether the field of linguistics could produce scientific knowledge that would aid legal professionals. A lengthy transcript of the interactions at that conference was subsequently published in the *Washington University Law Quarterly* (1995). In 2009, an interdisciplinary working group in Chicago (the NLR "Law and Translation" [LT] group) used that earlier transcript as the basis for their own discussion of issues arising from efforts to translate between law and linguistics (see Appendix 9.1).[3] This chapter at times draws on insights from that later 2009 working group discussion in analyzing the interdisciplinary interactions in the earlier 1995 conference. This approach follows a time-honored method in language-and-law studies that uses groups of researchers with interdisciplinary expertise to reflect on and analyze transcripts.[4]

9.2 "Translation" in Interdisciplinary Settings

Some might argue that the word *translation* is inappropriate for a process involving two people speaking the same language—and even what could be characterized as the same professional register (in this case, academic English). In a wonderful discussion of the art of translating between languages, David Bellos makes a case for this point of view, in entirely reasonable terms:

> . . . what a playwright does when he adapts a narrative text for performance onstage has no more relevance to translation than [transforming a ball of wool into a sweater] does. Jakobson's proposal to regard switching media as a form of translation is a red herring, and it's not clear to me why he should ever have come up with it . . . Translation does not extend in every direction. Its own field is quite large enough. (Bellos 2011, 312–314)

Bellos privileges translation "between languages" as the real thing (which does not actually differ that much, in my own opinion, from what Jakobson did when he denominated the movement between languages as "translation proper" (Jakobson 1959)).

Taking what is arguably an even more restricted view of the phenomenon of "translation" proper, Michael Silverstein proposed a trilogy of terms (*translation, transduction, transformation*) to capture the continuum of related, yet distinct, kinds of meaning shifts involved in moving from one semiotic formulation to another. (The word *semiotic* indicates the wide universe of ways that signaling of any kind can happen—not just linguistic, through language, but also through individual gestures, through a sign with an arrow painted on it, through a change in facial expression, or through silence.) Silverstein's typology limits the phenomenon of *translation* itself to something approximating equivalence relationships between *source* (language from which one is translating) and *target* (language into which one is translating) languages. These kinds of relationships can only be found in the most unusual of circumstances (say, when one can find forms in different languages that are both "inhabiting the communicative role of 'sender' or (loosely) 'speaker,' as opposed to 'receiver' or (loosely) 'hearer'/'addressee' as the focal notion ... of the grammaticopragmatic category of First Person" (2003, 81)). Beyond these narrowly comparable forms of speech, Silverstein notes that all shifts among language systems necessarily involve more change and fluidity in meaning. He distinguishes relatively smaller fluid shifts as *transductions*, and then more major shifts as *transformations* (2003, 83–95).

If I were to use this terminology, none of the shifts across disciplinary languages described here would properly be called "translations"; they would minimally be transductions, and often transformations. However, despite agreeing with the advantages of using a more precise set of analytic categories in examining these kinds of changes, I am for the moment using the less technical, more commonly understood vernacular word *translation* to indicate all the manners of transformation that happen when scholars attempt to communicate across established disciplinary boundaries. (Note, however, that both Michael Silverstein's own commentary in this volume, and Susan Gal's, use the more ambitious technical terminology, including the concept of *transduction*.) In examining what I'm calling "translation" in this chapter, I will focus in particular on the impact of metalinguistic norms, of language details and linguistic contexts, and of underlying epistemologies on the interdisciplinary translation process itself.

9.3 Metalinguistic Understandings and Language Contexts

The overarching question that provided an overt frame for the earlier 1995 conference was "What Is Meaning in a Legal Text?" In his book *Is That a Fish in Your Ear?*, translation studies scholar David Bellos makes a case for using a different kind of question. He notes that when he was an undergraduate, the students were all abuzz with the story of a junior don named Roy Harris who had refused to teach classes on translation until the senior faculty could define for him what "translation" was (Bellos 2011, 3). Of course, this turned out to be a terrific way to avoid the assignment, because the debate over this more abstract question could go on forever. As Bellos notes, "'What is ...?' doesn't usually provide a good prompt. It usually leads you headlong into hairsplitting disputes about the meanings of words"; thus Bellos finds it more productive to explore "stories and examples and arguments that circle around what seems to me to be the real issue—understanding what translation *does*" (Bellos 2011, 4).[5]

Belatedly, a number of those involved in the 1995 conference came to a somewhat similar conclusion: that is, they realized that "much of the difficulty in this discussion and throughout the conference was that the two sets of participants were trying to communicate by using the troublesome

yet crucial words *meaning* and *interpretation* before they had fully identified the different frameworks that gave each term different significance to
each profession" (Eskridge and Levi 1995, 1104fn.2). In other words, they
had not given sufficient attention to their own metalinguistic and disciplinary translation issues. Given the care with which the conference conveners
had considered the linguistic issues involved in their own conference—and
their degree of expertise in linguistics and legal language—this is powerful
testimony as to the difficulty of the enterprise. I would argue that the problem wasn't that this thoughtful group failed to define their terms at the level
of *semantics* (or acontextual meaning), but that they were unable to tame
the multiple underlying and conflicting *pragmatic* (meaning that depends on
context) frameworks in play.

In recent decades, the fields of linguistic anthropology and sociolinguistics have focused much attention on the way language depends on its contexts
of use for meaning (as noted, this is language *pragmatics*, by contrast with
semantic meanings that are less context-dependent—think of definitions in a
dictionary). While much work on language—in fields ranging from linguistics
proper to ordinary language philosophy—has proceeded as if the most important aspects of meaning were specifiable apart from specific contexts of use,
in another corner of the academic world, scholars have ventured further and
further into investigations of contextually based meaning. Even language philosophers thought to have been core contributors to theories of pragmatics—
like Grice and Austin—were shown to have missed the boat in terms of how
far down one has to reach into context to truly grasp how linguistic meaning
works in context.[6] This opened the door to new perspectives on the importance
of *metapragmatics*—that is, the meta-level ideologies, assumptions, and connections that surround and guide the use of language in context (see Silverstein
1979, 1993; see also (among many others!) Gumperz 1982 on contextualization
cues and Irvine and Gal 2000 on linguistic ideology). What, then, can we learn
from applying this form of pragmatic and metapragmatic analysis to interdisciplinary translations?

9.4 The 1995 Washington University/Northwestern University Conference

As I've noted, the results of the conference were subsequently published in an
issue of the *Washington University Law Quarterly* (1995). That issue included not
only a transcript [hereinafter *WULQ* Trans], but also articles by conference participants and by a set of invited commentators who had not attended the conference. The 1995 conference resulted from an earlier collaboration in 1993–1994
between professors of law and linguistics that had culminated in a *Yale Law
Journal* review article (Cunningham et al. 1995) and an *amicus* brief, both of

which were circulated to the Justices of the US Supreme Court (see Law and Linguistics Consortium 1994; see also Kaplan et al. 1995; Levi 1995). The professors called themselves the Law and Linguistics Consortium, and were encouraged when they saw their efforts rewarded by citations in three 1994 US Supreme Court cases. To follow up on this initial success, the scholars involved in the Consortium invited some new collaborators to join them, and held a conference in Evanston, Illinois co-sponsored by Northwestern University and Washington University.

Following on various preliminary discussions, the first full day of the conference was divided into four sessions:

1. The Meaning of Meaning: In Linguistics. In the first session, the linguists in the group attempted to explain to the law professors how linguists approach the question of meaning. Predictably, there were some differences among the linguists on this issue.

2. A Vehicle in the Park by Any Other Name. In the following session, the legal scholars challenged the linguists to use their approach to meaning to make sense of a classic legal problem. Given a statute that said "All vehicles are prohibited from Lincoln Park," would it be acceptable for an ambulance to cut through the park on its way to the hospital?

3. The Meaning of Meaning: In Law. Here the law professors in the group returned the favor and attempted to explain to the linguists how lawyers approach the question of meaning.

4. What Makes Linguistics a Science? In the fourth session, the linguists responded to questions from the lawyers about the status of linguistics as a science and linguistic analysis as having any privileged status in parsing the meaning of legal texts.

On the final day of the conference, the group considered three particular concrete legal problems: (a) a confusing premarital agreement; (b) a nineteenth-century legal hypothetical centered on instructions that were given to a servant about "soupmeat"; and (c) the famous legal phrase *reasonable doubt* in the context of jury instruction comprehension.

One impetus for this effort at interdisciplinary translation was to see whether linguistics as a discipline could be "useful"—whether it could add something to legal efforts at textual interpretation that would somehow resolve disputed issues or provide a scientific ground on which legal interpreters of texts could agree, regardless of their politics or policy concerns. This underlying goal may also explain the formulation of the fourth topic above: "What makes linguistics a science?" No parallel question is asked of law's authority, and the idea that linguistics needs to demonstrate its legitimacy as a "science" carries with it a not-very-implicit asymmetry. The question of how participants were negotiating their understandings of that asymmetrical goal became an important part of the interdisciplinary interactions.

9.4.1 TOPIC 1: IN THE ABSTRACT, WHAT IS MEANING IN A LEGAL TEXT?

EXCERPT 9.1[7]

JS [LINGUIST]: Clarify your term *conventional intent*.

BE [LAWYER]: I think "conventional intent" would be the intent we attribute to a body that has promulgated this language.

JS: I don't see how there's any "convention" involved in that.

BE: The "convention" would be the canons' interpretation. For a criminal statute we interpret the statute to have a mens rea requirement ordinarily.

JS: That's it, "interpretation"; that's not "convention."

BE: It's a convention—

JS: "Convention"—you use a certain interpretation or interpretive strategy, but when we linguists say "convention," we mean something very, very different.

(*WULQ* Trans, 873)

At another point in the transcript, as we'll see, the linguists explained "conventional" meaning as that which is commonly shared—and although they at time acknowledged that such commonality might be community-specific, at other times they appeared to insist that the "conventional" meaning of words is so widely shared that it is accessible to all speakers of a given language. (And, at the linguists' insistence, the lawyers shifted to using "conventional" rather than "literal"—but this created another problem, as the word "conventional" itself was linked to different underlying epistemologies and metalinguistic ideologies for members of the two groups.) Again, one of the most fascinating aspects of this transcript is the way that two groups of scholars, each quite sophisticated and self-aware in reflecting on language (including their own uses of language at the conference), nonetheless fell into fairly constant trouble in communicating across disciplinary lines.

This happened despite the fact that the conference participants took seriously that there were two different disciplinary "languages" in play; that some kind of translation would be necessary; and that they couldn't assume that everyone understood key words in the same way.

EXCERPT 9.2

MM [LAWYER]: But on your own view of "meaning" is there more to the meaning of the word than its function in a sentence that has truth conditions? Is there more to it or do we stop right there when we talk about meanings?

GG [LINGUIST]: Okay, I can't answer that question because it presupposes things that I don't agree with.

(*WULQ* Trans, 828)

Green here touches on a deeper problem, which the group attempted to discuss. Overall, however, in discussing the "meaning of meaning" at an abstract level, the group was drawn to what we could call a *metasemantic* form of explanation: that is, they were pushed to produce definitions of individual terms (including the word *meaning* itself) that held regardless of the terms' contexts of use. This frequently had the presumably unintended effect of relegating the pragmatic or indexical meanings of these terms within specific disciplinary contexts to the margins of discussion. It also implicitly imported a number of presuppositions into the conversation that wound up posing problems.

First of all, if we are to produce "dictionary-type" definitions for our terms, we need something like a dictionary—that is, we need a single authoritative source that can say "the word x means y for linguists."[8] A ubiquitous feature of the negotiations at the conference was that scholars had to speak in a single voice *for* their disciplines, despite the acknowledged fact that there are major disagreements about how to analyze "meaning" within both law and linguistics. The conversation would at one point name differences among linguists or legal theorists, but then veer back into attempts to find points upon which all linguists or all lawyers would agree, so that they could speak from the position of "linguistics" or "law" as unitary fields. This was reasonable in that context: the need to find those shared points—or at least to nail down the axes of disagreement within each discipline—was built into the frame of the linguistic event (the conference) itself. Thus we could say that the metapragmatic framework of the conference, billed as an intensive encounter between representatives of two disciplines, required speakers to talk not just as individual selves but as the voices of *intellectual* fields—which works best when each field is relatively homogeneous.

Within this framework, however, what were the participants to do about disagreements within fields, or moments when scholars from within the same field could not coordinate?

EXCERPT 9.3

GG [LINGUIST]: You can tell not everybody agrees with me. . . .

FS [LAWYER]: . . . Do all of you agree that the category that Mike refers to as *literal meaning* or *linguistic meaning* exists? . . .

MG [LINGUIST]: Shall we have a show of hands?

(*WULQ* Trans, 830–831)

EXCERPT 9.4

MG [LINGUIST]: Some contemporary formal semanticists in fact have taken to using the term *conventional meaning*, instead of *literal meaning*, because it more accurately conveys exactly what Jerry was talking about.

JS [LINGUIST]: Well, to know the entire semantic system, you also have to know the conventions about the applicability of complex items that are composed out of—

CC [LAWYER]: Right. I'm still trying to get the phenomenon out there that you're willing to call "literal." You are paraphrasing "literal" as conventions about the applicability of a word, and you said something about use.

GG [LINGUIST]: Could you say what you mean by *applicability*?

JS: No, that's the problem.

(*WULQ* Trans, 831–832)

EXCERPT 9.5

CC [LAWYER]: This is helpful. Of the six linguists in the room, none of them believe in a truth-conditional theory of meaning.

GG [LINGUIST]: That's completely false.

(*WULQ* Trans, 834)

Locating a single voice for linguistics as a field turned out to be quite difficult—and as noted, the burden was more on linguistics than law to represent itself in a single voice (i.e., that of a "science" that could provide some new form of certainty for lawyers dealing with language).

Thus the pressure to produce forms of scientific certainty from the field of linguistics also arguably encouraged some fuzziness about fissures within that field—despite many strenuous efforts for clarity. And the metapragmatic structure that envisioned two fields speaking to one another—while completely reasonable in many ways—created some additional dilemmas in terms of managing professional identities, coalitions, and courtesy.

9.4.2 TOPIC 2: IN PARTICULAR, WHAT IS A VEHICLE?

If asking a question about meaning in the abstract turned out to be problematic, what about more specific attempts to nail down meaning in specific examples? As noted in 9.4 above, one of the more specific topics at the conference involved how to define the word *vehicle*:

EXCERPT 9.6

CC [LAWYER]: Let me try this paraphrase, see if it works: All vehicles are prohibited from the park. Question 1 is: Does the literal meaning of *vehicle* include ambulances?

GG: [LINGUIST]: You're using "literal" meaning and I thought we were using "conventional."

CC: Okay, let's say "conventional"; does the conventional meaning of *vehicle* include ambulances?

GG: Yes.

CC: Do all the linguists believe that?

JS [LINGUIST]: I believe it only with some reservations.

CC: Then the next question is: Does the conventional meaning of *all vehicles are prohibited from the park* include [the meaning of] *all ambulances are prohibited from the park*?

MG [LINGUIST]: Yes.

(*WULQ* Trans, 839)

Here, at least, the linguists all agreed. In order to agree, the linguists had to converge on an approach to meaning that does not rely on the particulars of how, when, why, or where certain language is deployed. (They were more likely to do this when questions of grammatical/syntactic structure arose, not surprising in light of a strong appeal to Chomsky by the linguists' group.[9]) Interestingly, at numerous points in the discussion, Georgia Green, one of the linguists, did insist on a contextual way of determining meaning—one more in tune with a linguistic anthropological focus on pragmatics and metapragmatics in language (hence her earlier comment "You can tell not everybody agrees with me"). However, as a whole, the group of linguists at the conference (particularly when representing linguistics as a science) often stressed a very different approach—an approach under which the contexts in which words and sentences are uttered wouldn't matter. When explaining this more decontextual approach, the linguists stressed the use of introspection as a method (asking themselves, as speakers of language, whether certain linguistic constructions make sense and are grammatical).

This became confusing for the legal scholars, because at previous points in the discussion not only Green but a number of the other linguists had conceded that empirical research into actual language use can be important in determining what certain phrases mean in practice for particular populations.[10] The linguists' subsequent insistence on a decontextualized approach to determining "the" meaning of the word *vehicle* led something of a rebellion from one of the lawyers at the conference, who challenged the linguists on their methodology:

EXCERPT 9.7

BB [LAWYER]: How do you know [whether a prediction based in linguistic theories about syntax or semantics is correct]?

JS [LINGUIST]: Because we speak the language.

BB: What happened to all those conventions?[11]

GG: We try to discover the conventions.

BB: Yes, I know you try to discover the conventions, but I am astounded at your technique for doing so. You ask yourself!

JL [LINGUIST]: That's one way of asking—

BB: It's a terrible way.

GG [LINGUIST]: All right, we can ask each other. It makes no difference.

BB: Yes it does. You are a sub-community that —you're consulting each other for conventions and then claiming that they are the conventions of the larger community.

JS [LINGUIST]: This can be a problem. But we try to guard against it.

BB: Can be a problem—! . . . It's the central problem of communication that has been exemplified by the past day and a half.

(*WULQ* Trans, 910–911)

This lawyer then proceeded to insist on the importance of communities of discourse (a perspective that is well-represented in some areas of linguistic research, although not among linguists at the conference):

EXCERPT 9.8

BB: . . . let's suppose there is a discourse among lawyers in which we tend to attach certain meanings to phrases that are different from the meanings that are attached in the larger community. And I have been saying, how can you simultaneously say that meaning is conventional and refuse to recognize the conventions in the law-talk community as a possible sub-community with its own conventions?

(*WULQ* Trans, 911)

At stake in this struggle over universal static meanings, as opposed to meanings based in contexts and communities of discourse, was the question whether legal language depended on a distinct community with its own conventions of interpretation. As they debated the potential range of the word *vehicle*, the linguists insisted that under any interpretation based in standard English, an ambulance is a vehicle. It followed for them that if a statute prohibited all vehicles from the park, and an ambulance entered the park, then the ambulance driver had broken the law.

For the lawyers, interpretation of the words in the statute was a more complicated matter, one which could not be resolved by using a "dictionary definition" of the word *vehicle*. Here attention to differences in disciplinary linguistic ideologies might have been helpful to the participants. The actual practices of interpretation in legal communities do require lawyers and judges to move beyond abstract semantics or formal grammatical/syntactic analyses. This was forcefully asserted again and again by the lawyers at the conference, and there is a vast literature supporting them—including from the field of language-and-law (for summaries of this literature, see Mertz 2007, 26–33, 41–137; see also Ford and Mertz, this volume). However, if some important part of the interpretive expertise lies within the legal community of discourse, a question emerges as to how useful linguists can be to lawyers—and exploring this was one of the main goals of the conference. This is not to suggest that the linguists were responding instrumentally, but it does indicate that some interactional dilemmas were built into the conference's metalinguistic structuring of expert stance and role.

When this earlier transcript was discussed at the 2009 LT Working Group meeting, the metalinguistic structure at the later meeting allowed for a looser alignment within fields, and permitted the differences within linguistics to be aired without threatening the expert knowledge or validity of the field as a whole. The goal was exploratory, with no presumption that one discipline needed to prove its worth to another; indeed, the structure encouraged open consideration of whether it was even possible to translate some kinds of ideas across different disciplines. One law professor in the later LT group noted that the linguists at the earlier conference had been "disappointing the lawyers" when they admitted that there were disagreements within the field of linguistics as to how to study "meaning," since it seemed as if the lawyers wanted "what they did get from the micro-economists, a single theory or template that they can apply in a kind of literal way, to the problems that are defined within their world." Linguists participating in the later meeting spoke openly of deep divisions within their field. For example, one of the law professors in the LT group asked the linguists there whether they agreed that it was possible to single out a definitive "conventional" meaning for the word "vehicle," based on some kind of "ordinary" usage. Several of the linguists acknowledged that there was a strand of thought within the field of linguistics that would answer in the affirmative—but they also said that their own approaches led them to answer negatively. As one of them explained: "the notion that the literal meaning of a term is the convention of 'ordinary people usage' presumes that we are all using the word to denote the same thing"—and he went on to note that many linguists would find this presumption problematic. This led to an extensive and frank discussion of how linguists of various orientations, as well as different legal scholars, might approach the "vehicle in the park" example. One law professor summarized his understanding of the translation problem encountered in the original conference by saying that the lawyers at the conference "seem[ed] to be saying that ... we lawyers believe there is meaning within the language game that we play, and we don't necessarily need to look beyond it." This gets to a core question in interdisciplinary translation: are any parties to the conversation willing to be receptive to underlying disciplinary paradigms that differ widely from their own?

9.5 Interdisciplinary Encounters at the Meta-Level

In a conference whose goal is to demonstrate the utility of a science of linguistics to law, prioritizing the language game played by lawyers could certainly pose a considerable barrier to further conversation—unless the linguists could take account of the metalinguistic structures and norms viewed as central to that legal language game. (But to do that would forfeit claims of expertise based in universal language structure.) This very interesting transcript, then, provides numerous examples of the important role that meta-level assumptions can play in interdisciplinary dialogue—and especially meta-level assumptions about language as it functions socially (i.e., metapragmatics). Is the goal of talking to generate something useful, or just to achieve some mutual enlightenment (or one-way enlightenment) between disciplines? Who is speaking here—a discipline, a part of a discipline, or an individual scholar? Are there aspects of the immediate context, or the broader disciplinary and institutional contexts, that affect possibilities for productive communication? This section surveys some core metalinguistic issues that emerge from studying the transcript of the 1994 conference (continuing to draw here not only on my own analysis, but also on the observations of the LT group in 2009 as they read parts of the conference transcript).

9.5.1 WHAT'S THE POINT OF TALKING?

One way of assessing whether an interdisciplinary encounter was successful might be to ask what the participants' goals were. On the one hand, the explicit purpose for the gathering was clearly delineated and quite practical: as noted above, the linguists along with their lawyer colleague had achieved some success in being cited in US Supreme Court decisions, and they were exploring how and whether linguistics could be of further use to legal decision-making.

As it turns out, however, we find other threads of thought about the goal of the conference were woven through the transcript. One of the co-conveners, Judith Levi, for example, also stated a more free-form goal:

EXCERPT 9.9

... I'd like for us to be really creative and to feel free to brainstorm
    together and then just watch what comes out, without any prior
    expectations for what we have to produce. ... After all, we have
    no quizzes at the end, no frantic publication deadlines or funding
    deadlines. So let's just see what a weekend of talk that is both
    knowledgeable and naïve can accomplish and what it can create in the
    way of bridges between our professions.
(*WULQ* Trans, 801)

And indeed, after initial sessions in which participants were invited to spell out questions they wanted answered during the conference, the results were a mix of purely intellectual and more practical or applied queries, ranging from "How do linguistics and law treat the role of context in interpretation of language?" to "What can linguists offer as expert witnesses in a case that any (educated) speaker of the language, such as the judge or jurors, could not figure out themselves?" (*WULQ* 1995, 804–805). However, it bears noting that no similar challenges to law were posed, and that the quiet interactional hierarchy in which the linguists had to prove themselves to the lawyers persisted as an underlying tension throughout the conversation. (And, indeed, as a discipline, law demands answers that can be (and are) enacted in powerful ways, so the privileging of such a goal is already a move that situates the discourse in territory with which lawyers are more familiar.)

9.5.2 EFFECTS OF THE IMMEDIATE LANGUAGE CONTEXT

This hierarchy, in which the more powerful discipline of law could take or leave the offerings of linguistics, was one important effect of the immediate language context at the earlier conference. It is an aspect that would be very difficult to address frankly in this kind of setting, especially given that the people involved didn't know one another very well—particularly across disciplines (i.e., linguists might know one another professionally but were just getting to know the lawyers, etc.). It was an aspect of wider sociocultural context that was enacted in somewhat subtle aspects of the "local" interactions at the conference, and it arguably undermined some of the overtly expressed goals of interdisciplinary exploration and cooperation. When communication hurdles built into the context are both tacit and reflective of larger power structures, they can be quite challenging.

In terms of the "where" and "when" components of language context, it bears noting that the shorter, but regular meetings of the later LT group generated an atmosphere that differed from the more intense and finite tone of the interactions typical of groups at small one-time conferences that extend over several days, like the original conference analyzed here. This more intensive but short-term encounter of people from different disciplines may pose some additional communication challenges worth considering. In these settings, there has not been an opportunity for the participants to develop shared vocabularies or feelings of professional connection that might help them navigate difficult spots in the conversation. The short, intense format also led participants to attempt to encapsulate and summarize entire disciplinary traditions quite quickly, always a tricky task. (On a metalinguistic level, note also that disciplines might differ in how they weigh and contextualize shorter summaries of complex materials—with law having a very precise tradition around this kind of task.)

Another consequence of this context was a kind of formality one would expect from people who are meeting for the first time, especially when coupled with the need to explicate disciplines that are also in a sense encountering each other in this one-time setting. At a number of points, participants were asked to represent their disciplines and explain some aspect of their disciplines' position on relevant issues; these presentations were necessarily elliptical and somewhat formal. As we've noted, these abbreviated snapshots of disciplinary positions also took the form of "us in our discipline" as opposed to "you in the other discipline," as exemplified in the following exchange:

EXCERPT 9.10

BE [LAWYER]: Now here's my larger point, a challenge to the linguists. This returns to the themes that we had in talking about the vehicle in the park hypothetical and the *X-Citement* case. In all those cases you had the linguists lined up like a phalanx in a Spartan army. The linguists lined up saying "This is not the meaning of the statute when you say *vehicle* does not mean ambulances, when you say that *knowingly* modifies all those other terms." The phenomenon that is revealed by those cases, and I think now more transparently revealed by the conversation about my hypothetical, is that as circumstances change and what the speaker was not focused on comes to pass, then the importance of semantic meaning is reduced and maybe even evaporates.

MG [LINGUIST]: No.

(*WULQ* Trans, 948)

Here we see how many contextual strands flow together—strands of setting, timing, participation structures, identities constructed by the conference frame, larger disciplinary norms and social structures enacted locally, fluctuating and unspoken understandings about the underlying reason for attempting interdisciplinary communication. Much as Gruber, Matoesian, and Silverstein in this volume paint a picture of seepage or leakage in courtroom discourse—leakage that cannot be entirely contained through conscious intervention, we similarly find leakage here (even in a setting where much more attention is paid to the issues of translation). The power of quiet metapragmatic structures and assumptions, then, is considerable. With continued effort, analysis, and attention, it seems quite possible that we can make progress in bringing these metalinguistic effects into more conscious consideration—and also find ways to create better bridges. Of course, it bears asking whether all parties actually want to create those bridges! But if the answer is in the affirmative, then much potentially fruitful territory remains for further work. Perhaps humility about the limits of what can be accomplished might be an important tool in this effort.

It also bears noting that, perhaps ironically, the 1995 conference was much more of a success than some may have thought—depending on how we conceptualize its goal. If the goal was to come up with easily applied templates from linguistics that lawyers could use in achieving quick (and certain) answers about language use, then it was not very successful. If the goal was to begin a conversation that could yield clues about where and how the disciplines of law and linguistics might be able to connect in fruitful ways, then we must commend the participants for providing future scholars with an honest transcript—with data that were not cleaned up to make the interactions "prettier" than they actually were. The considerable effort that went into that gave us information that can be used to explore where, when, how, and why some interdisciplinary interactions involving the field of law falter or yield generative (!) results.

9.5.3 METACOMMUNICATIVE STRUCTURE
AND DISCIPLINARY EPISTEMOLOGIES

However, as we see in the next excerpt, a different interpretation of the exchanges at the conference was voiced by one of the participants at the end of the proceedings:

> **EXCERPT 9.11**
>
> KG [LAWYER/LINGUIST]: Well, I think if a sympathetic linguistic and a sympathetic law person got together and struggled with some of the theoretical problems we're discussing now, that would be interesting. But on the basis of the group discussion so far I would not feel optimistic about two people actually managing to combine to say something that was illuminating.
>
> JL [LINGUIST]: . . . can you be more specific about which theoretical issues? [. . .] Like meaning and language and interpretation[?]
>
> KG: Yes, and whether if lawyers have particular practices, that should be understood as the trumping of language or as a language of lawyers. The reason that I'm not optimistic is that my own conclusion is that it's a disciplinary matter. My perspective now is that a fundamental assumption of the linguistic discipline is that language has got to be general and have general rules. Therefore, there is a strong disposition to reject the idea that these kinds of things can possibly be looked at as a legal language, whereas the lawyers, I think, believe that's at least one way such a practice could be regarded.
>
> (*WULQ* 1995, 969)

In the excerpt above, KG paints a picture, his "take-away" point from the conference, of two clearly delineated disciplinary perspectives that are unlikely to interact productively. This summary is in many ways quite predictable from all of the metalinguistic (and specifically, metapragmatic) features we've discussed. Our analysis of those features indicates that this outcome was not inevitable, and might have looked different had some of the sociolinguistic structure of the encounter been altered—or had some specific features of the translation task been addressed explicitly.

As noted above, in analyzing the interactions among linguists and law professors at the earlier 1995 conference, the later 2009 LT group focused in on the sometimes spoken, sometimes unspoken metacommunicative assumptions behind the discussion. And as we've seen, the later LT group enjoyed a freedom that the earlier group had not had: they did not have to find ways to present linguistics as a single-stranded "science," but could explore how different kinds of linguistics might—or might not—interact fruitfully with different kinds of legal scholarship.

A more contextually oriented brand of linguistics might have to surrender its superior position if analyzing the language game of lawyers in its own right. What if the lawyers' worldview makes sense of language in a different way because of their normative commitments and charges? What if, then, the meaning of *vehicle* in a statute could never be determined without full consideration of the legal contexts in which it operates? On the other hand, linguists who pay attention to lawyers' language games might have a lot to say about the way those language games interact with other ways of approaching language. Lawyers who listened to the approach of these linguists might have to open their ears to other perspectives on how to interpret language or make meaning, especially when they are interacting with non-lawyers. Indeed, "[l]inguistics might challenge law's imperial belief that it generates itself as if ex nihilo, by exposing that law is embedded in a pragmatically-defined, normatively-laden tradition" (Mootz, 1995, 1023).

9.6 Translation: Not for Certainty, but for New Ways to Think

As this discussion has indicated, the difficulties inherent in translating across disciplines are complex, deeply contextual, and hard to summarize in sound bites. Nevertheless, mindful that some readers will want shorter "take-away" points, this concluding section suggests some key points to consider in working toward better interdisciplinary translation practices. In keeping with the approach advocated here, I focus on processes of thinking and talking—on questions—rather than on simple one-size-fits-all answers or templates.

This analysis has suggested that interdisciplinary communication is unlikely to flourish without attention to contextual structuring of language (including at the meta-level discussed here as metapragmatic). This is true at several levels:

(1) What are the assumptions structuring this particular interdisciplinary encounter in the minds of participants? What are some of the pitfalls that might follow from any of these assumptions? In what ways do aspects of the context contribute to these pitfalls?

(2) What are the communicative norms guiding scholarly discourse in each disciplinary community? Are there differences within disciplines that might be important to acknowledge? Are there productive ways to bridge differences between and within disciplines for purposes of this particular encounter (conference, working group, etc.)?

(3) Why are we seeking interdisciplinarity? For what goals, in what contexts, when do we want to insist on disciplinary boundaries, when to we want to elide them?

In his commentary on the *WULQ* transcript, Mootz aptly outlined how interactions between linguists and legal scholars at the conference reenacted an oft-repeated dance in which law turns eagerly to social science for greater certainty, only to be disappointed (1995, 1013–1015, 1023). This dance frequently proceeds on the assumption that the goal of certainty is (a) reachable only or best through disciplines that most closely approximate the natural sciences, and (b) the only or best gift that social science has to offer law. Like James Boyd White and others who have focused on translating the language of law, Mootz concludes that when law merely attempts to pluck the low-hanging fruit of severable "findings" or "methods" from social science, it is bound to miss much of the point (White 1990; see also Mertz 1992a, 1992b). Our examination of the interactions in this conference suggests that social scientists who use such a framework may also encounter difficulties. Note that this is a diagnosis that goes far beyond a failure to find matching "dictionary definitions" for shared terms; it goes to entire structures of interaction and the wider social structures of institutions behind them. We should also, however, applaud the courage and generosity of those earlier scholars in providing us with a transcript of their interactions on which to build in working to understand and talk across disciplinary boundaries. Examining their interactions has been very helpful in identifying promising new avenues for thought.

The authors in this volume provide ample support for paying close attention to the process of translation itself—and for asking about deeper structures affecting how and whether we communicate. This kind of questioning can lay the groundwork for a different approach to interdisciplinarity in law: one that begins by taking the translation process among disciplines more seriously—and that ends in asking how law itself could become a better translator of the social world upon which it casts judgment.

Notes

1. Within "technologies" I of course include the more obvious developments that have followed on the arrival of the Internet and ever-more-advanced computer-assisted forms of communication. But I also mean to indicate *knowledge technologies* as they've been discussed and analyzed in the field of science and technology studies—and especially in the nascent part of that field now turning its attention to studying social science (rather than just natural science). For example, Camic, Gross, and Lamont talk about "the basic tools and technologies of social knowledge making: focus groups . . ., survey interviews . . ., game-theoretic models . . ., and especially statistical models . . ." (2011, 12).

2. The participants in the 1995 conference included six legal scholars: Robert Bennett, Clark Cunningham, William Eskridge, Kent Greenawalt, Michael Moore, and Frederick Schauer; five linguists: Charles Fillmore, Michael Geis, Georgia Green, Judith Levi, and Jerrold Sadock; and one linguist who also had a JD: Jeffrey Kaplan (Washington

U. Symposium 1995, 785–790). (Legal scholar Cass Sunstein attended a small opening part of the conference but did not participate in the substantive discussions that are the subject of this analysis.)

3. The Chicago/NLR LT Working Group had a core group of continuing participants but also included several visitors from time to time. Present at the group's transcript reading in 2009 were Robert Burns (Law, Philosophy); Catherine Gruber (Linguistic Anthropology); William Ford (Political Science, Law); Gregory Matoesian (Sociolinguistics, Criminology); Elizabeth Mertz (Anthropology, Law); Michael Silverstein (Linguistics, Linguistic Anthropology); and Winnifred Sullivan (Religion, Law). Over its history, the group had also included visiting scholars from these fields and also from the fields of Psychology and Rhetoric. (The acronym NLR stands for New Legal Realism, a broader project concerned with encouraging more and better forms of interdisciplinary translation between the social sciences and law; see *Wisconsin Law Review* 2005.)

4. See Conley and O'Barr 1990, xii: "We listen to and record talk as it occurs, and then we meet with research assistants and colleagues to analyze the resulting tapes and transcripts." These group "reflection" sessions help researchers check and refine their emerging analysis. This is particularly useful in instances of translation (of many kinds), if the reflection group includes representatives of the divergent languages, cultures, disciplines, and/or other different perspectives at issue in the transcript. This was the case in the 2009 reflection group. I will explicitly note the points in my own discussion that emerged from the 2009 working group.

5. As we will see, Bellos is proposing a move from focusing on what linguistic anthropologists would characterize as the *metasemantic* level to instead examining what they would call the *metapragmatic* level. If we conceptualize the *semantic* meaning of a word as the aspect of its meaning that does not change in response to its context of use, then our attempt to explicate that meaning (which is a move to the meta-level) would be metasemantics. The best quick example of the metasemantic level is probably the dictionary, which attempts to specify the meanings of words at an abstract level that applies regardless of where, when, how, or for what reason that word occurs in particular situations of use ("An aspen is a tree of the genus Populus having flattened leafstalks that permit its leaves to flutter easily in the wind").

By contrast, *pragmatic* meaning is that aspect of language meaning that depends upon contexts of use. In recent decades, scholars in sociolinguistics, linguistic anthropology, and language pragmatics have resoundingly demonstrated the importance of this often-overlooked aspect of language to even arenas formerly thought to depend entirely on semantics (see Gumperz 1982; Levinson 1983; Silverstein 1976; also see introduction to concepts in Mertz 1985). As this line of thought developed further, the centrality of *metapragmatic* structuring to language meaning has also become increasingly evident (Irvine and Gal 2000; Lucy 1993; Silverstein 1979, 1993; Woolard 1998), although news of this discovery has been slow to reach some corners of the field of linguistics (and linguistic philosophy)—and that dynamic was fully displayed at the 1995 conference.

6. Building from roots in the Prague School (or Prague Linguistic Circle) and other scholarly traditions (see Mertz 1985 for overview), linguistic anthropologists followed the lead of Michael Silverstein (1979), who demonstrated how J. L. Austin's (1975) conception of *felicity conditions* actually miscalculated the contingent creativity at the heart of *performative language* (language that "does by saying"—like "I promise" or "I christen you"). In similar fashion, Stephen Levinson (1983) politely demolished core premises of

Gricean analysis, pointing out what had been obvious for some time to sociolinguists, psycholinguists, linguistic anthropologists, conversation analysts—and basically anyone studying how language actually works on the ground—that is, that there simply aren't universal maxims that apply across all language situations and cultures (see, among many others, Gumperz 1982 for examples). Indeed, adhering to one of Grice's (1975) maxims like "be brief (avoid unnecessary prolixity)" might get one into deep trouble in many cultural situations in which such brevity could be interpreted as curt and impolite—and this is just the beginning of the objections posed to such a list. Thus, two of the iconic philosophers of language deemed to have opened the door to contextual analysis and language pragmatics (while their contributions are obviously considerable and appreciated) have been shown to be analytically off-the-mark by those with actual empirical evidence of how language works in practice. From this point of view, one must examine particular social and cultural settings to find out under what circumstances a particular set of linguistic norms applies. There is much to learn, and the analysis has to become far more complex. Rather than positing a limited set of metalinguistic maxims presumed to govern speech everywhere, researchers have focused on the vast set of *metapragmatic* ideas and norms (or ideologies) that govern not just what we say but how we say it. And it turns out that the meaning of what we say hinges critically on structured relationships between our contexts of speaking and the meta-level ideologies of language and context in play while we speak.

7. Unless otherwise indicated, all excerpts are from the conference transcript.

8. The group did discuss the utility of dictionaries to lawyers, with one of the lawyers making the interesting (and revealing) point that dictionaries might serve as sources of authority on meaning that were good enough for legal purposes, given that "we cannot always hire a linguist" (FS, *WULQ* 1995, 823).

9. Noam Chomsky's research on "universal grammar" is an approach that looks for a deep structure of language that exists apart from use in context (Chomsky 1965). This approach stands in stark contrast to the tradition that goes back at least as far as the Prague School and Roman Jakobson's work in linguistics, which traces ways that even deep structures of grammar have to take account of use and context; Michael Silverstein has rendered definitive accounts of that tradition in the current time, along with other scholars from anthropological linguistics and sociolinguistics like Alessandro Duranti, Susan Gal, Charles Goodwin, Marjorie Goodwin, John Gumperz, Dell Hymes, Judith Irvine, Bambi Schieffelin, and many others (see generally Duranti 2005; see also Mertz 1985).

10. Under this approach, instead of asking oneself as a native speaker whether a certain linguistic expression makes sense (introspection), the linguist would have to do empirical studies to find out how particular speakers understood that expression—and preferably where possible would also examine language in action rather than just relying on speakers' self-reports.

11. When "conventions" were discussed at the conference, the importance of pragmatics and context tended to be highlighted more. Thus Green had explained that many linguists would talk about "conventional meaning" as "the meaning it would have in a normal context"—and while acknowledging that defining "normal" might be difficult, she summarized this as "the context everybody supposes everybody else supposes" (*WULQ* 1995, 838). Bennett, a legal scholar, then asked "Why is it that everybody has an understanding of what everybody else supposes?"—leading Green to respond that this would be "context-relative"

and "community-relative" (*WULQ* 1995, 838). At various points in the conference, linguists represented the division between more contextual studies of pragmatics and more decontextual studies of syntax and semantics as simply a division of labor that was not mutually contradictory (p. 836). At other points the potential contradictions between those approaches were acknowledged. Note that variation on this point would have implications for whether the group of linguists could speak from a singular "scientific" point of view that was undergirded by acontextual "universal" analytic principles.

References

Austin, J. S. 1975. *How to Do Things with Words* (2nd ed.). Cambridge, MA: Harvard University Press.

Bellos, David. 2011. *Is That a Fish in Your Ear? Translation and the Meaning of Everything.* New York: Faber and Faber.

Berk-Seligson, Susan. 1990. *The Bilingual Courtroom: Court Interpreters in the Judicial Process.* Chicago: University of Chicago Press.

Berk-Seligson, Susan. 2009. *Coerced Confessions: The Discourse of Bilingual Police Interrogations.* New York: Mouton de Gruyter.

Camic, Charles, Neil Gross, and Michèle Lamont, eds. 2011. *Social Knowledge in the Making.* Chicago: University of Chicago Press.

Chomsky, Noam. 1965. *Aspects of the Theory of Syntax.* Boston: MIT Press.

Conley, John, and William O'Barr. 1990. *Rules versus Relationships: The Ethnography of Legal Discourse.* Chicago: University of Chicago Press.

Cunningham, Clark. 1992. "The Lawyer as Translator, Representation as Text: Towards an Ethnography of Legal Discourse." *Cornell Law Review* 77: 1298–1387.

Cunningham, Clark, Judith Levi, Georgia Green, and Jeffrey Kaplan. 1995. "Plain Meaning and Hard Cases." *Yale Law Journal* 103: 1561–1625.

Duranti, Alessandro, ed. 2005. *A Companion to Linguistic Anthropology.* Malden MA: Wiley Blackwell.

Eades, Diana. 2008. *Courtroom Talk and Neocolonial Control.* Berlin: Mouton de Gruyter.

Eskridge, William, and Judith Levi. 1995. "Regulatory Variables and Statutory Interpretation." *Washington University Law Quarterly* 73(3): 1103–1115.

Grice, H. Paul. 1975. "Logic and Conversation." In *Syntax and Semantics 3: Speech Acts*, edited by Peter Cole and Jerry Morgan, 41–58. New York: Academic Press.

Gumperz, John. 1982. *Discourse Strategies.* Cambridge: Cambridge University Press.

Irvine, Judith, and Susan Gal. 2000. "Language Ideology and Linguistic Differentiation." In *Regimes of Language: Ideologies, Polities, and Identities*, edited by Paul Kroskrity, 35–84. Santa Fe: School of American Research.

Jakobson, Roman. 1959. "On Linguistic Aspects of Translation." In *On Translation*, edited by Reuben Brower, 232–239. Cambridge, MA: Harvard University Press.

Jasanoff, Sheila, ed. 1995. *Handbook of Science and Technology Studies.* Thousand Oaks, CA: Sage.

Kaplan, Jeffrey, Georgia Green, Clark Cunningham, and Judith Levi. 1995. "Bringing Linguistics into Judicial Decision-Making: Semantic Analysis Submitted to the Supreme Court." *Forensic Linguistics* 2: 81–98.

Knorr Cetina, Karin. 1999. *Epistemic Cultures: How the Sciences Make Knowledge.* Cambridge, MA: Harvard University Press.

Law and Linguistics Consortium. 1994. "Brief Amicus Curiae of the Law and Linguistics Consortium in Support of Respondents, United States v. X-Citement Video, Ind. (No. 93–723)". 115 S. Ct. Rep. 464.

Levinson, Stephen. 1983. *Pragmatics.* Cambridge: Cambridge University Press.

Lucy, John. 1993. "Reflexive Language and the Human Disciplines." In *Reflexive Language: Reported Speech and Metapragmatics*, edited by J. Lucy, 9–32. Cambridge: Cambridge University Press.

Mertz, Elizabeth. 1985. "Beyond Symbolic Anthropology: Introducing Semiotic Mediation." In *Semiotic Mediation*, edited by Elizabeth Mertz and Richard Parmentier, 1–19. New York: Academic Press.

Mertz, Elizabeth. 1992a. "Creative Acts of Translation." *Yale Journal of Law & the Humanities*, 4(1): 165–185.

Mertz, Elizabeth. 1992b. "Language, Law and Social Meanings: Linguistic/Anthropological Contributions to the Study of Law." *Law & Society Review* 26(2): 601–633.

Mootz, Francis J. 1995. "Desperately Seeking Science." *Washington University Law Quarterly* 73(3): 1009–1023.

Silverstein, Michael. 1976. "Shifters, Linguistic Categories, and Cultural Description." In *Meaning in Anthropology*, edited by Keith Basso and Henry Selby, 11–55. Albuquerque: University of New Mexico Press.

Silverstein, Michael. 1979. "Language Structure and Linguistic Ideology." In *The Elements: A Parasession on Linguistic Units and Levels*, edited by Paul Clyne, William Hanks, and C. Hofbauer, 194–247. Chicago: Chicago Linguistic Society.

Silverstein, Michael. 1993. "Metapragmatic Discourse and Metapragmatic Function." In *Reflexive Language: Reported Speech and Metapragmatics*, edited by John Lucy, 33–58. Cambridge: Cambridge University Press.

Silverstein, Michael. 2003. "Translation, Transduction, Transformation: Skating 'Glossando' on Thin Semiotic Ice." In *Translating Cultures: Perspectives on Translation and Anthropology*, edited by Paula Rubel and Abraham Rosman, 75–105. Oxford: Berg.

Strathern, Marilyn. 2011. "An Experiment in Interdisciplinarity: Proposals and Promises." In *Social Knowledge in the Making*, edited by Charles Camic, Neil Gross, and Michele Lamont, 257–283. Chicago: University of Chicago Press.

Trudgill, Peter. 1983. *Sociolinguistics: An Introduction to Language and Society*. London: Penguin Books.

Washington University Law Quarterly [cited as *WULQ*]. 1995. "Symposium: What Is Meaning in a Legal Text?" *Washington University Law Quarterly* 73(3): 769–1313.

White, James Boyd. 1990. *Justice as Translation: An Essay in Cultural and Legal Criticism.* Chicago: University of Chicago Press.

Wisconsin Law Review. 2005. "New Legal Realism Symposium: Is It Time for a New Legal Realism?" *Wisconsin Law Review* 2005(2): 335–745.

Woolard, Kathryn. 1998. "Introduction: Language Ideology as a Field of Inquiry." In *Language Ideologies: Theory and Practice*, edited by Bambi Schieffelin, Kathryn Woolard, and Paul Kroskrity, 3–47. Oxford: Oxford University Press.

APPENDIX: The Chicago NLR Working Group on Law and Translation

In 2009, as part of their ongoing discussions in the Chicago NLR LT Working Group, an interdisciplinary group read portions of the 1995 transcript out loud together, using that reading as the foundation for another conversation about translation between the fields of linguistics and law. (The version of the transcript from which they worked was somewhat different from the published version, which had been lightly edited.) Like the earlier group, the LT group included linguists and law professors, but also humanities scholars and social scientists from other fields. A number of participants in this more recent group held joint degrees in both law and social science. The LT discussion obviously built on the efforts of the 1995 conference, but it also drew on interdisciplinary practices that had emerged during years of its own working group meetings.

The group that met in 2009 reread portions of the transcript from 1995. This subsequent working group had been discussing issues surrounding interdisciplinary translation over several years, using readings from different disciplines to spur their conversations. One goal of the group was to notice whether and how different disciplinary traditions might be affecting interdisciplinary communication and comprehension (either in the materials we read, or in our own conversations). Law, linguistics, anthropology, religious studies, and political science were among the disciplines represented in the group.

The discussions of the 2009 group focused on two of the 1995 conference segments in particular: (1) part of a general discussion of how linguists and some philosophers of language approach meaning, and (2) a more particular discussion of how linguists and lawyers would make sense of prohibitions on "vehicles in the park." This selection permitted the 2009 group to compare interdisciplinary talk on more abstract (meaning) and more concrete ("vehicle") levels. The 2009 group read segments of the earlier transcript out loud, and then discussed the translation process at work in each segment. At the same time, the second group used this discussion of the earlier transcript to clarify their own understandings across disciplines.

In addition to paying close attention to the linguistic dilemmas arising from interdisciplinary talk, the 2009 LT group built upon years of conversations as a working group. Several members of the LT group (Silverstein, Mertz) had previously participated in ongoing interdisciplinary working groups organized by the Center for Psychosocial Studies in Chicago (later the Center for Transnational Studies). Those groups were based on a model of long-term conversations in which participants from diverse disciplines read and talked together over a period of years rather than days. The process of reading texts from different disciplines together gave participants a chance to develop a common vocabulary and set of understandings. The participants had an opportunity to struggle through differences and miscommunications, building a shared sense of purpose and intellectual connection. The LT Working Group in 2009 was partially modeled on the earlier Center for Psychosocial Studies working groups in its effort to cultivate in-depth interdisciplinary exchange within a group that met over a period of years—and which paid specific attention to the problems accompanying discussion across disciplinary boundaries. The resulting conversations at times explicitly focused on metalinguistic norms guiding discourse within different disciplinary traditions (as well as between them), in addition to focusing on linguistic details and contexts. Thus, while the method of group transcript analysis we employed (in examining the 1995 conference exchanges) was quite similar to that made common in language-and-law studies by Conley and O'Barr (1990, xii) and others, our approach also added features such as disciplinary diversity and conscious ongoing efforts at translation that had been typical of the earlier Center groups. This chapter draws on the 2009 discussions as part of the transcript analysis presented here.

10

Law's Resistance to Translation®

WHAT LAW AND LITERATURE CAN TEACH US

An Interview with Peter Brooks

> Legal interpretation must be held to some realist ethical standards. If the legal profession fails in this task, it may be time to bring in readers from outside law.
>
> —Brooks 2010, 355

> When legal interpretation issues in the mere assertion of mastery, perhaps it is time to bring in the professors of literature. They at least understand that the act of interpretation is an act of translation, of mediation.
>
> —Brooks 2010, 366

In the following transcript, Peter Brooks [PB] responds to a request that he speak about the issue of law's resistances: where, when, and why does legal language resist insights from law's "others"— whether they are disciplines or people? Elizabeth Mertz [EM] served as interviewer.

Professor Brooks began by discussing a US Supreme Court case, *District of Columbia v. Heller* (2008). Justice Scalia wrote the majority opinion in that case, which required the Court to interpret the following language of the Second Amendment to the US Constitution: "A well regulated Militia, being necessary to the security of a free State, the right of the people to keep and bear Arms, shall not be infringed" (*D.C. v. Heller* 2008, 576–588). Scalia paid scant attention to an amicus brief submitted by experts in language from the fields of linguistics and English that argued for a limiting role of the first phrase, concerning militias, on the right to bear arms, in accordance with eighteenth-century language usage (*D.C. v. Heller* 2008, 586). Brooks takes up the question of what Scalia was doing in marshalling evidence to support a broad interpretation of that Second Amendment language:

PB: In *Heller*, Scalia is actually enacting policy. He's overturning the acts of legislatures, he's overturning a tradition of legal interpretation which essentially left the Second Amendment alone. He's saying,

"I have such interpretive skills that I can read it for you." He begins part of his opinion by saying that he is turning now to the *meaning* of the Second Amendment, as if he could actually tell you what that is—and then, of course he claims that he's interpreting it in historical context. But, as the brief from the professors of linguistics and English shows, he really ignores what one could say about historical linguistic context and instead interprets it in fundamentally ideological ways.

The second part of my 2010 paper is about the narrative continuity in constitutional interpretation by the Supreme Court (Brooks 2010). I was particularly interested in what *Planned Parenthood v. Casey* had to say about *stare decisis*. The language in the joint opinion of Kennedy, Souter, and O'Conner in that case talks about the Constitution as a covenant that runs from one generation to another; it's language that is religious in implication, but also very much about narrative. The joint opinion talks about how each new decision has to realize the potential of the Constitution. This fits in with my idea about how narrative has to work backwards; each new episode gives meaning to the previous one, in a sense rewriting it. So, in this sense, narrative is essentially retrospective, looking backwards—but it always has to pretend that it's beginning at the beginning, as a logical entailment.

But to turn now to think about law's resistance, I think there is a resistance—to reading in the law. I've had some interesting debates about this. For example, Ken Abraham[1] has argued that in Torts, which is what he teaches, you are in dealing with those early torts cases acting as a kind of literary critic in trying to figure out what they mean and where they come from. I think that's true, but on the whole, law doesn't want to deal with reading in the kind of radical sense that we use it in literary study. In literary study, you have to take the entire rhetoric of a text into account, and not simply do what I see law students being taught to do with a legal opinion: a kind of "plum pudding" reading. In that kind of reading, you stick in your thumb and pull out a doctrinal plum.

Of course, the way students are taught, through casebooks, makes that almost inevitable, because you generally don't have the whole case. You just have the parts that are "relevant." Well, what makes them "relevant"? It's because of the consequence coming out of them, and the way it's been picked up by later cases, that they become relevant. And so the whole question of how we are spoken to in a traditional opinion gets lost. We lose sight of questions like how the judicial opinion is trying to persuade various audiences and make good on prior cases, all of that gets lost. But it seems to me that this is enormously important.

On the other hand, the kind of doctrinal reading that is taught in law schools is also important. Outsiders without legal training don't have the skill or savvy to do that. But in learning that "thinking like a lawyer" approach to reading, there can be a loss as well as a gain. I'm not arguing that the law has to change its methodology, so much as I'm trying to say, "Here are some of the things that were not taken into consideration in a classic legal reading, and if you pay attention to them, you might learn something interesting about what you're doing as a lawyer."

So, increasingly, the focus of all of these concerns is coming to rest on legal education. There is a feeling now that there is a crisis in law schools. There are all these JDs coming out with enormous debt, and they're not getting the jobs they used to have. So, what's going to happen to law schools? There are proposals coming out now to reduce law school to two years, and to make it more of a vocational training than it already is. When you think about that, a couple of things come to mind. One is, historically, how did this come to be? Why did the law school become a freestanding professional school rather than a department within the university—as happened in Europe? (Of course, after you get your BA in law in England, you go on to an apprenticeship in the Inns of Court.) And second, if law school were to become a two-year program much more focused on clinical work, what would happen to interdisciplinary work on law? It might well devolve to the liberal arts, just the way psychoanalysis in some senses left the field of psychology long ago and became centered in the humanities. It continues there because it provides such an interesting interpretive method.

Is there a loss in this? Well, it depends on what you want lawyers to be. If you think of lawyers as people who make motions and work things out through the courts, there might not be much of a loss. If you think of them as philosophically sophisticated, thoughtful people who are running American society (as they very often do!), then I think there'd be a tremendous loss.

So, in a recent interdisciplinary discussion I hosted at Princeton, we talked about what would happen if the deeper thinking about law wound up in the liberal arts. As Kathie Hendley[2] remarked, one thing you wouldn't want is simply "Con Law Light." This is often what people think they ought to teach when they deal with law in the undergraduate curriculum. When I teach undergraduates here at Princeton, I try to do something very different. In the class I'm teaching now, I try to match up and compare legal and literary approaches to certain narratives about crime (see Appendix). So what am I trying to teach? The core focus is on *law as a discursive practice* (if you'll excuse the terminology!) in American society. There seems to be an enormous thirst among undergraduates for understanding law and its social and intellectual roles.

One example of the kind of question we can examine in this broader frame for law would be the status of the confession. I use a videotape from a case involving an interrogation and forced confession from a man who was then imprisoned for life for killing his infant son (*Scenes of a Crime*, by Grover Babcock and Blue Hadaech). In the videotape you can see the cops just work this man over. I also include the *Frontline* film of the Norfolk Four, those four sailors in Norfolk, Virginia who were convicted and went to prison for eight to ten years; they finally were conditionally pardoned, but the governor said he couldn't give them a full pardon because the confessions were still on the books. I actually have transcripts of the confessions, so the students can take a look at those. The students also got very interested in the question of jury nullification, and so we read about that, and studied the role of juries. These are the kinds of larger questions that might get lost in a law school curriculum centered on skills.

My prior experience in teaching about law involved working with law students at Yale and at University of Virginia, and obviously I had to rethink my approach to teaching when switching from law students to undergraduates. When I was working with law students, I was trying to challenge their thinking—you know, to bring in interpretive approaches from another field, and to suggest that the readings that they'd been taught in law school had another side to them. So, for instance, I wanted them to see that you could read certain texts—say, the Torture Memos—from the perspective of someone interested in language, and show that it was a radical perversion of language that became the basis for all those horrendous acts. (It was Jane Mayer, the *New Yorker* writer, who said that the Bush administration began by perverting language.)

Or, in teaching law students, I also had them work on more positive readings—as, for example, in *Miranda*, asking how Warren goes about setting up his audience for this new reading which changes the contemporary understanding of criminal procedure so radically— making it seem as if it is entailed by the Fifth and Sixth Amendments.

EM: There is so much that is naturalized in this "learning to think like a lawyer" approach to reading legal texts. I know that many who have spent their professional lives trying to challenge that naturalizing reading have wound up very discouraged. How do you feel after attempting this kind of teaching; was there a moment where this alternative kind of reading seemed to translate—where it all made sense to your students?

PB: I had very varied reactions. The last time I taught such a course in a law school setting, I had very much the feeling that the law students went home largely unchanged. During previous times when

I'd taught the course to law students, I had some students come to me and say, "We learned more about law in this class than in anything else we've taken." Of course, that made me feel like a bit of a fraud, because I'm not teaching them law! I'm teaching them something about the language of law and about its rhetoric—which is not necessarily going to be directly useful to them, but which might help them to be more reflective about what they are doing as lawyers. So I had very different reactions when teaching law students. Now, teaching undergraduates and graduate students, I get a few students who have had legal training, either before they came here, or if they are pursuing joint JD-PhDs. (But these joint degree graduate students are already among the semi-converted, because they are seeking interdisciplinary training.)

At an institutional level, my primary experience teaching in a law school was in some ways disappointing. There was a time when there was a lot more interest in the insights that law-and-literature could bring to law teaching. But ultimately, the law school wound up being almost Teflon-coated, resistant to deep engagement with other perspectives. I had different experiences in the two law schools in which I taught, of course. But it was my experience that the more professional the law school, the more imperturbable and unthreatened it was, so that interdisciplinary work can be included unfettered—but it doesn't make much of a mark on the core of legal education in such places. In general, it is my impression that law schools have a way of insulating themselves. Sometimes it can be hard to get students from Arts and Sciences to come to the law school just because it is physically set apart. But even when the law school is right there, in the middle of campus, the law students can tend to insulate themselves—rarely leaving the building to go to any other classes in any other fields.

I think that the insulation and Teflon-coating have to do, finally, with the idea that law is a practice, and with the fear that if you drift away from this idea even a little, you lose the whole point of the training. I've seen even relatively open-minded law professors with interdisciplinary training adhere to this point of view—that this is why law has to be separated out from the rest of the university. Of course, it's true that law is a practice, but nonetheless in other countries and in other traditions, it can be studied within the university—and if you are going to insist that it's primarily a practice, then you have to ask, "What are law schools doing connected to universities at all? Why aren't you just 'reading law' in somebody's law office?" So I think that this insulation must have something to do with the dynamics of professionalization within American culture, and with the history of the law school. This would connect with the need that law schools had, as professional schools, to distinguish themselves from other kinds of training—and to establish the law school as a "university-worthy" field. So, in the late nineteenth century, for Christopher Columbus Langdell, the case method was actually supposed to lead to a set of scientific principles for studying the law. And I think that that idea, which was very typical of its time, had a lot to do with the law school setting itself off and eventually becoming what it is today.

EM: So, given the kind of Teflon coating and insularity that law-and-language scholars have found in the deployment of legal discourse, how would any other kind of reading be able to receive any attention within law? Where an alternative reading enters, what kind of effect could it plausibly achieve? Would you envision a hybrid discourse, or a form of translation, or something else?

PB: In my own thinking about different entry points—I think that's a good way to pose the question—I have shifted over time. Some would say that the moment of interest in hermeneutics and interpretation in law schools, which got a lot of attention from legal academics for a time, is past. Many of them have turned back to paradigms such as those provided by cultural history, or political theory, or forms of constitutional theory, and so forth; the interest in interpretation seems to have waned. I still think that that door should be open, and that people should be pressing professors on law faculties to keep their minds open to the lessons that can be learned from the disciplines that specialize in language and interpretation. I continue to think, transposing a remark made by Paul de Man, that law should be taught as a rhetoric and a poetics before it is taught as a hermeneutics and a history. In other words, law students ought to be taught something about how law speaks, independent of the actual cases that it solves. What are the grounds of meaning-making in the law? I suppose the most thoughtful ones actually do ask themselves that question. But where I would focus now is on how one would do an intelligent and thoughtful reading of law within the context of the liberal arts, as I've described.

EM: In a way, we could also ask if legal studies, like so many other fields, doesn't necessarily go through cycles in which there is a "new new" approach. And the legal academy's approach to this patterning is in part to borrow from other disciplines cyclically—to pick up some ideas and then to put them down again. But then what does that say about the real meaning of interdisciplinarity for a field like law? If the core frame is always centered on legal categories and perspectives, and insights from other disciplines are simply subsumed into that core frame—then it's unclear whether interdisciplinary work is truly possible.

PB: Yes, along those lines, it will be interesting to see what happens with the new PhD program in law at Yale. Dean Harold Koh used to talk about what he called an "interprofessional" degree, learning for example economics or political theory along with law. But this model might leave the study of law untouched by those other disciplines. One promising place for contact might be legal history, where both legal scholars and legal historians could find common ground. But one could argue that the law doesn't want what the historians would call "legal history"; law wants what we might call a "polemical history" that fits a particular case.

EM: So to me, this gets at a very fundamental question. If law and legal scholarship were to really incorporate interdisciplinary insights at a level that budged fundamental paradigms, what would the result look like?

PB: This gets us back to the question of what the law is really for. To the extent that you consider it always to have a pragmatic horizon, then yes, this creates a strong resistance to interdisciplinary insights. So you could ask: if your lawyer has read Stanley Fish, will he be better at defending you? I'm not sure that I know the answer to that—and I don't think that I have to provide the answer to that. I'm much more interested in asking questions about law, including law as an academic discipline, and asking, "What are you excluding?" Long, long ago—I'm talking about thirty years ago—David Apter, who was a sociologist and a political scientist, and I started a faculty workshop about the history of the discipline. It was called "From Repression to Guilty Knowledge." The notion was that every discipline, in the course of its evolution, had to repress certain things to become a discipline— it had to exclude certain things. But those things were still lurking somewhere as a "guilty knowledge" within the discipline. Within literary criticism, there are a lot of examples. The field is perpetually in crisis, so those "guilty knowledges" are not hard to find.

EM: In that, literary criticism is not unlike anthropology.

PB: Oh yes, anthropologists have put themselves in the stocks! But in some sense, anthropology has actually infiltrated many of the other disciplines. We all have to think a little bit like anthropologists about our own fields now. But I think that law doesn't want to deal with its "guilty knowledge." So that is one way of talking about law's resistance.

For example, in taking on criminal law (as I'm doing in my teaching right now), it would seem important to find ways to incorporate all the doubts that we've developed about how the criminal law works into the core scholarship and teaching in the area. We've of course always had doubts about how well theory translates into practice in criminal procedure, but lately they've become just rampant, there are so many examples. Just recently, the *Times* had a story about this guy named Louis Scarcella—he was a police detective who was great at getting confessions—and now they've decided to reopen all of his cases because of the dubious methods he used. For example, he let his suspects out to visit prostitutes in exchange for cooperation, and he used the same corroborating witness over and over again.

So what is the connection between what happens on the ground, and the conceptualizations we find within law, legal scholarship, and criminology about what is going on? The one place I've ever seen these come together is in the Lawyering seminar at NYU, with Peggy Davis[3] and Tony Amsterdam[4] and Jerry Bruner.[5] Tony Amsterdam founded something called the "Persuasion Institute," which is training public defenders essentially to write post-conviction petitions, in which I participated at one point. Just watching how Tony went about drafting a *cert* petition was the greatest lesson in narrative I ever had.

EM: Looking forward, how do you see the immediate future of interdisciplinary work in law?

PB: There are contradictory signs. At Georgetown Law School, Robin West[6] has a new program in Law and the Humanities. But as the financial crisis is hitting law schools, they are cutting back, and it's not clear how these sorts of programs will fare as that happens. And yet there continue to be these promising signals—BU Law School, for example, has been encouraging interdisciplinary work through a program of visitorships—in these times, such signals come as a surprise but a positive one. So, we'll see! My fear is that this will remain an entertainment on the fringes of the law, rather than ever come to really affect or change the law.

The other side of the coin—the presence of law in the undergraduate curriculum—I think that here one can be more optimistic. You don't want it to become a pre-law or pre-professional kind of training. You want it to be something that is valuable in itself—law as an intellectual discipline and as part of the culture. Law is part of a bigger cultural-literary-interpretive picture, and it belongs in that picture.

Notes

1. Kenneth Abraham is David and Mary Harrison Distinguished Professor of Law at the University of Virginia.

2. Kathryn Hendley is William Voss-Bascom Professor of Law and Political Science at the University of Wisconsin.

3. Peggy Cooper Davis is John S. R. Shad Professor of Lawyering and Ethics and the director of the Lawyering Program at the New York University School of Law.

4. Anthony Amsterdam is University Professor Emeritus at the New York University School of Law.

5. Jerome Bruner is University Professor at the New York University School of Law.

6. Robin West is Frederick J. Haas Professor of Law and Philosophy at Georgetown University Law Center.

Reference

Brooks, Peter. 2010. "Literature as Law's Other." *Yale Journal of Law & the Humanities* 22: 349–367.

Cases Cited

District of Columbia v. Heller, 554 U.S. 570 (2008).

Appendix: Sample Course Outline/Readings

Peter Brooks, Clues, Evidence, Detection: Law Stories. Fall Term, 2013

We'll look at stories *in* the law and *about* the law: court cases that turn on competing versions of a story, and how narrative "conviction" comes about, as well as fictional and nonfiction accounts of mystery, crime, investigation, and detection in literature and film. The course will introduce students to some issues in criminal law and procedure as well as to the analysis of narrative.

1. Thursday Sept. 12: lecture: Introduction: Conan Doyle, *The Adventure of the Speckled Band; The Musgrave Ritual*
2. Tuesday Sept. 17: lecture: *Brewer v. Williams*; Conan Doyle, *Silver Blaze*
3. Thursday Sept. 19: precept: Conan Doyle, *The Naval Treaty; The Final Problem; The Empty House*
4. Tuesday Sept. 24: lecture: *Nix v. Williams; Feldhacker v. United States*
5. Thursday Sept. 26: precept: Sophocles, *Oedipus the King*
6. Tuesday Oct. 1: lecture: Wilkie Collins, *The Woman in White* (first half)
7. Thursday Oct. 3: precept: *United States v. Llera Plaza; Kyllo v. United States; Florida v. Jardines*
8. Tuesday Oct. 8: lecture: *Miranda v. Arizona; Oregon v. Elstad; Missouri v. Seibert*
9. Thursday Oct. 10: precept: Wilkie Collins, *The Woman in White* (second half)
10. Tuesday, Oct. 15: lecture: Hitchcock, *I Confess* (film); *Scenes of a Crime* (video)

11. Thursday Oct. 17: precept: *Chavez v. Martinez*; Frontline, *"The Norfolk Four"* (video)
12. Tuesday Oct. 22: lecture (EW): Franz Kafka, *The Verdict (The Judgment); In the Penal Colony*
13. Thursday Oct. 24, precept: *The Rodney King Case* (video)
14. Tuesday Nov. 5: lecture: *Rusk v. State, State v. Rusk*
15. Thursday Nov. 7: precept: Michelangelo Antonioni, *Blow-Up*
16. Tuesday Nov. 12: lecture: *Mickens v. Taylor*, petitions and judgment
17. Thursday Nov. 14: precept: Sigmund Freud, *From the History of an Infantile Neurosis ("The Wolf Man")*
18. Tuesday: Nov. 18 lecture: Albert Camus, *The Fall; Old Chief v. United States*
19. Thursday Nov. 20: precept: Camus, *The Fall*; Susan Glaspell, *A Jury of Her Peers*
20. Tuesday Nov. 26: lecture: Barbet Schroeder, *Reversal of Fortune*
21. Tuesday Dec. 3: lecture: *Olmstead v. United States; Eldred v. Ashcroft*
22. Thursday Dec. 5: precept: Henry James, *The Aspern Papers*
23. Tuesday Dec. 10: lecture: *Brown v. Louisiana; U.S. v. Doherty*

PART FOUR

Concluding Remarks

11

Afterword

SOME FURTHER THOUGHTS ON TRANSLATING
LAW AND SOCIAL SCIENCE

Gregory Matoesian

In closing I offer several prominent themes on translation between the social sciences and law and consider promising avenues for future development between the two discourses. To do so, I employ several short data extracts for illustrative purposes.

Some years ago, I received several boxes containing over 16,000 pages of transcripts from numerous rape trials along with several boxes of trial material on old reel-to-reel tapes that the court reporter used as a backup for the transcriptions. While browsing through the transcripts I came across a page heard on one of the tapes but noticed that the transcript seemed "funny" compared to the recording. In the recording the defense attorney asked the rape victim (during cross-examination) if she could distinguish items that she remembered independently (preserved in memory) about the rape from items that she remembered only after reading her police statement (given some six months previously (right after the incident), but read a few days prior to the trial). Quite predictably, she failed to respond to the question, and after a lengthy pause of over six seconds the defense attorney asked, *Or don't you remember that?* After her *I don't know* response he followed up with the damaging assessment: *So you don't know what you do and don't remember?* A few moments later, the defense attorney continued this line of questioning but his delivery was fraught with dysfluencies and grammatical errors: *OK I-* **Mam-** *what items was it (.)* **Were-** *(pause)* **What were the items** *(longer pause) that you didn't remember until last Friday?* (boldface words indicate increased volume and stress, dash marks a cut-off on the word).[1] Moreover, the question evoked a robust spate of laughter from the jury and/or audience during the longer pause.

What was "funny" about the transcript was that the lengthy six-second pause had disappeared and the dysfluent question—not to mention the laughter—had been edited to: "What were the items that you didn't remember until last Friday?" Since then I've wondered why and how one text gets translated into something quite different. What is the function of translation? In the example above, the lengthy pause demonstrated the victim's state of indecision; the defense attorney subsequently performed "confusion" over the victim's testimony, not as some inner mental or cognitive state but emergent in speech dysfluencies, grammatical errors, and cut-off repairs. I thought this was his way of signaling to the jury his purported confusion over her confused testimony, perhaps also indicating that they should be confused too—confused enough to acquit his client.[2] In the remainder of this conclusion I outline a basic analytic framework to guide this idea of translation as dialogic performance in the concrete details of legal discourse, a framework organized around the following four concepts: intertextuality, identity, power, and multimodality. Attention to these aspects of translation at an analytical level is useful in achieving the goals articulated throughout this volume, of paying more attention to the norms, worldviews, and contexts that shape interdisciplinary communication—and especially of theorizing the translation process itself.

11.1 Intertextuality

Like most useful concepts, translation is an ambiguous term, and its use covers not just translation from a source to a target language or text, but also interpretation, meaning, and culture, to mention but a few.[3] Moreover, in both everyday and scholarly discourse it is common to speak of the language of law, language of social science, language of politics, language of gender, etc.; what we've done in this volume is to show how translation functions between the language of social science on the one hand and the language of law on the other (keeping in mind that the entire process gets overseen by culture and meaning). As Ford and Mertz note in the Introduction, a useful way to conceptualize translation would be to consider what linguistic anthropologists refer to as *intertextuality* (the relationship among texts, visible in the entextualization process): the decontextualization of discourse from one setting and its recontextualization into another. The crucial point about intertextuality is this: Whenever we extract discourse from its original setting and insert it into a new one we do so with an eye toward the interactional work at hand—that is, with an eye on what is happening to and through that discourse in its new setting. This move across contexts is of necessity an interpreter-mediated process rather than a neutral form of transmission between texts. As Hale (2006, 12) mentions: "If the interpreter believes her/his role to be that of a machine that robotically transforms words from one language to another, with no room for 'interpretation' or decision-making on their part, their renditions will very rarely be accurate." In her classic work (2004, xvi), she examines how interpreters "manipulate, filter and alter the messages of the main participants in their interpretation, and the impact such alterations have on the legal process." If this is so, then context is always co-constructed and interactive, never a passive "bucket" that merely surrounds and structures the integrity of texts.[4]

To illustrate this important point, I'll summarize some of the more prominent studies along these lines that show how intertextual translations affect the legal process in the United States and elsewhere. In her studies of court reporters, Walker (1990, 229) found that while court reporters are required to produce a verbatim transcript they routinely "clean up" the grammar of lawyers, judges, and expert witnesses while rarely doing the same for lay witnesses (as we saw in the above example). One of her most remarkable findings (Walker 1990, 235–236) was that appellate judges read transcripts not only to determine if the lower court had correctly applied the law but also to assess "character, intelligence and credibility" of attorneys and witnesses. In so doing, appellate judges are "actively engaged in forming impressions of the trial participants and are using those impressions in reaching their decision" (Walker 1990, 235).

In courtroom situations involving bilingualism, Hale (2006, 156–157; see also Berk-Seligson 2002, 142) found that interpreters translating Spanish into English regularly altered the form of witness's answers, often substituting powerless forms (such as hedges, hesitations, and grammatical errors) that were "detrimental to the evaluation of the witness's character and credibility." In her bilingual study of the protection order interview, Trinch (2003) observed how Spanish victim's stories of violence in the interview were transformed by English translators into the institutional demands of the written affidavit, often omitting key points and transforming euphemisms into more legally acceptable terms (such as "made love to me" becomes "rape"). In this process, the alteration leads to striking inconsistencies if and when the case goes to trial (often resulting in a denial of the protective order). All of these authors demonstrate in vivid detail a crucial aspect of translation: how the audience or projected audience shapes entextualized transformations and, consequently, the legal process.

11.2 Identity

And the object of that transformation includes, as we have seen above, identity: the dynamic and emergent process of signaling who we are and what we are doing at specific moments of discursive action. In the short extract below we can see how intertextuality, in the form of a direct quote attributed to the victim after the sexual assault, interacts with emotion to construct victim identity in the rape trial (Matoesian 2001, 48). *She calls Ann Mercer (.) and says (.) "I've been raped (.) come and pick me up."* The defense attorney animates the victim's voice in the reported clause using a flat tone of voice suggesting to the jury that this is an oddly stoic way to talk about the unsettling sweep of criminal events that had just transpired at the defendant's home.[5] Later in cross-examination the defense attorney asked the victim about Johnny Butler, the man who drove her to the hospital for the rape exam: *And he's your daughter's father right?* Using a triangulation of kinship reference, he mobilized a thoroughly unveiled allusion about the victim's sexual history, in particular, that she had a child out of wedlock along with the negative inferences that circulate around such an identity. In both cases, we can observe how the entextualization process is not a verbatim rendition or transparent translation from historical to current discourse but a moral evaluation or linguistic stance designed to accomplish interactional work in the construction of legal identity.

A useful way to conceptualize sociolegal identity relevant to translation is Erving Goffman's (1981) work on footing. Footing refers to the speaker's relationship to his or her utterances and the micro-organization of discursive identity in contextual situated interaction. The animator produces the words; the author composes the words; and the principal is the person who authorizes them. By dissecting discursive identities in such discriminating detail we can uncover instances where the translator projects the role of "mere" animator ("I'm just translating what other people said") while hiding the fact that he is also occupying author and principal roles. (In other words, some of the meaning conveyed in the translation is actually (and necessarily) authored and authorized by the translator.) We saw this dynamic in the direct quote above, where the defense attorney foregrounds his identity as animator of the author and principal's voice for strategic interactional and evidential purposes. In purportedly "just quoting" what the rape victim said, the defense attorney conceals the way he is authoring and authorizing a hidden message about the rape victim's "real" identity. We will return to this idea shortly.

11.3 Power

One of the most notable cases of linguistic translation and law occurred in1979 in the "Ann Arbor" trial (Labov 1982). The decision on habitual *Be* (or habitual aspect and other features of Black English Vernacular (BEV)) in BEV reveals the politics of translation and how it represents a negotiated power-driven process. In 1979 Judge Joiner ruled that the City of Ann Arbor, MI School Board violated the Equal Protection Clause of the 14th Amendment by failing to appreciate the differences between BEV (or African-American Vernacular English (AAVE)) and Standard English (SE). In essence the ruling supported the claim of several black students that sentences like *He makin sense but don't be makin sense* were not inferior and ungrammatical forms of SE but a separate language deriving from West African languages and that school teachers in Ann Arbor would have to translate such grammatical forms into SE as they would any other non-native language. Basically, invariant *Be* refers to habitual aspect or the duration of activity denoted by the verb. Thus the example above would be translated into "You've blundered into making an intelligible statement for once" (Dillard 1972, 46; see also Labov 1982, 190). What was most peculiar about the case was that the NAACP (as well as numerous black celebrities and politicians) supported the Ann Arbor School Board rather than the black students bringing the suit. Why? They realized that the black students would never succeed in business, politics, or education using such variant forms of English. And that is a matter dealing with power and language.

Indeed, translation always incorporates power: (1) power as the ability to make the translator's account matter in the fine-grained details of communicative practices (although this power in framing the translation is often invisible, as we've seen); and (2) power as linguistic ideologies or folk rationalization about language use (Silverstein 1979). To illustrate the former, Diana Eades (2008) shows how Australian defense attorneys exploit differences between the usage patterns of SE and Aborigine English to impugn the credibility of young Aborigine speakers. For example, Aborigine speakers remain silent for a time after a question, and their white cross-examiners use this to attribute blame. Martha Komter (2012) analyzes how reports of police interviews transform the defendant's words in the written case document, attributing sole authorship to the defendant, and erasing police questioning. Moreover, the judge and prosecuting attorney invoke the written "objective case file" to impeach the defendant's credibility when the defendant complains about file inaccuracies. In the case of Rodney King, where the police beating of an African-American man was captured on videotape, Charles Goodwin (1994) illustrates how an expert on police training interprets the taped beating as a legitimate use of force rather than police brutality by translating police violence into an "escalation–de-escalation" framework; in this "expert translation," King is portrayed as actually controlling police actions in and through his threatening behavior.

On the power exercised through linguistic ideology, Mertz (2007) demonstrates how the reproduction of law's power occurs through law school socialization rituals in which students learn new ideologies of language that bleach social, emotional, and moral contexts out of accounts of what happened in legal cases; this allows legal accounts to quietly claim an epistemologically privileged status for this socially constructed legal reality. Haviland (2003) considers the use of linguistic ideologies in a murder trial; he shows that court participants operate under the belief that translators should provide literal or verbatim renditions of Spanish into English (what Haviland calls a linguistic ideology of referential transparency), even when this is impossible and actually distorts testimony. As an example of belief in the possibility of referential transparency consider the work of Andrew Taslitz (1999). Taslitz proposes that rape trials (in the US adversary system) should use a "neutral translator" to translate the defense attorney's questions into less abusive forms while still maintaining the structural equivalence or integrity of the substantive text. On the one hand, this proposal admirably takes account of the ways the current system disadvantages rape victims. As the above examples reveal, however, the ability to mobilize linguistic resources always confers power on the translator to frame intertextual realities, to authorize the status of legal evidence, and to naturalize sociolegal identities (Angermeyer 2015; Ng 2009; Richland 2008; Shuy 1993). A translator is never a neutral animator a la Goffman or mere conduit for the transmission of discourse. How, for example, would one translate "baby" versus "fetus" into some morally neutral domain (Danet 1980)?

11.4 Multimodality

Perhaps the most taken-for-granted feature of law in general—and legal translation in particular—is the way that verbal and written forms of language integrate with bodily conduct (such as gestures, gaze, and movement) and the material/mediated environment (such as exhibits). Much hidden translation work is done at this level, and there is little insight into that level in scholarship on law and language to date. This area arguably constitutes one of the most promising avenues for future research on translation between social science and law (as intimated in the first sentence). (It bears noting that some scholars in the area have begun to excavate these issues, including in research by Alessandro Duranti, Hadi Deeb, and also in my own work.) For example, the legal system in France recently began to permit the use of video link hookups with the defendant in jail and, in bilingual cases, a translator in the courtroom (to save money in transporting the defendant from jail to the courthouse and back) (Licoppe and Vernier 2013). The video conference represents a type of mediated, multilayered translation in which the official translator has to speak loudly while the judge (who is also "translating," albeit less obviously) performs metalinguistic instructions for delivering the translation to accommodate the defendant via the video link. That is to say, the judge formulates the prosecutor's argument for the translator to deliver to the defendant in a type of double translation.[6] In less unusual but more pervasive contexts, attorneys and witnesses use gestures, gaze, and body movements to beat out the rhythm of their utterances, evaluate a witness' answer (for instance by turning the head, opening the mouth, and rolling the eyes), and organize and authorize a specific participation framework, as we saw in chapter 3. To illustrate, although attorneys may not overtly and verbally comment on the witness' answer (as in "give me a break"), they may comment covertly through bodily conduct. In Figures 11.1, 11.2, and 11.3, Roy Black turns his head, rolls his eyes (or eyebrow flash), and opens his mouth to indicate his skeptical stance from a witness' prior response.

FIGURE 11.1 **Bodily Conduct—Before.**

FIGURE 11.2 **Bodily Conduct—After.**

FIGURE 11.3 **Bodily Conduct—Eyebrow Flash/Mouth Open.**

11.5 An Integrated Framework

I would like to demonstrate a way to think about translation and law built around these concepts of linguistic ideology, identity, intertextuality, power, and the body. But now rather than consider them as autonomous concepts, I provide a brief demonstration of how they function as an integrated whole in the improvisational density of communicative practice.[7] In the following extract the defense attorney is questioning a witness when she makes an unexpected request to talk about items from the previous day in line 8.

Extract 1 (DA= defense attorney; AM=witness)

001 DA: You knew that you were going to be asked questions

002   only twelve hours ago. It was only twelve hours isn't that right?

003   (1.1)

004 AM: Yes.

005   (7.3)

006 AM: ((*slight head tilt forward and back at 7.0*))

007 AM: ((*lip smack/alveolar click and head movement forward toward microphone with thinking face display at 7.3*))

008 AM: I would like to complete my answer on uh:: the question (.)

009		about (.) saying that Senat[or Kennedy was watching.
010		[((gaze moves to DA))
011		(0.9)
012	AM:	((*raised and sustained eyebrow flash with mouth open-close co-occurring with three micro vertical head nods*))
013		(3.3)
014	DA:	Uh::: (.) which question are you answering now:: miss:://
015	AM:	You had asked me uh::: (.) yesterday (0.5) n'you also asked me
016		this morning (0.5) **about** my statement to the police
017	AM:	*I would like to complete that answer for the jury please.*
018		(0.9)
019	DA:	*You mean* this is an answer that I asked you yesterday you
020		now after thinking about it overnight want to complete the
021		ah::: answer[
022	AM:	[Ah::: No. I didn't have the opportunity to *answer your*
023		*question yesterday ((staccato delivery))*
024	DA:	I'm sorry I thought you had uh:: completed your answer.
025		If you want to say something to the jury that you've had
026		time to think about (.) please go ((lower volume))
027	AM:	No- it- >*I haven't had time to think about it.*
028		*I would have said the same thing yesterday when*
029		*you asked me.*< ((*Sped up with increased volume and stress*))
030		((Shifts upper torso and gaze downward in a thinking face display))
		((several lines omitted))
031		I had asked her (.) uh few questions (1.7) Uh:::
032		she repeated (2.5) th- that *he was watching, he was watching*
033		(2.8) I then, in return, asked her (.) who was watching (0.8)?
034		[*Was Senator Kennedy Watching?*
035		[((eyebrow flash)) ((multimodally signals the direct quote in 34))

In the above case the witness makes a request to "continue" her utterances from the previous day, an intertextual continuity between prior and current utterances. In response, the defense attorney evokes a linguistic ideology that shapes the epistemological criteria for gauging authenticity and truth: utterances that are planned or rehearsed (perhaps even being coached by someone else) beforehand represent inferior forms of evidential knowledge. Only spontaneous talk in the here-and-now contains truth and authenticity. By invoking this widely shared but never overtly discussed ideology, he can imply that her utterance is not a continuity with earlier discourse but an intertextual discontinuity, in which her animated words incorporate voices of some other projected author and principal (perhaps either her attorney or the victim or both). See Figures 11.4 and 11.5.

FIGURE 11.4 **Bodily Conduct—Before Torque.**

FIGURE 11.5 **Bodily Conduct—Body Torque.**

At a finer level of analysis, notice the contrast between the defense attorney's very (almost perversely) restrained *if*-conditional metapragmatic frame ("If you want to say something. . .") as it interacts with the witness' body torque, middle-distance, or "thinking face" gaze (line 30), embedded parenthetical *in return* (line 33), eyebrow flash (line 35), and sonorous defensive stance in line 27 (the increased loudness, stress, cut-off, and sped-up speech draw attention to the utterance).

This contrast frames the witness's forthcoming speech, undermining its epistemological status, and making it appear rehearsed (thus subtly invoking the negative inferences associated with rehearsed testimony). Put another way: her "interruptive" and prosodically marked "defensiveness" interacts with DA's metapragmatic structuring power to draw disparaging attention to the authenticity of her forthcoming quotes in lines 32–34. This in turn confirms the defense attorney's interpretation that she is speaking from a prepared script. This example, then, shows how translation is an inherently dialogic, thoroughly interactive, and power-driven negotiation in which the body plays a major role. It also demonstrates the importance of noticing how many layers work together to convey meaning in legal settings: intertextual references, invocation of linguistic ideologies, the linguistic and social construction of identities, power dynamics, and the input of multiple simultaneous signaling modes beyond just the words themselves (body language, intonation, and more: what linguists would call "multimodality").

In sum, there are always many levels of translation at work in legal settings, which are multiplied when we add to the mix the possibility of invoking relevant social science on law. This volume amply illustrates why it is important to pay attention to those levels. Frequently the unspoken dynamics at work in these subtle translations work to undermine overt goals of the legal system, in some cases making justice as it is imagined by participants impossible. At the same time, it may be impossible to avoid some of the creative, improvisational aspects of the quiet and constant translations at work in language use—wherever it happens. As elsewhere in everyday life, language exchanges in courtrooms construct part of the legal context itself, as participants shape one another's contributions. However, to the extent that knowledge from social sciences like linguistics can shed light on this always unfolding, evanescent process, it may be that uncovering layers of what is actually going on could contribute to larger goals of the legal system. It is in the hope that that might be possible that we, building on the work of many other social scientists, offer the insights gleaned from our research and interdisciplinary conversations on legal translations.

Notes

1. Dysfluencies are interruptions in an otherwise smooth flow of speech.

2. When speech form mirrors an idea that the speech content is attempting to convey, linguistic anthropologists would refer to that mirroring relationship as an "icon," in which the two resemble each other by virtue of a resemblance in form. Research indicates that this kind of relationship may be particularly powerful, especially as it tends to operate "under the radar" of conscious thought, reinforcing a sense that the content of a message is somehow "natural" because it fits with the form of that message.

3. Duranti (1997, 154) states that translation "implies an understanding not only of the immediate context but also of more general assumptions, such as people's worldview" and "involves a long series of interpretations and decisions that are rarely apparent in the final product."

4. See Mertz, Chapter 9 of this volume.

5. Even though her girlfriend stated that the victim sounded "hysterical" on the phone.

6. This means of course that the prosecuting attorneys must segment their speech to accommodate the translator's work, which requires a unique form of sequential collaboration to manage the intricacies of this speech exchange system.

7. I speak of this as "improvisational" because no matter how much the defense attorney or witness may have rehearsed what they were going to say ahead of time, when they begin to interact with each other they are forced to respond in the moment to whatever the other person is saying and doing. In this sense, when we translate, we have to respond both to the meaning in the original (or "source") language and the exigencies of the language into which we are translating (the "target" language)—and our choices are at every turn shaped by how we perceive the audience at which the translation is aimed.

References

Berk-Seligson, Susan. 2002. *The Bilingual Courtroom: Court Interpreters in the Judicial Process.* Chicago: University of Chicago Press.

Danet, Brenda. 1980. "'Baby' or 'Fetus'? Language and the Construction of Reality in a Manslaughter Trial." *Semiotica* 32: 187.

Dillard, J. L. 1973. *Black English.* New York: Random House.

Eades, Diana. 2008. *Courtroom Talk and Neocolonial Control.* New York: Mouton de Gruyter.

Goffman, Erving. 1981. *Forms of Talk.* Philadelphia: University of Pennsylvania Press.

Hale, Sandra Beatriz. 2006. *The Discourse of Court Interpreting.* Amsterdam/Philadelphia: John Benjamins Publishing Company.

Haviland, John B. 2003. "Ideologies of Language: Some Reflections on Language and U.S. Law." *American Anthropologist* 105(4): 764–774.

Komter, Martha. 2012. "Conversation Analysis in the Courtroom." In *The Handbook of Conversation Analysis,* edited by Jack Sidnell and Tanya Stivers, 612–629. New York: John Wiley.

Labov, William. 1982. "Objectivity and Commitment in Linguistic Science: The Case of the Black English Trial in Ann Arbor." *Language in Society* 11: 165–202.

Licoppe, Christian, and Maud Vernier. 2013. "Interpreting, Video Communication and the Sequential Reshaping of Institutional Talk in the Bilingual and Distributed Courtroom." *International Journal of Speech, Language and the Law* 20(2): 247–275.

Matoesian, Gregory. 2001. *Law and the Language of Identity: Discourse in the William Kennedy Smith Rape Trial.* New York: Oxford University Press.

Mertz, Elizabeth. 2007. *The Language of Law School: Learning to "Think Like a Lawyer."* Oxford: Oxford University Press.

Ng, Kwai Hang. 2009. *The Common Law in Two Voices.* Stanford: Stanford University Press.

Richland, Justin. 2008. *Arguing with Tradition.* Chicago: University of Chicago Press.

Shuy, Roger. 1993. *Language Crimes.* Cambridge, MA: Blackwell.

Silverstein, Michael. 1976. "Shifters, Linguistic Categories, and Cultural Description." In *Meaning in Anthropology*, edited by Keith Basso and Henry Selby, 11–55. Albuquerque: University of New Mexico Press.

Taslitz, Andrew. 1999. *Rape and the Culture of the Courtroom.* New York: New York University Press.

Trinch, Shonna L. 2003. *Latinas' Narratives of Domestic Abuse: Discrepant Versions of Violence.* Amsterdam/Philadelphia: John Benjamins Publishing Company.

Walker, Anne Graffam. 1990. "Language at Work in the Law: The Customs, Conventions, and Appellate Consequences of Court Reporting." In *Language in the Judicial Process*, edited by Judith N. Levi and Anne Graffam Walker, 203–244. New York: Plenum.

INDEX

CPSIA information can be obtained
at www.ICGtesting.com
Printed in the USA
BVHW030733150620
581447BV00004B/8